VICTORY GARDENS THEATER PRESENTS

VICTORY GARDENS THEATER

PRESENTS

SEVEN NEW PLAYS

FROM THE PLAYWRIGHTS ENSEMBLE

EDITED BY

SANDY SHINNER AND DENNIS ZAČEK

FOREWORD BY RICHARD CHRISTIANSEN

NORTHWESTERN UNIVERSITY PRESS
EVANSTON, ILLINOIS

Northwestern University Press
www.nupress.northwestern.edu

Printed in the United States of America

10   9   8   7   6   5   4   3   2   1

ISBN 0-8101-2346-0

JACKET PHOTOGRAPHS

FRONT TOP (LEFT TO RIGHT): Jerome Moore (David New)
and Ruth Moore (Roslyn Alexander), *Affluenza!* (photo by
Liz Lauren); Steve Burns (Phil Ridarelli), *Battle of the Bands*
(photo by Liz Lauren); Robert Wilson (Gary Houston) and
John Newton Templeton (Anthony Fleming III), *Free Man
of Color* (photo by Liz Lauren); Ted (William L. Petersen),
Flyovers (photo by Liz Lauren)

FRONT BOTTOM (LEFT TO RIGHT): Young Lillian (Bethanny
Alexander) and Young Ruth (Mattie Hawkinson), *Hanging
Fire* (photo by Liz Lauren); Barbara Jordan (Cheryl Lynn
Bruce) and Heart (Karla J. Beard), *Voice of Good Hope* (photo
by Liz Lauren); Jason Allcock (Daniel Oreskes) and Mediyah
(Celeste Williams), *Pecong* (photo by Jennifer Girard)

BACK TOP (LEFT TO RIGHT): Janet Burns (Jill Shellabarger),
Claire Sherman (Julie Ganey), and Gina Burns (Karlie
Nurse), *Battle of the Bands* (photo by Liz Lauren); Barbara
Jordan (Cheryl Lynn Bruce), *Voice of Good Hope* (photo by Liz
Lauren); Ted (Gary Cole), *Flyovers* (photo by Liz Lauren);
Young Lillian (Bethanny Alexander) and Young Ruth
(Mattie Hawkinson), *Hanging Fire* (photo by Liz Lauren)

BACK BOTTOM (LEFT TO RIGHT): John Newton Templeton
(Anthony Fleming III), *Free Man of Color* (photo by Liz
Lauren); William Moore (Richard Henzel) and Dawn
(Kim Wade), *Affluenza!* (photo by Liz Lauren); Creon Pandit
(Ernest Perry Jr.) and Jason Allcock (Daniel Oreskes),
Pecong (photo by Jennifer Girard)

The Biograph marquee photograph is by Shawna Seto.

Library of Congress Cataloging-in-Publication data are
available from the Library of Congress.

♾ The paper used in this publication meets the minimum
requirements of the American National Standard for
Information Sciences—Permanence of Paper for Printed
Library Materials, ANSI Z39.48-1992.

CONTENTS

FOREWORD

Richard Christiansen

Inspired originality, often wonderful and on occasion just a bit incredible, has marked the history of Victory Gardens Theater from its very beginning. For example, the theater indirectly acquired its name in 1974 from an off-the-wall suggestion by Warren Casey, coauthor of the musical *Grease* and the possessor of a remarkably askew sense of humor. Casey, one of the theater's eight—count them, eight—founders, suggested calling their new company Eight Great Tomatoes in a Can, a takeoff on a then-current advertising slogan for tomato sauce, but that title was judged just a tad too original, even for Chicago, where distinctive theater names such as Organic, The Second City, Body Politic, and Kingston Mines already had been coined.

Still, there was something catchy about Casey's concept, and after a while, and after much discussion, though the tomatoes were dropped, the name evolved into Victory Gardens, a title that summoned up images of healthful, homegrown, homemade products nourished in your own backyard. (It also blended nicely with the city of Chicago's Latin motto, *Urbs in horto*—"City in a garden.")

At that time, in the mid-1970s, the Chicago area was in the midst of a rousing period of expansion for resident, midsize theaters. The off-Loop scene, as it came to be called, produced one dynamic group after another. St. Nicholas, Wisdom Bridge, and Northlight were among the many youthful troupes that opened for business and added their voices to the growing chorus of creativity.

The founders of the Gardens—actors Cordis Heard, Roberta Maguire, Cecil O'Neal, and David Rasche; directors Stuart Gordon, Mac McGinnes, and June Pyskacek; and Casey—were all established theater workers in this scene, with their own separate careers to tend. But their new theater was meant to be something different, a communal effort, with everybody pitching in to develop Chicago theater artists and produce Chicago plays. To that end, seven of the founders put in a thousand dollars each for a start-up fund, and Gordon contributed a light board.

Their first offering, which was premiered in October 1974 in their slightly decrepit home at the Northside Auditorium, 3730 North Clark Street, was *The Velvet Rose*, by Stacy Myatt, directed by McGinnes. It was indeed original, a bizarre comedy/melodrama having to do with, among other things, cross-dressing and pussycats. It derived its funky, flamboyant style in part from a flourishing new strain of visual art, dubbed Chicago Imagism, that was being practiced by a group of brash young artists in the city. *The Velvet Rose* was an attempt to translate their kind of sassy, bold, and colorful urban surrealism into a popular theatrical equivalent. Unfortunately, it didn't work. *The Velvet Rose* was a flop, and Victory Gardens, which had barely started, was almost over.

Then, in November 1974, in the first of its many reversals of fortune, the theater had a hit, a country-western musical, *The Magnolia Club*, financed by an independent producer, with Victory Gardens providing the space for the show. A few months later, in May 1975, the auditorium housed another new work, *Sweet Bloody Liberty*, a ferocious revue/pageant staged by Paul Sills, the genius founding director of The Second City. It was a box-office failure; but at about the same time, in a coproduction with Goodman Theatre's Stage 2, the Gardens came up with a long-running success in *Three Women*, a vehicle for a trio of talented Chicago actresses, including Maguire, directed by O'Neal.

This hit-and-miss parade of productions added up to a rocky patch for Victory Gardens, an existence made all the more complex by the fact that there were eight people, each occupied with other career pursuits, in charge of setting direction and making decisions. The problem with this form of management was not lost on Allen Turner, the theater's future first board chairman. Seeing that this was perhaps too unique a way to run a theater, he proposed installing one single artistic director whose sole interest was fulfilling the Victory Gardens mission.

The man chosen for the job in 1977 was Dennis Začek, a native of Chicago's Southwest Side, a Northwestern University graduate, and an associate professor of theater at Loyola University Chicago who already had established strong ties with the theater. He had acted (slyly portraying a Bulgarian jewel thief in the original camp melodrama *Strangle Me*, by Frank Shiras); he had directed a sterling production of Harold Pinter's *The Caretaker;* and he was married to Marcelle McVay, the managing director, who had joined the Gardens in 1974 as its first salaried employee.

Life for them in the building at 3730 North Clark was busy but never easy. Začek, always careful in his words, admits that although at no time did he want to give up, there were times when he did think, "Boy, could we use a hit."

There were two performance spaces at 3730: the large proscenium stage on the second floor and a smaller studio space, where, in inclement weather, snowflakes and raindrops trickled from the roof down to members of the audience seated below.

Despite the hardships, Začek stuck to the theater's guiding principles of encouraging local talent. In his first few years he presented new plays by Chicago writers Alan Bates, David Blomquist, Alan Gross, Ruth Landis, William J. Norris, Nicholas A. Patricca, and Jackie Taylor, among others. He forged bonds with Latino and African American artists. For the theater's 1977–78 subscription schedule, he had Roger Brown, a leading Chicago Imagist artist, create the season's poster. And in 1979 he struck gold with the arrival of Sandy Shinner, a soft-spoken, self-effacing artist who joined the staff as audience development director and soon became the Gardens' associate artistic director, responsible for staging more than fifty plays in her long-running career.

In 1981, Victory Gardens said good-bye to the vagaries of Clark Street and moved south, sharing space and ownership of the two-story building at 2257 North Lincoln Avenue with the Body Politic Theatre. The two troupes combined forces for the Great Chicago Playwrights Exposition of 1987, a marathon program of new works, but in 1995, when the weakened Body Politic had to shut down for good, Začek, McVay, and company took over the entire building, which grew to include two main stages and two studio spaces.

Throughout this period, Victory Gardens continued to produce noteworthy new works by local authors. In 1985, James Sherman, a former Second Citizen, premiered his *The God of Isaac,* a sweet family comedy filled with home truths and sharp lines, and in 1989 he gave the Gardens its biggest hit ever with *Beau Jest,* directed by Začek, in which a nice Jewish girl snags a Gentile actor to portray her Jewish fiancé in order to please her parents. It broke box-office records in Chicago and went to New York for a record two-and-a-half-year run at the off-Broadway Lamb's Theatre.

Jeffrey Sweet, an Evanstonian who had moved to New York, launched his Chicago career in 1979 with the short *Porch,* the first of his eleven plays, most of which premiered at the Gardens. Claudia Allen, another prolific writer, came along in 1987, and there were dozens of additional works from such local writers as Jeff Berkson, Clifton Campbell, Rick Cleveland, Gloria Bond Clunie, Dean Corrin, Denise DeClue, Stuart Flack, Steven Ivcich, John Karraker, John Logan (who eventually turned to screenwriting such epic films as *Gladiator, The Last Samurai,* and *The Aviator*), Jamie O'Reilly, Douglas Post, Roger Rueff, Michael Smith, Studs Terkel, and Kristine Thatcher.

With premieres now making up a substantial part of the theater's seasons, Začek decided in 1996 to make official what had become obvious: Victory Gardens was a breeding ground for new plays. Positioning his organization for a special spot in the great Chicago-area theater market, he created the Playwrights Ensemble, made up of twelve individuals: Allen, Lonnie Carter, Steve Carter, Clunie, Corrin, Logan, Patricca, Post, Sherman, Charles Smith, Sweet, and Thatcher. Some of these writers have been much more active than others, but as a unit they form a group whose work is a driving force in filling the theater's stage and fulfilling its mission.

For Joyce Sloane, a founding member of the Gardens board, "it seemed the most natural thing in the world to do." The mission, simply stated, was centered on "serving playwrights and producing world premiere plays."

There were, and are, many theaters devoted to developing premiere work, but Victory Gardens stands distinctively apart from them in its ensemble structure. It provides a home base for its members, giving them, as part of the production process, a two-week workshop and a nine-preview run before a play's official opening.

Although the ensemble is at the core of production (a minimum of three ensemble plays is expected for each six-play season), new works by many other playwrights, local and national, are up for consideration, too. There has been a constant flow of original projects on the Gardens' stage, resulting in what Začek affirms is a record of "presenting more world premieres than any other theater in Chicago." (At the end of the 2004–5 season, the theater had produced 147 of them, 65 by ensemble members.)

That the theater has survived this noble and tricky course is due to the steadfast commitment of Začek, McVay, and Shinner and, in large part, to the enduring loyalty of its subscribers, who gladly support and encourage the varied, variable work put before them.

But producing new plays is by nature a risky business. There is no track record of performance on which to rely. There is no guarantee of consistent quality. And heaven knows how critics and audiences will take to the untested and unexpected.

These uncertainties can lead to frustration and dissatisfaction, and in the autumn of 2000 it led to near disaster. Board members, impatient with the new plays' season and eager to strike out with a more popular direction in a much larger theater, temporarily subverted Začek and McVay's authority, seeking to put them under control of a new executive director. After a stormy couple of weeks, however, the board revoked its earlier move, and, as Shinner says, "the mission of the theater was preserved."

Less than a year later, in a remarkable endorsement of their formerly embattled leadership, Začek, McVay, and Shinner stood on a Broadway stage to accept the 2001 Tony Award for regional theater, given in recognition of their theater's history of "displaying a continuous level of artistic achievement contributing to the growth of theater nationally." As with Chicago's Steppenwolf and Goodman in earlier years, the Gardens had reached the high prestige and national recognition that comes with the Tony. Začek, grateful and exultant, noted: "It couldn't have come at a better time."

Spurred by the Tony acclaim, the theater in 2004 set up plans to buy the Biograph movie theater at 2433 North Lincoln Avenue (where John Dillinger was gunned down by FBI agents in 1934) and convert it into an "American center for new plays," at the same time keeping the old building at 2257 North Lincoln as a rental facility for other off-Loop troupes.

Meanwhile, the original works kept coming: Sweet's *Immoral Imperatives* and *The Action Against Sol Schumann* (both in 2001), Corrin's *Battle of the Bands* (2002), Joel Drake Johnson's *The End of the Tour* (2003), Charles Smith's *Free Man of Color* (2004), and Lonnie Carter's *The Romance of Magno Rubio* (2004), to name but a few.

In these years, actors such as Harold Gould, Irma P. Hall, Julie Harris, William L. Petersen (an alumnus of Začek's acting classes in the 1970s), and Esther Rolle performed as guest artists alongside Chicago actors. And in 2004, Fritz Weaver gave a brilliant portrayal of a great man in decline in Joanna McClelland Glass's two-character drama *Trying*. Weaver, a Broadway and film veteran not used to the small confines of an off-Loop theater, took on the role with some reservations, but after a hit run in Chicago and a 2005 transfer to off Broadway in New York, he said, "Most places I've performed, it's all about the business. At Victory Gardens, it's all about the work."

A small fraction of that work is contained in this first anthology of plays that have received their premieres at the Gardens. They are similar in their use of small casts, which is appropriate for a small theater (195 seats) that works under a relatively small budget, but their styles cover a broad range, from the sharp social comedy/drama of Sweet's *Flyovers* to the ingenious contemporary verse comedy in the Molière mold of Sherman's delightful *Affluenza!*

All of them are by ensemble members, and all of them, of course, are original. Enjoy.

PREFACE

Dennis Začek

One Saturday morning approximately ten years ago, I was asked to speak extemporaneously about the Goodman, Steppenwolf, and Victory Gardens. The request for this compare-and-contrast exercise took place at a weekend meeting of the board of directors. After briefly listing the obvious differences of location, budget, and longevity, I focused on the essential drive and identity of each organization. I concluded that the Goodman, under the artistic direction of Robert Falls, was essentially a directors' theater and that most of the artistic programming choices emanated from Mr. Falls and his very capable staff of stage directors. As to the Steppenwolf, it seemed quite evident that the genesis of artistic choice came from the needs and talent of the ensemble of actors working under the dedicated leadership of Martha Lavey. Finally, I opined that Victory Gardens was a playwrights' theater. I explained that each year I selected a season based on the playwrights and their most relevant work. I sought out premieres that most clearly "spoke to the condition" of our audience. At this point Alvin Katz, then chairman of the board, said, "In other words, Victory Gardens has an ensemble of playwrights." Relieved to have survived the compare-and-contrast exercise, I responded with a resounding yes.

Less than a week passed before my phone started to ring. Numerous calls were placed by playwrights who had an association with Victory Gardens. Their inquiries could be reduced to a number of basic questions: "When was this ensemble established?" "How big is the ensemble?" "Am I part of it?" At this point it became clear to me that the time for a formalized establishment of an ensemble of playwrights had come to pass. As I reflected on the possible candidates for inclusion, I was certain that the group should in some way reflect the diversity of our great city of Chicago. After considerable reflection, I chose to establish an ensemble of twelve playwrights. While the ensemble is not a perfect example of the variety of voices present within our community, consideration for inclusion was given to age, gender, race, sexual preference, and religious background. Once the Playwrights Ensemble was established, the vitality, strength, and identity of our theater grew to a palpable level. There is no doubt in my mind that the creation of the ensemble led inexorably to the moment in which we received the 2001 Tony Award for excellence in the regional theater category.

While the ensemble members continue to create work in their own individual styles, their collective energy informs another distinctive nurturing mode. Since the writers view Victory Gardens Theater as their artistic home, they all benefit from a sense of security as well as a responsibility to the organization *and* to each other. We hope that this initial anthology will provide the reader with a sample of some of the work that has emerged from our unique environment.

VICTORY GARDENS THEATER PRESENTS

PECONG

STEVE CARTER

PLAYWRIGHT'S STATEMENT

There are those of my plays for which I take full blame, and there are those for which I take full responsibility. Fortunately (for you), you'll never get to see or read sixteen for which I take full blame. I didn't like them, so I shredded all copies except a copy of one I couldn't locate. It's out there somewhere to plague my spirit long after I'll have quit the scene. Along with *Eden, Nevis Mountain Dew, Dame Lorraine, Spiele '36, One Last Look, Primary Colors, Terraces, Mirage*, and *The Inaugural Tea*, *Pecong* is one for which I take (and happily so) full responsibility. All the aforementioned and some of the unmentioned, even those which I destroyed but nevertheless are still my "children," mean something to me. *Pecong*, however, is the play that was the most enjoyable for me to write, so it is extra special to me. I was having so much fun writing it, I deliberately did things to prolong the finishing of it, such as running out of paper and typewriter ribbons on the weekend so that I'd have to wait until Monday when the store opened to replenish my supplies. Yes, I said, type-writer ribbons. Remember them?

I won't go into any details about the philosophy of the play, the reasons that I wrote it, and all that. You read it and draw your own conclusions. I will say that I am forever indebted and grateful to the Victory Gardens Theater for providing me with the time, the space, and the wherewithal to write *Pecong* and for showing their faith in me and the play by rewarding me with its very first production. Usually when a prospective producer calls to say that he or she would like to present it at his or her theater, I say, "Thank you for your interest. Now, tell me the 'buts.'" That's when they start with, "Well, if you could cut this or change that . . ." That's when I thank them as politely as I can (not easy for me) and tell them to find a play that will meet all their needs and priorities. I thank the Victory Gardens Theater for including *Pecong* in its first anthology and giving you the opportunity to read the play as I wrote it and, with your imagination, see the play as I see it. They never had any "buts"!

This play is dedicated, with love, to my family: my late mother, Carmen; my sister, June; my nephew Scott; my nephew Steven and his wife, Denise, "de niece"; my two grandnephews, Steven II and Leeland; and my grandniece, Elise Sophia. Many special thanks to my friends Jerry, Sandy, and Alexandra Shinner Wilson and Zachary, Dennis, and Marcie McVay Začek and all the very special staff at the Victory Gardens Theater; to Michele Swanson, "Ms. Wonderful," for being in the Boyces' pool at just the right time, and the Boyces for having the pool; and to Graham Brown, for whom the role of Creon was written and who, in April 2002, finally got to play it, for his faithful and tireless efforts on behalf of the play. *Pecong* was written through the courtesy of the Marianne and Michael O'Shaughnessy Playwrights' Development Fund with grateful appreciation.

PRODUCTION HISTORY

Pecong, by Steve Carter, was first presented by Victory Gardens Theater, Chicago, Illinois, in January 1990.

PRODUCTION TEAM

Director	Dennis Začek
Set	James Dardenne
Costumes	Claudia Boddy
Lights	Robert Shook
Sound	Galen G. Ramsey
Composer	Willy Steele
Choreography	TC Carson
Production Stage Manager	Galen G. Ramsey
Assistant Director	Sandra Jean Verthein

CAST

Granny Root	Pat Bowie
Jason Allcock	Daniel Oreskes
Creon Pandit	Ernest Perry Jr.
Persis	Catherine Slade
Faustina Cremoney	Wandachristine
Sweet Bella	Diane White
Mediyah	Celeste Williams
Cedric	Gary Yates
Oppidans	Feleccia C. Boyd, Shanesia L. Davis, Lydia R. Gartin, Shawn Goodwin, Thomas W. Greene V, Alison Halstead, Dexter L. Warr, Christopher Williams

The play was subsequently produced by Tricycle Theatre, London, England, in 1992; Newark Symphony Hall, Newark, New Jersey, in 1992; the American Conservatory Theater, San Francisco, California, in 1993; and the Phillip Sherlock Centre for the Creative Arts, Kingston, Jamaica, in May 2003.

CHARACTERS

Mediyah, *an Obeah queen*
Granny Root, *her grandmother, also an Obeah queen*
Cedric, *twin brother to Mediyah*
Faustina Cremoney, *an island woman and a minor "prophetress"*
Persis, *sister to Faustina*
Creon Pandit, *the own-all, do-all, and existing Grand King Calabash*
Sweet Bella the Silent, *daughter to Creon*
Jason Allcock, *a visitor from a neighboring island*
Damballah, *played by the actor portraying Creon*

Additional characters include townspeople, dancers, musicians, and so forth. The number of townspeople can vary from theater to theater. It has been done with as few as two and three musicians, but it does tend to make the production look rather spare.

STAGING

Time: Well in the past
Places: Trankey Island (Ile Tranquille), an "island of the mind" in the Caribbean, and Miedo Wood Island, a dark, mysterious place

PROLOGUE

[*The wee hours before cockcrow on a lushly verdant Caribbean "island of the mind." On the floor of a hut,* MEDIYAH *sleeps on a pallet. Lantern in hand,* GRANNY ROOT *enters, thrice circles the figure of her sleeping granddaughter, utters some "mysterious" words, and gestures, symbolically.* MEDIYAH *stirs.*]

MEDIYAH: Is you, Granny?

GRANNY ROOT: Who else?

MEDIYAH: I try to stay up, but you was gone so long, I had was to doze off.

GRANNY ROOT: Plenty to do. Get up from there and wipe the sleep from you eye. We have t'ing and t'ing to do, and we ain't have much time.

MEDIYAH: I ain't want this t'ing to happen.

GRANNY ROOT: It have to pass, darlin'. This old heart done beat long past she time. These old bone, them tired. Is about time this body get throw in the dirt and cause new tree and food to grow.

MEDIYAH: But I ain't want you to die.

GRANNY ROOT: Ain't I done told you I ain't like that word? I ain't want you to use it! Ain't I done tell you I goin' alway be with you? Is through you, you old granny goin' live forever.

MEDIYAH: I know you say this, but how I know it true?

GRANNY ROOT: You callin' Granny "liar" to she face?

MEDIYAH: I ain't mean it that way. I just want to know if I reach me hand, I could touch you?

GRANNY ROOT: Better than that! Better than anybody "touch"! You goin' feel Granny. Granny goin' be there!

MEDIYAH: I goin' see you?

GRANNY ROOT: Only you, darlin'. Only you.

MEDIYAH: You make me promise?

GRANNY ROOT: I goin' told you this one last time. You goin' see Granny when you want to see she. Granny goin' let you see she when she want you to see she. And since Granny always goin' want you to see she, you goin' see she. No make me say that again. Now, give me you ear. Time flyin'. Is a lot of thing I never tell you.

MEDIYAH: I all the time know that when you want me to know thing, you goin' tell me, and if you ain't want me to know thing, you ain't goin' tell me.

GRANNY ROOT: Well, you granny goin' meet she maker and still she no say too much, but certain thing you have to do. Certain thing you have to know. Is only one person in this world I ever love like you and that is you mother. I try me best to love you brother, but is you take me heart. You is you mother all repeat. Cedric have too much of he father in he.

MEDIYAH: But, Granny, Cedric and me . . . twin. We have the same daddy.

GRANNY ROOT: You hear what I say? You is all you mother! Cedric . . . all he father!

MEDIYAH: Yes. Cedric even look like . . .

GRANNY ROOT: Hush! Don't even utter that name! We ain't never mention that name. If you have suspicion, keep it in you head and you heart. You ain't need that name in you mouth. Now, we have to go past all that 'cause t'ing already set in motion. I been out doin' and doin'. Come here to me!

[GRANNY ROOT *firmly grasps* MEDIYAH's *arms.*]

Before,
all you did know, for sure,
was herb and root and bush to cure
a pauper at death door.
Now, darlin' granddaughter,
you goin' know more.
Granny leavin' you
for you own appliance,
all she power and she science.

MEDIYAH: Don't leave me, Granny.

GRANNY ROOT: All is ready.
T'ing in motion.
You can't stop tide or wave
in ocean.
Once you was baby,
then you wean.
So you was princess,
now . . . you queen!
Stand up tall
and wipe you eye.
You is queen
and queen don't cry.

MEDIYAH: What about Cedric?

GRANNY ROOT: Cedric is man! Only woman does have power and knowledge of science in this family. Nothing Granny can do for Cedric no more. You do for him what you can, if you willin'. He you brother and he not a bad sort, but he too much he father and that same father cause me and you grief. Now hear me 'cause I think it goin' soon day. The minute I shut me eye, you reach with you hand and pull out me heart. Wrap it in tingus leaf while it still beat. If anybody want, all you could have you funeral funnery and t'ing, then throw this ol' carcass in the hole that I done dig out back. Then, you and only you take me heart and bury she on Miedo Wood Island.

MEDIYAH: Miedo Wood Island? But, Granny, I can't go there. Nobody can go there alone. Since I been live on this earth, only one person me ever see go there and come back to tell it . . . and that is you.

GRANNY ROOT: And now, you goin' be the only one go there.

MEDIYAH: But that place have all wild animal and serpent and haunt and t'ing.

GRANNY ROOT: Mediyah! You queen now. No place hold badness for you. You born on Miedo Wood Island like you mother before you and me. You have nothing to fear! You the queen of Miedo Wood Island. It belong to you now. Nothing touch you! And if you feel to take somebody there . . .

MEDIYAH: Somebody? . . .

GRANNY ROOT: . . . nothing touch he, either.

MEDIYAH: Granny, what you talkin'?

GRANNY ROOT: Remember, you power is great.

Make you no misuse it.

Make you no abuse it.

Make you no confuse it.

Or, dear heart, you could lose it.

But you could have lickle bit of fun now and then. I always have lickle fun doin' t'ing to that Faustina Cremoney. She of the great trifling effort. But the gods, them know I ain't mean she no real harm. She can sometime be lickle botheration, but she not too bad a sort. Have some toleration with people like she. Howsoever, if somebody do you a true and harsh badness, defend youself with all you power. Bring down rage and destruction. Don't care who it is and no mind the cost to you, so long you have honor and standin' when you see you face in you glass. Now I goin'. I hear cock stampin' he foot and clearin' he throat to sound "Mornin'!" Come! Let Granny caress you one next time.

MEDIYAH: I ain't want this time to come!

GRANNY ROOT: What I tell you 'bout that, eh? Granny goin' all the time be with you.

When it dark. When it light.
When it day. When it night.
When it sun. When it storm.
When it breeze. When it warm.
Well, you goin' stand there and let me go to me grave without kiss?
MEDIYAH: Oh, Granny. Granny.

[*From offstage comes the lilting rhythm of Calypso music. In the distance, a dancing figure clad like a chanticleer struts and prances.*]

GRANNY ROOT: It time! Remember me! Think of me and you mother and let we have vengeance. Good-bye, darlin'.
MEDIYAH: What?
GRANNY ROOT: Bye, girl. Now.

[*Suddenly, there is a cock crow, and the dancing figure mimics a real rooster. Simultaneously,* GRANNY ROOT *lifts her arms to heaven, and* MEDIYAH *screams and plunges her hand into* GRANNY ROOT's *chest and pulls out her pulsating heart. She wraps it in a large leaf as* GRANNY ROOT *falls back, lifeless, in her chair.* MEDIYAH *sinks to the ground at her grandmother's feet. The scene brightens just a bit, and the dancing figure is revealed to be* CEDRIC. *He is exuberantly tipsy and is accompanied by an entourage that consists of two overly attentive dancing ladies and some musicians.*]

CEDRIC: Mediyah! Mediyah! Rouse youself and make you come out here and greet you brother, the champion!
I win again! I win again!
Four time in a row
I win again! I win again!
King of Calypso.
I vanquish all me rival
and scuttle all me foe.
I put them to rout
with sweet word from me mout'.
All I do is sing out,
and down they go.
Is then when they fin'
this night made for me, one, to shine.
And I win again! I win again!
Ain't I told you so?
I win again! I win again!

Four time in a row.
One more time to go
and the permanent title of
Mighty, Royal, Most Perfect, Grand King Calabash
is mine.
Yes, girl. You shoulda see you brother. I all the time magnificent and
superb, but tonight . . . I go past that. Tonight, I sing better than God!
I win again! I win again!
Me put them all to shame.
I win again! I win again!
Them too sorry that them came.
Them saga boy so wilted
them faint right to the floor.
Them kick up them feet
and can't compete
no more!
I win again! I win again!
I lash they with me tongue.
I win again! I win again!
I King of the Pecong.
I bring home the medal,
the cup, and the cash.
Higher than high is how I does rate.
Climb out you bed and celebrate.
I win the title four time straight.
One next time and I permanently be the great
Mighty, Royal, Most Perfect, Grand King Calabash.

[CEDRIC *and his companions are dancing vigorously when* MEDIYAH, *now clad in mourning, comes out of the hut with the wrapped still-beating heart in her hands.* CEDRIC, *on seeing her, sobers immediately.*]

All you, less that noise! I say, "Quiet!" nuh?

[*Everyone goes silent, staring at* MEDIYAH.]

The ol' lady gone, eh?

[MEDIYAH *nods.*]

She go peaceful?

[MEDIYAH *nods.*]

She ain't have no pain?

MEDIYAH: No.

CEDRIC: Then, she go good. What more all we could want? She run a long and good race, so why you look so baleful. All we have to pass. Who know that better than she? No, Sister . . .

We ain't have to be sad.

We ain't have to feel bad.

Let we take she and put she in the ground,

Pronounce some pleasant word, then prance around.

Let we sing and take libation.

Then let we make some lickle celebration.

Mop up you face and let we see you smile.

Granny Root goin' home . . . in style!

[*He gestures to his musicians.*]

All you boy, help me pick she up and tote she to she restin' place.

MEDIYAH: She hole already dig in the yard. Put she in it gentle.

CEDRIC: Where you go?

MEDIYAH: Elsewhere!

CEDRIC: What you do?

[MEDIYAH *holds the leaf-wrapped, audibly beating heart aloft. Thunder. Lightning flashes.* CEDRIC *is suddenly trancelike.*]

I understand!

MEDIYAH: All you, be gentle with she remains!

[CEDRIC *and the men pick up the corpse and, joined by the two dancing girls, do symbolic, ritualistic movement, then exit. As* MEDIYAH *prepares to leave,* GRANNY ROOT, *now clad in black veiling and holding a large opened black umbrella trimmed with the same black floor-reaching veiling, appears.* MEDIYAH *still holds the heart aloft.*]

Remember, Granny. You make me a promise to all the time be here.

GRANNY ROOT: And since when Granny Root fail to keep she promise?

Granny goin' all the time be with you, girl.

MEDIYAH: I the granddaughter of Granny Root.

Let everybody know it.

I the granddaughter of Granny Root.

Let everybody know it!

[MEDIYAH, *followed by the ghost of* GRANNY ROOT, *exits. Lights!*]

ACT 1

SCENE 1

[*Some weeks later. Cockcrow on the island. In her hut,* PERSIS *sleeps on a straw pallet.* FAUSTINA, *garbed as befits an Obeah queen, enters with authority.*]

FAUSTINA: Persis!

PERSIS: What is it, Faustina? I just lay down me head from me revels and here
   you come. What you want?

FAUSTINA: Rise, woman! Is a brand-new day.
   You want to sleep you life away?

PERSIS: Be-shite!

FAUSTINA: The sun done rise. The cock done cry.
   It time for you to ope' you eye.

PERSIS: Woman, stop! I sick to death with this rhyme business. Every mornin'
   you wake up, you chantin' rhyme like you is some high priestress or some
   such. Just 'cause all of a sudden you learn how to read lickle piece of card
   and t'ing.

FAUSTINA: Aha! So that what do you of late? You jealous 'cause I get the gift.
   You been so ever since I get Granny Root card, them. Well, m'dear,
   I ain't ask and I ain't make deal.
   I ain't beg and I sure ain't steal.

PERSIS: There she go again!

FAUSTINA: I dream Granny Root come to me just 'fore she die,
   and she voice let out one baleful sigh.
   "I goin' soon," she say. "'Twon't be long,
   but you know how I does like me rum strong.
   So if you put a crock o' you best grog 'side me stone,
   I goin' leave you the gift of prophecy for you very own."

PERSIS: Deliver me!

FAUSTINA: When it come to brewin', you know I better than good.
   All the time boil up cane and t'ing better than you could.
   You act like is me fault that me brew up the best
   and make rum stronger than you and the rest.
   'Taint me fault when me get home and open me door,
   me find Granny Root tarot card sittin' on me floor.

PERSIS: I still think you does find them old, worn-out card in Granny Root trash. Why she leave them to you? She make rum better than anybody. She ain't have to seek from you.

FAUSTINA: She did always confess a secret admiration for me brew.

PERSIS: You too fool and you think me one, the same. You does march round here makin' utterance sound like they is pronouncement from on high. If Granny Root let you have them card, she only funnin' with you like she all the time used to do or she plannin' some special trick. She ain't leave you no book or potion or scientific power.

FAUSTINA: Well, after all, I ain't relate to she.
   Blood thicker than water.
   And all them kind of recipe,
   she leave to she black-face granddaughter.

PERSIS: You better hush you mouth 'fore Mediyah hear you and work gooz-zoo on you hind part.

FAUSTINA: Long as I wearin' all these amulet,
   I ain't have the first thing to fear.
   'Sides, that black monkey-face creature
   ain't nowhere near.

PERSIS: Hah! The woman have ear like bat. You better watch you tongue, 'cause you ain't know what she capable of. Granny Root all the time say when that girl come into she own, she goin' be even more powerful than she. You and me both does know that still water does run deep, deep, deep and all that glitter far from gold!

FAUSTINA: And, pray tell, what that does mean?

PERSIS: Nothin'! I just feel to say it. You think you is the only one could make pronouncement?

FAUSTINA: Well,
   speak of the devil and here come she brother.
   All fill up with heself . . . and no other.

PERSIS: Hmmm. He and he entourage!

[*Enter* CEDRIC, *quatro in hand, and his ragtag band of followers.*]

   Mornin', Mr. Cedric.

CEDRIC: Is me you a-talk to?

PERSIS: Who else passin'?

CEDRIC: If is me you want to address,
   you must say, "His Mighty and Royalness."

PERSIS: Oh, man, shut you face, Mr. Big Shot. The rule say you have to win Pecong and Calypso five time consecutive 'fore you can lay claim to bein'

Mighty, Royal, or Grand. You ain't win but four. Only ol' Creon Pandit and he daddy 'fore he win five time. And come what you bet, if Creon did have a boy instead of he daughter, Sweet Bella the Silent, them Pandit would still have claim to the title. Maybe you think you is a Pandit. Come to think of it . . . Now that I does look . . . you does have the look of Creon 'bout you, you know. 'Specially round you eye, you nose, you mouth, you ear, you chin. You ain't think so, Faustina?

CEDRIC: I better than all them Pandit.

PERSIS: Is what you think. You voice like a rasp. I ain't see how come you win four time . . . much less . . . one. I know the judge them have substance and honor, so you must be use some big magic or some such to get them pick you, Mr. Cedric.

CEDRIC: Cedric the Magnificent is no more me name.

I now the Mighty, Royal, Most Perfect,

Grand King Calabash of substance and fame.

PERSIS: Oh, God. Save me from this rhyme to-do!

CEDRIC: I, one born Calypsonian. Who better to rhyme?

Whomsoever come to challenge me, just waste up they precious time.

PERSIS: Shite!

CEDRIC: And what do you, Auntie? How come you so closemout'?

FAUSTINA: Ain't none you damn auntie,

so no call me such.

You can't see what I doin',

Mr. Know So Much?

You can't see that I readin' card?

Just use you eye. That ain't too hard!

PERSIS: Double shite! Now the two of them rhymin' . . .

CEDRIC: Them card look for all the world like no other

than them that did belong to me old grandmother.

FAUSTINA: Where them come from is my affair,

'long as I get them fair and square.

PERSIS: Stop! I say stop!

It like one bad dream.

If I hear one more rhyme,

I goin' scream . . .

Oh, be-Christ! Them have me doin' it!

CEDRIC: Pay she no mind. Is me you readin'?

FAUSTINA: I just readin', but it look like you in the deck.

CEDRIC: What them say 'bout me?

FAUSTINA: You ain't want to hear.
CEDRIC: You think I does frighten? You think I does scare?
    Nothin' does fright me. Nothin' dare!

[PERSIS, *almost silently, screams.*]

    I think you does forget what is the trut'.
    That I is the grandson of Granny Root.
FAUSTINA: That ain't mean a t'ing.
    All we know is only the female in you line
    that does have power to do science and divine.
CEDRIC: You better tell me now,
    you wrinkle-up ol' cow!
PERSIS: Why you mout' so nasty? Tell he the bad news, Faustina.
FAUSTINA: I too happy to do so.
    These card, them say some new singer comin' roun',
    and it look like Cedric goin' down!
CEDRIC: Who? Who risin' to challenge?
    Where the man?
    Let he show he face, if him can!
    Find me the man so skill at rhymin'!
    Find me the man who have the timin'
    that this Mighty Calabash possess.
    Oh, yes.
    Find me the man who can beat me.
    If him so willin',
    tell the villain
    to step forth and try to unseat me.
    I raise me sweet voice, loud and clear,
    and issue challenge to all who can hear.
    I say to all assemble here
    and far and near,
    in melodious combat, come and meet me
    and see if you is the one
    who can lose he life,
    he home, he wife,
    he fork, he knife,
    he stress, he strife.
    The time most rife,
    me son,

for tryin' to defeat me.
Defeat me? Hah! Never!
I am the Mighty, Royal, Most Perfect,
Grand King Calabash . . . forever!

[CEDRIC *and his "groupies" play and dance furiously. Then, at a signal from him, they march off.*]

PERSIS: See how them young gal hang off he?
Like them 'fraid to let go he arm.
Like them 'fraid him goin' vanish into thin air.
Like him so much Mr. Charm.
FAUSTINA: Eh-eh! You rhyme?
PERSIS: It contagious.
Him think him the end-all and be-all,
but pride does goeth before the fall.
FAUSTINA: Yes, Miss Adage, I done already read he card.
Him goin' fall and him goin' hit hard.
PERSIS: You see that, eh?
FAUSTINA: Yes, man. It plain like day.
And when him fall and hit the groun',
is someone from he own house goin' bring he down.
Hahoii! But look who crossin' now.
PERSIS: Them two! Hmmm!

[CREON, *followed by his daughter,* SWEET BELLA. *She walks seductively, giving the eye to every male she sees.*]

Mornin', Creon Pandit! Mornin', Sweet Bella Pandit!

[SWEET BELLA *smiles, condescendingly.*]

CREON: All you here as usual, eh? So, what the news? For I know if there any, all you would know it, 'cause you all the time on sentry duty like two sentinel. So, who pass durin' the night? Who doin' rudeness with who? Who deliver baby for who? Who fart?
FAUSTINA: You ol' buzzard. Me goods come in?
CREON: Them lickle piece of cloth you does order been come into me emporia long time. It there waitin' for you. You have the cash to pay for it?
FAUSTINA: I have credick. You know I alway pay me bill.
CREON: Credick, shite! The last time were almost two year 'fore you pay me.

FAUSTINA: Brute! Who tell you to put me business on the road. Well, I guess you can't help youself. Is all that Chinee, Syrian, and Indian blood mix up in you.

CREON: What you say?

FAUSTINA: As I does so often say, too much strain for you vein!

CREON: You of Zulu. I ain't have the first piece of Chinee in me.

PERSIS: How you know? You daddy keep record of he ramblin'?

FAUSTINA: And who you callin' Zulu? We ancestor come here straight from Egypt!

CREON: Strike me blue and holy shite!

Cleopatra think she white!

[*He surrenders to convulsive laughter.*]

PERSIS: I ain't see nothin' a bit funny. Both of us descend straight from the Nile.

CREON: Ooh-hoo! You hear that, Sweet Bella?

Both of they does come from the Nile.

Well, so does crocodile!

Come! Let we go 'fore these two North African lift up they shift and pull two asp from 'mong them old basket of fig and sic they on we.

FAUSTINA: I readin' you card, Creon Pandit. Somethin' dire goin' befall you.

CREON: Hahoii! Somethin' dire already befall. I see you the first thing this mornin'. What more "dire" than that, eh? Come, Sweet Bella.

[SWEET BELLA, *silently laughing, obeys her father and they go off,* CREON *still convulsed with laughter.*]

She ancestor from Egypt! Is a wonder she even know Egypt. Is a wonder she know Egypt a-tall!

FAUSTINA [*calling after him*]: The card, them say you goin' have big trouble.

PERSIS: That man still pretty, you know!

FAUSTINA: He too pretty, and he still have plenty big stone for a man he age.

PERSIS: But that don't diminish with age, m'dear. Only it ability to rise up and dance round. I still like the way him pant fit he. You ever take he?

FAUSTINA: Is for me to know and you to mind you business. You?

PERSIS: I ain't shame to say. Yes!

FAUSTINA: You too lie!

PERSIS: 'Twas too dear and precious a moment in me life to debate with you. Who comin' next, Miss Oracle?

FAUSTINA: Yes. Change subject. Is Mediyah.

PERSIS: I does feel sorry for she sometimes. She look so sad and different since Granny Root pass. Like she ain't know life. Like she dry.

FAUSTINA: Ain't you would be dry, too, if you ain't never have man for moist you? Man don't want she. It run in the family. Creon Pandit ain't never even think 'bout marryin' she mother. Even when he find she carrying she and Cedric in she belly for he.

PERSIS: Careful, woman! Mediyah might could hear you.

FAUSTINA: She still far off.

PERSIS: Remember she know science and t'ing. She still Granny Root granddaughter.

FAUSTINA: All we know Granny Root the queen of science and t'ing, but this granddaughter ain't she. We ain't have the first sign that the woman pass on she power to this one. She have yet to let we see one lickle miracle. All we know Mediyah know herb and bush for healin', but who ain't know that?

PERSIS: But Mediyah all the time know more than anybody. It come natural to she. And she still the only one can go to Miedo Wood Island for special herb and bush and root and t'ing and come back. Ain't no animal, haunt, or t'ing does ever bother she. She charm! Sometime she does talk wild and crazy, and when I peep me eye in she window, she 'lone and solitary, but I swear, and on more than one occasion, me hear she sayin', "Granny, this . . ." and "Granny, that . . ."! Hup! It she, for true!

[MEDIYAH *comes on, pulling a small boat on wheels in which the ghost of* GRANNY ROOT *sits with a small earthenware crock of rum, from which she occasionally sips. She is unseen by* PERSIS, FAUSTINA, *or anyone else onstage except* MEDIYAH, *who, unnoticed by* PERSIS, *gives* FAUSTINA *a casual but significant glance . . . at which* FAUSTINA *freezes.*]

Hello, Mediyah. Where you a-go on this hot day?

MEDIYAH: Ah? The day feel hot to you? It feel cool to me.

PERSIS: Now that I does hear you say it, it do feel cool.

MEDIYAH: Yes. It cool with just a trifle too much heat.

PERSIS: I notice that. It cool, yet it hot!

MEDIYAH: You was all the time quite perceptive.

PERSIS: So, where you travelin' on this cool, hot day?

MEDIYAH: I goin' where I goin', to do what I goin' do. If you friend, the minor prophetress, could move she mouth, she might could tell you, but I had was to still she for a lickle bit 'cause I ain't care for she tone. Faustina darlin', I only havin' lickle fun with you 'cause, number one . . . you no worth me energy or me true power and, number two, I in a very good mood. But you remember, I ain't never smell fart in me life. You want know why? 'Cause no matter how silent they does come out a person hind part, I able to hear them and move out the way. So you must figure, if I able to hear silent fart, not that I fully comparin' you to a silent fart . . . mind you, but if I able to hear silent fart, you know I can hear when people say vicious thing 'bout me and me family. You get that? Now, Persis, after I move on, make you count to seven and this ol' rag will regain she speech and movement. She so light in substance, all I need is me thought, alone, to send she to oblivion if me want. She could hear me, it true, but I feel you should tell she. That way, we make sure you know it, too.

[MEDIYAH, *pulling the little boat, goes off.* GRANNY ROOT, *motionless throughout the preceding, now turns to look at the two women and laughs uproariously, but silently. As soon as they're out of sight,* PERSIS *bolts to* FAUSTINA.]

PERSIS: Faustina? Oh, God! Faustina?

[MEDIYAH *returns.*]

MEDIYAH: Oh, yes. Tell she to get some tan bark and weave it into a true collar for wear round she neck if she want some lickle protection from me. So long, darlin' Persis. So long, creature.

[MEDIYAH *goes again.*]

PERSIS: Oh, God, God, God! You see what you and you mouth get you? One! Ain't I tell you the woman could hear a mosquito makin' pee-pee on welwet? Two! I tell you the woman have extraordinary power! Three! She know science! She have skill! Four! And you goin' bait she just 'cause you could read lickle piece of card and sign! That ain't power! Five! Is a wonder she ain't change you into a she-goat! Is a wonder she ain't make soldier crab chew on you titty and make wart all over you face! Is a wonder she even tell me to count to seven!

[FAUSTINA *doesn't move.*]

I say, "Seven!" Wait! Maybe I miss. Make I recount. One, two, three, four, five, six, seven! I say it right! Seven ain't the right number. Faustina, I can't break the spell. I 'fraid you done for. I 'fraid you speechless forever. Well, at least you ain't die!

[MEDIYAH, *pulling her boat, returns.*]

MEDIYAH: Ain't I tell you I was funnin'? Now, I goin', for true.

PERSIS: But wait, kind Mediyah. You tell me the number is seven. I count to seven, and me poor sister still ain't move.

MEDIYAH: Oh, yes. I lie! I tell you I was funnin'. The number is ten. For true! Better say it fast for she look for all the world like she goin' pass monumental gas if she don't let out some word soon.

PERSIS: One, two, three—

MEDIYAH: No! You must wait till I gone, and I ain't in no big rush. I just goin' tra-la-la at me own pace. Take me own sweet time, tra-la-la, tra-la-la, tra-la-la . . .

[MEDIYAH, *pulling the cart with the veiled and silently chuckling* GRANNY ROOT, *goes off. This time,* PERSIS *follows her a bit to make sure she's gone.*]

PERSIS: One, two, three, four, five, six, seven, eight, nine . . . and I hope she ain't havin' more hilarity with we this time. Believe me, Faustina, I ain't even see the woman when she put on spell.

[FAUSTINA, *almost out of the spell, looks as if she's about to explode. She makes muffled noises and tries to stamp her foot.*]

Oh, yes. Ten!

[FAUSTINA *stomps free of her enforced trance and gasps for breath.*]

FAUSTINA: Bark! Strip me some bark, woman! The succubus try to turn me to stone. Fetch me piece bark! That damn criminal try to choke me! Bark! Bark!

PERSIS: You ain't learn? You still spoutin' insult?

FAUSTINA [*in a more cautious whisper*]: Fetch me the bark, woman! The witch . . . I mean . . . she . . . that one try everything she know to take 'way me vitals. Bark, woman! Hurry, nuh? Fetch me a big piece o' bark!

PERSIS: I fetchin'. I fetchin'.

[PERSIS *runs offstage as* FAUSTINA *continues gasping for breath.* PERSIS *returns, carrying some strips of bark from a tree.*]

Here!

FAUSTINA: Why you a-hand me them for?

PERSIS: Ain't you yell and scream so 'cause you want it? Ain't you cause me to run round like damn wild Indian and damn near bruck up me foot lookin' for this damn shitey bark?

FAUSTINA: But ain't you the one so Miss Artful with she hand and needle and thread and t'ing. Weave me a collar, nuh?

PERSIS: You hear the ingrate? "Weave me a collar, nuh?" Well, you could tell me when the word "please" distappear from the English language, eh?

FAUSTINA: No time for no "please"! I think I dyin'.

PERSIS: If wish was dream and you should live so long!

FAUSTINA: Weave, woman. Weave!

PERSIS: Rass!

[*Lights.*]

SCENE 2

[*Miedo Wood Island.* MEDIYAH, *pulling the boat with* GRANNY ROOT, *enters. Rocks and branches of palm trees are arranged to look like two thrones.* GRANNY ROOT *sits on one of them and seems to be listening for something or someone.*]

MEDIYAH: Okay, Granny, we here. Maybe now you could part you lip and tell me why I have to come here today. I ain't need to come here. I already have enough herb and bush and root in the house where I ain't have to forage for another fortnight or two unless is a breakout of some plague or epidemic or some such. Why you have such urgency for this place today?

GRANNY ROOT: Hush, girl.

MEDIYAH: Why you have you ear on a-cock so for?

GRANNY ROOT: Aha! All in readiness. It soon time.

MEDIYAH: Soon time for what?

GRANNY ROOT: Somebody soon come.

MEDIYAH: Granny darlin', everybody, them know Miedo Wood Island have all sort of haunt and wild animal and t'ing. Who so fool to brave all that by comin' here?

GRANNY ROOT: Somebody brave and fool.

MEDIYAH: Well, whoever 'tis, too much fool for me. I ain't want to meet such.

GRANNY ROOT: Somebody comin'. Granny know! Granny always know! You ain't want to own it, but you does know, too.

MEDIYAH: Sometime I does forget you dead, you know.

GRANNY ROOT: Ain't I told you 'bout usin' that word?

MEDIYAH: I does forget that, too, 'cause ever since you . . . that word you ain't want me to say, you ain't leave me 'lone long enough to get used to the fact that you is really . . . that word you ain't want me to say. And, what is more, you ain't been . . . that word you ain't want me to say, long enough for me to get used to the fact that you really . . . that word you ain't want me to say. You know what I tryin' to say, Granny darlin'?

GRANNY ROOT: You know, sometime you does miss you pass. We have to be serious, girl. I leave lickle something quite untidy on this earth when me bone get the call from yonder. I thought I could rectify in me own time, but voice greater than mine say, "All thing in they own time!" So, it fallin' to you to take care of everything for Granny. So it be! Aha! Footfall! He comin'!

MEDIYAH: He? Man comin' to defy this evil wood?

GRANNY ROOT [*chanting*]: You Granny Root granddaughter. You be the best.
You do this thing for Granny, then Granny rest.
You give youself over to all them God of Greatness.
Give youself over to all them old God of Greatness
and Blackness.
Give youself over.
Let they take you.
Give youself over.
Let they make you
Granny Root granddaughter, for true.
Give youself over.
I goin' be here.
Give youself over
and let he see, here
Granny Root granddaughter is you.
Give youself over.
Give youself over.
Give youself over.

[*There is a flash of lightning and a roll of thunder. For an instant* MEDIYAH *and* GRANNY ROOT *seem to be frozen in time. There is another flash of lightning, more thunder, and an agonizing scream from a man somewhere in the wood. At that scream,* GRANNY ROOT *disappears.*]

MEDIYAH: Granny, you hear that? But, wait. Where you a-go? Granny? Granny?

GRANNY ROOT [*from offstage*]: You ain't need to see me. Go see who scream in the wood.

[MEDIYAH *obeys. Shortly after, she comes, aiding a young man* (JASON) *with much difficulty. His clothes are torn away to the point where, except for a piece of rag here and there, he'd be naked. He collapses on the ground at the feet of* MEDIYAH.]

MEDIYAH: Oh, God! But you is a pretty piece of flesh!

JASON: Thank you, missy. Is so woman all the time tell me. Thank you, God, for lettin' a woman be the last thing I see 'fore I pass.

MEDIYAH: Pass? But you is too pretty to die.

JASON: Me know that, but I think I cashin' in me chips all the same.

MEDIYAH: Well you could tell me you name 'fore you make all you good-bye and t'ing.

JASON: In life I was Jason Allcock from Tougou Island. Known the entire length and breadth of Tougou as Jason the Ram, born Calypsonian, extraordinaire.

MEDIYAH: And tell me, Mr. Jason Allcock, you pretty ram goat, what you doin' here in this wild, lickle piece of spit in the ocean. This wood have haunt. This island death to human being. You ain't hear that?

JASON: I am one born Calypso . . . Oh, I say that already. I come here because a ol' dead-face woman come to me in a dream and tell me to come here. She say in this wood does grow the calabash tree. This calabash tree does have the best wood in the entire world to make quatro. She say, too, that here it does have a cat blacker than thought . . . which if I could catch it and rip out she entrail, it gut does make string for the quatro. She say if I combine the calabash wood and the cat gut, I would have heaven for a voice and a quatro that sound like golden harp.

MEDIYAH: And why you must have such?

JASON: For the challenge!

MEDIYAH: What is this "challenge" and why it so important you risk up you life?

JASON: I hear 'bout this pretender to the throne of Royal, Mighty, Most Perfect, Grand King Calabash. Them say him win four time and goin' for five, then him Calabash for life.

MEDIYAH: I hear such.

JASON: I here to put a stop to that, 'cause no man can match me when it come to Pecong and t'ing. But this same ol' woman tell me in the dream, quatro from this wood not only the best but make me completely invincible. I hear this selfsame, so-call champion nightingale get he wood and gut string from here.

MEDIYAH: Is so you hear?

JASON: Is so. But this same ol' hag no tell me this forest so brutal and vicious. When I come to this place, a tempestuous storm lash out at me and over-turn me craft. I had was to swim ashore fightin' and dodgin' all kind of shark, them. Then I pull meself here, and all kind of wild t'ing snap and spit at me and me clothing tear off and leave me lookin' like bare-ass pickney.

MEDIYAH: Bare-ass pickney lookin' sweet to these eye.

JASON: Thank you, sweet thing. On a regular day I would done long time grab you and pitch you to the floor and do you a rudeness, but I ain't have the strength today. I dyin'.

MEDIYAH: Is so you think?

JASON: Well, like I say, all them wild critter does rear and tear at me, but I fight them off with me cutlass. I swingin' machete at all of them, but they too numerous and them chase me right to the calabash tree. It like I could see golden quatro dangle from every leaf. I take me cutlass, and I 'bout to fell the tree, when . . . yarrak! A cat, bigger and blacker than the universe, jump from the topmost branch and land 'pon top me. I tell you, we havin' some punch-up before I give she a final cuff. She scream like a ol' woman and fall out. I slit she open and rip out she gut. Is while I tendin' to this with me back turn, I feel . . . doop! The damn, dread calabash tree cobra strike me a fatal blow. Look you! You see the mark? So I ain't have long. And worse yet, I done leave me wood and me gut in the damn jungle. This the first time you could call me a fool. I believe in a dream. I guess I must be goin' now, 'cause you standin' over me and everything already lookin' dark.

MEDIYAH: What you mean by that, mister?

JASON: I mean the blacker the berry, the sweeter the juice. Lord, it make me think . . . Is only three thing I regret I ain't do 'fore I kick out. One! I ain't leave no son. I ain't leave son, the first, behind me!

MEDIYAH: Pretty ram like you?

JASON: I have plenty daughter all over Tougou, but that ain't no 'complishment.

MEDIYAH: No?

JASON: None of them woman, them, ever bring me boy. All man need son to carry on he name. Gal pretty, but they can't sing Calypso in the tent. The rule say no woman for sing in the Calypso tent!

MEDIYAH: If you dyin' like you say, you wastin' time. What the next two regret?

JASON: I ain't goin' be here to challenge this four-year upstart for the championship. Oh, woman, if I was not 'bout to meet me creator, I would compose a lickle lilt for you. Words like honey I tell you, for I mellifluous like hell.

MEDIYAH: Ah-hah!

JASON: It true, Star Apple. I open me mouth to sing, and I ain't ever find woman who could resist.

MEDIYAH: I ain't say you lie. Regret three?

JASON: Well, I always did say when I check out, I want to have a woman 'neath me and me mouth all over she.

MEDIYAH: Eh-eh? But you got some brass!

JASON: I ain't suppose you could do lickle somethin' 'bout number three, eh?

MEDIYAH: Boy, you too bad. You does have some lawless mouth, you know.

JASON: Is me charm. Woman always find me so. Can't help it. I born that way. I makin' love to woman from me cradle. I think all that goin' now 'cause I don't even feel I have strength to do you one small rudeness. At least you could bring you face down here and leave me have one kiss 'fore I pass, nuh?

[*He pulls her down to him.* MEDIYAH, *far from resisting, is more than enthusiastic. At the moment of their kiss,* GRANNY ROOT *appears and gestures symbolically. Lights flash and there is thunderous sound.* GRANNY ROOT *again disappears.*]

Be-Jesus! Thunder and lightning and all the element in you mouth, woman. Me lip, me teeth, me tongue, me throat . . . all aflame. I comin', God. Now ordinarily when I say I comin', I does mean just that. Howsoever, I 'fraid that this time when I say I comin', I mean I goin'! But this is one terrible damn time to pass, eh? Shite! I already see the face of God.

MEDIYAH: Hear me good, you altogether gorgeous thing.
I listenin' while you pretty mouth spoutin' you charm
and you pretty head restin' in the crook of me arm.
You think I 'bout to let the smallest piece of harm
come to you?
I look dumb to you?
You must be crazy in you head
if you think I goin' let you dead.

JASON: But who you is? How come you here in this beastly wood and no animal or haunt try for make meal out you?

MEDIYAH: You notice that at last, eh? Well, I born right here and I special.
I Granny Root granddaughter.
I all herb and bush and Miedo Wood water.
Is with a priestress of science and healin'
you dealin'.
You ain't feel, since I touch you, you fever 'batin'?
Whoever want to claim you life have to keep on waitin',
'cause is me, Mediyah, now holdin' you fate in
she hand.
Understand?

Yes! Is me who snatch you from the mouth of hell
and goin' make you pretty, handsome carcass well.
Close you eye and sleep, 'cause truth be to tell,
I goin' 'range meself 'bout you
and suck the venom out you.
Oh, yes, man. I goin' lift
up me shift
and give you the gift
of new life.

JASON: I can't keep me eye open. I sorry. Bye, gal!

MEDIYAH: Yes! Sleep on, me beauty! I goin' into the wood and get you wood
and gut string you leave there, and I goin' make you the most fine gold
quatro you did ever see. Yes! You sleep, Mr. Sugar Tongue. I goin' keep you
right here on this island with me till it time for you to win Pecong at the
Carnival. You goin' sleep all the time I ain't here, so that when I are here,
you ain't goin' have nothin' but energy . . . which you goin' truly need. Oh,
man, is new life for you. In the meantime, God, I can't wait no longer.

[MEDIYAH *throws herself savagely on* JASON, *who, though asleep, reacts in kind.
The lights go down on them but come up on* GRANNY ROOT *perched in a tree and
laughing eerily and evilly.*]

GRANNY ROOT: No, m'dear. 'Taint for you to die of love for this man or any
one of they. Love? Hah!
Love does make you mind go simple
and make you face swole big with pimple.
Is hate
should motivate
a woman fate.
But have no fear.
Granny goin' always be near
and she goin' steel you 'gainst foolishness
and approachin' bitterness.
Yes!
However, 'taint no reason why you can't have lickle fun on the road to
heartbreak and vengeance!

[GRANNY ROOT *cackles as the lights go out.*]

SCENE 3

[CREON's *store.* SWEET BELLA *is behind the counter.* FAUSTINA, *in a somewhat more sober-colored version of the clothes in which we last saw her, and* PERSIS *enter.*]

FAUSTINA: Where you daddy?

[SWEET BELLA *indicates the back of the store.*]

Creon Pandit, you old bandit. Come out here!
CREON: Who takin' me name in vain?

[*He comes out.*]

Oh, is only Cleopatra and she handmaiden. What you want?
FAUSTINA: I come for me goods.
CREON: What goods? You ain't have no goods here. All a ol' crocodile like you could have is bads.
FAUSTINA: Don't rag with me, man. I come to pick up me cloth.
CREON: What cloth? You have cloth here?
FAUSTINA: Don't get me wroughted, nuh! All you know you have cloth for me here.
CREON: You mistake. Is me, one, who have cloth here. Is when you have some shillin' for show me, is then I have some cloth for you. Till then, the cloth mine.
FAUSTINA: You ol' pirate. Is them warrin' faction in you blood that does make you brutish so, you know. Bring me me cloth, nuh!
CREON: Show me you money, woman!
FAUSTINA: Here! Is three Moravian coppers. Now bring me me cloth, and I want me change!
CREON: Change? What change? You think you have change comin'?
FAUSTINA: Don't trifle with me, you ol' fart!
CREON: I hangin' on to this cloth so long for you, you ain't think I entitle to storage charge?
FAUSTINA: Now the man tryin' to t'ief me money. You better bring me me cloth and me change 'fore me take a torch to you and you lickle store.
CREON: Try it, beldam. You seem to forget I also the magistrate. You just threaten the law. I could have you tail throw in jail, if I want.
FAUSTINA: Is so you would treat ol' friend, eh? No wonder you house goin' soon fall. I done read you card, you know.
CREON: You can't even read English, much less piece of card.

PERSIS: You know, you two is trial. Sometime both of you act like you don't have no brought-upsy a-tall.

CREON: Here you damn piece of change. Next time you goin' know better. I ain't like me merchandise lay fallow on me shelf.

FAUSTINA: You talkin' chupidness. Is only two week since I order.

CREON: You too lie! The cloth have two foot dust, it there so long. I had was to wrap it so it ain't fade.

FAUSTINA: I have a good mind . . .

CREON: Since when? . . .

FAUSTINA: . . . to carry me trade elsewhere and not come in here a next time. You ain't deserve me patronage.

PERSIS: And, you would please tell me, to which next establishment you would favor with you trade, since Creon Pandit store the only one round here?

CREON: Make she know it! Even if somebody have enough craziness to try to raise emporia and want to rival with me, he ain't goin' be so fool as to sell goods to you. Bella, reach me that roll of black bombazine from the shelf and let we get this ol' crow from out me shop.

PERSIS: Black bombazine?

CREON: And, careful. Blow off the dust! I ain't want you to dirty you frock.

PERSIS: Black bombazine? You order black bombazine?

FAUSTINA: Creon Pandit, you mouth too big. Who authorize you to put me business on you clothesline?

CREON: You ain't tell me is secret.

PERSIS: You order black bombazine?

Who you think you is? The queen?

FAUSTINA: And what, pray tell me, causin' such hilarity?

PERSIS: Oh, forgive me, nuh!

I succumb to jollity

'cause you think you quality.

FAUSTINA: I is a augurer now. I can't walk round here like I ordinary.

PERSIS: Oh, God! Me heart! Me heart!

FAUSTINA: Shut you fool mouth! I have to have proper dress for Carnival when it come. You think I can make appearance in costume, rag, and bead like common jamette? All you mere mortal can wear all them color and be the rainbow if you so choose, but I have standin' and station. I have responsibility. Me life dictate by the card, them. They probably goin' ask me to sit on the bench and be a judge.

PERSIS: Oh, God! I goin' die, and I ain't even make out me will.

FAUSTINA: As soon as you through playin' fool, you think you can run up this bombazine into something that look dignify without makin' too much distress on the cloth?

PERSIS: Whoop! You hear that, Creon Pandit? She majesty goin' trust me to stitch up she coronation robe, underlin' that I am. I surprise she ain't want to chance needle and t'read sheself.

FAUSTINA: You the seamstress! I the priestress!

PERSIS: But you is too comical.

FAUSTINA: Creon Pandit, you have stranger comin'! No! Two! No! Three!

CREON: Who comin'?

FAUSTINA: You goin' see one just now. I ain't say no more.

PERSIS: Is Mediyah!

CREON [*shaken*]: Granny Root granddaughter? What she want here?

PERSIS: I ain't know. I ain't see she for some month.

[MEDIYAH, *brightly dressed, enters.*]

Hello, Mediyah.

MEDIYAH: Hello, ladies. Faustina, you ain't have to hide in the back stall. I ain't feel for mischief today.

PERSIS: I never see you come in Creon Pandit store 'fore now.

MEDIYAH: You right! Hello, Creon Pandit!

CREON: What you want here? You come to cause ruction?

[*He takes a heavy chain with a cross on it and puts it around* SWEET BELLA's *neck.*]

Bella, go to the back!

[*He practically pushes* SWEET BELLA *out.*]

I ain't want no pass with you!

MEDIYAH: I goin' ignore all that! I need several piece of cloth and some other t'ing. You can take it from this lickle piece of coin.

CREON: That gold!

PERSIS: Gold?

MEDIYAH: Gold!

CREON: It real?

MEDIYAH: You could try it out on you tooth.

CREON: But I ain't have change for this.

MEDIYAH: Who tell you I goin' need change? Is a whole lot of cloth and t'ing I needin'. Here me list! You could fill it?

CREON: Yes, mistress. Sweet Bella, help me gather these item, them.

[SWEET BELLA *returns and helps her father to gather items.*]

PERSIS: So, Mediyah, where you was all this time? Is so long I ain't see you. I does ask you brother, Cedric, for you all the time and him, that sweet-singin' boy, say he ain't know where you is. Sometime I does pass by you house, tryin' for a glimpse, but the shutter always shut and I ain't hear you singin' inside like I always was used to.

MEDIYAH: What for you want to get in me business?

PERSIS: I ain't mean no harm.

MEDIYAH: Persis, you does make me chuckle. Don't fret youself! I decide to stay on Miedo Wood Island!

[PERSIS *and* FAUSTINA *elbow each other's ribs.* CREON *and* SWEET BELLA *look aghast.*]

I decide to build me a little castilla over there.

PERSIS: But that is one angry lickle piece of sand in the sea. How you could live there?

MEDIYAH: Careful! Is me home you talkin' 'bout. Creon Pandit, I want them thing deliver . . .

CREON: I ain't have nobody so fool to go to Miedo Wood Island, and I, for sure, ain't goin' . . .

MEDIYAH: Who ask you for do such? I ask you for do such?

CREON: But you say . . .

MEDIYAH: You ain't let me finish "say." Now I want them thing deliver to me old house. Me granny house.

CREON: I ain't goin' there neither. Everybody know you granny house hold badness and animosity for me and all Pandit.

MEDIYAH: How you could say such? Cedric there! The house ain't have no badness and animosity for he. Even though he ain't have the name, he a Pandit!

CREON: Ain't nobody 'live could prove that!

MEDIYAH: You right! Nobody 'live could prove it.

[PERSIS *and* FAUSTINA *have not stopped elbowing each other's ribs.*]

So how could the house have haunt and botheration for you if Cedric there? And you and he . . . relate.

CREON: I ain't claim that!

PERSIS: But, Creon, all of we does know the whole story.

CREON: Ain't nobody know no whole story . . . nothin'!

PERSIS: Faustina, tell the man.

FAUSTINA: Me ain't know nothin'! I does mind me business. Me lip . . . seal!

MEDIYAH: You grow wise since I last see you. Creon bring—

CREON: Creon don't bring! I the owner! I the magistrate! I don't bring nothin'. I have delivery boy for that!

MEDIYAH: Then why you causin' such ado? Surely, me granny house ain't have no bad spirit for you delivery boy. Unless, unbeknownst to all we, he a secret Pandit, too. Well, have them thing deliver to the porch if he ain't feel to come inside. I could, ha-ha, spirit them to me island. I got me ways, you know. Oh, and by the way, I see that fine white cloth frock coat you have in you window. Put that in with me purchase, too.

[PERSIS *and* FAUSTINA—*elbows and ribs.*]

CREON: But that coat is for man!

MEDIYAH: You think I blind and ain't know that?

CREON: But you can't just buy man coat, so! You have to know size and fittin', and that coat ain't look, to me experience eye, like it goin' fit Cedric, unless you goin' alterate it.

MEDIYAH: And who, in the heaven you know, tell you I buyin' coat for Cedric? Me brother buy he own clothin'. Ain't you or nobody else have to bother you head with worriation. The coat plenty fit for the one who goin' wear it. Now, fold and box it nice. While I thinkin', you could throw in two, three of them white trouser. Here! I want you wind this piece of red ribbon round it and tie me one big bow.

CREON: You still have change comin'.

MEDIYAH: I know that!

CREON: I ain't want you to think I cheat you.

MEDIYAH: Creon Pandit, is no way you could t'ief me. You know that. You hold on to them coin I have comin'. I establishin' credick. Bye! Bye, ladies. Faustina, you could talk now, and the two of you could stop hunchin' one another. You rib must be black and blue. I ain't comin' back today. I give you me word.

[*She goes and then pops her head back in the door.*]

Of course, sometime I does lie and me word ain't mean a t'ing.

[*She laughs, raucously, then leaves.*]

FAUSTINA: Woman, you have me rib sore.

PERSIS: And you me! You ever hear such?

FAUSTINA: You better hush you mout', woman, and wait till she get out of earshot!

CREON: Sweet Bella, take this coin and put it in the coffer. You two bush rat goin' have to vacate, 'cause I closin' down. I think I goin' rum up meself, lickle bit.

FAUSTINA: Don't rush me, nuh! You think she goin' give you she patronage all the time? Hah! You got a next think comin'!

PERSIS: That gold part of Granny Root legendary fortune, come what you bet! But I wonder who them coat and pant for?

FAUSTINA: Come what you bet, them for the same mysterious person plant them two alligator pear seed in she belly.

PERSIS: What you say? What you say?

FAUSTINA: You ain't see, eh? Well, of course, you ain't have the power of foresight and divination. You ain't have the gift, and you ain't have the card. She carryin' two piece of something in there. Ain't I say is three stranger comin' to Creon Pandit shop?

CREON: Is so you did say!

FAUSTINA: So? She is the one stranger, for she never set she foot in here before. And she carryin' two in she oven. One and two does always come out . . . three . . . if I does know my mathematic.

PERSIS: I thought she did look sorta . . . different . . . But no! You pickin' leaf from the wrong bush, woman.

CREON: She look the same to me. Lickle cleaner, maybe, but . . . Oh, you ol' man-eater, you. How you a-know so much?

FAUSTINA: You forget me card?

CREON: Oh, yes. I does forget you is the all-seein' oracle. Well, you could tell me, Sybil, who she lay up with?

PERSIS: Yes! That what I want to know. Better still, who lay up with she?

FAUSTINA: How I should know?

CREON: I thought you could read so much card.

FAUSTINA: Is card tell me she carryin'.

PERSIS: Then card should tell you who she carryin' for.

CREON: I surprise such a monumental occurrence like who pumpin' pipe and tool to Mediyah escape you eye. Well, it look like the two of you goin' have to trilly over to Miedo Wood Island if you want find out. Shark won't molest you if you swim. They scare. You two is the only other two I know could go there and come back without all them haunt and animal and t'ing bother them. They know you is they relative. Get outta here now. I tell you I closin' me shop!

FAUSTINA: We goin', you brute!

PERSIS: You too rude. Bye, Sweet Bella. Is a shame you can't speak, but is you father disposition that get the curse put on you.

CREON [*most angry*]: Get out, you two ol' harridan!

[*They go.* SWEET BELLA *regards her father.*]

Sweet Bella, you mustn't mind what them say. Both of them is bitter, bitter woman. They soul sour with invective and vinegar. Don't look so at you daddy. You daddy love only you and you mother, rest she soul. I never play ram on she. I marry she, and I stay in faith till she pass. Sure, I do plenty t'ing 'fore I marry, but I supposed to. I a man, and when I young, I had was to run with the wind and be wild thing. You think I handsome now? God, you should see me then. When me hair was thicker and blacker than a night without moon. I was a sheik. I could teach any damn Casanova a thing or two, believe me. Then one day I see this black, black girl. She hair . . . short and tight . . . like a clench fist. She lip like it 'bout to bust with too much honey, and she voice like a breeze. She eye burn hole right through me. She skin? Ah, she skin. She skin was a miracle of black velvet with the sun shinin' behind it. I never see nothin' like that. I completely bewitch by she and she skin. That same skin I couldn't bring to me father table. Ah, girl. You ain't understand. I ain't make the world. T'ing is t'ing, and I ain't set that rule. I was important. I was Mighty, Royal Most Perfect, Grand King Calabash. I did win Pecong five time consecutive. Only man ever do that is me daddy. I was important. The girl was . . . black!

[SWEET BELLA *looks at her father. The veiled figure of* GRANNY ROOT *passes silently through the room. They both shudder, as if a cold wind had passed over them.*]

Still, I would rather you had all the black skin in the world if I could just hear you voice say, "Daddy, I love you." I know that ol' woman curse me when she daughter pitch sheself off Devil Cliff. She deliver twin, and then she pitch sheself into the wind. She body never find in the water. She mother swear sheself against me line from there on out. You come out without voice. I do it to you. And I too, too sorry. I love you so, but you is me only regret. Oh, Sweet Bella, I was young, and I ain't had better sense than to be young. Go, now. Go fetch one of them lickle black boy from the back and tell he he have delivery to make.

[SWEET BELLA *starts to go.*]

No! Wait! On second thought, I think I goin' take this one over meself.

[SWEET BELLA *looks understandingly at her father.* PERSIS *comes back in, calling to the offstage* FAUSTINA.]

PERSIS: Just wait there! Ain't no need for you for come in. I sure I leave me purse on the counter. Creon?
CREON: I close!
PERSIS: Oh, shut up, man. Here ten shillin'. Put me 'side ten yard of them black bombazine, and I pick it up when I come in next time. And hear me! Nobody say you have to be town crier and put me business in the ear of all and sundry creation. You follow?

[*She goes, calling to* FAUSTINA.]

I find it! I told you, ain't I?
FAUSTINA: Oh, you find it where it drop on the floor?
PERSIS: How you know it drop on the floor, dear sister?
FAUSTINA: I read it in the card, poopsie! The card make me see all thing.

[CREON *and* SWEET BELLA *smile at each other as he locks the door of his shop. Lights.*]

SCENE 4

[*The old hut.* CEDRIC *is sprawled, drunkenly, on the floor. Jugs, bottles, wooden wine cups, and other things indicate there have been many lengthy parties going on.* CEDRIC's *two dancing girls are sprawled, inelegantly, on either side of him.* MEDIYAH, *followed by the ever-present* GRANNY ROOT, *enters. Both are horrified at what they see.* GRANNY ROOT *picks up an old besom and starts after* CEDRIC, *but* MEDIYAH *wrests the broom from her hands before she can strike.*]

GRANNY ROOT: The place look just like ram and she-goat live here.
MEDIYAH: Don't wrought youself. I goin' take care of this.

[*Broom in hand, she stands over the sleepers. She doesn't speak loudly.*]

You two courtesan, wake you worthless tail up!

[*The two girls stir, drowsily.*]

Wake up, you good-for-nothin' but good-time wenches!

[*The two wake with a start and are about to scream, but a gesture from* MEDIYAH *silences them.*]

Not a sound. Vacate these premise 'fore I take this besom and sweep you into eternity. Make haste!

[*The two quickly gather their things and, terrified and trying to scream, run from the hut.*]

GRANNY ROOT: You do good, girl. You does bring such joy and laughter to me spirit. Come what you bet, if them have on undergarment, they soil them.

MEDIYAH: Cedric!

[MEDIYAH *pitches the contents of a water pitcher in* CEDRIC's *face. Sputtering, he lashes out blindly with his cutlass.*]

CEDRIC: Aaiieeee! I goin' kill . . .

MEDIYAH: Get up!

CEDRIC: You brain come loose? Why for you pitch water at me for?

GRANNY ROOT: Criminal!

MEDIYAH: 'Cause you ain't wake when I call you name!

CEDRIC: Tyrant! You crazy?

MEDIYAH: Look how you does have this place. Pig does live cleaner than this.

GRANNY ROOT: Like you ain't have the first bit of brought-upsy!

CEDRIC: Who fault that? Where you was all this time?

MEDIYAH: What you say?

CEDRIC: Is well over three, four month since you set foot in here.

MEDIYAH: So?

CEDRIC: So, so don't bring you errant self in here complainin' 'bout the place look like pigsty if you ain't here to clean it!

GRANNY ROOT: What gall!

MEDIYAH: But you is a ol' bitch, you know that? What you think I does be? Maidservant and you the king? You too fool. You waitin' all this time for me to do you service?

CEDRIC: Who else? I the man here!

MEDIYAH: Hear him, nuh! 'Cause he have something dangle 'tween he leg, him can't pass broom 'cross the floor. I should kick you in you vital and make you stone inoperative.

GRANNY ROOT: Blackguard!

MEDIYAH: Since you does so need woman to pick up behind you, why you ain't make them two wilted blossom I just chase from here do such, eh? How them could lay up here cross you and you smellin' so foul? This a island with water on all side. Ain't no reason for man to smell worse than ram goat in summer.

CEDRIC: You better hush you mouth 'fore I vex and tell me where you was all this time.

MEDIYAH: On Miedo Wood Island. Why you eye open so agape? That place ain't hold no fear for me.

CEDRIC: I know that. Is only that is 'bout this same Miedo Wood Island, and you I been thinkin'. I need you to go and ax me off piece wood from the calabash tree. I need a next quatro.

MEDIYAH: What do you old one?

CEDRIC: It mash up! Me and me compay, them, saunter into Creon Pandit cantina for some merriment and libation, and we sittin' there mindin' all we own business when this bunch of bum—say them from Tougou Island—come at we to issue challenge for Pecong at Carnival. Tell me them have some dilly with voice and brain better than me, and him goin' cause me to fall in the contest. Of course, I accept the challenge 'cause no way me and me magic quatro could lose. Well, that devil grog that Creon Pandit does sell in he place is the cause of it all. 'Fore you know it, one thing does lead to a next, and one of them Tougou boy, full of drunk, sayin' some nastiness 'bout me ancestry . . .

MEDIYAH: Eh-eh?

GRANNY ROOT: I hope you kill he . . .

CEDRIC: . . . and I had was to grab he by he collar and butt he . . .

GRANNY ROOT: Good!

CEDRIC: . . . and before you know it, he boy, them, jump in and we havin' one grand punch-up in the place . . .

GRANNY ROOT: I hope you wreck Creon Pandit cantina.

CEDRIC: . . . and we havin' fun, fun, fun! Then one of them devil get lucky and catch me a vicious blow back me neck, and I fall quite on top me quatro. It turn serious then. I ain't utter a word. I get up. Is the first time I ever knock off me feet, you know, and I evil now. I pick up what used to be me quatro and look at it. It mash flat. It like it collapse. The ruction stop . . . and you could cut the silence, it so thick. I look at me compay, them. Them lookin' at me. A look pass 'tween we that tell them is all me fight now. Them Tougou boy ain't know what happenin'! Suddenly, without warnin', I scream and spring like cat and pitch meself 'mong them. Me arm and cutlass flailin' like windmill. You ain't see hurricane do more damage than me. Most of them run, but they is two who ain't goin' push nobody on quatro no more. I tell you, I was so full up, I had was to grab both them sweet brown gal you chase 'way and wear them out at the same time. Anyway, I need you to bring me some wood from Miedo, and I could fashion me a next quatro in time for Carnival. Is just enough time for the wood to cure proper, and I could use the same string so you ain't have to kill cat for me.

MEDIYAH: I can't do that, Cedric.

CEDRIC: What you say?

GRANNY ROOT: She say true!

MEDIYAH: I say I can't do that. Brother, is only one time I could get wood for each person from Miedo. You done have you share.

CEDRIC: You sayin' you can't get no more wood?

MEDIYAH: I could get plenty wood, but no more for you. Is one time only for each person.

CEDRIC: But you could do it. You special. We special. We born there.

MEDIYAH: No! Is only me born there. You forget. You born in the boat on the way. Is only after we land and Granny bring Mother ashore that I come out.

CEDRIC: It ain't matter. You have the power.

MEDIYAH: But if I break the law of science, I lose me power.

CEDRIC: So, you ain't goin' help me? You twin brother? You desert me, eh?

MEDIYAH: You desert youself.

CEDRIC: Okay, Sister. I ain't goin' beg! No need to worry you head. You brother still have he voice. He still have he brain. He could still sing Calypso and shout Pecong better when he drunk and sick than any foot jam who sober. I ain't need you or you quatro tree for help me.

MEDIYAH: Where you goin', Brother?

CEDRIC: 'Taint none you damn business, but I goin' to join me friend, them. Is one thing I did alway say: When you family ain't stand by you, you alway have friend. I come into this world. I ain't ask, mind you, and ain't nobody ask me, but I come. The first thing they tell me is I ain't have me daddy name and me mother kill sheself. Then me granny kick out, and now I ain't even have a sister. Well, thank be to God, I have friend who love me and would buy me a cup of grog when I feelin' low. I ain't have no family would do so.

[CEDRIC goes.]

MEDIYAH: Cedric!

GRANNY ROOT: You can't stop him. T'ing is t'ing and they can't change. Everything charted and goin' 'long. It all plan by greater than we.

MEDIYAH: Granny, I ain't feel too sorry for Cedric. How come that does be so? After all, he and I is twin. I should be feel somethin' more than I does feel?

GRANNY ROOT: I already tell you. T'ing is t'ing. That is all.

MEDIYAH: Okay, Granny.

GRANNY ROOT: Now, on this particular matter I ain't interfere before . . . but I think . . . when you get back to the island and wake Jason Allcock from he induce slumber, you better tell he that he goin' be daddy to you twin you carryin' in you belly.

MEDIYAH: You know, eh? You ain't say nothin', so I thought I had put one over on you.

GRANNY ROOT: Oh, child, I tired tellin' you . . .

GRANNY ROOT AND MEDIYAH: . . . "Granny see everything! Granny know everything! Granny goin' alway be here . . ."

MEDIYAH: . . . Yes, Granny, I know. I goin' tell him today. I think is time. But first, make I clean up this place lickle bit.

GRANNY ROOT: Leave it! Cedric ain't goin' need this place a next time. You ain't goin' have no more use for it.

[*From offstage,* CREON *calls.*]

CREON: Hola! Hola! Who in there?

GRANNY ROOT: Himself!

MEDIYAH: What you want, Creon Pandit?

CREON: I bring all them thing you purchase. I transfer them to you boat already, and I goin'.

MEDIYAH: Wait!

[MEDIYAH *goes out to* CREON, *who seems rooted to his spot.*]

CREON: What you want?

MEDIYAH: My brother and some boy, them have a tumble and bruck up you cantina?

CREON: Yes!

MEDIYAH: Why you ain't say nothin'?

CREON: You brother sittin' there mindin' he business when them Tougou rascal come in and start botheration. Well, I a Calabash. The only one 'live to claim such, and it look like Cedric goin' soon join me in me advance state. I ain't like it the way them fellow come in and make challenge and—

MEDIYAH: And?

CREON: Them say something they ain't have no cause to say. Cedric well within he right to knock them over.

[MEDIYAH *takes some coins from her pocket.*]

MEDIYAH: Here!
CREON: What this for?
MEDIYAH: Damage!
CREON: But—
MEDIYAH: I ain't want no child of me mother to owe a thing to you.
GRANNY ROOT: You do well, Granddaughter.
CREON: You ain't have to do this . . .
MEDIYAH: We get this far without you help, and we ain't need it now.

[CREON *backs away, cautiously, but hides behind a tree. Of course, he can see only* MEDIYAH *as she kneels on the ground and bends her body in supplication.* GRANNY ROOT *puts her hands on* MEDIYAH's *shoulders and stops her movement.*]

GRANNY ROOT: Creon Pandit watchin'!
MEDIYAH: I know!
GRANNY ROOT: Then let he see. Bye, old hut! We ain't need you no more.

[GRANNY ROOT, *her hands on* MEDIYAH's *shoulders, as if passing power into her, looks upward.* MEDIYAH *thrusts her arms out, and the hut "bursts into flame."* CREON, *in terror, runs from the scene. Lights.*]

SCENE 5

[*The hut of* MEDIYAH *and* JASON *on Miedo Wood Island.* JASON, *surrounded by flowers and baskets of tropical fruit, sleeps soundly and blissfully.* MEDIYAH, *the beribboned suit box in her arms and followed by* GRANNY ROOT, *enters.*]

MEDIYAH: Each time I does look at that man, I does want to jump he.
GRANNY ROOT: He quite pretty.
MEDIYAH: All over and all the time.
　　In the sun or in the night,
　　He pretty by day or candlelight.
GRANNY ROOT: And you body all a-jumble
　　when him act all rough and tumble.
　　Even when him claw and clutch you,
　　it still feel soft where him touch you.
MEDIYAH: I know you does always say you does live through me, but you could feel he, for true?
GRANNY ROOT: He know how to make woman say, "Wuppi-wuppi!" He know he art. He a skill practitioner, and if you ain't careful and hold you-

self . . . just so . . . you could lose you power as well as you heart. It time to wake he and tell he you news. I goin' off on some revel.

[GRANNY ROOT *disappears.* MEDIYAH *approaches the sleeping* JASON, *taking a small vial from her neck and a leaf from her pocket. She puts the vial to his lips and, after emptying it of its contents, passes the leaf over his face.* JASON *stretches, yawns, and wakes.*]

JASON: Hi, gal. Make you drop you shift and get in this bed so I could do you. Then I want me sayuno, and after I eat, I goin' do you a next time. I feelin' like a bull ram today, and I ravenous for everything in me sight. Bring you face down here and let me attack it.

MEDIYAH: Man, how come we ain't lash up 'fore this time?

JASON: Be thankful for now, gal. Don't have regret for the past. Is that same past does lead us to this same now.

MEDIYAH: Well, philosopher, I have lickle piece news for you. I know for long time now, but I happy with me news . . . so I keep it to meself.

JASON: Eh-eh? I hear this tone million time already. You knock up?

MEDIYAH: How you does know?

JASON: You think I does born yesterday? Ain't I tell you plenty gal in Tougou make baby for me?

MEDIYAH: I remember is so you say, but none of them wench give you boy like I goin' give you.

JASON: I hear that before, too!

MEDIYAH: This time it true.

JASON: How you know?

MEDIYAH: Jason, look me in me eye! You does know me to lie? You ain't know by now I special? I real special! When I find you, you body all chew up and mew up and have scar and t'ing. Where them scar now? You see them? When I find you, you ain't think you goin' see the next day, you body weak so and creak so. Since that time, you does feel one ache? You ain't been nothin' but young and strong and givin' me body all the pleasure with you youth and you strength. You ain't even have a memory of how tear up and sear up you was when I first see you. When I leave off from you, I does go 'bout me business here and elsewhere. With all the wild animal they does have here, any does come to give you aggravation? No! I does put up barrier that no haunt, spirit, or wild t'ing could breach. You belong to me, Jason Allcock, and nothin' goin' change that. I put charm all over you. So when I tell you you goin' have son, believe it. And when I tell you you goin' have two son, you better believe that, too . . . for it too true.

JASON: You tellin' me I goin' have twin boy?

MEDIYAH: I, yet, goin' convince you of me power. You feelin' young and strong?

JASON: Yes!

MEDIYAH: You feel for give me lickle tumble?

JASON: All the time!

MEDIYAH: You feel for make me body sing with you music?

JASON: Like you the quatro and I the picker!

MEDIYAH: You feel for make you mouth run rampant all over me terrain?

JASON: Woman, you have me hotter than Satan fire! Bring youself over to me.
Let me have at you.

MEDIYAH: No, doux-doux.
You come over here and get me.
Come over here and let me
give you all the love
and fulfillment of
all you dream
and treasure.
Come over here and take me.
Come over here and make me
tingle with delight.
Make me fill you night
with sweet scream
and murmur of pleasure.
Come! Come! Come, sweet man!
Come! Come get me if you can!

[JASON *struggles but can't seem to rise from the bed.*]

JASON: What happenin'? I can't move! What you do to me?

MEDIYAH: You know how you does enter
me center
and bury youself to you hilt
while all the time you croonin' lilt
and drippin' sugar word in me ear?
Them word does sometime cause me eye to tear.
Them alway cause me heart to flame.
Well, try to lullaby me now!
I bet all
you can call
is me name.

JASON: Mediyah, Mediyah Mediyah Mediyah! Mediyah, Mediyah Mediyah Mediyah, Mediyah?

[JASON, *suddenly angry, calms himself and looks coolly at* MEDIYAH.]

MEDIYAH: So you must believe me when I tell you that I carryin' two boy for you . . . right here in this belly. You tell me about all them silly, flirty t'ing who make baby for you. Well, I ain't like them and them ain't like I! I the most different woman you goin' meet. No other like me. I givin' you boy 'cause you say you want them. Jason, I give you anything you want.

GRANNY ROOT [*from afar*]: Mediyah?

MEDIYAH: You want to be Grand King Calabash, and I goin' see to it. All you have to do is ask.

GRANNY ROOT: Mediyah?

JASON: You mighty impressive, but you ain't know me. Plenty woman does love me. Why? Them know I wayward and never goin' make they legal. Them know, too, that I good to all me daughter. Every one me daughter have me love and me name, and the first straight-leg rogue who even look like them come to do they badness with him stone in him hand have me machete where him leg meet. I a rascal, but I honest, and I ain't want nothin' from nobody I ain't work for meself. When you find me in this same wood, all mash up and slash up, I ask you for anything except youself for me to kiss and do a little smooch? No! And you could refuse me, you know! I ain't beg! I ask you to heal me and seal me and do all this kindness? No! I come here with me machete in me hand, and I prepare to do me own battle or die! Is me way! I make me own way and me own fate! Is me strip me wood from calabash tree! Is me strangle wildcat and pull out she gut. Is you make up me quatro, true, but I ask you to do that? No! And, be-Christ, is me who goin' win Pecong and t'ing by meself! On me own! Now, I ain't ungrateful. I too glad you find me and mind me and sure me and cure me and love me and carryin' two boy for me. But I rather you take them two boy and yank they out you belly. I rather be all scar up and mar up. I rather you let all me blood run out and get drink up by the earth. I rather you leave me die than deny me the right to win the contest on me own. I ain't need magic! I ain't need conjure! I ain't need sorcery! I only need me! Me! Me! Me! Now, if you want to spout incantation and work spell and do me badness and sadness and evilness, go to it. I come into this world a honest man, and I go out the same. I ain't scare of a livin' arse—excuse me language—in this world, so do you worse!

MEDIYAH: Jason, you make me love you . . . too much.

GRANNY ROOT: Mediyah!

MEDIYAH: I ain't want to be nothin' but the only woman in you life!

GRANNY ROOT: Mediyah!

MEDIYAH: I ain't care for be nothin' but she who have you all the time!

GRANNY ROOT: Mediyah!

MEDIYAH: Tell me, Jason! Say it! Tell me you ain't love nobody but you Mediyah, and I do anything you tell me. Anything you say! Anything you ask! The world goin' belong to you if you say you love me the same like I love you. I use me power to give you anything! Everything!

[GRANNY ROOT *appears. Lights flash.* MEDIYAH *and* JASON *freeze.*]

GRANNY ROOT: Mediyah, you ain't have no power. You just give it to this man. He hold power over you now. You surrender to he. You just a ordinary woman now. You goin' have to leave this island. Granny goin' see you out safely, but you must go. Both you and he. You can't protect he no more. You can't make he sleep with secret potion and t'ing. You goin' have to go 'fore cockcrow or you doom. Obey me!

[GRANNY ROOT *gestures.* MEDIYAH *moves.*]

MEDIYAH: Granny, what happen? I ain't know a feelin' like this before. I burnin' up. Me stomach all a-churn.

GRANNY ROOT: You fall too much in love. That is all. You lose control.

MEDIYAH: I ain't like it. It hurt. It like a million jamette dancin' Carnival and trampin' in me head. Me body feel like Damballah heself pitchin' rock and flame at me.

GRANNY ROOT: I did almost know that feelin' once. Long time ago . . . but I check it! I see the way of the world, and I say, "No!"

MEDIYAH: Take it away, Granny! Take away this feelin'!

GRANNY ROOT: Is only you can do such.

MEDIYAH: How? Tell me how! I do it right now!

GRANNY ROOT: Remove the man!

MEDIYAH: What?

GRANNY ROOT: Banish he from you heart! Call down thunder and lightnin' to strike he from here! Cast he into the pit! Cause flame to rise up round he. Conflagrate!
Immolate!
Incinerate!
Use science! Use skill!
Kill! Kill! Kill!

[MEDIYAH, *aroused by* GRANNY ROOT's *fervor, gestures wildly. Nothing happens to* JASON.]

MEDIYAH: Nothin' ain't happen!

GRANNY ROOT: 'Cause you ain't want it to. In you heart, you ain't want it to.

[MEDIYAH *gestures again, falls to her knees in prayer, dances wildly, prostrates herself, does all manner of things, but nothing happens.*]

Is like I say, darlin', you too much in love. A woman too much in love ain't have no power! Now you have to prepare to leave here. I can give you only to cockcrow. Then you must follow me close or you mighty love goin' be you miserable death!

[MEDIYAH *sinks to the ground, sobbing.*]

Poor, ordinary woman!

[GRANNY ROOT *disappears as* JASON *returns to normal.*]

JASON: No! I can't say them word you want, 'cause I ain't feel to say such. I ain't tell lie to you or no other woman. I ain't find she yet who could make me feel and say them word. When I find she, I goin' know it. When I find she, I goin' feel it. When I find she, I goin' be proud to say it. I truly fond of you. For true, no gal ever treat me so good like you, but more than this, I can't say. Bring me boy, them, safe to this world, and I give you honor and paradise. Now on them term, you want me still? Tell me now. We could fall down on the grass, this night, and see heaven. We could know beauty and bliss like we never know, for I feelin' young and strong and a little extra of me juice good for them two boy you have in there! We could . . . eh-eh? What do you? Why you a-cry?

MEDIYAH: Jason, we have to leave this place before cockcrow!

JASON: Why? You no more happy here?

MEDIYAH: Listen!

[*We can hear animal sounds and horrible noises that are almost inaudible. They grow louder and louder.* JASON *picks up his weapon as* MEDIYAH *clings to him for protection.*]

I scare. I can't protect we no more. We must leave this place.

JASON: Before cockcrow, you say?

MEDIYAH: Yes, darlin'.

JASON: Then we still have lickle time.

MEDIYAH: We should go now.

JASON: Before cockcrow, doux-doux. We have time.
 I goin' make all them tear
 distappear.
 I goin' whisper rudeness in you ear.
MEDIYAH: We ain't have time.
JASON: Two spice bun bakin' in you oven.
 It take time.
 Just like you and me
 out to do some lovin',
 it take time.
 We can't go rush and reelin'.
 It don't pay goin' fast
 if you want the feelin'
 to last.
 You and me
 havin' lickle funnin'.
 It take time.
 Then we flee
 'fore we let the sun in,
 but it take time.
 So lay back now,
 and I will sing you flower,
 cover you with kiss
 till the mornin' hour,
 touch you with me hand
 is only me hand reach you,
 sing honey in you ear
 that way I will teach you
 the meaning of the word,
 a word you've only heard,
 "sublime."
 But it take time.

[*They fall to the ground, oblivious to the once-again-rising sounds of animals and jungle horrors.* GRANNY ROOT *appears, the noises fade gradually, and* JASON *and* MEDIYAH *are in embrace.* MEDIYAH, *still apprehensive, tries to urge him out of the wood.*]

 Slow, slow, slow!
 I ain't used to runnin'.

I take time.
Time to show
me cleverness and cunnin'.
Take we time.
So lay back now,
precious little flower.
Lay back now.
Only I does have the power
to ease you every fear.
Nothin' here goin' haunt you.
Even ghost can see
just how bad me want you.
We can beat this jungle.
Ain't no mountain we can't climb.
But it take time.

[GRANNY ROOT *trails her veil over the prone pair.*]

GRANNY ROOT: All thing take time, but time goin' soon done!

[*She disappears.*]

JASON: Slow, sweetness. Cockcrow a long way off. We ain't have no rush. We just go easy.

[MEDIYAH *surrenders . . . completely.*]

ACT 2

SCENE 1

[*Months later. The hut of* MEDIYAH *built on the site of the old one. It is overgrown with vines and weeds. Inside,* MEDIYAH *sits in an old rocking chair. Very much pregnant, it's obvious she has not cleaned the place in a while. Outside,* PERSIS *and* FAUSTINA *approach furtively. They wait until they are directly within hearing distance, then elbow each other in the ribs and gleefully and deliberately speak aloud.*]

FAUSTINA: Persis?

PERSIS: What is it, Faustina?

FAUSTINA: Is a lovely day for Carnival, ain't it?

PERSIS: Oh, darlin' Sister. True. It quite lovely. And this one goin' be so special, too. That drunken Cedric goin' for he number five win.

FAUSTINA: It look like he goin' take all the prize and t'ing.

PERSIS: But, wait! Some time ago you did tell me that you card say ain't no triumph for Cedric this time. What happen? You did read them wrong?

FAUSTINA: As mare does find new he-horse,
   so hart does find new hind.
   As wind does find new chart to course,
   so card does change them mind.

PERSIS: You mighty prophetic and profound this mornin'. Yes, I sure goin' to this one set of Carnival. Me wouldn't miss it.

FAUSTINA: Me too, neither. I wish everybody could go, but some people can't go 'cause them too shame to show them face.

PERSIS: Oh? You could tell me why?

FAUSTINA: Plenty people have plenty reason. Some shame 'cause them belly big, big, big, and them ain't have man to give they legality, properness, standin', or he name.

PERSIS: You does say true? Such people does exist? No! You ain't mean it. You can't know such sinful people. You ain't raise to know such.

FAUSTINA: Me card bring me in contact with all kind.
   High and low.
   Up and down.
   Fast and slow.
   Square and roun'.

PERSIS: You ain't say.

FAUSTINA: Oh, yes. I does know some people so shame 'cause them once so high and mighty and laud and lord theyself all over the place like peacock, but now them topple. Them drab like peahen and them hiney bare like pickney.

PERSIS: Oh, miseration. It too sad to see somebody once them think them empress and now them ain't even have chamber pot. That how the world go. One day you a good morsel. The next you nothin' but somebody fecal deposit.

FAUSTINA: But wait. We so busy chattin' and feelin' sorry for them what come low like snake, we ain't realize we passin' Mediyah hut.

PERSIS: No! You wrong, Sister dearest. This ain't Mediyah hut. At least it ain't the hut of the Mediyah I does know, for this place have weed all grow up on she. The Mediyah I does know does keep she place. She does trim she grass and have lovely flower all red and yellow and white and t'ing. This place does look wild like somebody what ain't have man to love they. No! You truly wrong! This place ain't belong to our Mediyah!

FAUSTINA: No! It belong to she! Oop! We ain't stop to think. Maybe she does sick and can't pick up after sheself, and that why she estate look so wild and tempest.

PERSIS: Let we go in and see after she.

[MEDIYAH, *broom in hand, comes to the door.*]

MEDIYAH: The first ol', never-use, dry-up tart put she foot through me portal without me permiso, I goin' take this one besom and t'ump she into the future.

PERSIS: Oh, look, Faustina. Is Mediyah. I glad to see you on you feet. We thought you did sick. You goin' see you brother go for the crown tonight?

MEDIYAH: You two ol' fart better vacate me premise 'fore I cleave you head.

FAUSTINA: You does have to humor she, Sister. You does get quite prickly when you carryin' baby for invisible man.

MEDIYAH: How you does know? The two of you barren like a ol' empty tortoise shell.

FAUSTINA: We does forgive you you outburst, 'cause we know it hard when woman does have to bring forth she lickle nameless offspring and she ain't have man.

MEDIYAH: You could look at me and say I ain't have man? Is only you two ol' ghost could make baby from spirit! The first fool fellow try to fit he flaccid fiber 'neath them frowsy frock to fondle and feel you fallow, infertile, infecund, faded fruit does faint from foul and fetid fragrance of you flatulence. I should long ago turn you into the serpent you is, but I 'fraid mongoose would bite you and die from you venom. Get off me place 'fore me choke you.

FAUSTINA: Come, Persis. The woman demented. We can't help she. Them devil plant in she belly by she phantom lover done drive she insane.

[MEDIYAH *disappears into her hut.*]

PERSIS: Somethin' tell me all we better haul arse.

[MEDIYAH *returns, holding something behind her back.*]

MEDIYAH: All you say I ain't have chamber pot? I not only have pochamb, but it decorate . . . inside and out. Here!

[MEDIYAH *flings a flowered and filled "pochamb" at them. It misses them as they flee.*]

PERSIS [*from a safe distance*]: The woman crazy and she content . . . foul.

FAUSTINA: Is a good thing I ain't have on me bombazine. She would soil it if she did connect. But she aim as good as she name, and all we know she ain't have that.

[GRANNY ROOT *appears and gestures at the departing duo. They scream.*]

PERSIS: Oh, God! Abomination!

FAUSTINA: The bitch must have two pochamb!!!

PERSIS AND FAUSTINA: Aaaiiieee!!!

[GRANNY ROOT *goes into the hut.*]

GRANNY ROOT: It do me heart good to see them two dry whore so dirty. Look this place, nuh? Everything all awry. How you could stay in such disarray?

MEDIYAH: I ain't feel to clean. I have too much burden here.

GRANNY ROOT: Other woman does carry and still keep she place. How you could expect somebody to see you house so filthy? What this in the pot?

MEDIYAH: Lanty pea soup. Jason tell me he comin' today, 'cause it the beginnin' of Carnival. The contest, later, you know.

GRANNY ROOT: How you expect the man to eat in so filthy a confine? You soup smell good, but if I was 'live, I wouldn't eat it. You know what them always say.

Dirty kitchen, dirty pot!

Dirty woman, dirty lot!

MEDIYAH: Don't scold me, nuh! This place too much for me. This belly too much for me. I want to have these baby and done. I tired carryin'. I can't do nothin', I so tire. Me foot all swole up so, me can't take four step without I have agony. The sun shine and I weepy. It rain and I worse. Jason only does come once in a blue moon, and when him come, him only stay lickle piece of time. He ain't have no talk for me. He ain't touch me and is him do this thing to me, you know. He ain't look at me. He only say him want to know how him two son comin' 'long. He come late . . . when it dark . . . and he gone 'fore mornin'. After all this t'ing over, I goin' rip out me tube. I ain't goin' through this a next time. Never!

GRANNY ROOT: Such a much complaint.

MEDIYAH: Granny, I miserable! And, oh, God . . . them kick me again! How baby not even born could do they mother such cruelty?

GRANNY ROOT: You is a ordinary woman. You havin' ordinary pain. You makin' ordinary complaint. The magic gone, child. Havin' baby is most real! Jason comin'. I goin'!

[GRANNY ROOT *disappears.* JASON *enters.*]

MEDIYAH: Hello, darlin'.

JASON: This place filthy! I can't stay here! How you feel? Me two son all right?

MEDIYAH: They fine and kickin'. I make lanty pea soup for you.

JASON: You ain't expect me to eat nothin' from this place? How I know you pot clean?

MEDIYAH: I make the soup for good luck!

JASON: I ain't need no soup for win!

MEDIYAH: I know, but don't rush off. Plenty time 'fore the festivity, them.

JASON: I can't find place to stretch out or sit. I goin'! After I win, I might could come back and let you peek at me trophy, but you better pick up this place . . . else I not settin' foot in here. Me mother ain't raise me in no dirty house, and I ain't want me son raise in no dirty house. You goin' wish me *bon chance?*

MEDIYAH: Yes. I gettin' up just now.

[MEDIYAH *rises and offers her lips for* JASON *to kiss. He offers his cheek. She kisses it.*]

JASON: Careful! Don't dirty me suit. Why you don't go to the pond beneath Yama Fall and have a dip and cleanse youself. At least, woman, you could fill a basin and drop a rag in it and then pass it over you body. I ain't like no unclean woman. I ain't like no unclean woman for the mother of me son. I have to go. Bye!

[JASON *leaves.* MEDIYAH, *abject and sobbing, sinks to the ground.* GRANNY ROOT *appears.*]

GRANNY ROOT: Ordinary woman! Ordinary woman!
Ordinary woman! Ordinary woman,
less than whole.
Give 'way she brain,
she heart, she soul.
Now she playin'
ordinary role.
All because
she lose control.
Ordinary woman
feelin' sad.
Ordinary woman
feelin' bad.
Ordinary woman
soon get mad.
Then ordinary woman
once more glad!
MEDIYAH: Granny, you did say somethin'?
GRANNY ROOT: No, darlin'. Granny ain't say nothin' a-tall.

[*Lights.*]

SCENE 2

[*Carnival! Music! Dancing! The townsfolk . . . masked and colorfully costumed!* CREON, *resplendent in gold, a blue ribbon of honor across his chest, a silver and gold cape, bejeweled cane, and a crown on his head, leads the revelers.* SWEET BELLA, *costumed as a radiant Cleopatra, dances with some of the men.* FAUSTINA, *in her somber bombazine dress, enters regally with the air of a great lady dispensing alms to the poor. Her dress is betrayed, however, by the many gauzy fiery yellow and red petticoats that peek from beneath the hem of her dress.* PERSIS *enters in a more joyous manner. Her costume features more gauzy orange and red petticoats than that of her sister. Her parasol is trimmed with the same material.* FAUSTINA *turns her nose up at her sister and dances sedately.* PERSIS, *riant, is having the time of her life. As* CREON *passes the sisters, he uses his cane to lift their skirts.*]

CREON: Mornin', ladies. I always did think all you have secret fire 'neath you skirt, them.

[FAUSTINA *"objects," but* PERSIS *lifts her skirt even higher to show more.* CREON *laughs and whoops. Everyone swirls around a slightly elevated square festooned with gaily colored bunting, giving it the look of a boxing ring.* CEDRIC, *in his chanticleer costume, pompously enters with his entourage. They parade, ceremoniously, as* CEDRIC *steps into the ring. He spars, much in the manner of a boxer.*]

PERSIS: Well, it look like you card finally make up them mind. Cedric done vanquish all he foe. Is only one final mystery challenger to go.

FAUSTINA: Ain't I tell you, miss? The card, them don't lie. Them ain't like some people I does know who, when you does turn you back, does make them dress out of all me extra piece of black bombazine.

PERSIS: Oh, hush you mouth. Is me own black bombazine. You think you is the only one could call sheself lady?

FAUSTINA: Lady t'ief!

[*Suddenly, there is a hush. The music and the hubbub stop. The crowd parts, and* JASON, *clad in a black figure-revealing costume topped by a black close-fitting hood with the horns of a ram and wearing a black mask, appears . . . golden quatro in his hands. He walks silently around the square and then, suddenly, leaps into the ring. Standing in the corner diagonally opposite* CEDRIC, JASON *stares, piercingly, at his opponent. As the crowd comes back to normal,* CREON *steps into the center of the ring.*]

CREON: Ladies and gent, as all you does know,
I win Pecong five time in a row.
Is so!
I the only livin' Mighty, Royal,
Most Perfect, Grand King Calabash.
Only me daddy 'fore me do what I do . . .
and win this verbal clash.
But young Mr. Cedric here
givin' it a try and he biddin' fair.
So far today, as all you does know,
him done vanquish all him foe.
Him only have this last to go.
Is so!
So, without much further ado,

make I present to you
Mr. Jason the Ram
from the Isle of Tougou.
Yes, him come all the way
from he lickle village . . .
come all the way here
to t'ief and pillage
the crown quite out from Cedric han'.
Yes!
Jason of Tougou, the mystery man.
Gentlemen, all you 'proach the center of the combat zone, if you please.

[CEDRIC *and* JASON *step to the center of the ring to receive instructions and engage in a stare down.*]

Yes, this Jason come to make invasion,
and Cedric a-boil with indignation.
So on this auspicious occasion,
I goin' judge this conflagration.
I tell you, nobody better qualify than me
to judge and referee.

[*The crowd goes wild as* CEDRIC *prances around.*]

Well, all you know the regulation.
You entitled to one legal hesitation.
If you does try for a double . . .
Oh, man. Trouble, trouble, trouble
on top of trouble.
So let we have the competition!
No gallivantin'!
Both you shake you hand
and come out chantin'!
Be keen like blade and sharp like pin!
And may the best man win!
PERSIS: That Jason look plenty, plenty sweet in he array.
He look to have plenty heavy stone.
I think I goin' wager a copper or two on he leg alone.
FAUSTINA: Fool! I tell you what the card say.
PERSIS: Um-hmm, I does hear you . . . but
somethin' seem to catch me eye

when I see that mound 'tween him thigh!

CREON: All you pay 'tention to the gong.

When you hear it sound, begin Pecong!

[CREON *hits the gong. Pecong! Music plays. Raucous Calypso rhythm. The two opponents come out of their respective corners and dance around each other, feeling each other out in the manner of boxers or, if you will, fighting cocks. The Pecong is a contest in which each man insults the other. When one man does, the other reacts as if he's been struck by a blow. With each verbal blow, the crowd reacts, as if at a prizefight, and roars its approval.*]

CEDRIC: Come on, Mr. Challenger.

Come, if you dare

Come on, Mr. Big Man.

Come, see how you fare.

Come, come, come.

Take you lickle chance

Make you lickle chant.

And then me word goin' kick you

right in the middle of you shitey pant.

FAUSTINA: Cedric open with wit and style . . .

JASON: You will pardon me if I does make so bold,

but you empty t'reat does leave me cold.

I does hear how you is so much "Master,"

but me tongue too fast and me brain too faster.

So, Mr. Cedric, if you please excuse,

no way I could lose.

PERSIS: You hear that?

CEDRIC: Well, step up, boy, if you does dare.

You ain't goin' get a next opportunity so rare.

I just hope you life complete

if is me you goin' try to beat.

Come on, challenger, but I hope you make you peace

and say you prayer 'fore you heartbeat cease . . .

'Cause me word too strong and you blood too thin

to ever 'low you to win!

FAUSTINA: Hahoii? Cedric have it in the bag!

JASON: T'reat, t'reat, t'reat

is all I does hear!

T'reat, t'reat, t'reat

ringin' in me ear
But when you goin' say? When you goin' do
some damage to this Jason of Tougou?
It look like I goin' have to make the start
and jab you right straight to you heart . . .
and say, "Cedric, you man of smallish part,
you underarm have odor like ragged fart!"

FAUSTINA: Oh, God!

PERSIS: Whoop!

CEDRIC: I does hear people talk 'bout you
and use bad word, you lout, you.
Them does see you seek you pleasure
and all the time chewin' on the treasure.
I does say, "Stand aside, all you.
Be calm! Don't push
when Jason have he face bury in some young gal bush!"

PERSIS: Raucous!

FAUSTINA: Foul utterance!

JASON: It true! I does like them gal so young
and does have them taste on the tip of me tongue.
But at night I does sleep with innocence and joy
because me ain't like you. I ain't sleep with boy!

PERSIS: I, too, enjoyin' this, you know!

CEDRIC: I does see you on the make,
out there huntin' female snake
with you little tool in you hand
doin' battle
with whatever hole underneath she rattle!

FAUSTINA: A veritable blow!

JASON: And I does see what you does give
to all you sundry relative.
None safe from you . . . not even you mother,
not even you brother.
You would mate with you sister,
copulate with a mister.
You would even rape a fever blister!

PERSIS: Cedric reelin'!

FAUSTINA: Shut up!

CEDRIC: You mother behind ain't never see tub.

She mout' nasty and, here the rub,
me too clean to go 'tween she hip,
and I ain't want that ol' haunt lip
nowhere round me billy club.

FAUSTINA: A good return!

JASON: I layin' in me bed. I feel this crunchin'
quite at me vitals, I feel this munchin!
I pull back me sheet and see you mother lunchin' . . .
. . . eh-eh . . . gnawin' with she rat teeth on me truncheon!

PERSIS: Riposte! Riposte!

CEDRIC: All you family ugly with wart on them face.
Them not even part of the human race!

JASON: You does have the nerve to mention face
when you ugly like a mongoose backin' out a fireplace?

CEDRIC: You mother too crazy for me part.
She even see it in she dream.
She does rub it and caress it,
she does reach down and she press it,
but she can't take too much, les' it
make she wet she drawers and scream!

FAUSTINA: Aha! A good hit!

JASON: You mother does quite act like crazy fool.
She jaw go slack and she mout' does drool.
But I think she goin' have to go back to school.
She amateur when it come to nyammin' tool.

CEDRIC: It too bad it have to be this way.
You not so ugly as them all does say.
You know what you face does call to mind?
A wilted, bare-ass baboon behind
that run into one big meat grind
and lose the fight!
That right!

JASON: I does give you gal friend yardstick.
I fill she to she core.
I tell she, "Me name not Richard!"
but she screamin', "More, Dickie, more!"
Then I does have to fight she
to keep she from me waist.
I box she, then I bite she,

but she screen for lickle more taste!
PERSIS: The boy is a born composer, you hear!
CEDRIC: When last you does have woman?
  When last you try it out?
  With petite dangle 'tween you leg
  that always pointin' sout'.
  I does feel so sorry for it,
  lyin' there for dead
  while mine jumpin' and mine pumpin'
  and you no can raise him head.
JASON: I sorry you let out we secret.
  I woulda say you can't.
  But now you done tell the world
  you familiar with inside me pant.
  I wouldn'ta tell nobody
  'cause I ain't want you disgrace,
  but now all does know
  you does bend low
  and could tell them how me taste.
  I was savin' me nether
  for when I get together
  with some gal or the other.
  But you nyam it all,
  bat and ball,
  and ain't leave none for you mother.
PERSIS: Jason of Tougou pullin' out all the stops!
CEDRIC: I ain't have no time to babble
  or hang round with no rabble.
  I goin' put a end to you once and for all.
  I goin' take out me fleshy cutlass
  and stick it up you butt, lass,
  'cause you cryin' out for bed on which to fall.
FAUSTINA: That ain't such a worthy rhyme, Cedric.
PERSIS: What you card say now?
FAUSTINA: Them say hush you fool mouth!
JASON: Is me you callin' lassie?
  I ain't know you was so classy,
  but if you thinkin' I is woman,
  you is wrong.

'Cause if you thinkin' you have slugger
and is me you try to bugger,
I goin' mash you with somethin' mighty strong
and long.
You surely does mistake me
if you think that you could take me.
You confuse if you think me ass cover with lace.
'Cause I have somethin' here . . .
You could pet it.
You could pucker you lip,
take you tongue and wet it,
but have a care that me don't let it
rear back he head and spit in you face.

CEDRIC: I . . . I . . . I . . .

PERSIS: Cedric falter! Cedric falter!

CREON: Yes! Cedric does falter!

CEDRIC: Hush you mouth, all you!
All you, shut you yap!
I still have resource
me ain't begin to tap.
All you think that Cedric dozin'.
Hah! You got a next think comin'!
I still composin'!
Okay! I got it!
You mother swear she smart
when she latch on to me part.
She scream and yell,
"Take me to hell!
I give you everything you think you lack!"
But when me eye glance down
and see what mufflin' round,
I send she by sheself,
and she ain't come back.

FAUSTINA: Come on, Jason of Tougou. You have him now!

PERSIS: Traitoress!

[JASON *begins a slow circling stalk.*]

JASON: I lyin' in me bed alone.
You mother jump me like dog after bone.

She make a leap. Land top me with a crash.
She does mout' me till I ain't know which.
I wake up in the mornin' and have private itch.
Is then I see I drippin' and have ugly rash.
And when I go to make wee-wee,
I burn so . . . God! I say to she,
"May the bloody pile torment you
and corn grow on you feet.
May crab as big as roach
crawl in you bush and eat!
May the whole world turn again' you,
and when you a total wreck,
may you fall through you own asshole
and bruck you goddamn neck!"
FAUSTINA: Cedric gone now.
PERSIS: Yes. Just like you card does say.

[CEDRIC *staggers. The crowd is silent.* CEDRIC *tries to say words, but they won't come. Of course, nobody can see the veiled figure of* GRANNY ROOT *holding her umbrella over* CEDRIC's *head.* CEDRIC, *unable to speak and disgraced, runs off in spite of* JASON's *outstretched hand.* GRANNY ROOT *stays on. There is a great shout from the crowd, and the scene erupts with music and dancing.* CEDRIC's *band runs after him.* PERSIS *grabs* JASON *and kisses him.*]

You is one beautiful and elegant lad, and you cause me to win quite a few
shekels. You is a born Calypsonian! You does have girlfriend?
FAUSTINA: I win some, too! Me card tell me all along you was goin' be the
winner, so me wager lickle bit of penny. Move, woman. Let the man kiss
me!

[*Before this can happen, however,* JASON *is hoisted onto the shoulders of some men, and they parade him around.*]

CREON: Young man, I does like you attack.
Is through you me title still intac'.
You throw Cedric to the ground . . . and mash he up.
You smartly earn this year Pecong Cup.
You is one quite excellent fella.
Make I introduce you to me daughter, Sweet Bella.

[SWEET BELLA *comes forward with a wreath for* JASON's *neck. The moment she places it and their eyes meet,* GRANNY ROOT *gestures and all except* JASON *and*

SWEET BELLA *seem to freeze.* GRANNY ROOT *sprinkles some dust into the Pecong Cup and gives it to them. They each drink.* GRANNY ROOT *retrieves the cup and drains it.* JASON *and* SWEET BELLA *begin a slow, sensuous, sinuous dance. There's not a half inch of space between them. Even though the crowd is frozen, they are not unaware of* SWEET BELLA *and* JASON. *The impression should be given that the crowd is moving at a considerably slower pace than the dancing pair.*]

SWEET BELLA: Jason . . .

CREON: Me daughter speak!

PERSIS, FAUSTINA, AND ALL: Sweet Bella the Silent speak!

JASON: What sound is this!

SWEET BELLA: Jason! Jason!

CREON AND ALL: She speak again!

JASON: I ain't never hear a sound so. It like bird! It like bell! It like music! It like heaven!

SWEET BELLA: Jason!

CREON AND ALL: Miracle! Is a miracle!

CREON: The man make me daughter speak! He make she speak! She ain't never 'fore utter sound, and she speak when he and she eye meet up. He done bruck the spell cast on she. The man a prince! Better than a prince. Him a god!

JASON: It feel like I can't speak. It feel like I can't make rhyme. Confusion runnin' wild in me head and elsewhere. Me breath gone! Is like I seein' woman for the first time in me life.

SWEET BELLA: Is not the same with me. I see you before, Jason. I see you so many time, I can't count.
I see you when I wake.
I see you when I sleepin'.
I see you when it sun
or when the moon come creepin'.
I see you in the moon
every moment of me life before.
I swimmin' in the sea.
There ain't no danger to me
because you watchin' me.
You ain't no stranger to me,
I know you comin' soon
every moment of me life before.
I just find word to say
what I could not express.

Thing people does say every day.
For instance,
word like "love" and "tenderness."
I see you in me dream.
I can't help me dreamin'.
I wake up from me dream
and in me heart, I screamin',
screamin' out you name
and hopin' you just outside me door.
I see you in me eye
in every tear I cry,
each sigh I sigh,
each lie I lie.
In each hello . . .
in each good-bye,
every moment of me life before.
I couldn't speak before.
I save me first word for you.
It take me all me life
to tell how I adore you.
I ragin' like typhoon
tearin' up the tropic shore.
Yes, I does see you
every moment of me life before.
Yes, I see you before, Jason.

JASON: Sweet Bella, I never say this before, I feel to say it now. I does love you. I ain't know why I say it, but I ain't scare to. It just come out. I does love you. It don't even feel strange. I does love you! Yes, that what this feelin' I does feel. Yes! I does love you, Sweet Bella Pandit, I does truly love you. I ain't even have more word than that.

[*All the others return to "normal speed."*]

SWEET BELLA: Daddy, I could speak!
CREON: Praise be! I know it was true! Praise be!

[CREON *falls to the ground in gratitude and thanks.*]

SWEET BELLA: Daddy, this man want to talk to you.
CREON: I figure so.
JASON: Mr. Creon Pandit, Mighty, Royal, Most Perfect, Grand King Calabash,

all me life I ain't see nobody like you daughter. I know you ain't know nothin' 'bout me, but I not a too bad fellow. In me life I know a whole lot of gal, and I tell you, out in the open, that quite a few does make baby for me. I know me duty to them children, them, and I does do it, but I never feel for none of they mother or any gal what I does feel for you daughter, Sweet Bella. My heart and entire soul ragin' with flame what like come from the center of the earth. I can't make no procrastination. I say to you before all assemble here. I want to marry you daughter. I want to marry she. Now!

PERSIS: Oh, God! The man fast!

FAUSTINA: The man faster than fast. Him rapid!

JASON: I can't explain what come over me. I see she and me heart just gone.

CREON: It true I ain't know much 'bout you, Jason of Tougou Island. But I does know this. Me daughter born without speech. You does see she for the first time . . . and she talk. Is a true sign. Is a supernatural occurrence. A true sign from the God, them. Sweet Bella, you want this man?

SWEET BELLA: Is more than just want, Daddy. I have to have him. I thinkin' . . . I feelin' . . . if I ain't have he soon, I goin' fall down right at he foot and die and the earth could swallow me and I ain't care a t'ing. I feelin' if you ain't let me have he and he have me, I goin' climb a scarp or Devil Cliff and pitch meself right into the wind. I feelin' if I ain't take he soon, I could throw meself right into the flame, and when I meet Satan, I would kill he.

PERSIS: Faustina, you ever know such passion was runnin' wild so, inside she?

FAUSTINA: I struck speechless!

CREON: Sweet Bella, you me only child. I ain't never hear you speak before. Even if it a miracle, I can't just throw you to the man. I does just hear you voice, sweet like a bird, for the first time. You want to deprive you daddy of that sweet sound so soon? Everything makin' fast current, but I ain't a proper daddy if I just . . . let you go. Of course, this the answer to all me dream. The man have the proper look and coloration, and since I ain't have son to carry on me name, I could at least have grandson to carry on me blood. And who know, one day this same grandson could be Mighty, Royal, Most Perfect, Grand King Calabash. Give me three day to make plan and t'ing. Till the end of Carnival. If the two of you still does have no let-upsy, then as magistrate, I, meself, will perform the ceremony just before midnight . . . last day of Carnival. What you does say, Mr. Jason? If you does love she like you does say, three day is a eyeblink.

JASON: Three day is torture! A man could die in three day, but I does love this gal. So even if it ain't fine with me, she too worth the wait. Okay!

CREON: Well spoken! Sweet Bella?

[SWEET BELLA *thinks and, finally, nods assent.*]

> Don't nod, gal. You have voice sweeter than mornin' wind in the mountain. Don't deprive you daddy from hearin' it.

SWEET BELLA: Yes, Daddy. I could wait . . . but three day is all. If you ain't keep you word, I goin' run off with he, even if it Lent! I ain't care.

CREON: Then since all you willin' to wait, I give me consent. I quite happy, you know. Just think, I goin' have me some grandson at last!

[*The crowd erupts! Music! Dancing! Whatever! The crowd is at its frenzied peak when* GRANNY ROOT *comes out of her trance.*]

GRANNY ROOT: Now we does begin!

[*Thunder! Lightning!* MEDIYAH *appears.*]

MEDIYAH: Jason! Jason! Jason, you son, them comin'! Come! Hold me hand! Help me! I havin' you son, them, for you, Jason darlin'.

[*Even* PERSIS *and* FAUSTINA *are speechless.*]

CREON: Jason of Tougou, you does know this woman?

JASON: Yes! I does know she!

CREON: You does know she is sister to Cedric, who just fall to you in Pecong?

JASON: No! I ain't ever know that. She ain't ever tell me such!

CREON: You did lay up with she?

JASON: I did lay with she, yes, but no more!

CREON: You ain't love she or promise youself to she?

JASON: Sweet Bella, as the God, them, me judge and witness, I ain't love nobody but you in the whole of me life, 'side me mother and she long depart from here. This just one of them gal who I does jook up long ago when I was wicked. That then, sweetness! I does love you now with all the heart you does leave me when you take it so complete.

[MEDIYAH *lets forth a horribly agonizing scream and falls, writhing, on the ground.*]

MEDIYAH: Jason! Jason! Jason, with all you does leave of me heart, I hate you. I does curse you, and before all here, I swear I goin' have me vengeance. Aaaiiieee!!!

GRANNY ROOT: Aha! You Granny Root granddaughter again.

MEDIYAH: Aaaiiieee!!! Granny! Granny, call all the God, them. Attend me!

CREON: She delirious! She talkin' to she dead granny! She talkin' to air!

PERSIS: All you hard back man, get 'way from here. Go stand someplace and hide you eye. All you woman, surround me. And one of you, tear off you petticoat and give me.

[*The men obey, as do the women, encircling* MEDIYAH, *who is being attended by* PERSIS *and* FAUSTINA. JASON *and* SWEET BELLA *stand off, alone.* CREON *stands apart, watching them.*]

SWEET BELLA: I does love you, Jason of Tougou. I ain't give a care what you do before I see you. I sorry for Mediyah, but you does belong to me. I sorry for she, but I ain't care. I does love you.

JASON: I does love you, Sweet Bella Pandit.

SWEET BELLA: Three day, Jason! Three day till Carnival end, and then I goin' have you.

JASON: Three day!

SWEET BELLA: Just 'fore midnight on Carnival Night!
'Fore four-day mornin' come in sight!

JASON: Oh, God!

[SWEET BELLA *walks off, leaving* JASON. GRANNY ROOT *passes her umbrella over the crowd. There is an audible gasp. Seconds later there is another.* PERSIS, *after a bit, approaches* JASON *carrying two petticoat-wrapped bundles.* JASON *is allowed to see the contents of the bundles, but when he reaches for them,* PERSIS *pulls back.* JASON *walks off.* GRANNY ROOT *passes her umbrella over* CREON's *head. He starts, frightened. Looking over his shoulder,* CREON *goes.*]

GRANNY ROOT: Yes, Mediyah. You hatred make you Granny Root grand-daughter again.

[GRANNY ROOT *cackles. Lights go out.*]

SCENE 3

[MEDIYAH's *hut, and it's still far from neat.* MEDIYAH, *on her pallet, stares into space.* GRANNY ROOT, *eyes focused on her granddaughter, stirs something in a pot. Two rough-hewn cradles are in evidence.*]

GRANNY ROOT: You brother comin'.

MEDIYAH: I know.

[CEDRIC, *drunk and angry, enters. He surveys the condition of the hut and his sister. His eyes alight on the two cradles.*]

CEDRIC: So it true! You make two baby! I does hear 'bout it from all who get ecstasy when they could spread ondit! And you name in everybody mouth. I now see why you say you can't help me to get wood for a next quatro. You pitch over you own brother for help some man who ain't give a fart for you. He load you up with pickney, them, and then he cut out. Right now he languishin' in the arm of Sweet Bella Pandit. Right now he croonin' lilt in she ear . . . the same like he mussie done to you. Right now he t'umpin all we half sister. Right now you ain't even in he memory, 'cause he too busy addin' another notch to he count. Good for you!

[GRANNY ROOT *gestures to silence* CEDRIC, *but* MEDIYAH, *her eyes still rooted in space, raises her hand to indicate that she wants* CEDRIC *to talk on.*]

You know what that man do to me? This man who you lay on you back for. You know what him do? Him shame me! Him cause me to cast me head down and not be able for lift it. Him cause everybody who did have respect and fear for me to laugh and stamp them foot with glee as I does pass. He does cause everybody to have only toleration for me like they does have for bug! You know how that does feel? Well, I hope you know it soon. I curse you, Sister! I hope you blood and you milk does turn to ugly, hellacious green bile. I hope you body dry up and turn to black powder. You help to kill you brother, Mediyah. It like I tear up into lickle piece and throw to dog for eat. I hope both you boy know the pain you cause me. I could have be like king in this place, but you abdicate me. Damn you, Sister! Damn you!

[CEDRIC, *drunkenly, stumbles out.*]

GRANNY ROOT: Too bad!

MEDIYAH: Part of Cedric curse already true. Ain't nothin' runnin' through me vein but bile and bitterness.

GRANNY ROOT: You need more than bitterness.

MEDIYAH: I know.

GRANNY ROOT: I know you know, but I makin' sure. [*She tastes her concoction.*] It ready. I even put in somet'ing even you ain't know 'bout. You had long sleep. I had was to wait for you to wake. I ain't even able to talk to you in you dream.

MEDIYAH: I ain't need you in me dream. Only room in me dream for me hatred of Jason of Tougou.

GRANNY ROOT: Jason is man . . . and man does inspire hatred. Tell me hatred done replace love in you heart. Tell me hatred of man does replace love in you heart!

MEDIYAH: I done told you!

GRANNY ROOT: No! You tell me hatred of Jason. Tell me now is hatred of man you feelin'.

MEDIYAH: Yes!

GRANNY ROOT: Tell me again and swear it!

[*She grabs* MEDIYAH'*s hands and spits in the palm of each.*]

Swear it!

MEDIYAH: I does swear it! By all the God, them, I does swear it!

GRANNY ROOT: Good! Aha! Right on time.

[PERSIS *and* FAUSTINA *enter.*]

PERSIS: Mediyah! Mediyah!

FAUSTINA: Mediyah, we could come in?

MEDIYAH: Yes.

PERSIS: Thank you. How the two little baby keepin'?

MEDIYAH: Them sleep!

PERSIS: And we shoutin' and keepin' noise and t'ing.

FAUSTINA: Shame on you!

MEDIYAH: Is all right. They does sleep sound. They ain't wake till them want to.

PERSIS: Is always such a joy to have lickle baby cryin' in the house.

MEDIYAH: Them don't cry! Baby only cry 'cause them can't tell you what do they. I know what do these two, so them don't have for cry. They ain't cry when them born, and them never goin' cry.

PERSIS: As long as them have them health . . . that what count, I suppose.

FAUSTINA: Mediyah, we could help you pick up round here?

PERSIS: We could do so if you want for we to do so. I mean, we ain't want for interfere, but if you does need some help to . . .

MEDIYAH: Why all you does want to do this. All we ain't friend! I does thank you for deliverin' the baby, them, but we ain't waste no love or like on weself.

FAUSTINA: Mediyah, is time we does put all this ruction aside. The man do you a horrendous dirtiness. I never see such in all me life.

PERSIS: Never! You deliverin' the man baby. Two of them . . . as if one ain't hard enough. You twitchin' in the dirt, and he rejectin' you right on the selfsame spot.

FAUSTINA: It like he grab hold of all we woman and slap all we. It like he rainin' blow on all we arse!

MEDIYAH: You come to tell me this?

FAUSTINA: We come to tell you that Creon Pandit makin' big weddin' plan for he daughter and that rapscallion who did have he way with you.

PERSIS: Them goin' marry at Carnival finish tomorrow night!

FAUSTINA: Before midnight! It goin' be the highlight.

PERSIS: But even worse . . .

FAUSTINA: . . . The man on he way here now . . .

PERSIS: . . . Comin' to you hut for . . .

MEDIYAH: He comin' for take he two son 'way from here.

PERSIS: You does know this?

FAUSTINA: You ain't goin' 'low he to have he way?

PERSIS: No! You couldn't condone such action.

FAUSTINA: No! I ain't goin' believe that!

MEDIYAH: I say what I goin' do?

FAUSTINA: But you does have a certain look in you eye that does say . . .

MEDIYAH: You does see look in me eye? I ain't know you could see look in me eye. But you is most observant. Keep lookin' in me eye! That right! Both you keep lookin' in me eye. Closer, ladies.

[PERSIS *and* FAUSTINA *are enchanted.*]

GRANNY ROOT: Yes, Granddaughter, you does have you power back.

MEDIYAH: Now, all you go wait just outside till I does call you to come in.

PERSIS AND FAUSTINA: Yes, Mediyah.

[*Obediently, they go.*]

MEDIYAH: You does know me mind?

GRANNY ROOT: Yes! Steel youself. He comin'.

MEDIYAH: I know!

[JASON *enters, wearing the suit* MEDIYAH *bought him.*]

JASON: Hello!

MEDIYAH: Jason.

JASON: You does feel all right?

MEDIYAH: I fine! I ain't perform no feat! I ain't do nothin' ain't ordinary. I only have twin . . . for you. Nothin' special.

JASON: I see them two woman outside you place dawdlin' round.

MEDIYAH: Them help deliver you son, them. Them came to inquire after they health. That what you a-come for?

JASON: Mediyah, you still have this place unkempt. Well, I ain't come to lash you with more word over you bad housekeepin'. I goin' be brief. You does know I fall in love with Sweet Bella Pandit and does plan to marry up with she 'fore Lent mornin' come.

MEDIYAH: Is so I did hear. I offer me congrats.

JASON: You ain't vex?

MEDIYAH: Why I should vex? You ain't love me. I distapoint, true . . . but I ain't vex . . . no more. I find you on Miedo Wood Island all hack up and wrack up. True! I heal you and comfort you. True! I give you wood and wildcat gut for fashion quatro for you to win Pecong. True! I give you two boy you say you want for so long and never have. All that true, but I ain't vex. Why I should vex?

JASON: Good! I glad you does feel so, 'cause I ain't want to make you no hurt. Well, as you does say, I always want some son. Now I does have them, and now I does want them.

MEDIYAH: With you!

JASON: With me! Boy belong with them daddy!

MEDIYAH: Them ain't nowhere yet near wean.

JASON: If you had kick out, them two boy would have to find some other woman to give them titty. I win Pecong. I have lickle cash to buy fertile titty from woman in that business. You ain't truly want them boy, you know. You ain't need no reminder of me. I just a scalawag, you know, and it best you does forget me.

MEDIYAH: You will pardon me, Jason, but I ain't never goin' forget you.

JASON: Well, I ain't see how you could, but me charm aside, the boy, them, goin' be better off with me. I marryin' well, and Creon does like me.

MEDIYAH: Of course! You make he daughter chatter after a life of silence, and you does have good tint. Match it with he Sweet Bella, and the two of you could make grandchild with pleasin' coloration.

JASON: True!

MEDIYAH: What about these two boy?

JASON: Them fair enough, thanks to me. Them ain't goin' get too much darker 'cause I did peek at them ear when them birth.

MEDIYAH: I see.

JASON: Anyway, them goin' be taken good care of. So give me them, nuh!

MEDIYAH: Them goin' soon wake up and want they milk. You better leave me nurse them a next time. You could go someplace and then come back after them suck. Then you could have them.

JASON: You ain't goin' give me trouble?

MEDIYAH: Why I should do such? What you does say true! Boy belong with them daddy. I ain't carve out to be mother. 'Specially to you children. Look how I does keep this place. Like you say, you ain't want no son from you . . . raise in pigsty.

JASON: True!

MEDIYAH: True! So you go, take a trot, then come back and . . .

JASON: I know you was goin' have good sense. Sweet Bella tell me you was goin' cause some aggravation 'bout this. I tell she, she wrong 'cause I does know you.

MEDIYAH: But she ain't know me. I ain't goin' cause no excitement. I, too, glad she talkin', you know.

JASON: You ain't upset with she?

MEDIYAH: You look at she, she look at you, and she speak. That a great omen. A sign from up there. I can't find no fault with what the God, them, does decree. What happen ain't she fault. And I no more upset with she than I upset with you. All you want is for raise up you son, them. True?

JASON: True! Give them they last milk, and I goin' come back. Oh, yes. I did never thank you for the quatro. So I do it now. Thank you!

MEDIYAH: Oh, you most welcome. Thank you for the twin!

JASON: You welcome, too.

[JASON *goes.*]

GRANNY ROOT: Worthless dog! Vile pig!

MEDIYAH: Granny, what dog and pig do to you, you does insult they so?

GRANNY ROOT: I make apology to all the animal I confuse he with. It all I could do to keep from doin' somethin' to he.

MEDIYAH: Mr. Jason of Tougou,
    I goin' get marry, too.
    I sendin' you a special invite
    to me nuptial night!
    Since *you* special, I makin' room
    for you, right 'tween me and me groom.

GRANNY ROOT: Hahoii!!! Give youself over, girl!

MEDIYAH: Come to me, all you God from the old country
    and the old time.
    Come to me and make me harder. Steel me!
    God of Thunder, speak in your most angry temper!
    God of Lightning, wreak you havoc and illuminate the
    darkest hour with you blindin' power!
    God of Wind, be extreme in you violence and blow the

path of gentility to hell.
God of Cold, plant icy river in me heart.
God of Hell, attend me!
Sun, Moon, Star, hide you face and let through
the God of Vengeance
to marry and consummate with me
and spew the foul content of we marriage bed
over Sweet Bella Pandit
and that bastard thing she choose for sheself.
Make me blood like hot oil
to burn and smother all life
from they and all they line!
Fill me with hate
and let that hate never depart!
God of Vengeance, stay with me forever!
God of Hate, stay with me forever!
God of Screamin' Quiet and Quiet Scream,
be all my life.
God of Vengeance and Hate, make me you wife!

[*She goes to the cradle and regards the inhabitants.*]

And for these . . .
. . . these that come from them two regrettable seed he plant
in me,
make me milk
pure boilin', bubblin', bitter, and burnin' bane.

[*She picks up the babies and places them, one at each breast. Lights swirl, flicker, and dim.*]

Now, Jason, you can come for you two boy.
Take they to you bride and enjoy.
GRANNY ROOT: You do well, me daughter. You please all the old God, them, and you please Granny, too!

[GRANNY ROOT *laughs, malevolently. Lights.*]

SCENE 4

[MEDIYAH'S *hut. Moments later. She has nursed the babies and returned them to their cradles. She goes to the doorway.*]

MEDIYAH: Attend me here!

[PERSIS *and* FAUSTINA *obediently enter and, drinking from wooden goblets offered them by* MEDIYAH, *sit as she directs.* GRANNY ROOT *indicates by gesture that* JASON *approaches.*]

I know! Come in, Jason. These two lady help deliver you baby. They not only have plenty interest, but them does have plenty milk. They does, therefore, provide one pair of titty for each one you boy. If you ain't want them, you ain't get the baby, them. Agree?

JASON: Agree!

MEDIYAH: Good!

JASON: You two ain't mind?

PERSIS: No! How we could mind?

FAUSTINA: No way we could mind.

PERSIS AND FAUSTINA: In fact, we quite "enchant" to do such!

JASON: Good! I sure make two healthy-lookin' boy. I think they goin' suck you dry within the week.

MEDIYAH: Jason, if you ain't mind, I have weddin' gift for you bride. Is to show you and she me heart in the right place. I guess you want know what inside. I tell you. Is a thing I purchase in Creon store. A night frock so pretty and silky, I did plan to wear it on me weddin' night . . . if you did ever so choose to marry up with me. But you ain't choose to marry up with me, so I think Sweet Bella should have it. At least it still serve a bride. I put thousand petal from flower and quite some sweet herb in the parcel to give it scent and wishes for the future.

JASON: Flower and herb?

MEDIYAH: Yes. I had mean to enchant you like any young gal on she night of night would enchant she princely groom, but since that rule out, Sweet Bella will wear it and maybe take you to paradise.

JASON: On she behalf, I does thank you. Is a kind and gentle gesture. You does surprise me.

MEDIYAH: Jason, I goin' turn me back. Persis! Faustina! Take the baby and go with he. When I turn round, I ain't want to see none of you here. Go!

JASON: You two lady, *suivez-moi!* Good-bye, Mediyah! I ain't expect to see you a next time. I think you goin' have it much better if you ain't stay in this place. If you ain't think of yourself, think of these two boy. Yes! It goin' go much better for you if you leave here. Remember, the magistrate goin' be me daddy-in-law! Good-bye!

[PERSIS *and* FAUSTINA *gather the two babes and follow* JASON, *who carries the* "gift."]

GRANNY ROOT: Death! I wishin' a hard and evil and fast death to Jason of Tougou.

MEDIYAH: No! I ain't goin' permit that! Take back you wish! It wasted on he. I already see to it that Jason of Tougou goin' live. He goin' have the most long and most slow life of remembrance. Now, Granny, content youself in some business or whatever you please. I goin' sit here and 'wait the news.

[*As* GRANNY ROOT *eyes her,* MEDIYAH *arranges herself to receive the news. She stares, vacantly, humming to herself as she rocks . . . and waits.*]

SCENE 5

[*Darkness. There are screams of utmost horror. Townspeople run to and fro in utter confusion. The lights come up to reveal* MEDIYAH *sitting impassively and* GRANNY ROOT, *anxious to swallow every word from* PERSIS *and* FAUSTINA, *who come running up, exhausted, in tears and filled with revulsion.*]

PERSIS: Oh, Mediyah . . .

FAUSTINA: Oh, God! Mediyah! Mediyah!

PERSIS: How could you manipulate we so?

How you could do such?

FAUSTINA: How? How? How? How you could hate so much?

PERSIS: Oh, Mediyah, you is one hard—

FAUSTINA: Harsh—

PERSIS: Bitter—

FAUSTINA: Sour woman!

[MEDIYAH *sits like a stone.*]

MEDIYAH: You will relate the event.

PERSIS: Me and Faustina find weself in Creon Pandit house. We does hear some laughter, and we realize the weddin' festivity afoot.

FAUSTINA: For we part, we ain't know how we get there. It like me and Persis wakin' from some dream. We in some room. Everything sorta haze, and we eye gettin' 'custom to we surroundin' when we does each feel somethin' strange.

PERSIS: Both of we scream out simultaneous.

Both of we look down.

Both of we does have one pitiful baby at we breast.

Baby all purple and discolor.
Two baby who ain't ask for this world.
Two baby—

PERSIS AND FAUSTINA: Dead!

FAUSTINA: We scream and scream and scream and scream and scream.

[*In the background, under separate spotlights,* JASON *and* CREON *appear to mime out the action.*]

And Creon and Jason of Tougou come runnin'
and bruck down the door and,
still in them weddin' costume,
cutlass in hand,
whoosh in!
Them see the baby in we arm.

PERSIS: The dead baby in we arm.

FAUSTINA: Jason fall down with horrible cry-out
and thrash the floor.
He knuckle bleed as he whimper to heaven,
"Why? Why? Why?"

PERSIS: I never hear man cry with such agony and sorriness.

FAUSTINA: Creon grab we and shake we and yell so at we
that we does kill these two baby.
When we does tell he we ain't know what happen
or how these baby does come to be dead,
Jason jump up and attack we.
He cutlass swingin' and flingin'
and flailin' and sailin' in the air.

PERSIS: The only reason he metal ain't seriously catch we is all the tear in he
eye leave he foot unsteady and him aim faulty.

FAUSTINA: Then we hear a sound. A scream—

PERSIS: So high,
so sharp,
so pierce.
More keen than blade.
It halt Jason in he track
and cause all we to stand stiller than death!
When all we leg free, we run to that scream
that even God would fear.
It comin' from the nuptial chamber.

We pitch open the portal
and, oh, what we see!
FAUSTINA AND PERSIS: Oh, God! What we see!
What we see!
What we see!

[SWEET BELLA, *her nightdress aflame, writhes and screams in excruciating agony.*]

FAUSTINA: Sweet Bella have on the very night frock you gift she with.
Sweet Bella, it seem only a few hour since she find she voice.
PERSIS: Sweet Bella. She voice so sweet
and so like a little bell that tinkle.
Sweet Bella. She voice now like a grate.
Yellin' and roarin' and grindin' and raspin'.
PERSIS AND FAUSTINA: And she body . . . aflame!
Aflame! Aflame!
She entire body aflame!
FAUSTINA: Creon pitch heself on he daughter.

[CREON, JASON, *and* SWEET BELLA *mime the action.*]

PERSIS: Jason . . . pitch heself on he bride
and he new in-law daddy.
But the flame too hot and mighty.
Creon burn too bad,
but him stay clamp to he daughter
in they incestuous dance to the death.
Jason . . . fall away
screamin' with no sound from he mouth.
It too late.
FAUSTINA: What used to be Sweet Bella
now only ash and dust and smoke and steam
and burn flesh and smell that does make you
sick to you bowel.
PERSIS: A stench like you never smell.
FAUSTINA: Creon, burn and disfigure,
skin meltin' 'way from he carcass,
run and stagger till he leg no longer carry he.
He fall 'pon top Sweet Bella and
mash she corpse to charcoal.

He last breath come from he mouth like a sad whistle . . .
   and he pass into history.
PERSIS: Oh, Mediyah, what that gal do to you?
   What she do to you so bad she earn such a dispatch?
   What Creon do so bad he no longer have breath
   to breathe?
PERSIS AND FAUSTINA: Ah, Mediyah, you is a hard, harsh, bitter, sour
   woman!
MEDIYAH [*stonily*]: What of Jason?
PERSIS: We comin' to that.
FAUSTINA: But we have a next bitter news.
PERSIS AND FAUSTINA: Tragedy 'pon tragedy.
   Sorrow 'pon sorrow.
   Bitterness 'pon bitterness.
   Sadness 'pon sadness.
PERSIS: And strangeness . . . 'pon strangeness
   for as we runnin' here to tell you all this occurrence,
   we see Cedric, you brother.

[*In the background,* CEDRIC *appears, dangling.*]

FAUSTINA: Cedric the Rhymer now defeated.
   In he hand, he quatro mangle.
   He eye . . . agape and starin' straight to heaven,
   and he once-proud body dangle
   . . . dangle from a tree
   where there were no tree before.
PERSIS: A calabash tree that spring up overnight.

[CEDRIC *disappears.*]

MEDIYAH: What of Jason?
PERSIS: Woman, you can't take lickle time to mourn the dead?
FAUSTINA: You have no sorrow for none of these people?
PERSIS AND FAUSTINA: Poor Mediyah. You is a hard, harsh, bitter, sour
   woman!
MEDIYAH: What of Jason?
PERSIS AND FAUSTINA: We only have sorrow
   and sadness for you.
   Such a hard, harsh, bitter, sour woman!
   Pity! Pity! Pity!

MEDIYAH: What about Jason of Tougou?

PERSIS: Jason? That poor waste man?
    Jason, as we say, thrash heself on the ground.
    He eye shed more water than Yama Waterfall.

FAUSTINA: More than the river.

PERSIS: Then it dawn on he that he should dead like Creon,
    'cause he ain't nothin' more to live for,
    but he ain't have the courage to bear the pain
    and grab it like Creon.
    And he commence to reprimand heself
    with blow after blow,
    and he run 'bout the room
    pitchin' heself 'gainst all four wall.
    I never see such a pitiful madness.

FAUSTINA: Then, with brutal suddenness, him halt!
    Him livid and turn this dull blue and gray tint
    right in front of we very eye.
    He body and he glance grow cold.
    A cold like we never feel in this island.
    We had was to grab shawl and throw 'bout we shoulder,
    the man radiate such cold.
    Then he walk over to them what used to have life,
    and he look down.
    He come over to we,
    for we still have he dead, shrivel-up baby, them,
    in we arm.
    He relieve we of them
    and he look down.
    Then he give they back to we
    and he look down.

PERSIS: Then he pick up he shiny machete
    and say to we . . .

JASON: Go! Tell the witch, Mediyah, to prepare sheself!
    Tell she I comin' with heavy, ponderous, sorrowful, sad,
    and deliberate footstep to kill she!
    To rid this poor world of she!
    To send she back to the very bowel of hell
    from which she spring!
    Go! Tell she all this!

Tell she who grind and mash and tear and break
and poison and burn me heart
all this! Go!

PERSIS: Is so him say and is so we do!
All we beg you leave to go.
Please don't trouble youself to show
further botheration for we.

FAUSTINA: If perchance you does see we takin' we custom,
please to turn you head
and treat we like people dead
and gone.

PERSIS AND FAUSTINA: You cause we eye to be full with tear
and we heart to be heavy with stone
and youself to be forever . . . alone!
Good-bye!

[PERSIS and FAUSTINA, *tearful, leave.* MEDIYAH *and* GRANNY ROOT *sit in respective attitudes of impassiveness and waiting. In the distance a drum beat, signaling approaching heavy footsteps. Soft, muted, and measured at first, their sound gets louder and louder until at last* JASON *fills the door frame.* MEDIYAH, *defiant, turns to face him. He raises his weapon, grasping the hilt with both hands high over his head, as if to cleave the stone-faced* MEDIYAH *in two.*]

JASON [*screaming*]: Mediyah!!!!!!!!

[JASON *brings down his machete with all his might and purpose, but the blade stops inches above the head of* MEDIYAH, *whose gaze continues to "fix" him. Whimpering, he slowly crumples to the floor in an abject heap. On his knees and at the feet of* MEDIYAH, *she—slowly and disdainfully—raises a foot and, scornfully, pushes him over . . . leaving him prostrate and sobbing.*]

Mediyah! Mediyah! Mediyah!

[MEDIYAH *begins a slow circular walk, with* JASON *crawling, abjectly and snakelike, after her.*]

MEDIYAH: And is so you will be from now. A crawlin', grovelin', slitherin' thing that people does see and set them dog on and spit at. 'Low me, if you please, to be the first.

[*She spits at him.*]

You did cause me some pain and hurt.

So forever eat sand and mud and dirt!
Eat dust and t'ing what does drop from dog!
Eat worm and t'ing what does hide 'neath log!
Yes! Know only sand and mud and dirt!
Raise you head only high as the hem of me skirt!
Stay down in the gravel where you does belong,
Jason of Tougou, master of Pecong!
Master of lilt! Master of rhyme!
Master of filt'! Master of crime!
As long as you does continue to be,
you ain't never, never, never, ever goin' forget me!
Wherever you crawlin' take you,
be it far or be it near,
make you take you this name for carry
forever in you ear . . .

[*She bends down and screams in his ear.*]

MEDIYAH!!!

[*She, disdainfully, points him toward the door. Painfully, slowly, and still sobbing,* JASON *crawls from the scene on his belly.*]

GRANNY ROOT: It all done now. You revenge. All man what does do you
    harshness . . . gone! My daughter, you mother, revenge! Creon and all he
    line . . . gone! There ain't goin' never be a next Creon Pandit!
MEDIYAH: All Creon line not gone. I still here.
GRANNY ROOT: You ain't Creon seed. You different seed from Cedric.
    You all herb and bush and root and air and fire and smoke
    and earth and wild forest.
    You want to see you daddy?
    You want to see who spew heself forth into you mother
    at my prayin' and incantation
    so she shame could be avenge?
    You want to see who cause you to birth?
    Behold! Behold!

[GRANNY ROOT *gestures. Smoke! Thunder! Lightning! Fire! The awesome figure of* DAMBALLAH *appears and menacingly but silently laughs. He dances . . . prances . . . a puff of smoke, and he disappears.*]

When you mother come to me

and say she power gone,
she beg me not to damn he,
for she so love he, this Creon.
But Granny Root pray
and Granny Root do.
Spirit appear . . .
and out come . . . you!
You . . . all Granny Root perception.
You . . . all spiritual conception.
You . . . all Granny Root revenge.
You . . . all Granny Root say you was
and . . . that all you was.
Come!
You and me off to Miedo Wood Island.
Is we home.

MEDIYAH: So! That Jason I did love
and that Jason I did hate.
Now I ain't feel nothin' for he
'cause me passion 'bate.
I ain't feel he a-tall!
I ain't feel nothin' a-tall!

GRANNY ROOT: To Miedo Wood Island, child.
You and me goin' say we good-bye there.
Me spirit tire and me can sleep . . . now!

[MEDIYAH *and* GRANNY ROOT *disappear. Lights.*]

EPILOGUE

[*A group of revelers, stragglers from Carnival, noisily cross the scene. Still dancing and swilling from rumpots, they're drunkenly trying to keep the spirit going.* PERSIS *and* FAUSTINA *open their slatted windows.*]

PERSIS: All you . . . less that noise! You ain't know what time it is?

FAUSTINA: You ain't know what day it is? Carnival over! It Lent and Carnival over!

PERSIS: You ain't know that?

FAUSTINA: What do you?

PERSIS AND FAUSTINA: Is time for all you 'semble here
to low you eye and be austere.
Go home! Go home! Until next year.
Carnival over! You hear?

[*The revelers reflect for a moment, wave off* PERSIS *and* FAUSTINA, *and go off, still shuffling to their beat. Still drinking in the morning heat,* PERSIS *and* FAUSTINA *regard them, shrug their shoulders, regard each other, shrug their shoulders, and go off to join the merry band.*]

FLYOVERS

JEFFREY SWEET

For Lindsay

PLAYWRIGHT'S STATEMENT

Flyovers was developed through a series of private readings and explorations. My thanks to the various actors, writers, directors, and friends who helped me find my way on this one, among them Polly Adams, Lindsay Crouse, Kit Flanagan, Peter Frechette, Tim Halligan, John Christopher Jones, K. C. Landis, Melissa Manchester, Kristine Niven, Jeff Perry, John Rothman, James Sherman, Marc Vann, and the members of Ensemble Studio Theatre. Special thanks to the folks at Naked Angels for a particularly valuable workshop: Jace Alexander, Nicole Burdette, Jodie Markell, and Geoffrey Nauffts.

The title of the play came from a story I heard about a network executive talking to a producer who had pitched him an ambitious TV project. "They'll get it in New York, and they'll get it in Los Angeles," the executive said, "but will the flyovers get it?" (Friends living in the Midwest tell me that the term has some currency there.)

I do a fair amount of traveling, and I've noticed that the resentment of New York and Los Angeles is almost palpable. This has been the subtext of a startling number of conversations I've had with people around the country—this anger on the part of many that so much of the culture is dictated to them by people on the coasts who are blithely indifferent to what's going on elsewhere. This often is expressed in comments like "Well, maybe being from New York this won't look like much to you, but we like it." Ted may be Oliver's bully. New York and L.A. are widely perceived to be the twin bullies of the United States.

This isn't restricted to cultural concerns, of course. In this era of corporate executives reaping millions by putting into place economies and cost-cutting plans that translate into the decline of whole towns, it's easy to see why those newly unemployed might be pissed at the urban centers where most of these corporate executives live and work.

Anyway, these ideas were on my mind when the play was being written.

PRODUCTION HISTORY

Flyovers, by Jeffrey Sweet, was first presented by Victory Gardens Theater, Chicago, Illinois, in May 1998.

PRODUCTION TEAM

Director . . . . Dennis Začek
Set . . . . Mary Griswold
Costumes. . . . . Jeff Bauer
Lights . . . . Todd Hensley
Sound . . . . Andre Pluess and Ben Sussman
Production Stage Manager . . . . .Shane Spaulding

CAST

Iris . . . . Amy Morton
Ted. . . . . William L. Petersen
Lianne . . . . Linda Reiter
Oliver . . . . Marc Vann

Gary Cole and Teddi Siddall took over the roles of Ted and Iris during the extension run of *Flyovers* at Victory Gardens.

CHARACTERS

Ted, *in his forties*
Oliver, *in his forties*
Iris, *in her forties*
Lianne, *in her forties*

STAGING

The primary location of the play is the deck of Ted's house in a town in Ohio. The second scene takes place in the living room of Iris's home. We see the front door, a bit of the kitchen, and a door that leads offstage to a bedroom. There should be no intermission. The time is 1998.

SCENE 1

[*The deck of* TED's *house. A barbecue, outdoor bar, etc.* TED *is making a drink for* OLIVER. OLIVER *wears a jacket and tie. The scene begins at twilight and continues into the night.*]

TED: You really get into it sometimes, the two of you. You and uh—

OLIVER: Sarah.

TED: Sarah, yeah. Sometimes you seem to be really—

OLIVER: Well, that's part of the fun of it.

TED: —really pissed at each other.

OLIVER: No, not pissed.

TED: She doesn't tick you off? Her attitude: "Of course you'd like that piece of crap, Oliver, it's got explosions and butts and boobs. Cuz you're a guy." That doesn't make you—

OLIVER: That's part of the act.

TED: The act? You mean it's a phony?

OLIVER: No, the opinions we have are the opinions we have. But the idea of the show—the thing that makes our show different from Siskel and Ebert or those other guys—is that it's a man and a woman. The idea—the way we sold it to the syndicator—was a lot of couples go to the movies together—

TED: I think they call those dates.

OLIVER: —and they end up talking about the same kind of stuff, *issues,* we get into on—

TED: So you're, what? Representing these couples?

OLIVER: Sort of.

TED: She's talking about the movie from, like, the woman's point of view, and you're doing it from the guy's?

OLIVER: More or less.

TED: So you're supposed to be the male point of view. What? Representing?

OLIVER: Pretty much.

TED: Representing, for instance, me?

OLIVER: You?

TED: I'm a male. I have a male point of view.

OLIVER: You put it that way—

TED: Hunh. You like movies with subtitles, right?

OLIVER: I like some of them.

TED: I like none of them. So right there, you don't represent me. You don't speak for *my* male point of view.

OLIVER: I don't have your confidence.

TED: Not when it comes to movies.

OLIVER: Well, no two people are going to have the same taste, the same perspective.

TED: But my bet is that you and that woman—

OLIVER: Sarah.

TED: —yeah, see more eye to eye about movies than you and me would. That the two of you would probably agree with each other more often about what is or isn't a shitty movie than you and me. This, despite the fact that you and me, we're both guys, which is something you and she don't have in common.

OLIVER: Your point?

TED: I think I just said it.

OLIVER: I guess I missed—

TED: You and her—a man and a woman—have more in common than you and me, who are two guys. But you'd normally think it would be the two guys who have more in common.

OLIVER: That's the point you're making?

TED: Yes. That's my point.

OLIVER: Fair enough.

[TED *refills* OLIVER'S *glass.*]

TED: You ever get it on?

OLIVER: Get it on?

TED: You and Sarah.

OLIVER: No.

TED: People ask you that a lot, don't they?

OLIVER: Anytime people see a man and a woman together, they think there's that possibility.

TED: They think it's a possibility because there *is* that possibility. Any man, any woman, the possibility exists. As long as your equipment is functioning. Unless there's been some horrible accident that makes it impossible—

OLIVER: No, but thank you for your concern.

TED: But the idea has occurred.

OLIVER: What?

TED: You and her.

OLIVER: I'm married.

TED: And that proves what? You like movies with subtitles so much. Anytime somebody in one of those movies is married, you *know* they're gonna be jumping on someone else. That they're married is the tip-off. They're married *so that* they can cheat.

OLIVER: Hey, I just *review* movies. I don't live them.

TED: So you and her—never?

OLIVER: Well, if we did, Ted, you'd be the first person I'd tell.

TED: Right.

OLIVER: Would fifty bucks be useful?

TED: For what?

OLIVER: You were talking before about a plaque. For Mr. Kelly when he retires.

TED: That's generous.

OLIVER: Well, what the hell, he was always nice to me. So, what do you figure for the inscription?

TED: Inscription?

OLIVER: On the plaque. Something about the occasion or the purpose or whatever.

TED: *You're* the writer—what do you think?

OLIVER: Okay. "To Mr. Kelly in acknowledgment of, uh, recognition of . . . uh, with *thanks* for"—how many years?

TED: Thirty-six.

OLIVER: —"thirty-six years of inspiration as a teacher and a friend." Something like that. Maybe an engraving of a test tube or a Bunsen burner.

TED: Sure, that ought to bring a tear to his eye. That chair of yours looks wobbly.

OLIVER: I'm sorry?

TED: The chair you're on. Something wrong with the leg.

OLIVER: Seems okay—

TED: No, no, move back and forth. Come on.

[OLIVER *hesitates, then does it.*]

I thought so.

[TED *heads to the door to the kitchen.*]

Last thing I need is the chair collapses under you, you break your ass, and your insurance company comes after—

OLIVER: Where are you—

TED: Just gonna get—

[*He disappears into the house.* OLIVER *remains sitting for a second. Then he moves back and forth on the chair to test the leg. Beat. He stands up and moves over to lean against the railing.* TED *returns with a screwdriver.*]

This'll just be a second.

[*He turns over the chair.*]

Just what I thought—the screw's nearly out.

[*He begins to work on the chair.*]

If we *really* wanted to thank him for years of being a teacher and a friend—Kelly—we'd help him escape this place.

OLIVER: Escape?

TED: This town.

OLIVER: What's wrong with it?

TED: Nothing, if you like corpses.

OLIVER: I don't know.

TED: No, you don't.

OLIVER: No, I didn't mean—I didn't say "I don't know" as in "I don't have a clue."

TED: No? How then?

OLIVER: More in the spirit of "I'm not sure if I agree with you." With what you said. The opinion you—

TED: It's not an opinion. This town—if we had any decency, any feeling for what this place means or used to mean—to some of us anyway—we'd haul in a huge fucking pile of dirt—a mountain—and just dump it on top, maybe put up a cross. Honor its memory, sure. Visit once in a while with flowers, but let it just be what it is, which is—

OLIVER: Dead?

[TED *finishes futzing with the chair, turns it over, offers it to* OLIVER.]

TED: There.

OLIVER [*sitting*]: Yes, I can tell the difference.

TED: Why don't you take off your jacket? Get comfortable.

OLIVER: Why not.

[*During the following,* OLIVER *takes off his jacket and drapes it over the chair. He takes off his tie, too.*]

TED: Do you get paid extra if they put your name in the ads?

OLIVER: Paid?

TED: Something I was wondering. I see your name in the ads. Quotes from you. "Bruce Willis's best since *Hudson Hawk!*"

OLIVER: I didn't say that.

TED: "A film to touch the heart and stir the soul."

OLIVER: I might have said that. About something. Not *Hudson Hawk*. But no, they don't pay me.

TED: That doesn't seem right. They're your words. They use them. Your words put butts on the seats in the theater. Your words help them make money. No, I think they ought to pay you.

OLIVER: But then there would be doubt—

TED: How?

OLIVER: —about whether I really like the movie.

TED: Well, they'd only pay you if you really did.

OLIVER: But how would they know that?

TED: Because you said, "I really like this movie."

OLIVER: Yes, but how would they know whether I said so because I really did, or because I'd like to pick up some change so I said I liked something I didn't like?

TED: Because you wouldn't do that.

OLIVER: Yes, but people know I wouldn't do that because there isn't any *reason* for them to suspect my integrity.

TED: Okay. I see what you're getting at.

OLIVER: The whole point of credibility as a critic is that you have the reputation of someone whose opinion you can trust. Not that you necessarily agree with it, but that at least—

TED: —they think you're honest.

OLIVER: Yes.

TED: That's important—honesty. What you said, integrity.

OLIVER: Well, it's important in general, of course—

TED: Sure.

OLIVER: —but in what I do—

TED: Sure. I see that.

[*Beat.*]

You'd probably be glad, right? If this place gave up the ghost.

OLIVER: Glad?

TED: This town. What does it mean to you, anyway? Memories? Not ones you want to remember, I bet. We made your life hell here. And we intended to.

OLIVER: Oh, I'm sure—

TED: No, we didn't like you. "We"? Okay, I. Though I wasn't alone. First time I saw you, I think it was in Miss Kingman's class, first time I saw you—the pens in your pocket, the glasses—I didn't know your name, I didn't know if you were Jewish or Greek or Albanian. But you carried your books like a girl—well, you *did*—and you had a crease in your slacks—

OLIVER: So my fate was sealed.

TED: Dead meat on sight. First time I see you, I can already picture you trying not to cry and crying anyway. And the next day you coming to school with some kind of tape wrapped around the middle of your glasses to hold them together where I snapped them in two. I was a mean little bastard. And don't you say you "don't know," because that's something you *do* know. You of all people. I was an asshole. I beat you without pity.

OLIVER: Okay, accepted.

TED: What?

OLIVER: Oh, I thought that was an apology.

TED: Really.

OLIVER: I thought that's what you were leading up to. I mean, you did the confessional part—the acknowledgment of responsibility for past crimes—

TED: Crimes?

OLIVER: —so I thought next we were going to get contrition.

TED: "I'm sorry, forgive me"—that sort of thing?

OLIVER: In that general neighborhood.

TED: You think I owe you one?

OLIVER: I think it's possible you might think so.

TED: Because of how much I've learned in the meantime? How much I've grown?

OLIVER: I hope we've *all* grown. Jesus, what's the point if we haven't? You know, what have we been doing?

TED: Can I get back to you on that?

OLIVER: Sure.

TED: Is that something you want? An apology?

OLIVER: Doesn't make any difference.

TED: How's your drink?

OLIVER: Fine.

[TED *pours a little more into* OLIVER's *glass. Beat.*]

TED: But that wasn't why you came?

OLIVER: Nope.

TED: Hoping that you and I would—maybe after all these years, some satisfaction—

OLIVER: I didn't come with any expectations. I just—

TED: You just came.

OLIVER: Something else I was supposed to do fell out at the last minute. I remembered the reunion was happening this weekend, so why not? And I'm glad I did. I really am.

TED: You probably haven't thought about me in years anyway, right? Who the hell am I, anyway? You've got enough people to fill your mind without dredging me up. More pressing things to occupy your—screenings. Parties. Stuff to crank out for that newspaper of yours. Celebrities to interview.

OLIVER: You make it sound so impressive.

TED: Maybe it isn't impressive in New York or L.A. Maybe it's something people are used to there. Like you run into Woody Allen waiting his turn for his prescription at Walgreens. Sinus medication, don't you think?

OLIVER: Good chance.

TED: And there's Kim Basinger telling the laundry to be careful with her lingerie.

OLIVER: Yeah, she's a stickler about that.

TED: Maybe L.A., New York, living with these people as your neighbors, swimming in the same goldfish bowl, it's not such a big deal. But out here in the boonies—in flyover land—

OLIVER: Flyover—

TED: Isn't that what you people call us? You people who live on the coast, one of the coasts. Flyovers? On your way, back and forth between L.A. and New York, we're the ones living down here in places you'd never even think of actually touching down and visiting.

OLIVER: Hey, am I here, am I visiting?

TED: I'm not criticizing.

OLIVER: "Flyover." What a crummy word. Where'd you hear it, anyway?

TED: Isn't that one you people use?

OLIVER: I'm not a "people." I'm just me. And, no, I don't use it. I mean, the whole idea of it—talk about condescending.

TED: But don't words happen because they're needed? Something exists, if you want to talk about it, you got to put some sounds together that mean that thing. The word exists because the idea, the attitude, exists.

OLIVER: Okay, maybe there are some jerks who think like that, who would make up a word like that. But the idea that you can just discount most of this country, most of the people in this country—

TED: It offends you.

OLIVER: It does.

TED: All right, but let's just take a look at a couple of things that are true. Most of the stuff on TV, in the movies, where is that made? L.A., right? Most of it. Okay, maybe every now and then someone says, "What do you say we put a car chase in a cornfield," and so they haul out a map of Kansas, and they sail in and for five or six days they stay in the local Holiday Inn and complain how they can't find a decent bagel anywhere.

OLIVER: I don't defend behavior like that.

TED: And where are most of the decisions made?

OLIVER: People make decisions everywhere.

TED: I'm talking about the ones that have an effect. How many decisions made here in Ohio are going to change anything about your life? Like what the interest rate is gonna be if you want to take out a home equity loan or something?

OLIVER: Well, interest rates—that's pretty much the Fed, isn't it? In D.C.

TED: D.C.—they're part of the flyover club, too. D.C., L.A., N.Y. Do you think the people who live in these places give a damn about the effect of what they decide or do on people they never see?

OLIVER: But not everybody you're talking about is from those places. I mean take Clinton, for instance—he's from Arkansas.

TED: Yeah, the important word there is "from." Do you think, when he's finished being president, you think that's where he's going to go live? Clinton? I'm betting L.A. Hell, you're "from" Ohio. Does that make you an Ohioan?

OLIVER: Well, obviously something resonates. I'm here this weekend.

TED: Okay, you and some of the others, I'll give you that you may have *started out* in other places. But if you're making the decisions—government, the media—like I said, it's D.C., L.A., N.Y. And you visiting here, this is not the rule. This is the exception. Not that I'm claiming there's any reason you or any of the others *should* visit. What the hell is here anyway? And whatever there *was* here, there's even less of it now, so there's even less reason to come here. Or stay here. Which goes a long way to explaining why we don't bump into Woody Allen or Kim Basinger on Main Street.

OLIVER: Well, I don't see what that has to do with me. I'm not Woody Allen, I'm not Kim Basinger—

TED: You spend time with these people.

OLIVER: I'm just, for professional reasons, sometimes in the same place.

TED: But they look at you. They see that you are there. You are real to them. You have their attention.

OLIVER: But it's not because of *me*. It's not that they're talking to me, really. They're talking to who I write for, and because I do the TV thing. And that I write reviews they'd like me to like them so when I write about them I'll want to say nice things. I'm an instrument they talk through to get publicity. But don't confuse me with these people. I'm not one of them.

TED: Okay.

OLIVER: You don't sound convinced.

TED [*shrugging in response*]: Why *did* you come? You had a free weekend, you say. Why'd you decide to spend it here?

OLIVER: Same reason you did probably. High school. Wherever you go, you carry that with you, right?

TED: Like the clap.

OLIVER: Oh, come on.

TED: No, you're right. High school.

OLIVER: A chance to see old friends.

TED: Did you have friends? At Buchanan High?

OLIVER: Actually, you'd be surprised.

TED: I probably would. No, I'm not being fair.

OLIVER: And I think it's one of the ways you measure stuff, how far you've gone. Or haven't.

TED: Then I'm shit out of luck. I haven't moved two miles.

OLIVER: Not just geographically. There are other kinds of progress. Other measurements.

TED: So you came to measure yourself?

OLIVER: That's probably part of it. But it's always there, isn't it? Who you were. So you go to one of these things and go into the gym and you see the crepe paper—I mean, my God—*crepe* paper. How many years since I actually saw crepe paper close up—

TED: Real thrill, hunh?

OLIVER: —and there they are—all these people who haven't seen you since you were who you were. Sometimes you can almost read their minds when they see you. "Oh, his skin finally cleared up. Isn't that nice?"

TED: "Oh, he's not serving time."

OLIVER: And maybe you show up just to show that you're around *to* show up.

TED: Yeah?

OLIVER: You know what I'm saying?

TED: No.

OLIVER: Well—

TED: I'm fucking with you, man. Of course I do.

OLIVER: But to say, "See, I exist beyond what you thought I was in high school. I own a car. I have a bank account. I'm not a virgin anymore."

TED: No kidding, that's great news.

OLIVER: To say I've escaped the bounds of who you thought I was, what you thought I was back then.

TED: Well, just the fact that you're alive I consider a victory.

OLIVER: Oh?

TED: You attracted people like me to beat up on you in high school. I figured that in the larger world there would be larger people out there to beat up on you.

OLIVER: There were. There are.

TED: But you're not dead. No, that's great. Maybe I'll take a little credit for that.

OLIVER: I'm listening.

TED: You know in the movies: the son-of-a-bitch sergeant who rode your ass, and you hated his guts, but he toughened you up so you wouldn't get your head blown off in battle. Like I was your own personal one-man boot camp.

OLIVER: Or like a vaccine.

TED: How?

OLIVER: I can't remember which one—Salk, Sabin? One of them, they inject you with weakened polio. A weakened version of the disease. It stimulates the immune system. Builds up your antibodies so later you're ready to take on something stronger.

TED: So I helped you build up your antibodies? I'm a weak version of a disease?

OLIVER: It's an analogy.

TED: No, I'm glad if I was useful. But you know what was going on.

OLIVER: When?

TED: Back in high school. I mean, it was obvious. Here you were, you were making your grades and writing for the school paper and winning prizes and scrolls and things. And I knew where you were going.

OLIVER: Where was I going?

TED: Where you went. Out of here.

OLIVER: That made you angry?

TED: And I knew I was going to end up staying, probably working at the plant. Which I did. I'm not complaining. But I would have liked—it would have been nice to have a choice.

OLIVER: Why didn't you go to college? Ohio State.

TED: Right. Could you see me in college?

OLIVER: Why not? You could still—if you wanted to. A lot of people do. Midcareer schooling.

TED: I don't have a career, Oliver. I *work*. We could use some lights.

[TED *turns on the deck lights. As the scene progresses, it will get darker in the area off the deck.* TED *is about to refill* OLIVER'S *glass.*]

OLIVER: I have to ask—

[*He stops.*]

TED: Ask. What?

OLIVER: What do you want?

TED: Do I have some kind of agenda?

OLIVER: *Do* you?

TED: Of course.

OLIVER: I mean, inviting me here, your place—

TED: They're opening a new Taco Bell in town, and a letter of recommendation from someone of your stature would be real—

OLIVER: Sure. You got it.

[TED *pours,* OLIVER *drinks.* TED *starts lighting citronella candles.*]

TED: No, I can understand why that's something you'd ask. My intentions. My motives. I can see why you'd be—I'm surprised you took me up on coming here.

OLIVER: You think after all this time, that I would—?

TED: Maybe. Sure, you could. You'd have a right to.

OLIVER: Well, no. I mean, come on. What would be the point?

TED: Do people always do things because they have points?

OLIVER: I like to think *I* do. I like to think that my life is built on some rational basis.

TED: Well then, good for you.

OLIVER: But, hell, we really aren't the same people. Twenty-five years. Don't the scientists say that all the cells in our body are regenerated every seven years?

TED: Regenerated?

OLIVER: Replaced. New version of the cell comes along, taps the old one on the shoulder. "Hi, I'm here. You can go die now." And so every seven years, you're a whole new you.

TED: Then the me that gave you shit was three or four versions back.

OLIVER: There you go.

TED: Hey, if you think of it that way, nobody should be sentenced to more than seven years in jail. Seven years would make you a lifer.

OLIVER: I think you're onto something.

TED: After seven years, no matter what you've done, you can say that wasn't me that did that rotten thing. That stuff was done by my bad old cells. They're all gone now. I've got me nothing but new good-guy cells now. Of course, you want to work on it that your new cells really are an improvement. Don't want to have a lot of backsliding cells fucking up your progress.

OLIVER: Sure, got to be vigilant.

TED: Though, today at the lunch—looked to me like some of the gang, their new cells were major backsliders.

OLIVER: Mitch?

TED: Oh, man, you ever see anything so pathetic?

OLIVER: What happened?

TED: A major taste for the booze has to be part of it.

OLIVER: But you don't know?

TED: Haven't seen him in years.

OLIVER: You used to hang out, I thought—

TED: No. Not for years. I think he lives in Cleveland. Not a place I get to.

OLIVER: When you think of what he used to—

TED: He did not get good replacement cells. You like Bruce Willis?

OLIVER: He's done some good work.

TED: You ever meet him?

OLIVER: Did an interview once.

TED: You know what gets me? Here he is married to Demi Moore. Between them, they must have all the money in the world. And he still lets her take her clothes off so everyone can see. You tell me how that's different from Larry Axelrod, this guy I used to work with at the plant, carries a picture of his wife in his wallet. Lying naked on the pool table in his rec room. "Like to see what I got?" This expression on her face of "Take the goddamn picture already, will you?" And he pulls this out, says, "This is mine. You can look, but you can't touch. *I'm* the only one gets to touch." Like I would want to, you know? You see her in the supermarket, trying to decide which brand of spaghetti sauce to buy. I have to keep myself from saying, "Lady, I've seen your bush."

OLIVER: Hmmmm.

TED: So how is he different from Bruce Willis? He goes to a premiere of one of her movies. All these stars around them—Danny DeVito, Sharon Stone, Denzel Washington—the media, sitting there in a crowded theater, and up there's Demi—forty feet high. Some actor putting his hands all over her. End of the movie, lights come up, Bruce probably gives her a kiss, says, "Good work, honey."

OLIVER: Actually, the rumor is they may be breaking up.

TED: Really?

OLIVER: That's the rumor.

TED: But, you know, I think people like them—they do it to piss us off.

OLIVER: I'm sorry, people like who, do what?

TED: Like Larry Axelrod and Willis. The whole "look, but don't touch" thing. Of course, there's a difference, depending where you are on the—you know—scale.

OLIVER: Scale?

TED: If you're a guy on the street in a raincoat and you flash, you get arrested. If you do it at like one of those topless clubs out by the airport, you're this pathetic thing one step up from a hooker. But if you're Kim or Demi or Sharon Stone or Michael Douglas and you get paid seven million dollars to wave your stuff around, you can pretend you're an artist. And people wonder what's wrong with this country. Another?

OLIVER: Hunh? Sure.

[TED *starts to make him another drink.*]

TED: I'm gonna have to go inside, get some more ice.

OLIVER: That's okay.

TED: It's not a problem.

IRIS [*from offstage*]: Hello?

TED: Yes?

IRIS: Ted?

TED: Back here! Iris?

IRIS: Yes.

TED: In the back. The deck.

[IRIS *appears.*]

Look at you.

IRIS: The girl I thought I was going to have to fill in for—her shift—[*Aside to* OLIVER] A restaurant.

[OLIVER *nods his comprehension.*]

TED: She showed up after all?

IRIS: I guess she's feeling better. Or she needs the money. Something.

TED: Well, that's good news.

IRIS: Yeah, except, of course, I could use the money, too.

TED: How much you need?

IRIS: You got a spare seven or eight grand?

TED: I left my checkbook in my other life. What about you, Oliver?

IRIS: Don't you go giving Oliver shit.

TED: Actually, I was gonna get more ice for his drink. You want something?

IRIS: Well, I wouldn't say no to a Scotch rocks.

TED: Your turn to get waited on, hunh?

[TED *exits*.]

IRIS: Same old Ted.

OLIVER: Oh, I don't know. I think he's—

IRIS: What?

OLIVER: Matured.

IRIS: Matured? Ted?

OLIVER: Well, he hasn't broken my glasses yet.

IRIS: You aren't wearing glasses.

OLIVER: He's being friendly.

IRIS: He ask you for money?

OLIVER: Does he need money?

IRIS: Oliver, everybody in this town needs money.

OLIVER: I didn't realize things were so depressed here.

IRIS: Take a look over there. See that building?

OLIVER: That's the plant—

IRIS: You see any lights in the windows?

OLIVER [*understands*]: Ah. What happened?

IRIS: Some conglomerate bought the plant. Eltar. We were going to be a division of Eltar. "The world at your doorstep through electronics."

OLIVER: Seems to me if the world were at your doorstep, it would be pretty hard to open the door.

IRIS: We were going to be a division. Part of Eltar's big happy extended corporate family. And then someone in New York looked at a balance sheet and I guess figured out that there was fifty cents to be saved by shutting the plant down. So much for family feeling.

OLIVER: When did this happen?

IRIS: When did it finally shut down? About seven months ago.

OLIVER: I didn't know.

IRIS: Stuff people used to do over there is now being done in Malaysia. Is it Malaysia or Malaya?

OLIVER: Malaysia sounds right. I think it's on the Malay Peninsula.

IRIS: Where is that?

OLIVER: Somewhere east is all I know.

IRIS: Well, somewhere east a bunch of Malaysians are plugging components into boards that people here used to plug. Hunh.

OLIVER: What?

IRIS: You came back. You actually came back.

OLIVER: Why is everyone so surprised I came back?

IRIS: I saw a documentary on TV. On PBS probably. Yes, I sometimes watch PBS. This woman—this Jewish woman—she's visiting the concentration camp she was in during World War II. She's taking these filmmakers around. Showing where all this stuff happened to her, to people she knew. Where people died. Her sister. I couldn't understand that either.

OLIVER: There *is* a difference between Buchanan High and Auschwitz. A pretty crucial one actually.

IRIS: What I said was dumb.

OLIVER: I didn't mean to jump on you.

IRIS: No, you're right.

OLIVER: I was rude.

IRIS: And that's the worst thing that ever happened to me. Forget it.

OLIVER: I really didn't have that bad a time here. Everybody thinks I was miserable here.

IRIS: You enjoyed being beaten up?

OLIVER: Oh, kids get beaten up everywhere.

IRIS: Doesn't mean that it was right for them to do that to you.

OLIVER: No permanent damage.

IRIS: Do you remember who I am?

OLIVER: Iris.

IRIS: He called me that. If he hadn't, would you have—do you remember *me*?

OLIVER: You used to go with the drummer.

IRIS: You *do* remember!

OLIVER: What was his name—Ken? He used to carry his sticks with him and drum on his desktop in study hall.

IRIS: Yeah, I could pick 'em, couldn't I?

OLIVER: Sure, I remember you.

[TED *returns with a tray, carrying drinks and munchies. He serves in a parody of a cocktail waitress.*]

TED: Here we go—

IRIS: What is that? That you're doing?

TED: The bunny dip.

IRIS: What the hell is that?

TED: It's how they served drinks at the Playboy Club. The girls. They had ears that they wore, and tails on their behinds, and they would serve like this.

IRIS: I'm sure I wouldn't know.

TED: I was in the club in Lansing once. Back when I was I don't know how young. Somebody's uncle took us. We were impressed, I've got to tell you.

IRIS: Wow, real live women with actual breasts.

TED: Yeah, those were pretty much my thoughts.

IRIS: If you want to get technical, they probably weren't actual breasts.

TED: I think the tails were real, though.

OLIVER: I hope so.

IRIS: *Some*thing to believe in, hunh?

TED: Tell you the truth, I was hoping to meet your wife. See what she looks like.

OLIVER: A real live woman with actual breasts.

TED: No tail?

OLIVER: Probably had the operation before I met her.

TED: A little scar at the base of the spine?

IRIS: You're both amusing the hell out of me.

TED: Are we being gross, Iris?

OLIVER: No, she's right.

TED: Iris has delicate sensibilities, don't you?

IRIS: Yeah, I blush easy.

TED [*toasting*]: To fellow veterans.

[*They join him in the toast.* OLIVER's *phone goes off.* OLIVER *reaches into his jacket pocket and pulls it out.*]

Your phone?

[OLIVER *looks at the number on his phone.*]

OLIVER: Damn, looks like I have to take this one.

TED: Caller ID?

OLIVER [*nodding*]: Sorry.

TED: What's to be sorry about? You're a busy guy, an important guy.

OLIVER [*overlapping, answering*]: Hold on for a second. [*To* TED] You mind if I take this inside?

TED: A little privacy. Sure.

OLIVER: Sorry.

TED: No, fine.

[OLIVER *goes into the house.* TED *turns to* IRIS.]

I didn't think you were going to join us.

IRIS: I didn't think I was either.

TED: What changed your mind?

IRIS: Who says it's changed?

TED: You're here.

IRIS: You know what your problem is?

TED: My problem is people keep telling me what my problem is. Like I give a shit about their opinion.

IRIS: Fine.

TED: I'm sorry, Iris. Were you about to give me constructive criticism? Were you about to tell me something that if I took it to heart, it would turn my whole life around?

IRIS: Far be it from me—

TED: I hope so. I should fucking hope so.

IRIS: Maybe I'll just finish my drink and go.

TED: Do what you want to do.

IRIS: I don't need this.

TED: No, you just need, what is it—seven or eight grand?

IRIS: You assume the whole world is like you—

TED: I assume that people have needs and will do what they have to to meet them.

IRIS: Yeah, but there are limits.

TED: When did you start teaching Sunday school?

IRIS: Fine. How's your wife?

TED: What's that supposed to mean?

IRIS: Why does it have to mean anything more than the words I use?

TED: What's her name?

IRIS: Lianne.

TED: So why don't you say that? Why don't you ask, "How's Lianne?" How's my wife.

IRIS: Fine. How's Lianne?

TED: She's visiting her mother. She and the kids.

IRIS: So she's not around.

TED: No. Did you want to have a conversation with her?

IRIS: Conversation?

TED: Did you want to do some heart-to-heart feminine thing? Bonding?

IRIS: Right. I want her to tell me all of your secrets.

TED: And what would you do with them?

IRIS: I'd use them against you, of course. I would conspire with your enemies and I'd bring you down. God, do you know the meaning of the word "paranoid"?

TED: Okay.

IRIS: Can't I express concern?

TED: Is that what you were doing?

IRIS: "How's Lianne?" Yes, I think so.

TED: All right, sorry. I'm an asshole again. Sorry. She's—what am I going to say? She's fine?

IRIS: Anyway, I wouldn't bond with her. I think that's what *men* do. They bond.

TED: What do women do?

IRIS: Confide, console.

TED: Well, what if *I* want to confide and console?

IRIS: Who to? Another guy?

TED: I'm not saying I'm actually thinking of doing this—

IRIS: I think if you were going to confide and console with another guy it would probably be read as bonding.

TED: I just want to know how this works.

IRIS: I'm not an expert.

TED: But, Iris—

IRIS: What?

TED: If you ever catch me consoling or confiding or bonding with some guy—

IRIS: Unh-hunh?

TED: I want you to shoot me. Right here.

IRIS: But not otherwise?

TED: Fuck you, too.

[*She laughs. Beat.*]

IRIS: I heard some talk—did you hear this—?

TED: You have to tell me before I can say yes or no.

IRIS: Right.

TED: I don't read minds.

IRIS: Just that there's some talk about putting together some deal to buy the plant back.

TED: Oh, yeah, yeah—

IRIS: I mean it sounded serious. There are other places where people—the employees—they bought back their company.

TED: I'm supposed to help buy back the company? Quick, let me cash in all my vast portfolio of stocks and bonds.

IRIS: I think they did this up in Dayton.

TED: It's easy to talk.

IRIS: What I hear is that there's some serious possibility. What's-his-name, the union—

TED: Dunphy?

IRIS: The other one.

TED: Stetlano.

IRIS: Stetlano, yes. Word is Stetlano says there's some interested money. It would mean new contracts, but basically we'd be working for ourselves.

TED: Oh, don't kid yourself. Somebody would still have the power to hire and fire. Somebody would still make policy. Decide whether to change the shape of the buttons or what color plastic would be used in the shell. You'd still have to keep somebody above you happy.

IRIS: Do you prefer unemployment?

TED: I'm not saying that. But whenever you have to answer to somebody else, there's always somebody else you've got to—

IRIS: —to answer to?

TED: Unless you work for yourself. Like make pottery in the basement.

IRIS: Well, there's your answer. Get yourself a potter's wheel—

TED: A what?

IRIS: That's what they make pottery on. A wheel. Didn't you ever see *Ghost*?

TED: The movie?

IRIS: Demi Moore. She's making pottery. She's got a potter's wheel.

TED: Is this before or after she takes off her clothes?

IRIS: I don't think she does it in that one.

TED: Too bad.

IRIS: Who cares? God, do you think of anything else?

TED: I'd tell you only I'm afraid you'd think I was confiding.

IRIS: I thought you would find it interesting, is all. I mean, if they can pull this thing together at the plant—

TED: When it happens, they can call me. If my phone hasn't been disconnected.

IRIS: Giving up isn't the answer.

TED: I'm not giving up. But I'm not gonna hold my breath.

[OLIVER *returns.*]

What was it—L.A. or New York—that called?

OLIVER: New York.

TED: Everything okay?

OLIVER: Scheduling. Someone had to change a date on me. Studio wants some retakes on this picture, that means someone I was supposed to interview—

TED: An actor?

OLIVER: Actress. She isn't going to be in the country when we were scheduled to talk. So we have to figure out another time. So her people call my people—

IRIS: You have "people"?

OLIVER: In the office.

TED: You and your people—you have a flag? An anthem?

OLIVER: I should look into that.

TED: T-shirts, sweatshirts—

OLIVER: Actually, they're employed by the production company. The TV show. As I am. And Sarah. So I don't hire them so much as they're hired to help me.

TED: You all call each other by your first names?

OLIVER: Sure. Why not?

TED: So you're *good* to your people.

OLIVER: I try to be good *with* them.

TED: "With," not "to."

OLIVER: Yes.

[*He has reached into the jacket draped over the chair and taken an electronic organizer out of his pocket and starts typing.*]

TED: You're a walking electronics outlet—the phone, this—

OLIVER: It's how I keep my schedule straight. And, you know, appointments and addresses and phone numbers.

TED: How many numbers can it hold?

OLIVER: A few thousand, I guess.

TED: You know that many people?

OLIVER: I didn't say I filled it all.

TED: Put me in there. Me and Iris. We want to be in your organizer.

IRIS: Speak for yourself.

TED: You don't want to be in Oliver's organizer? You too good to be in Oliver's—

IRIS: Oliver hasn't invited me to be in his organizer.

OLIVER: You want to be in my organizer?

IRIS: Okay now—

OLIVER: McCarty, right? Iris McCarty?

[*He fiddles with the keyboard.*]

IRIS: You don't have to.

OLIVER: No, I think it—there we go. McCarty. *M-c* not *M-a-c,* right?

IRIS: Right.

OLIVER: Here.

[*He offers it to her.*]

IRIS: I should type it in?

OLIVER: Why not?

IRIS: All right.

[*She starts typing her particulars in.*]

What do I do now?

OLIVER: Just hit save. Right there, see?

[*She does it.*]

TED: My turn, my turn!

[OLIVER *hands the organizer over to* TED.]

Jeez, you need fingers like, what's his name, the guy from *Fantasy Island?* "The plane, the plane!"

OLIVER: If you want me to type it—

TED: No, I can do it.

[*He types.*]

Well, I guess this is possible.

OLIVER: I wouldn't want to write a long article on it.

TED [*pressing a button*]: Save.

[TED *doesn't hand it back to* OLIVER.]

So, who we in there with?

OLIVER: Oh—my accountant. The liquor store. Bruce Taybor, my producer.

TED: Sarah—

OLIVER: Yes, Sarah's in there.

TED: John Travolta?

OLIVER: No.

TED: If I look under *T* in here, I wouldn't find John Travolta's home number?

OLIVER: No.

TED: But there are famous people in here. People I've heard of.

OLIVER: Mostly their offices. Maybe their managers.

TED: How do you like that, Iris? We're in the same organizer as some famous people's managers.

IRIS: You want to give that back to him?

TED: I'm sorry, of course.

[*He hands it back to* OLIVER.]

Probably a lot of Jewish names in there, too, right?

IRIS: Oh, for God's sake!

TED: I'm not saying anything!

IRIS: "A lot of Jewish names" and you aren't saying anything?

TED: What, there aren't a lot of Jewish people in show business? You're gonna tell me there aren't a lot of Jewish people in show business? Oliver, you're Jewish, right?

OLIVER: Yes.

TED: You're in show business, right?

OLIVER: Yes.

TED: A lot of the people you know in show business—

OLIVER: A lot of them are Jewish too, yes, so?

TED: So nothing. It's just an observation. There's something about being Jewish, probably, that—probably some cultural thing about talent. A lot of the comedians, stand-ups—

OLIVER: Yes.

TED: Paul Newman.

IRIS: He is?

TED: You didn't know that?

IRIS: No.

TED: Everybody knows that. Tell her I'm right.

OLIVER: He's right.

TED: Paul Newman's Jewish. You know who isn't, though—I read this, I didn't believe it, but it's true—

OLIVER: Tell us.

TED: Rod Steiger.

OLIVER: I didn't know that.

TED: How about that? I know something you don't know. About your own business.

IRIS: Are you sure?

TED: Surprising, isn't it? You'd think if *anybody*—

IRIS: And so how does this change your world, your life?

TED: Not saying it does. It's just interesting. It just goes to show you that your prejudices, your stereotypes, things aren't what you—you see what I'm getting at, don't you, Oliver?

OLIVER: Yes.

TED: Just because Steiger plays pawnbrokers and Mexican bandits and stuff doesn't mean he's necessarily Jewish.

IRIS: Why would playing Mexican bandits mean you're Jewish?

TED: Because they do a lot. Eli Wallach.

OLIVER: Actually, here's how it works, Ted—if you're in my organizer, you're automatically Jewish.

TED: Hey, cool.

OLIVER: That's how it works.

TED: Well, I'm honored.

OLIVER: The yarmulke will arrive in the mail. Allow ten business days for delivery.

IRIS [*holding up her glass*]: You mind if I—

TED: Help yourself. Naw, a lot of the most talented people—

IRIS: You still on that?

TED: I think it's interesting. Spielberg, Woody Allen, Streisand. Though, jeez, did you see that Streisand special, how many years ago? She's up there singing. Madison Square Garden, Vegas, or someplace. But she's up there singing, and there are these shots in the audience. And there are all of these shots of, like, old boyfriends. Maybe Ryan O'Neal, that hairdresser guy, I think, Elliot Gould—

OLIVER: Another Jew—

TED: Yeah, but that's not my point. It was like, let's look at the club. You know, the club of people who had things with Barbra Streisand. And she's up there singing, a love song probably. And smiling while she's singing, and in the audience there are these people who are veterans of Barbra. But they're looking up at her as she sings this song. Maybe a song of eternal love or something. To people she's mostly dumped. But I guess if you're part of that scene, it's kind of expected of you.

OLIVER: Expected?

TED: That after a couple of years you'll costar opposite someone else, do a love scene—a nude scene—and switch to *them*. People would be disappointed if you didn't. These people get married—the question isn't if they'll break up, but when. Sometimes, you know, I think *I* could do famous better than some of them. You wouldn't see *me* in embarrassing headlines, the check-out line at the grocery. Punching out photographers, racking up frequent-flier mileage at Betty Ford—

IRIS: You talk a lot of shit, you know that?

TED: You think so?

IRIS: I'm saying it, aren't I?

TED: You think I'm wrong?

IRIS: Right, wrong—what does it matter? Why are you talking about this? Celebrities, for God's sake—

TED: Don't forget, you're talking in front of a guy who makes his living—

OLIVER: No, I actually kind of agree.

TED: That I talk a lot of shit?

OLIVER: That celebrities—they really aren't that significant.

TED: But it's what you spend your life—

OLIVER: I review movies and sometimes I do interviews. And I have fun, sure, sometimes, but it's not like this is important. Not seriously.

TED: So you're doing something that isn't important. Your work, it isn't—

OLIVER: Well, I guess people have to have some diversion. I guess that serves a function. But no, compared to the real stuff—

TED: Politics—

OLIVER: The real issues—

TED: The spotted crane, civil rights, the national debt—

OLIVER: All that—

TED: So why do you do it?

OLIVER: It's what I do.

TED: But if it isn't important—

OLIVER: It's what I do. It's what someone is willing to pay me for. People end up in jobs, and, Ted, that's what they *do*. Their *jobs*. Their work. They get salaries. To earn them, they do their work—

TED [*with heat*]: If they *have* work. If they're lucky enough to *have* salaries. If they're lucky enough to have jobs they get paid salaries to hang around with famous people in New York and L.A. and make judgments like nobody else is entitled to have an opinion.

[*Beat.*]

OLIVER [*rising*]: Maybe it's time for me to—

TED: No, please look, I—apologize. I just—please. You know, this kind of—it means something to me. You visiting like this. Because, yeah, it's bothered me.

OLIVER: What?

TED: You think I don't look back, I don't know what I was? How rotten I—

OLIVER: Hey, I already said—

TED: Yeah, but it's not only what *you* say, it's how I feel about *myself.* So, please—

[LIANNE *enters from around the side of the house. She carries a large stamp album. She looks at* OLIVER, *her mouth open.*]

OLIVER: But it's getting late, and there are things I want to do tomorrow. Other people I want to catch up with. Some sleep—

[*Now* OLIVER *sees her.*]

Hello?

[TED *turns and sees* LIANNE.]

LIANNE: Where's your wife?

TED: Honey?

OLIVER: My wife?

TED: What are you doing here, honey?

LIANNE: I see you with her all the time.

OLIVER: You see me—

TED: She's confused. She means Sarah. On TV.

OLIVER: Oh.

TED [*to* LIANNE]: That's not his wife.

LIANNE: Sure, she talks like—

TED: No, honey, that's someone else. That's a friend of his.

LIANNE: Oh.

TED: Somebody who works with him.

OLIVER: But a lot of people make that mistake. It's okay.

TED: It's an actress.

OLIVER: Well, not an actress exactly—

TED: But not a real person—

LIANNE: But the way you talk to each other—

OLIVER: Yes, well—

LIANNE: The way you fight—

TED: They don't fight.

OLIVER: Does it look like we're fighting?

TED: She gets confused. [*To* LIANNE] Lianne, honey, what are you doing here? You're supposed to be with your mama today. [*To* OLIVER] Her mother lives at the other end of the development. About a half mile down that—

LIANNE: I took a walk.

TED: But, Lianne, that's not what you were supposed to do. You and the boys were supposed to visit with your mama today. Remember?

LIANNE: She fell asleep—Mama. We were watching something and—

TED: She fell asleep?

LIANNE: They all did. The boys, too. [*To* OLIVER] We have two boys. [*To* TED] We were all watching this movie. It was old. They fell asleep. Black and white. The people in it are all dead. God, you forget how many dead people there are.

TED: A lot of them.

LIANNE: Seems like there didn't used to be so many. Or is it me? It must be me. You didn't say you were going to have a party.

TED: This isn't a party. We're just—

OLIVER: I'm Oliver.

LIANNE: I know. The TV.

OLIVER: And you're—Lianne, is it?

LIANNE: He's my wife. I mean, I'm his—

OLIVER: Oh. Well, hello.

LIANNE: Stupid.

OLIVER: No. Anybody can get confused. I get confused all the time. I'm confused right now.

IRIS: How are you, Lianne?

LIANNE: Iris.

IRIS: You want to come sit down?

TED: Tell you what I'm worried about—if your mama wakes up and finds out that you're gone? She'll wonder. She'll be concerned.

LIANNE: But I'm with you.

TED: She doesn't know that.

LIANNE: You could call.

TED: But then I'd wake her maybe.

LIANNE: If she's asleep then she's not worried.

TED: But she might wake up. Or the boys. They're gonna wake up.

LIANNE: Well, that's okay—they're at Grandma's. I'm thirsty.

[*Beat.*]

TED: I'll get you a Coke.

LIANNE: That's not what *you're* drinking.

TED: Do you want the Coke?

LIANNE: I'm just saying—

TED: *Do* you want the Coke? Honey, do you want the Coke?

[*Beat.*]

LIANNE: Sure. Yes.

[*She drifts onto the deck as* OLIVER *remains standing.* TED *fetches the Coke for her.*]

OLIVER: You weren't at the luncheon today.

LIANNE: No, I was over at Mama's.

TED: Lianne mostly doesn't know the people I went to high school with. And she gets a little nervous in crowds.

LIANNE: Too many people, they use up the air. That's not scientific, I know, but it feels like it.

OLIVER: Yes, I've noticed that.

LIANNE: So I'm not crazy.

OLIVER: What's that you've got there? The book?

LIANNE: Oh, this, yes. Ted, I think this is it.

TED [*handing her a Coke*]: What's that?

LIANNE: This is—I was going through some of my dad's stuff in the basement. [*To* OLIVER] My dad died a month ago.

OLIVER: I'm sorry.

LIANNE: He was a real good man. I miss him a lot. But I was going through some of his stuff. Mama was asleep and I found this in a box, and I thought maybe it could be—

TED: *What* could it be?

LIANNE [*to* OLIVER]: Do you know anything about stamps?

OLIVER: You mean, to collect?

LIANNE: Some of them are valuable. I know this. Some stamps. I've heard—

OLIVER: I think you're right. Yes. The rare ones can be—some of them can go for—

LIANNE: How much?

OLIVER: Well, different stamps, different prices. And, you know, collectors—

LIANNE: If you have a stamp that a collector wants—

OLIVER: Sure, some of them, thousands of dollars. Tens of thousands even. Depending on how rare, what condition they're in, whether they're postmarked—

LIANNE: Postmarked is when there are black lines on them?

OLIVER: Right. Means that they've been—

LIANNE: Used?

OLIVER: Used, yes, right. Canceled. You see a stamp that's got those black, wavy lines on it—

LIANNE: Maybe *I* should wear some black, wavy lines—

OLIVER: Oh?

LIANNE: 'Cross my forehead. What, do you think it would catch on?

TED: Lianne—

LIANNE: So serious, so serious. But canceled is no good?

OLIVER: It's *less* good. Like I say, the better the condition—

LIANNE: Of course.

OLIVER: Mint condition is best.

LIANNE: You know more about stamps than you said.

OLIVER: No, just a little. When I was a kid.

LIANNE: You collected stamps?

OLIVER: Nine or ten years old. God knows where they are now.

LIANNE: Would you mind taking a look?

TED: I'm sorry, Oliver, you shouldn't have to—

LIANNE: He can say no if he wants to.

OLIVER: It's okay, Ted.

TED: You didn't come out here to appraise—

OLIVER: Actually, I'm kind of interested.

[LIANNE *hands* OLIVER *the stamp album.* OLIVER *begins to look through it.*]

LIANNE: Cuz it would be great if you saw anything that was actually worth something in there. Something that we could sell.

OLIVER: Ah.

LIANNE: We're broke, you know.

TED: Lianne! [*To* OLIVER] We're not broke.

LIANNE: That's why we can't get the dryer repaired?

TED: The guy doesn't have time for an appointment another couple of weeks.

LIANNE: Oh, then I got it wrong.

TED: I'm in between jobs, is all. So's half the town. Christ, you make it sound like it's time to invest in a tin cup.

OLIVER: Hey, it's happening everywhere. Downsizing.

IRIS: Don't you love that word?

OLIVER: I have writer friends, they can't understand how if there's eighty million cable channels to choose from, how come they can't get work.

TED: Somebody has to write that stuff Peter Graves says. Or the narration, the *National Geographic.*

OLIVER: A lot of the channels, they're putting on old shows, reality shows. Or documentaries of World War II.

TED: So they're not hiring actors.

OLIVER: I guess not.

TED: What do you need someone to play Hitler for some TV movie, when you've got all that stuff of the real thing yelling his head off?

LIANNE: Oh, *he's* in here!

TED: Who's where?

LIANNE [*flipping through pages in the album*]: No, see, I'll show you. There, see? Lots of Hitler. German stamps.

TED: Yup, that's Hitler.

LIANNE: They must be worth something, don't you think? Everybody's heard of Hitler.

OLIVER: Well, it isn't really how famous the people on the stamps are. It's how rare.

LIANNE: Oh, so because there's a lot of Hitler stamps—

OLIVER: Right.

LIANNE: Okay, this makes sense. I follow this.

OLIVER [*looking through the book*]: You know, I remember some of these.

LIANNE: The hinges, they're getting loose—

OLIVER: You know something—

LIANNE: What?

OLIVER: I think this one—

LIANNE: The pink one?

OLIVER: This could be. You might have something here. Yes, I remember. The Springfield commemorative. This is one of the ones I could never get. I saw it in a stamp store once when I was a kid. I was there with my dad. I said, "Dad, this one." He asked how much. I told him. He just laughed, like "Dream on."

LIANNE: Expensive?

OLIVER: It would have meant a lot of weeks without allowance, let me put it that way. So it's one of the ones I never got. This is in good condition. You should have someone who knows this stuff take a look at it. I mean really knows. Or buy a guide.

LIANNE: There are guides?

OLIVER: Oh, yeah—the value of different editions and so forth. I wouldn't be surprised if there's some stuff in here that's really appreciated in value.

LIANNE: Well, that would be real good news.

OLIVER: Actually, you know what?

LIANNE: What?

OLIVER: I'd like to buy that stamp.

LIANNE: The pink one?

OLIVER: Yeah.

TED: Do you collect stamps now?

OLIVER: No. But there's something about—this is one I always wanted. Like an itch I never got to scratch. I told you, my dad—

TED: If you don't collect, what would you do with it?

OLIVER: Maybe put it into one of the little plastic windows in my wallet.

TED: Keepsake kind of thing.

OLIVER: Something I always wanted and there it is. You must know the feeling. When you were a kid, something you wanted, never got.

TED: Sure—a hand grenade.

[*He laughs at his own joke.*]

OLIVER: You willing to sell?

LIANNE: Why not?

OLIVER: Shall we say a hundred dollars?

LIANNE: Is it worth that much?

OLIVER: It's worth what someone's willing to pay, and I'm willing to pay a hundred dollars.

TED: I guess this is your lucky day, Lianne.

LIANNE: Well, yeah, okay. But that's not why I showed it to you—

OLIVER: I know.

LIANNE: You're our guest. You don't have guests in your house to sell them stuff.

OLIVER: It was my idea, remember. I'd consider it a favor.

TED: Lianne, the man's waiting for you to make a decision.

LIANNE: Okay then.

OLIVER: Okay?

LIANNE: Yuh.

OLIVER: Good.

[*He takes a hundred out of his wallet and gives it to her. Then he delicately takes the stamp out of the book and slides it into his wallet.*]

There.

LIANNE: The fastest hundred dollars I ever made.

OLIVER: You're happy, I'm happy. This is a definition of a good deal.

TED: You know what, though, honey—

LIANNE: What?

TED: I think I'd better drive you back to your mom's. Her feelings are going to be awful hurt if she wakes up and you're not there. She's going to think you don't like her.

LIANNE: Oh she knows better—

TED: But still, I think it's a good idea.

LIANNE: Well—

TED: I'll just do that. [*To* OLIVER *and* IRIS] Give me a minute or two and I'll be back.

OLIVER: It was nice meeting you, Lianne.

LIANNE: You too.

IRIS: You look pretty today, Lianne.

LIANNE: Oh?

IRIS: I like your hair.

LIANNE: Oh, yours too.

TED: I'll just be a few minutes.

[TED *gently escorts* LIANNE *off the deck, around the side of the house, and off-stage. The sound of a car starting and driving away.* OLIVER *and* IRIS *are alone together.*]

IRIS: She was on good behavior. You should take that as a compliment. Something about you calmed her down. I have to hand it to Ted, his patience. I mean, you saw—

OLIVER: How long—

IRIS: Well, she's always been a little unsteady. But it's been worse lately—first, the plant closing, then her father dying. The things that have always been there suddenly not.

OLIVER: Losing a parent is real hard.

IRIS: Your folks?

OLIVER: Both gone. Yours?

IRIS: My dad's still hanging in there. He and an old buddy named Hank and Hank's wife share a place down in the Florida Keys. I went down to visit, and I got the feeling that they'd moved a lot of stuff around before I got there, for my sake.

OLIVER: Cleaned up?

IRIS: More hiding the evidence.

OLIVER: Evidence of what? They running drugs or something?

IRIS: I think when it comes to Hank's wife, it's share and share alike.

OLIVER: Hank's wife puts up with that?

IRIS: Actually, I think it was more or less her idea. Apparently Hank has slowed down some.

OLIVER: Oh.

IRIS: And she hasn't.

OLIVER: And your father?

IRIS: Well, he's always tried to make himself useful.

OLIVER: They didn't want you to know this?

IRIS: I guess they thought I might have opinions.

OLIVER: You don't?

IRIS: At this point in their lives, jeez, if they can put together something that works for them, who am I to—

OLIVER: Sure.

IRIS: Kind of a hoot, though, when I think back to how hard I tried to hide the stuff I was doing from *him*—my dad. And that he threw me out of the house for being a tramp.

OLIVER: Did he?

IRIS: Yeah.

OLIVER: That's kind of harsh.

IRIS: Well, I got knocked up. The summer after I got out of high school. He wasn't too happy about that.

OLIVER: Ken the drummer?

IRIS: Somebody else. I was smart enough not to marry him, though. What can I tell you—I was a wild kid. And now my kid's a wild kid. My daughter. Twenty-four now, not such a kid. You're looking at a grandmother.

OLIVER: I don't believe it.

IRIS: You're not the only one. But the same guy, you know—my dad—same guy who gave me grief about what I did back then, now here he is in a seniors' threesome. And it seems kind of okay. They're all getting along, nobody's getting hurt—

OLIVER: Maybe different rules apply at different ages. There's stuff that we think is okay for people over eighteen to do that we think twelve-year-olds shouldn't. So maybe there's a later stage where stuff that would be upsetting, disturbing in people in their thirties, forties, fifties—maybe there's a point where it starts being almost—cute?

IRIS: That's just the word I want to associate with my sex life. "How's your sex life?" "Cute." You got kids?

OLIVER: Nope.

IRIS: You came here alone. Your wife—

OLIVER: This wouldn't be her scene.

IRIS: She stayed in New York.

OLIVER: My reasons for coming here weren't anything she'd be interested in.

[*He gets up and pours himself another drink.*]

You want another?

IRIS: Actually, yes, I would.

OLIVER: What about you? Married? Not married?

IRIS: Not.

OLIVER: Not now, or not ever?

IRIS: Both.

OLIVER: Oh. Any particular reason?

IRIS: Not a lot of guys that interested in taking up with you when a baby that isn't theirs is part of the deal.

OLIVER: And when she stopped being a baby?

IRIS: By then I was used to not having someone else underfoot. Don't get the wrong impression—

OLIVER: What impression do you think I'm getting that might be wrong?

IRIS: Skip it.

OLIVER: Why?

IRIS: Oh, it's just a lot of horseshit.

OLIVER: What is?

IRIS: Come on—I say something about my life, you make sounds like you hear me and understand or sympathize, and tomorrow or the day after, you climb back onto a jet and fly to whichever coast and what's the point? That you feel good about yourself?

OLIVER: Why would I feel good about myself?

IRIS: Because you've—you think—you're under the impression that by listening to me you—

OLIVER: I what?

IRIS: —you've done something.

OLIVER: Done what? What have I done?

IRIS: Exactly.

OLIVER: I'm sorry?

IRIS: What *have* you done?

OLIVER: I don't know. You tell me. You've got the floor.

IRIS: Look, why don't I just say to you that I really and truly believe that you are a good guy and the rest of the dance isn't necessary.

OLIVER: But I *am* interested. I wouldn't ask if I weren't.

IRIS: Fine, and what good does that do? You're interested. How does that make either of our lives better? Waste of time, Oliver. Full credit for good intentions, but waste of time.

OLIVER: What are we arguing about?

IRIS: We're not.

OLIVER: Then why do I get the feeling you're mad at me?

IRIS: I'm not.

OLIVER: Okay.

IRIS: I'm not mad at you.

OLIVER: Okay.

IRIS: Just because I may disagree with you about something, that doesn't mean—

OLIVER: Well, yeah, see that's what I want to know—

IRIS: What?

OLIVER: What we're disagreeing about.

IRIS: Look, are we having a good time?

OLIVER: Yes.

IRIS: So why don't we just have it and not analyze it. This job of yours—this movie reviewing—keep it to the movies. I don't want to worry how many stars you're giving me for this conversation.

OLIVER: I wouldn't do that. I don't do that.

IRIS: Hey, how much is it really worth?

OLIVER: What?

IRIS: The stamp. How much?

OLIVER: Oh, maybe four thousand dollars.

IRIS: Gee, I would have thought more.

OLIVER: Well, maybe I underestimate. Maybe six, seven—

IRIS: Maybe six or seven *cents*.

OLIVER: You think Lianne might have put one over on me?

IRIS: That's right, it was her doing.

OLIVER [*handing her the drink, smiles*]: You were wrong about my not remembering you.

IRIS: Oh?

OLIVER: I think you might be surprised how much I used to think about you—

IRIS: About me how, as if I can't guess.

OLIVER: Well, aside from that.

IRIS: You never said anything.

OLIVER: What was I going to do, ask you for a date?

IRIS: People do. People did.

OLIVER: But there was something about you—

IRIS: What was about me?

OLIVER: This is going to sound sort of—

IRIS: Never mind what it sounds—

OLIVER: I thought—the crowd you hung out with?—I thought you were better than them.

IRIS: Better?

OLIVER: Not to put down the gang you hung out with—

IRIS: Even if they were lowlifes like Ted?

OLIVER: Well—but that there was more there. That you—

IRIS: I wasn't just a wild kid.

OLIVER: There was something—

IRIS: I had potential. I was a diamond in the rough. If you had the nerve, you would have shown me there were better things in life, finer things—

OLIVER: Put it that way, I sound like an asshole.

IRIS [*waving his comment aside*]: You'd introduce me to symphonies and the *Mona Lisa*. Expand my horizons. That it?

OLIVER: And poetry. Don't forget poetry.

IRIS: Shakespeare.

OLIVER: Emily Dickinson.

IRIS: So you'd introduce me to Shakespeare and Beethoven and that crowd. And what was I supposed to introduce *you* to?

OLIVER: Oh, I didn't think directly about that. Not straight on. I didn't paint any pictures. I just thought that I'd show you this world of higher thought and beauty and it would awaken in you this desire to—

IRIS: Jump your bones?

OLIVER: Not exactly the words I would have used then. Or now.

IRIS: What words *would* you use now?

OLIVER [*not answering the question*]: And what if I *had* asked you for a date? Back then.

IRIS: I probably would have been flattered. That you looked down and noticed me.

OLIVER: Oh, come on, "down." I was a geek. How can a geek look down on anyone?

IRIS: You think everybody didn't know good stuff was going to happen for you? Why do you think Ted beat you up? He was paying you back ahead of time.

OLIVER: But you would have gone out with me? If I'd asked?

IRIS: No, actually, I probably would have made some kind of crack, and then I would have told the gang, and they would have given you shit, too.

OLIVER: You would have told them?

IRIS: Yes, I would. You had too high an opinion of me. I mean, I wasn't that nice a person.

OLIVER: Oh, don't do that. I mean, kids, for Christ's sake, teenagers—they're all too concerned with not being laughed at to worry about perspective, kindness, any of that. I mean, I don't expect, much less blame—but you know this. You must have seen it in your own kid, your daughter. What's her name?

IRIS: Natalie.

OLIVER: Nice.

IRIS: You realize, she's older now than you and I were the last time we saw each other?

OLIVER: Wait a second. Let me—say that again—

IRIS: You're older, no, *she's* older now than you and I were—

OLIVER: —the last time we saw each other. Right.

IRIS: It's true.

OLIVER: Senior prom, was it?

IRIS: Probably.

OLIVER: You looked great that night. In case you didn't know.

IRIS: You remember vividly.

OLIVER: Kind of a dark blue dress, off the shoulders.

IRIS [*disturbed*]: Hey—

OLIVER: What's the matter?

IRIS: What are you doing?

OLIVER: Just remembering.

IRIS: Well, don't.

OLIVER: Oh?

IRIS: Let it alone.

[*Beat.*]

OLIVER: I'm sorry.

IRIS: No, it's okay. I mean, I'm not offended.

OLIVER: No?

IRIS: But it's—

OLIVER: Okay.

IRIS: We're here right now. All that other stuff—

OLIVER: No, I agree.

IRIS: Good.

OLIVER: Except that's sort of the point, isn't it? A reunion. These are the kinds of thoughts that'll come up.

IRIS: Except I chose not to go, remember? You didn't see me at the luncheon.

OLIVER: That's true.

IRIS: So it's not like that's something I'm really eager to revisit.

OLIVER: But you decided to come by here to see me in particular?

IRIS: That's different. Ted called me—

OLIVER: Called you at your job?

IRIS: We talk about you sometimes, so he knew that I'd be interested you were coming to visit.

OLIVER: You talk about me?

IRIS: I watch you on the tube, on the TV—

OLIVER: Really.

IRIS: It's not like I know dozens of people who have TV shows. And sometimes Ted and I, yes, we talk about some of what you say. Not that my opinion's worth all that much, but I like what you do. I like what you—I think you make good points.

OLIVER: It never particularly occurred to me that you'd watch the show.

IRIS: Oh sure.

OLIVER: What do you know?

IRIS: Sure.

[*Beat.*]

OLIVER [*very directly*]: You and Ted—the two of you—you never—

IRIS: What? Did he ever get into my pants? No. Somehow I missed that treat. Why? Would it damage your opinion of me—

OLIVER: I didn't think you had.

IRIS: Is that a load off your mind?

OLIVER: I hoped you hadn't.

IRIS: You hoped?

OLIVER: It's something that—it's none of my business—something I couldn't help but wonder.

IRIS: When?

OLIVER: Back then, in school. And tonight.

IRIS: Wondering tonight about back then, or wondering tonight about—what—now?

OLIVER: The thought, the question occurred. Some of the looks you were giving each other—

IRIS: You're reading in.

OLIVER: It's none of my business anyway.

IRIS: Believe it or not, he's pretty nuts about Lianne and the boys. Whatever else there is about him, that part—I've never heard anything but that he walks the real straight and narrow when it comes to his family. He really is good with Lianne.

OLIVER: I'm glad to hear that. She's somebody who needs to be cared for. Looked after.

IRIS: From what you can see.

OLIVER: Which, yeah—here I am, shooting my mouth off. Fifteen minutes and I'm—sorry. But, you know, my heart went out to her.

IRIS: Oliver?

OLIVER: Okay.

IRIS: She's not yours to rescue.

OLIVER: No, of course not.

IRIS: The hundred bucks was a nice gesture, but let it go at that.

OLIVER: No, of course. It would be presumptuous. Of course.

IRIS: And, about me and Ted—news flash: it *is* possible to be friends with a guy without making it with him.

OLIVER: I'm sure.

IRIS: Or don't you have any women friends?

OLIVER: Many.

IRIS: And do you sleep with all of them?

OLIVER: Hardly any.

[*Beat.*]

Gee, I wonder if I've had enough to drink. What do you think?

IRIS: Loosen your leash. You're not driving.

OLIVER: Yes, true. Do you think he's going to be long? Dropping off Lianne?

IRIS: Her mama's just down the road. But, you know, there's a chance he might get stuck in one of those family things.

OLIVER: Yeah, I've heard about them.

IRIS: Family things?

OLIVER: No, I was just wondering. See, Ted gave me a lift out here—

IRIS: Oh, right.

OLIVER: Not that I haven't enjoyed myself.

IRIS: Sure, how often do you get conversation this profound in New York?

OLIVER: When I think of how afraid I used to be of him—do you know—well, maybe I shouldn't say this—

IRIS: Say anything you feel like—

OLIVER: He said earlier, before you were here—he made this comment about how I probably haven't thought about him in years. I wasn't going to tell him, but I think about him every day.

IRIS: Really?

OLIVER: When I was a freshman, I was standing in the boys' john, you know, at the—

IRIS: Urinal?

OLIVER: There was a whole row of these ones that go all the way down to the floor.

IRIS: Okay, I get the picture.

OLIVER: So I'm standing there, and I'm—

IRIS: Yes, and?

OLIVER: —and suddenly I feel this hand in the middle of my back and a push. I step forward to catch my balance, and my foot's in the thing now, and down my right leg there's this trail.

IRIS: Ted?

OLIVER: He laughs. I go into one of the stalls and close the door and wait for it to dry. I was late to class, and I was sure everybody knew, could tell. All the times he pounded me, those I've mostly forgotten. But I go into a public john, particularly if there's a lot of noise and rowdiness—at a ballpark?—I feel my back tense up—

IRIS: Waiting to be pushed again?

OLIVER: Like that's something you needed to know, right? Well, maybe this visit will turn out to be therapeutic.

IRIS: Because you've made peace with Ted, you'll stop tensing up in the men's room?

OLIVER: You know, it would be worth the whole trip.

[IRIS *laughs.*]

IRIS: Would you like a lift back? Where are you staying, the Taylor Arms?

OLIVER: Good guess.

IRIS: I'll take you back.

OLIVER: If it's no trouble.

IRIS: It's what I have a car for.

OLIVER: Well, great. What about Ted? He comes back, we're not here—

IRIS: We'll leave a note.

OLIVER: Right.

IRIS: Or call him when we get where we're going.

OLIVER: "When we"—

IRIS: Or however it turns out.

OLIVER: Sure.

IRIS: Ted is not a problem in any case. You ready?

OLIVER: Let me finish my drink.

[*He is sitting in his chair as he drinks. She drifts over. He puts down his glass. She swoops down and kisses him on the lips, then stands up straight again. He is a little startled, but not displeased. He looks up at her, a little bemused. Lights fade.*]

SCENE 2

[*The living room of* IRIS's *home. We see the door to the front road. We also see a bit of the kitchen and a door that leads offstage to a bedroom. In half-light, under music,* OLIVER *and* IRIS *enter, a little unsteadily. They are laughing and all over each other. He tosses his jacket over a chair and turns to* IRIS, *who points him in the direction of the bedroom and gives him a little shove to propel him woozily offstage. She turns around to check the front door handle, making certain—as we will realize later—that it is unlocked. Then she turns and begins to take off her blouse as she herself enters the bedroom. The door to the bedroom is left ajar. The music fades, and the lights come up a bit, indicating the passage of time. The sound from the bedroom gives evidence of hot and heavy activity. In the middle of this, the front door opens. It is* TED, *carrying a tote bag. He gently closes the door behind him and makes his way to the bedroom door to check on their progress. He opens the tote bag and pulls out a flash camera. The sound from the bedroom begins to build in intensity.* OLIVER *is evidently approaching climax.* TED *watches for his moment, then slips through the door. A series of four or five white flashes erupt from the bedroom as well as sounds of confusion.* TED *now ambles out of the bedroom. He turns on the lights in the living room and sits in an easy chair where he can have a good view of the door to the bedroom. He waits. A beat or two and* OLIVER *enters, having hastily put on his pants and a T-shirt. He looks at* TED.]

TED [*affably*]: Got to tell you something, Oliver—got to compliment you. You looked like you knew what you were doing in there.

OLIVER [*bemused*]: You took pictures.

TED: Five of them.

OLIVER: Pretty fast shooting.

TED [*holding up the camera*]: Motor. Advances the film automatically, recharges the flash. Fast shutter, fast film—when I blow them up, won't be any doubt who it is. A side of you your TV viewers have never seen in sharp, clear shots.

OLIVER: What are you planning to do with these sharp, clear shots?

TED: Thought I'd send them to your wife.

OLIVER: So what you told me before wasn't strictly the truth. When you said you had no agenda.

TED: No, I had an agenda.

OLIVER: This was your agenda.

TED: This was my agenda.

OLIVER: Why you invited me over to your place, why you kept filling my glass, why Iris so conveniently appeared—

TED: Yup.

OLIVER: I didn't see it coming.

TED: You underestimated me.

OLIVER: I don't know if I'd put it that way.

TED: I really don't care *what* way you'd put it. I'm pretty fucking *tired* of you *putting* it, okay? All your opinions. And the attitude tonight like I was supposed to be grateful to you for sharing this crap. Like you were the grand high rabbi of New York granting me an audience. Like you really have something meaningful to tell me. That you even *believe* you do. That I should look to you for wisdom? What movie to see, how to be a good human being? You tell me, "Oh, I couldn't take money for saying something nice about a movie, that wouldn't be *honest*. I have *integrity*." Well, buddy, I've got a camera full of your integrity.

OLIVER: I'm sorry if I offended you.

TED: The only thing that makes you sorry is that I'm sitting here with this. Otherwise you wouldn't give two shits about what I think. Isn't that right?

OLIVER: Actually, no, I don't think so.

TED: No, you don't think so what? You wouldn't give two shits or you would?

OLIVER: I might even give three.

TED: Well, you're gonna give more than that.

OLIVER: Or else you send these pictures—

TED: To your wife.

OLIVER: My wife. Wow. What if I tell you that someday you'd be embarrassed that you did this? That maybe you'd dislike yourself kind of a lot?

TED: Not be able to face myself in the mirror in the morning?

OLIVER: We have to live with what we do. With the consequences.

TED: Well, the consequences here are that we'll have money we didn't have before.

OLIVER: "We"?

TED: I have a partner.

OLIVER: Of course.

TED: How do you think I got in?

OLIVER: She left the door unlocked.

TED: But, see, I know what you were doing—

OLIVER: What was I—

TED: Just now. What you were trying to do: appeal to my better nature.

OLIVER: Didn't work too well, hunh?

TED: I enjoyed watching you try. There's one thing I wish—

OLIVER: What?

TED: That you were wearing glasses. For old times' sake.

[*He mimes breaking them.*]

OLIVER: I could take my contacts out.

TED: Would they go crunch under my heel?

OLIVER: They're the soft kind. Probably just make a little squish.

TED: Not worth it.

OLIVER: Sorry.

TED: Oh, before I forget—

[TED *reaches into his pocket and pulls out the hundred-dollar bill.*]

I want the stamp back.

OLIVER: Excuse me?

TED: The pink stamp. Give it to me.

OLIVER: I bought it. Your wife and I made a deal.

TED: Null and void. Here's your hundred dollars. You think I don't know what you were doing, you fuck?

OLIVER: Buying a stamp.

TED: Buying *some*thing, that's for sure. *Thinking* you were buying something. She's *my* wife. She has problems, it's *my* job. You want to play the big man, descend from a fucking cloud with alms for the poor. What gives you the right? As if we'd accept a handout from you.

OLIVER: You don't want my money.

TED: No, I don't.

OLIVER: Unless you can take it.

TED: I don't care if you get it or not.

OLIVER: No, I understand. If you accept something from me that might smell of concern, sympathy—

TED: Pity—

OLIVER: —that makes you a wuss. Blackmail, on the other hand—

TED: You *owe* this to me.

OLIVER: Okay, this part I'm having trouble following. I haven't seen you in twenty-five years, how can I—

TED: Where do you put your money, Oliver?

OLIVER: Where everybody—my wallet.

TED: No, I don't mean your cash, I mean your *money.* Stocks? Mutual funds?

OLIVER: Some real estate and, yeah, mutual funds.

TED: Been pretty good for you lately, hunh? Mutual funds.

OLIVER: Doing okay.

TED: All those companies in the portfolio, streamlining their operations. Getting rid of dead wood. Getting rid of divisions that aren't performing up to par. Closing down plants that aren't showing a good enough return.

OLIVER: Did you have any particular plant in mind?

TED: How much did your portfolio go up? How much did you make while some people filed for unemployment?

OLIVER: So this is what—reparations?

TED: Call it whatever you want to call it. [*Calling*] Iris, come on out here.

[*Beat.*]

   Iris!

[*Beat.* IRIS *appears wearing a robe. She avoids looking at* OLIVER.]

IRIS: Something you need me for?

TED: Toss me his coat.

IRIS: You can't get it yourself?

TED: I want you to do it.

[*Beat.* IRIS *gets it, hands it to* TED. TED *reaches into the inside pocket, pulls out* OLIVER's *wallet, opens it, takes out the stamp, puts the hundred-dollar bill back in the wallet, and puts the wallet back into the pocket. Feeling around,* TED *finds* OLIVER's *checkbook and tosses it to him.*]

   This is how it's going to go: you're gonna write me a check. After I cash it, I'll send you the film.

OLIVER: A check?

TED: Fifty grand.

IRIS: Wait a minute. You said twenty. On the phone, you said—

TED: I changed my mind.

IRIS: You said twenty, we'd split twenty.

TED: So now we'll split fifty.

IRIS: That's not what we agreed.

TED: Look at him, he can afford it. Besides, in a way it's a bargain, compared to what he'd have to shell out for a divorce—

IRIS: That's not the point.

TED: You couldn't use twenty-five grand?

IRIS: I don't need that much.

TED: Fine, take what you want. More for me.

IRIS: You can't just change things—

TED: Hey, whose idea was this? Whose plan?

IRIS: Like this is so brilliant? You think this is inventing the wheel? Discovering Velcro?

TED: It's gonna solve some problems, isn't it?

OLIVER: Sorry to interrupt, but I still have a question or two.

TED: Ask.

OLIVER: If I don't write the check—

TED: Old business. I send the pictures to—

OLIVER: —to my wife, yes. But what size were you thinking of sending?

TED: Size?

OLIVER: Of the pictures? The prints? Five by seven? Eight by ten?

TED: What does it matter?

OLIVER: Just want to have a complete grasp of the situation.

TED: Eight by ten.

OLIVER: Matte? Glossy?

TED: I like glossy. Is that enough of a grasp? You gonna write that check?

[OLIVER *hesitates, then writes the check and tears it off.*]

[*To* IRIS] Bring it here.

IRIS: Ted—

TED: Do you want your share?

IRIS: I think I've done enough for my share. I think I've done *more* than enough for my share.

TED: Oh?

IRIS: You were supposed to come in sooner. You were supposed to come in before—

TED: Before he slipped it to you?

IRIS: I've done my share.

TED [*to* OLIVER]: You think she's mad at me?

OLIVER: Could be.

TED: Iris, you mad at me?

IRIS: Another thing you didn't do the way we said. The way we agreed.

TED: Iris, I'm at a loss here. I'd offer you more money by way of compensation, for my bad timing when I came in, but you just said you don't want more. Of course, even if you decided to do me the favor of accepting more, we'd still have to figure out how much your compensation should be.

[OLIVER *gets up and hands* TED *the check while* TED *is still looking at* IRIS.]

OLIVER: Here.

TED [*to* IRIS]: Just how much is it worth, Iris? Your what—your honor? What would be an appropriate figure? Give me an estimate in round numbers.

IRIS: Very funny, Ted.

[TED *laughs as* OLIVER *moves back across the room.* TED *looks at the check. His expression changes.*]

TED: What's this supposed to be?

OLIVER: My bet is glossy eight-by-tens go for fifteen bucks a pop here. Five times fifteen is seventy-five, a little extra for tax and postage and an envelope. You can mail them to her care of the address at the top of the check there. The mail will be forwarded to wherever she decides to live.

TED: Wait a second. What are you playing here?

OLIVER: She left me two weeks ago. My wife.

TED: Left you?

OLIVER: Packed up her bags and took off. It's one of the reasons I came to the reunion. Something to do with myself. She and I were supposed to go to St. Thomas this weekend. But she announced two weeks ago that she had other plans with somebody else for the rest of her life. I think she's being optimistic about the "rest of her life" bit, but the upshot is she's gone. And frankly, it wouldn't upset me all that much if she got some evidence that I'm managing okay. That I'm not lacking for company. I hope I'm smiling in at least one of those shots. But the point is you don't have a situation here with blackmail potential. The conditions don't exist.

[*Beat.*]

TED: This is—you're just making this up, right? You're bluffing.

OLIVER: No, it's the truth. But if you don't believe me, call my bluff. *Make* the prints. Send them to her.

[*He begins to laugh.*]

The joke's on me, really. I wanted to believe that you'd pulled it together. I wanted to believe that you—I don't know why. Probably the sentimental streak in me. Probably the part of me that believes in midnight basketball for troubled youth and rehabilitation programs in prisons and buying UNICEF cards. But, Jesus Christ, you were a putz in high school and you're still a putz. Only difference is now you're an older putz.

[*Beat.*]

I should probably get dressed now. Pardon me, Iris.

[*Brushing past* IRIS, *he heads for the bedroom. Beat.* TED *puts down the camera and begins to head for the bedroom.*]

IRIS: Ted, now don't—

[TED *pushes her aside and disappears into the bedroom. The sound of violence as* TED *is evidently working* OLIVER *over pretty badly.* IRIS *stands at the door.*]

Ted! Stop! Don't!

[*She heads into the bedroom but is shoved out quickly as the beating continues. She looks around the kitchen. She is about to reach for a knife but thinks twice and grabs a heavy skillet. She goes into the bedroom, and there is a sudden bonging sound. Then silence. Now* TED, *bleeding from the back of his head, stumbles into the living room and falls down, dazed.* IRIS *returns to the room, still holding the skillet.* TED *turns to look at her.*]

I told you to stop.
TED: You some kind of maniac?
IRIS: You were hurting him.
TED: He laughed at me.
IRIS: Are you okay?
TED: You hit me with a fucking skillet, what do you think? Shit, I'm bleeding.
IRIS: I want you out of here. Out of my house.
TED: This is because I came in late, right? Because I let him do it to you?
IRIS: I won't be part of beating somebody up.
TED: What do you call what you just did to me? Stupid bitch.

[OLIVER, *sporting a bloody nose, appears in the doorway to the bedroom.*]

IRIS [*brandishing the skillet*]: You want more?
TED [*shrinking*]: All right, all right.

[IRIS *picks up the camera, opens it, takes the film. Closes the camera and tosses it to* TED.]

IRIS: Go.

TED: You realize what you're doing?

IRIS: I'm gonna miss getting your Christmas cards.

TED: You know what you're forgetting, Iris? You live here. You live here, and I live here. This clown, he didn't live here even when he did. Which one of us you going to be seeing next week at the Texaco? Or if by some miracle the plant actually does open again, the line in the cafeteria? Or you're at the bar and Stuart lets you persuade him to serve you one drink more than what you know is your limit—and what Stuart knows is your limit—and you're in no shape to get behind the wheel—which one of us you gonna turn to for a lift home? Who's gonna be there?

[TED *exits.* IRIS *puts the skillet down. She goes to the kitchen and grabs a fistful of paper towels and hands them to* OLIVER.]

OLIVER: He gave me a twenty-fifth anniversary beating. My homecoming is complete.

[IRIS *doesn't react.*]

How are you? You okay?

IRIS: I'm swell.

OLIVER: You look a little woozy.

IRIS: I'm not used to handing out concussions.

OLIVER: Maybe you ought to sit down, put your head between your legs, do some deep breathing.

IRIS: Excuse me?

OLIVER: Could do you some good. Why don't you try it?

IRIS: What the fuck's the matter with you?

OLIVER: The matter?

IRIS: Don't you understand what just happened here? Don't you get it?

OLIVER: Sure.

IRIS: I set you up. Ted and I were in this together.

OLIVER: Okay.

IRIS: Do you understand that?

OLIVER: Yes.

IRIS: I was part of trying to get money out of you. I got naked and got into bed with you, I let you put yourself inside me so that he could take pictures so that we could get money out of you.

OLIVER: No, I figured that much out.

IRIS: It's called blackmail. Extortion. It's a crime. You were going to be the victim of a crime. You *are* the victim of a crime!

OLIVER: No, really, you don't have to shout.

IRIS: So what is this attitude about? This concern shit?

OLIVER: Well, I figure you must have had your reasons for doing what you did.

IRIS: My reasons are I wanted money.

OLIVER: Because you needed it.

IRIS: Of course I needed it. You think I would have done this for pleasure?

OLIVER: Well, a guy could hope.

IRIS: That was the point. You showed up. You didn't bring your wife—

OLIVER: Ted smelled an opportunity. He called you—

IRIS: And I did it. I actually did it. Dumb.

OLIVER: Well, not *that* dumb. Four or five weeks ago, it would have worked. No question. You just had the bad luck of depending on my wife to play the wifely part the way she was supposed to. Believe me, I share in your disappointment. No, four or five weeks ago, I would have written the check.

IRIS: But four or five weeks ago, if you still thought your marriage was solid, would you have hopped in the sack with me?

OLIVER: Hmmm.

IRIS: Probably not.

OLIVER: Well, the impulse would have been there. The impulse has always been there. I think I'm paying you a compliment. If you consider it a compliment. Anyway, that's not what we're talking about.

IRIS: What do you think we're talking about?

OLIVER: Why you agreed to do this thing with Ted you wouldn't have done otherwise. You're not somebody who would do something like this if you weren't desperate. You want to tell me about it?

IRIS: No.

OLIVER: If you need money so bad—

IRIS: Who doesn't need money?

OLIVER: Well, actually, I don't. Not at the moment. But you told Ted before you only wanted to take what you needed.

IRIS: So?

OLIVER: So it sounded like there was a specific sum you had in mind. A specific sum, which suggests a specific something you need it for.

IRIS: Everybody has problems. Nothing unusual. No big deal.

OLIVER: Something to do with your daughter? With Natalie? Or her kid?

[*Beat.*]

IRIS: Actually, yes, she needs open-heart surgery. My granddaughter.
OLIVER: Really?
IRIS: No!!! Jesus Christ, I could tell you *anything*! How do you stay alive?
OLIVER: I just want to understand. You did this thing. This thing you wouldn't do unless you were desperate. But you see, I understand cuz I'm going through my own stuff. You're desperate, I'm not in the greatest place in the world—
IRIS: You miss your wife.

[*This hits home. Beat.*]

OLIVER: You know what, maybe this was supposed to happen. No, no, hear me out—
IRIS: This was supposed to happen? You were supposed to get blackmailed and beaten?
OLIVER: Well, not that exactly, but here we are—
IRIS: Give me a break—
OLIVER: You and me. Maybe there's some good that's supposed to come out of this.
IRIS: What is this "supposed to"? If something was "supposed to," then that means that someone had to do the supposing. Who? Some higher power? Do you think this is part of some higher power—some *plan*—*God*? You think that God put you in my bed and had Ted work you over so that we were *supposed to* find each other? For what?
OLIVER: Comfort? Consolation?
IRIS: You know, right now I almost want to beat you up myself. Where do you get this shit?
OLIVER: I'm sorry.
IRIS: What, now you're gonna apologize to *me*?
OLIVER: What do you want me to do? Tell me what you want me to do. Do you want me to yell at you? Call you names? Would that make you feel better?
IRIS: Then you might be recognizably human. You should be furious. Right now, if you were a human being, you'd want to run Ted over with a truck and—
OLIVER: And do something to you? What? Beat you up? Slap you around?
IRIS: I'm not saying I want you to do that. But at least it's something I'd understand.
OLIVER: Okay, what don't you understand?

IRIS: Is it a Jewish thing? This thing you're doing?

[OLIVER *looks at her for a second, then begins to laugh. She looks at him sternly for a second, then she begins to laugh, too. They laugh long and hard. Finally, they subside.*]

How's your nose?

OLIVER: Fine.

IRIS: You going to do anything about Ted?

OLIVER: Like maybe press charges? No.

IRIS: Any particular reason?

OLIVER: It would mean sticking around this town some more. That's not something I'm real eager to do.

[*Beat.*]

What do you say you come back with me?

IRIS: Come back with you?

OLIVER: To New York. I'm serious.

IRIS: Oliver, I don't have any stamps to sell you.

OLIVER: Do you have somebody right now?

IRIS: None of your business.

OLIVER: You don't. You don't, I don't. It could work.

IRIS: Sure.

OLIVER: Why not? Why not? If we decide we want it to? What's to keep it? If we just decide. If we just decide this is what we want to do. This is what we want to be. That it's our choice how our lives turn out. Think about it.

IRIS: We would last maybe three weeks.

OLIVER: Okay, fine, I'll settle for that.

[*As she stands, he takes hold of her arm. Pressing his head against her stomach, he begins to cry. She hesitates, then she puts her arms around him. The grief pours out of him.*]

IRIS: Okay now. Okay.

[*She holds him as the lights fade.*]

VOICE OF GOOD HOPE

KRISTINE THATCHER

To the Honorable Thomas S. Eveland, with love and respect

PLAYWRIGHT'S STATEMENT

Barbara Jordan was elected to the Texas state senate in 1966, becoming the first black senator since 1883. Six years later she became the first black woman from the Deep South elected to the United States House of Representatives. During the 1974 House Judiciary Committee's deliberations on the impeachment of Richard Nixon, Jordan's calm and reasonable defense of the United States Constitution gained her a reputation as a politician who could cross party lines to an American public in need of a steady voice.

It was during the impeachment hearings that I heard Barbara Jordan speak for the first time. In 1976 I heard her again, delivering the keynote address at the Democratic National Convention. I remember having read pieces of her Harvard commencement address in 1979. In the ensuing years I might catch her on the *MacNeil–Lehrer News Hour* or *Meet the Press*. I would read about her in the papers from time to time. The last time I heard her speak was when she addressed the delegates at the 1992 convention. I had always been a member of her fan club, but on the day she died I experienced a sense of personal loss that seemed out of proportion to the handful of times I'd heard her speak. I wanted to find out more about her. And as I read about her, I knew I wanted to write about her.

Molly Ivins once wrote that Barbara Jordan "sounded like the Lord God Almighty." It's true; Jordan had a command of public address that most politicians only wish they possessed. I discovered, however, that what fascinated me most about her was not her vocal skill or her impeccable use of the English language but her unflinching personal integrity, her encyclopedic knowledge of the law, and her absolute power of reason. While we have made progress in achieving what Jordan called a "national community," she also understood that each generation deals anew and in its own particular way with the poison of racism.

When she was awarded the Presidential Medal of Freedom in 1994, two years before her death, President William Clinton called her "the most outspoken moral voice of the American political system." He went on to say, "She has captured the nation's attention and awakened its conscience in defense of our Constitution, the American dream, and the commonality we share as American citizens."

PRODUCTION HISTORY

Voice of Good Hope, by Kristine Thatcher, was first presented by Victory Gardens Theater, Chicago, Illinois, in March 2000.

PRODUCTION TEAM

Director	Dennis Začek
Set	Jeff Bauer
Costumes	Karin Kopischke
Lights	Joel Moritz
Sound	Andre Pluess and Ben Sussman
Dramaturg	Sara Freeman
Production Stage Manager	Melissa Renee Miller

CAST

Heart	Karla J. Beard
Barbara Jordan	Cheryl Lynn Bruce
John Ed Patten	Kenn E. Head
Julie Dunn	Yvonne Huff
Robert Strauss	Daniel Mooney
Nancy Earl	Meg Thalken
Karen Woodruff	Kim Wade

The play was subsequently produced by Luna Stage, Montclair, New Jersey, in 2002; Ensemble Theatre, Cleveland, Ohio, in January 2003; and Stage West, Fort Worth, Texas, in November 2004.

CHARACTERS

Barbara Jordan   Heart
Nancy Earl   Julie Dunn
Karen Woodruff   Robert Strauss
John Ed Patten

STAGING

I have been extremely nearsighted since a wild and crazy cycling mishap in my youth and admit that, as a result, I have learned to respect and surrender to more sharp-eyed individuals to make visual sense out of the words of my plays. My characters walk from place to place, making certain demands about where the desk should be, where the painting should be, where the rags should be. I think I know what I'm doing as I write. I try to visualize the physical problems, but more often than not, it takes my director or the designers to show me an easier way. I have learned to heed their advice, and my rewrites often contain their solutions to sticky problems. In terms of *Voice of Good Hope,* I suppose each director might benefit, due to the rapid changes of scene, if they set the play in as neutral a territory as possible. Figure out a place that might encompass every place, where every prop, every piece of furniture, and all light cues might work together in some harmonious fashion. Once the play gets going, it mustn't stop for anything, including scene changes. During the first production meeting at Victory Gardens, the director, Dennis Začek, remembered a pair of underwear from his youth and declared the design team should spin off that image. I didn't quite understand and was even slightly appalled but wisely kept my mouth shut. The result was a background reminiscent of the American flag—except that the stripes were black and white. It worked so beautifully that I can't imagine how anyone could conceive a better arena, although I would love to see as many directors and designers as possible try. My nightly dreams are visually splendid, but when I awake in the morning, the colors, the places, the objects tumble out of my mind and down through the back of my head. I can vividly remember and report what was said, but rarely can I describe what I saw. When it comes to visual unity, I leave that to my betters. Leave me out of it. However, if you want to talk about how the play should sound, particularly in terms of incidental music, I'm in: gospel and blues all the way!

PROLOGUE

[The House Judiciary Committee Rayburn Building, July 25, 1974, 9:00 P.M. It is Congresswoman JORDAN's *turn to speak on the impeachment of Richard Milhous Nixon. The portions of the famous speeches represented in the play should be staged as one might stage the chorus in a Greek drama. They should be memorized. There should be no regular speaking area, no podium. Rather, she should be allowed to roam the stage, speaking directly to the audience. All speeches should flow directly out of the preceding action.]*

JORDAN: "Mr. Chairman, earlier today we heard the beginning of the Preamble to the Constitution of the United States, *We, the people.* I felt somehow for many years that George Washington and Alexander Hamilton just left me out by mistake. But through the process of amendment, interpretation, and court decisions I have finally been included in *We, the people.*

"Today I am an inquisitor. I believe hyperbole would not be fictional and would not overstate the solemnness that I feel right now. My faith in the Constitution is whole, it is complete, it is total. I am not going to sit here and be an idle spectator to the diminution, the subversion, the destruction of the Constitution.

"The fact is that yesterday, the American people waited with great anxiety for eight hours, not knowing whether their president would obey an order of the Supreme Court of the United States.

"Beginning shortly after the Watergate break-in, President Nixon has engaged in a series of public statements designed to thwart the lawful investigation by government prosecutors. He has made public assertions bearing on the Watergate case which the evidence will show he knew to be false.

"If the impeachment provision of the Constitution of the United States will not reach the offenses charged here, then perhaps that eighteenth-century Constitution should be abandoned to a twentieth-century paper shredder. Has the president committed offenses and planned and directed and acquiesced in a course of conduct which the Constitution will not tolerate? That is the question. It is reason, and not passion, which must guide our deliberations, guide our debate, and guide our decision."

[August 1994. A private room in Brackenridge Hospital, Austin, Texas. The room is dark, and a figure sleeps soundly in a chair. Appearing in the doorway, but backlit

so we cannot see her face, is a middle-aged blond woman. She comes quietly into the room, leans over the chair, and gently touches the face of the chair's occupant. The figure in the chair stirs.]

Bennie?

EARL [*rising*]: No, B.J., it's Nancy.

JORDAN: Is it morning or afternoon?

EARL: It's two o'clock, Barbara. Afternoon.

JORDAN [*struggling to sit up*]: I dozed off.

EARL: Did you see the newspaper?

JORDAN: What are you doing here?

EARL: Dr. Briggs told me that the specialist was coming in to look you over. I didn't want to miss her. Did you see the paper?

JORDAN: Mm-hmm.

[*She indicates a barely touched newspaper on the table.*]

EARL: Are you happy?

JORDAN [*sitting up*]: I had a dream about John Ed. He came to visit me here in the hospital. He brought a few rags to fold.

EARL: True to form.

JORDAN: I remember my dad quoting from scripture about a man who left the church and went down from Jerusalem. Whenever he saw John Ed, my father used to badger him about how when you leave the church, "you go down! Down from Jerusalem!" Even as a child I wanted to say to my dad, "If you even get to heaven, John Ed is going to be there opening the gates for you."

EARL: How did this dream turn out? When John Ed appeared, what did he say?

JORDAN: That's the thing. I heard him laugh just the way he used to. So sweet. The only problem is, I couldn't make out a goddamned word he was saying . . . I could use a real toothbrush.

[JORDAN *produces a cigarette and puts it between her lips.*]

EARL: I brought you a real toothbrush last night.

JORDAN: No.

EARL: A purple toothbrush. It's standing in a cup beside your Colgate.

JORDAN: No.

[JORDAN *produces a match.* EARL *grabs the cigarette and trashes it.*]

EARL: Has no one combed your hair since last night?

JORDAN: I certainly haven't.

EARL: Should I open the shades, let a little light in?

JORDAN: On pain of death.

[JORDAN *pulls the walker toward her.*]

EARL: Where are you going?

JORDAN: Jerry Ford is expecting me on the golf course.

EARL: Why don't you just take the chair?

[*She indicates a nearby wheelchair.* JORDAN *stares at her.*]

Let me wheel you over. It's a wonderful invention: one second you're here; next second you're there.

JORDAN: I'll take the walker.

EARL: At least let me help you up.

[*She holds out her arms.*]

On three, okay?

JORDAN: Get away. Go over there.

[*She waves to a corner of the room.* EARL *takes a step.*]

Go *way* over there.

[EARL *stands aside while* JORDAN *launches herself.* JORDAN *goes approximately two feet.*]

EARL: Slow down!

JORDAN: I've gone two feet here.

EARL: Just watch what you're doing.

JORDAN: Shit!

EARL [*pulling out a chair*]: Sit down. Just sit down.

JORDAN [*sitting*]: When is she supposed to be here?

EARL: Any minute.

[*She helps* JORDAN *get settled at the table. Then she rolls up the wheelchair and sits in it herself.*]

Briggs says Woodruff is the best.

JORDAN: Speaking of Briggs . . .

EARL: You will see him at four. He does have other patients, you know.

JORDAN: When this specialist gets here, I'll do the talking, okay?

EARL: Of course.

JORDAN: I mean it. *I'll* do the talking.

EARL: I said fine!

[JORDAN *slaps her cigarettes on the table in an unspoken challenge. She deals a hand of solitaire.* EARL *watches.*]

JORDAN: So, have you turned the swimming pool into a giant planter yet?

EARL: I've got a load of dirt coming on Saturday.

JORDAN: Hah!

EARL: I *am* tempted to drain the damned thing.

JORDAN: Don't you dare.

EARL: Then you stop sneaking in there when I'm not home!

JORDAN: It was hot. I was bored.

EARL: I don't want to hear it was hot, you were bored!

JORDAN: Well.

EARL: Barbara, you scared the hell out of me. You have no idea what I went through.

JORDAN: I know. How are things at home?

EARL: The oxeye daisies are in bloom. Lupines and Indian paintbrush are popping up in the ditches by the driveway.

JORDAN: Lord.

EARL: I haven't seen the cardinal in days.

JORDAN: It's that new seed mixture.

EARL: I don't think so. The female still comes around. I can't figure it out, unless one of the cats got to him.

JORDAN: It's obvious. He misses me, so he's flown the coop.

EARL: He's gone, that's all I know.

[*Pause.*]

I've hired a carpenter. There will be a ramp when you come home. You can use it or not at your own—

JORDAN: Get this straight. I'm going to do what I want to do until I can't do it anymore.

[WOODRUFF *enters.*]

WOODRUFF: Hello?

JORDAN: Oh, shit!

EARL [*rising*]: Yes?

WOODRUFF: I'm Karen Woodruff.

EARL: Nancy Earl. I'm Barbara's housemate.

WOODRUFF: Hello. [*To* JORDAN] Oh, dear.

[*She takes a deep breath.*]

It's an honor.

[*She extends her hand to* JORDAN.]

Professor, I mean Ms.—no—Congresswoman Jordan.

JORDAN: You had it right the first time.

WOODRUFF: Oh, good. What did I say?

JORDAN: Why don't you just call me Barbara? That will simplify things.

WOODRUFF: It might take me about five minutes before I can have a normal conversation with you. This is so unprofessional!

JORDAN: I spent six years in the U.S. Congress, don't worry about it.

EARL: Dr. Woodruff?

WOODRUFF: Yes.

EARL: Barbara is on quite a combination of drugs. She'll just give you a rough time. Think of me as the responsible adult here.

WOODRUFF: I'm sorry.

[*She holds out her hand.*]

You told me your name, and I—

EARL [*shaking it*]: Nancy Earl. We're curious about how the heart attack may have affected the MS.

WOODRUFF: Yes, well, of course. [*Composing herself*] I've looked at all the records and talked extensively with Dr. Briggs. They took some blood this morning?

JORDAN: I'm down about a quart.

WOODRUFF: I want to ask a few questions, and then I'll go have a look at the results of the blood work. In about ten minutes, we'll take you to rehab for an evaluation. Dr. Briggs told me that prior to the incident you were experiencing problems with your vision. It would break up? Hard to focus?

JORDAN: I need new glasses.

EARL: She changed her glasses prescription three times last year. It didn't help.

WOODRUFF: Numbness in your arms or legs?

JORDAN: They slept a little.

EARL: Every fifteen minutes her legs went to sleep. I finally got her a walker.

WOODRUFF: How is that working out? The walker.

JORDAN: Now she's trying to push a wheelchair on me.

WOODRUFF: Have you suffered mood swings? Depression, fatigue?

JORDAN: No.

EARL: They had her on lithium, but she stopped taking it.

JORDAN: I couldn't wake up to do my work.

WOODRUFF: Any unusual stress lately?

EARL: She's taken on an extra class.

WOODRUFF: I'd just like to have a look at your eyes. Follow the light.

[WOODRUFF *puts a hand on* JORDAN's *forehead to hold her head still and moves the light from side to side as* JORDAN *tracks it with her eyes.*]

You've cut out caffeine?

JORDAN AND EARL: Yes.

WOODRUFF: Good.

EARL: She smokes two packs of cigarettes a day.

JORDAN: I *buy* two packs of cigarettes a day.

EARL: And she takes at least three shots of Cutty Sark every evening.

WOODRUFF: I don't have to tell you what that's doing to your immune system, do I?

JORDAN: I've heard the lecture.

EARL: I've taken the liberty of giving her some dietary supplements and making herbal teas to try to counteract the damage.

WOODRUFF: Are there any new sensations or sudden lack of sensations you may have developed since the incident?

JORDAN: No.

WOODRUFF: Any new feelings or emotions?

JORDAN: No.

WOODRUFF: Nothing?

JORDAN: No.

[*Beat.*]

WOODRUFF: I can't be of much use to you, Ms. Jordan, if you won't help me a little here.

[*Pause.*]

EARL: Thank you, Dr. Woodruff.

WOODRUFF: Okay, then . . . I'll be back in about ten minutes.

EARL: We'll be ready.

WOODRUFF [*to* JORDAN, *cheerfully*]: By the way, congratulations. You must be very pleased.

[*She exits.*]

JORDAN: Pleased? Pleased about what?

EARL: Let me get this straight. You've seen the paper, but you haven't actually read it, have you?

JORDAN: Strom Thurmond had another baby?

EARL: Barbara.

JORDAN: What?

EARL: Listen up.

[*She retrieves the paper, opens it, creases it, and tosses it on the table between them. She stabs her finger at an article.*]

You are being awarded the Presidential Medal of Freedom.

[*Pause.*]

JORDAN: By whom?

EARL: By the president of the United States, I would assume.

JORDAN: What for?

[EARL *surrenders.*]

EARL: Where's your comb?

JORDAN: In the bathroom, on the sink, right next to my purple toothbrush.

EARL: In other words, you haven't found your comb, either?

JORDAN: I want my slippers.

EARL: I'll get them.

JORDAN: No. *I'll* get them.

[*She rises with difficulty and, using the walker, shuffles toward the bathroom.*]

And thanks for letting me do all the talking, by the way.

EARL: It was all I could do to keep my mouth shut.

JORDAN: I'm sure.

EARL: You say you can't hear what John Ed is trying to say? Why does that make total sense?

[PATTEN *enters, pushing a cart. While he sets the stage the way he wants it, he keeps a watchful eye out for his "heart."*]

Barbara?

JORDAN: What?

EARL: If you go on like this, you're not going to make it.

[HEART *enters, distracted, hurriedly pushing a bicycle.*]

JORDAN: Spare me.

PATTEN [*speaking to* HEART]: I didn't think you were going to make it.

EARL [*as she attends to the scene change*]: I am tired of your sarcasm and denial.

HEART: I'm here.

JORDAN [*to* EARL]: And I am tired of this conversation.

HEART: [*to* PATTEN]: What do you need?

[PATTEN *unloads the cart and sets the stage.*]

EARL: I did not sign up for this.

[*She finishes her part of the scene change and exits.* JORDAN *remains onstage looking at* PATTEN.]

PATTEN: These rags need tying up.

[HEART *lays her bike on its side.*]

ACT 1

SCENE 1

[*Summer 1948. The Fourth Ward, a pocket of black America that borders the heart of Houston. All that is required to set up* PATTEN*'s junkyard are rags, a couple of crates to sit on, and perhaps a tire swing suspended on a rope.*]

PATTEN: You got a standard on that bike?

HEART: Yes, sir.

PATTEN [*gently*]: You'll wreck the finish if you don't use it. That's a Schwinn, child.

HEART: Sorry. We're tying up bundles?

PATTEN: Old Man Moses is coming later to take them to the scale.

[*She parks the bike upright.* JORDAN *exits with the walker.* PATTEN *suddenly sees the girl's condition: her hair is still shining and fixed, but her clean dress has been smudged with dirt. One elbow is badly scraped, and a thin line of blood has trickled down from her right knee and is staining her anklet.*]

What happened to you? Is that blood?

HEART: I took a tumble.

PATTEN: You fell off your bike?

HEART: I fell.

PATTEN [*calling offstage*]: Mama!

HEART: No, sir, please! It's just a scrape or two. Don't call Mama!

PATTEN: You're bleeding!

HEART: Don't call Mama.

PATTEN: Why shouldn't I call your grandmother?

HEART: She'll just make an ungodly fuss.

PATTEN: Nothing she does is ungodly, child. I thought you knew that by this time.

HEART: I don't need any kind of fuss at the moment.

PATTEN: What *do* you need?

HEART: Your handkerchief will do.

[*He surrenders it.*]

Thank you.

[*She takes it, and he watches as she presses it to her stinging knee. He fetches a bucket filled with water and sits beside her. He takes the handkerchief, dips it in water, and gently dabs at her knee and elbow.*]

PATTEN: I shouldn't have got you that bike. You're still too small for it.

HEART: I didn't fall off the bike.

PATTEN: What happened then?

HEART: You fed Pidge and Dewey yet?

PATTEN: They wait for you on Sunday.

HEART [*rising quickly*]: Should I go—

PATTEN: Your grandmother gave them a few sweet potatoes. They can wait their turn for you, but I can't. Sit beside me for a little and work. Dewey's getting fat anyway.

HEART: Everything that's old gets fat. Especially mules.

PATTEN: I'm old. You see any fat on me?

[*She lifts her eyes toward him for a brief moment and goes back to her work.*]

HEART: I'm not saying whether I do or don't.

PATTEN: And here I am thinking I'm in the prime of my life.

[*They work.*]

You hungry? Because I went to the back door at Matthew Garner's and got us a bag full of reg'lars. He's getting stingy, old Matt. I pay for them, but the bag gets lighter every week. Mama's keeping them warm for you.

HEART: No, sir, I'm not hungry. Just yet.

PATTEN: Say the word.

HEART: Pretty soon.

PATTEN: Here's the money Moses gave me last Monday. Put it away.

[*He chucks a roll of twenties at her.*]

HEART [*picking up the roll*]: Mother thinks we should be putting your money in the bank.

PATTEN: Tell her that you're my bank.

HEART: Well, I've got a lot of money stuffed in odd places.

PATTEN: Toss that rag. It's too dirty.

[HEART *does so.*]

Hand me your twine. And let go of that knife.

HEART [*flaming*]: I'm twelve years old!

PATTEN: I know how old you are, Heart. But the fact remains I would be derelict in my duty to your folks if I were to let you cut the rope with that knife, especially since I know how you're going to do it.

HEART: How do you know how I'm going to do it?

PATTEN: Because I'm *looking.* You got your left fist on the twine, and you're about to pull up with the right. That razor will make a swift and accurate beeline for your eye . . . It hasn't got a thing to do with how old you are. It's about how smart you are.

HEART: I'm smart.

PATTEN: No. You're wise. Smart will come later.

[*Beat.*]

You think you'll do me any good in my old age with your right eye gone?

[*She surrenders the knife.*]

Handle first. You've shed enough blood for one day.

[*She turns the handle toward him.*]

I think I asked you for that twine, too.

[*She hands it to him. He cuts twine for her.*]

So how come you're so late?

HEART: I met up with some friends. We were playing a game.

PATTEN: Not those children in the next row, I hope. You don't need to be associating with those children.

HEART: Not them. Some others.

PATTEN: You don't need to be like them.

HEART: Like what?

PATTEN: Ignorant.

HEART: I wasn't playing with those ignorant children.

PATTEN: That's good.

HEART: I was playing with some *other* ignorant children.

PATTEN: She thinks she is so clever, Lord.

[*Beat.*]

HEART: How come you don't go to church?

PATTEN: I got my church right here.

HEART: I don't see no church.

PATTEN [*correcting her*]: Any church. What do you see?

HEART: Your backyard. Rags, newspapers, tin cans, and manure. No pulpit.

Only busted chairs. No praying. Just chat. And we never dress up back here. Mother makes me put on my oldest clothes to come see you. Nobody testifies.

PATTEN: Those are your oldest clothes?

HEART: We tie up bundles and eat reg'lars.

PATTEN: And that worries you, does it?

HEART: I'm not worried.

PATTEN: What are you, then?

[*Beat.*]

HEART: It's a stupid game anyway.

PATTEN [*it takes him a moment to rewind*]: Then don't play it.

HEART: They make me.

PATTEN: Who makes you, baby? I can fix it so you don't have to play any game you don't want to.

HEART: They don't make me, exactly. But they can't play the game if I don't.

PATTEN: What is this game called, if you don't mind my asking?

HEART: The Sinner Game. The Christians and the Sinner.

PATTEN: Just one sinner?

HEART: I'm the only one who can play the sinner.

PATTEN: Why are you the only one?

HEART: Because I'm the only one who ain't been saved yet.

PATTEN: What happens in this game? Do they make you testify or what?

HEART: They throw me into the hellfires, which means they push me down into the ditch beside Lawson's Gas Station.

PATTEN [*quietly*]: They do what?

HEART: I have to scream and beg for my soul. Then they laugh or pray or weep. Whatever suits 'em.

PATTEN: It's always you they push into the ditch?

HEART: Today it got a little . . . out of hand.

PATTEN [*rising*]: How about you and me take a walk?

HEART: A walk?

PATTEN: Let's take a little stroll on over to the next row!

HEART: You won't fix anything. Even if you could, we'd have to stroll a lot farther than the next row. I don't know what the big deal is about being saved. It doesn't turn you into a different person, does it?

PATTEN: Not that I've noticed.

HEART: Anyway, you haven't been saved, so I don't suppose I want to be, either. It's a matter of principle, I guess you could say. I'm . . . you know . . . I'm with you.

PATTEN: On what grounds have you decided that "you're with me"?

[*She doesn't understand the question.*]

And for your information, I have, too, gotten myself saved.

HEART [*surprised*]: When? When did you? Where was I?

PATTEN: You were down in El Paso herding sheep.

HEART: Grandpa.

PATTEN: It's my way of saying it was years before you were born. I got myself saved, and since I was saved, I felt I could relax a bit.

HEART: So if I get myself saved, I can relax?

PATTEN: Well—

HEART: Maybe not go to church quite so often?

PATTEN: Now, don't get me into trouble here, Heart. I simply choose not to attend formal church services. And nobody misses me.

HEART: I bet Mama misses you at church.

PATTEN: Your grandmother does *not* miss me at church. She's nervous as a tick whenever I go. I'm a hopeless old sinner, and she's happy I'm not sitting beside her belching and rolling my eyes.

HEART [*on her feet*]: Who told you that you were a hopeless old sinner?

PATTEN: What?

HEART: Nobody's gonna call you a hopeless old sinner!

PATTEN: And nobody did. Settle down, child.

HEART: You're not a hopeless old sinner!

PATTEN: Okay. I'm young and pure.

HEART: Well, you're not!

PATTEN [*in total surrender*]: No, I'm not. I'm fine. I'll see you in heaven, okay?

HEART: Just tell me, and I can arrange it—

PATTEN: Darling child, you don't have to arrange nothin'. I am not a hopeless old sinner, and you do not have to arrange a thing.

HEART: Neither do you, then.

PATTEN: What?

HEART: If you can take care of yourself, so can I. You don't need to worry about ignorant children.

PATTEN [*quietly*]: Lord, I am in deep water here.

[*Beat.*]

HEART: So you actually went and got yourself saved without telling me.

PATTEN: My mama saw to it in pretty short order.

HEART: Why did you stop going? What's wrong with church?

PATTEN: There's not a thing wrong with church, Heart. Not a thing.

HEART: Then why don't you go?

PATTEN: I don't go like your folks do. I don't go like my own woman does. I'd rather give up the ghost than listen to your grandpa Jordan carry on the way he does.

HEART: He has a mighty fine speaking voice. That's what they say.

PATTEN: He has a fine voice. Just makes me itch all over, on those special occasions when I hear it.

HEART: Easter Sunday is the only time you hear it. I go one hundred and fifty-five times more than you do, every single year.

PATTEN: You've figured it out, have you?

HEART: And it's not fair if you ask me.

PATTEN: Nobody's asking, have you noticed?

HEART: Why does he make you itch?

PATTEN: I don't possess his particular slant on the matter of faith. I deal in weights and measurements. Just like a Supreme Court justice.

HEART: How are you like a Supreme Court justice?

PATTEN: A judge weighs in on fundamental disagreement. I weigh in on people's trash. I figure me and any judge you can name are in the same business. Now, I don't actually have a certificate, a degree that tells the world exactly who I am and what I know. My diploma comes from the school of hard knocks, heavy weights, and accurate measurements.

HEART: I don't think judges talk as much as you do. You sound like a preacher to me.

PATTEN: So be it.

HEART: I think I mostly resemble your side of the family.

PATTEN: Why?

HEART: Church is a misery. I never thought of it giving me the itches, like you said. It gives me the fidgets. I love to sing there. I love to sing. But I don't just want to sing the hymns. I want to sing the blues, too. Know what my favorite song to sing is?

PATTEN: All ears.

[*A smile plays across* HEART's *face. She makes room for herself; moves and sings with abandon one stanza and the chorus of a blues song like "Money Honey." When she finishes,* PATTEN *approves and applauds.*]

That was just fine!

HEART: The message of that song is not, I guess, such a fine thing, because when I tried to sing it at Good Hope Baptist, Rose Mary and Bennie told me to pipe down.

PATTEN: Well, you can sing it here, Heart. Anytime you want.

[*Beat. Suddenly, he pipes up, remembering the song and repeating the verse. She listens and watches him, taking him in with wide eyes. When his voice fades, he chuckles.*]

[*Mostly to himself*] And *that's* how you sing the blues.

[*He looks at her, smiling, but his rendition of the song has stirred something in her, and she's open and ready to get down to business.*]

HEART: You know how people write or say, maybe, "She's black in her heart," "It was a black day," "He was a black guard"?

PATTEN [*pronouncing it for her*]: Blackguard.

HEART [*wrinkling her face*]: Bla-gurd?

PATTEN: Never mind, just go.

HEART: So Bennie's telling me the other day about the first thing Daddy said when he saw me newborn. She said it made Ma'am cry. You know what I'm talking about?

PATTEN: What did Bennie say?

HEART: You know the thing I mean?

PATTEN: I might.

HEART: Is it true?

PATTEN: You surprised him, Heart. You were an intense person, even newborn.

HEART: Did Ma'am cry?

PATTEN: Your mother cries if her shoes don't match her dress.

HEART: So she cried.

PATTEN: Your daddy wasn't thinking straight. He hurt your mother's feelings.

HEART: Bennie thinks he was hoping for a boy, and then I came out. Not only was I a girl, I was too black. Bennie says he asked, "Why is she so black?" Was that my first sin?

PATTEN: No.

HEART: Why *am* I so black?

PATTEN: Because you're perfect.

HEART: You think my heart is black?

PATTEN: You're doing something with that word "black." Making some judgment which I forbid you to make. You know old Bill down the street?

HEART: Who collects spiders. And he's got a funny tooth. He looks like a rhino.

PATTEN: Bill, who collects spiders and has a funny tooth—

HEART: I don't like to say it, but he looks like a wild boar or something.

PATTEN: The man has an upside-down tooth! That's not the point! Is Bill too white? Does he have a white heart? Can we make any assumptions at all about Bill's good or bad behavior because he happens to be a white man?

HEART: Then why did my daddy say it? Like it was something bad? I don't think he likes me, even to this day. I'm always the one in trouble with him.

PATTEN: Not because you're too black. Because you're too smart.

HEART: No, I'm "wise. Smart will come later," right?

PATTEN: That kind of remark is exactly what I mean. That kind of remark drives your father crazy . . . "Too black." There's no such thing. It was just your father's foolishness, and I know you can find it in your heart to forgive him.

HEART: It's not just him that thinks so.

PATTEN: Do those children tease you about your color?

HEART: Not just them.

PATTEN: Who else?

HEART: My teacher is colorstruck.

PATTEN: She's what?

HEART: That's what I call it. I've noticed that if she thinks your skin "has no light in it," if you have to get your hair combed with Excellento, she thinks you're maybe a little backward, too.

PATTEN: What sort of pinhead teaches children to put down one of their own!

HEART [overlapping]: That's why I like to prove the teacher wrong every chance I get. She doesn't like that.

PATTEN [overlapping]: As if we don't have enough trouble on our hands.

HEART: Let's face facts.

PATTEN: Let's do.

HEART: I'm awful black. And I'm always the one in trouble.

PATTEN: And you think there's a correlation there, do you?

HEART: Grandpa.

PATTEN: You think those two things are related to each other?

HEART: I don't know. I'm only asking! Bennie thinks I'm like you, too. She says you was always in trouble, too.

PATTEN: Your sister has been a busy girl.

HEART: She's busier than anybody.

PATTEN: I'm beginning to believe it.

HEART: She said she heard Mother and Daddy talking late one night. She said they were talking about Mother's brother, the one that died while you were in the penitent.

PATTEN: Your sister told you about that?

HEART: Bennie believes in digging for the truth.

PATTEN: Yes, indeed, Bennie is the busiest girl I know. So, come again? You figure you're like me because we both—

HEART: Cause trouble. We're troublesome creatures. And very black.

[PATTEN's *head drops for a moment while he tries to unravel the meaning of her words. She grows still and watches him.*]

PATTEN: Heart . . . I did cause trouble at one time in my life, it's true. I'm going to tell you about it because I think you're old enough to hear it, and I don't want you to hear it from anybody but me. I want the facts straight, you understand?

HEART: Yes.

PATTEN: You can make up your own mind then, once and for all, whether or not I'm a hopeless old sinner.

HEART: Okay.

PATTEN: And it's not the penitent. It's the penitentiary. Prison. Back when your grandmother was as young and pretty as a filly, and your mother was a little girl, I owned a candy store over there on San Felipe Street. I was sitting up there late one night doing some inventory, and nursing a little gin, when I heard someone calling from the street. This person said he needed change, so I opened the door to him. The day's receipts were stacked on the middle of the counter. Just as I get around behind it, he makes a jump for the money. He rakes it into his hand and bolts out the door. I have a gun in the back room, so I go and get it. When I come out of the shop, I am fit to be tied. I see this fellow running down Heiner Avenue. I take off after him and stumble over the streetcar tracks. Like I say, I have a little gin working on me. I pick myself up and I hear somebody call, "Catch that nigger. He's got a gun." Next thing I know somebody is shooting at me and I'm running as fast as I can. Just as I round the corner on Saulnier and see there's no place to go, I stop, turn around, and put my hands up high in the air. And whosn'ever he is, once I turn to face him, with my hands high up, he takes the opportunity to put a bullet through my left palm. It went in here.

[*He shows her his left palm.*]

And it came out here.

[*He shows her the back of his left hand.*]

By this time I'm pretty—I am a little agitated by this time. I swear to you, Heart, I don't remember any of what happened next, but they tell me I started to shoot. Turns out I was shooting at a white policeman, and I hit him, too. Hit him three times.

HEART: Did you kill him?

PATTEN: No, missy, the Lord was looking after both of us that night.

[*Beat.*]

That policeman lived to testify against me in court before a jury who convicted me pretty much on his word alone.

HEART: A white policeman, a white judge and jury.

PATTEN: Before you draw any conclusions, guess who it was sitting every day in the court ready to testify as to my character and my behavior that night. Guess who it was that raised a five-thousand-dollar bond to get me out of jail so I could continue to support my family while the appeals were pending.

HEART: Who?

PATTEN: The white shopkeepers on San Felipe Street. White men and women and their children were sitting in that courtroom every day. On my side. Old Man Moses weighs one bale of newspapers at a time, doesn't he?

HEART: Yes, sir.

PATTEN: That's just how you take the measure of a human heart. One individual at a time. Seven years into my sentence, Ma Ferguson got herself elected governor. Her first act was to pardon a goodly number of Negro convicts who had been wrongly convicted. Ten years to the day of my incarceration, I was among the first to be set free. A full, unconditional pardon. So there. Now you know. What do you think of your old grandpa now?

HEART: I still like you just fine.

PATTEN: Good.

HEART: Only more so.

PATTEN: All right, then. Came out, went into the junk business, and I have been a cheerful man ever since. Happy ending. I always liked being in business for myself, especially after my experience in prison. Never wanted a soul between me and the Lord. What have I always told you?

HEART [*by rote*]: "The world is not a playground but a schoolroom. Life is not a holiday but—"

PATTEN: Yeah, I've told you that, but I'm thinking about something else.

HEART: "I take the narrow way with the resolute few who dare to go through—"

PATTEN [*laughing*]: I have filled your head. No, no. I was thinking this time about "You just trot your own . . ."

HEART: "Trot your own horse and don't get into the same rut as everybody else."

PATTEN: Do what you're going to do and don't get sidetracked. That's the path Christ took. You don't need a soul in this world operating between you and the Power. It's the Power, Barbara, that sets you free. Don't waste your gifts.

HEART: What gifts?

PATTEN [*enthusiastically*]: Have you ever heard your mother speak?

HEART: She talks all the time.

PATTEN: I mean at prayer meetings.

HEART: Yes, sir, at meetings.

PATTEN: Do you understand she has more power in her voice when she's simply chatting with a neighbor than Grandpa Jordan has during his most inspired orations?

HEART: She's pretty loud, yes, sir.

PATTEN: I'm not talking volume; I'm talking resonance. Resounding intellect, resounding spirit, resounding voice. Her voice can bring people to their knees, you understand.

HEART: It's done that to me on many occasions—but it's the palm of her hand you've *really* got to watch out for.

PATTEN: Are you listening to me?

HEART [*slightly offended*]: Yes, sir.

PATTEN: Your mother was meant for bigger things, and she didn't heed the call. I was almost out of hope, until you came into this world. You've got something your mother never had.

HEART: What's that?

PATTEN: Perspective. Your mother saw the world from deep in the valley. That was my fault, I expect. You see the world from a mountaintop.

HEART: I've never seen a mountain in my life.

PATTEN: Just look beneath your feet.

[*Beat.*]

HEART: Mama's right.

PATTEN: About what?

HEART: You *are* a perplexing individual.

PATTEN [*looking toward the back door*]: Well, it takes one to know one.

HEART: I'm gonna go get myself saved, I expect. I'm not gonna get saved because you did, because I wouldn't jump off a building if you did, much as I like to follow you around.

PATTEN: That's a mercy.

HEART: I'm not gonna get saved because I always have to play the one bankrupt sinner who gets herself cast into the eternal hellfires. Okay, maybe—maybe that's a little bit of the reason. If I get myself saved, it's sort of an insurance policy for after I'm dead. Jesus can just look in the book and see I got myself saved, and that'll be one particular load off my mind.

PATTEN: Mine, too.

HEART: My sisters say they are "happy in the Lord." I'd like to get me some of that happiness. For a long time I've felt sad in the Lord. It's not like the Lord bears a grudge against me.

PATTEN: Course not.

HEART: I don't think he's even *noticed* me! Getting myself saved might make me "smart" enough to handle a knife. Maybe my daddy wouldn't talk against me. There are a hundred reasons why I could go and get myself saved, but there's only one that makes sense to me. You know what it is?

PATTEN: I can't imagine.

HEART: Because I just plain *feel* like it.

PATTEN: You "just plain feel like it"? That's it?

HEART: Yes, sir, that's the heart of the matter. It feels like the right thing to do. I figure a body can't know a thing in this world until she experiences it for herself. Experiences it for her own sorry self.

PATTEN: Stop talking, Barbara.

HEART: Okay.

[*She looks at him, expecting something.*]

PATTEN: Jesus himself entered the Temple at age twelve.

HEART: That settles it, then. Next Sunday I'm gonna march my bankrupt bag of bones to the front of the church and get myself saved.

PATTEN: I may put on a tie and come to church just to see such a glorious sight.

HEART: Really?

PATTEN: I make no promises.

HEART: Don't come if you don't want to. It's up to you.

PATTEN: There is one thing your Grandfather Jordan and I have in common, after all. One small, pure, decent thing.

HEART [*rubbing an eye*]: What?

PATTEN: Don't ask what, ask who. Stop rubbing your eyes like that. I think you might need glasses.

HEART: No, I don't.

PATTEN: That's what your mother said until she ran into that stone wall with her bike.

HEART: I see fine.

PATTEN: Then find your way to your grandma's kitchen, wash yourself up, and bring us back some of those reg'lars. After we're fed, we'll find some oats for those fat old mules.

HEART: Yes, sir.

PATTEN: Barbara!

[HEART *stops and* JORDAN *enters.*]

Take your shoes off on the porch. Your grandmother's on the warpath. If you think church is a misery, try crossing her newly waxed kitchen floor in anything but your stocking feet.

HEART: Yes, sir.

[HEART *kicks off her shoes, picks them up, and hollers "Mama" as she exits. Mama calls back, mentioning something about shoes.* JORDAN *watches* PATTEN. *He sits for a moment. He looks at the blood on his handkerchief and takes a deep breath. Then he puts the handkerchief in his breast pocket and goes to work clearing the stage.*]

SCENE 2

[PATTEN *places the stools into his cart and pushes off. The lights go down on all except* JORDAN *as* HEART *enters with an easel.* DUNN *enters and moves the table back into position.* STRAUSS *enters. He places a portrait on the easel and leans back admiring it as* JORDAN *continues to speak.*]

JORDAN: "Who speaks for the Negro? . . . The Negro has always had the faith, an almost blind faith, in what the country promised to become. The Negro stands, silhouetted against a thriving and abundant America, and his presence, his very presence on the American scene, speaks for itself. What does he want? He wants 'in.' He wants you to hear him, understand his condition. He feels that if you do this—if you really listen to him as he speaks through his presence and understand his condition—he feels that you will save him. And that in the process of saving him you will also save this country. And in the process of saving this country . . . you save yourselves."

[HEART *hands a set of files to* JORDAN *and then exits.*]

ACT 2

[*Winter 1975. U.S. Congresswoman* JORDAN's *inner office.* STRAUSS, *chairman of the Democratic National Committee, stands alone admiring a portrait that dominates the room. It depicts an elderly black gentleman bending tenderly toward a tiny black girl.* JORDAN *addresses him, her arms full of files.*]

JORDAN: Chairman Strauss.

STRAUSS: Barbara.

JORDAN: I'm sorry.

STRAUSS: Don't be. I'm early.

JORDAN: I've been running all day. I can't seem to get hold of the time. How are you?

STRAUSS: This painting wasn't here the last time I stopped by, was it?

JORDAN: I don't know. I've had it awhile. I commissioned Polsky Morgan to do it for me. You like it?

STRAUSS: It's beautiful.

JORDAN: It makes this office feel like home. Did Bud offer you something to—

STRAUSS: He did. No thanks. I've had enough coffee for one day.

JORDAN: Have a seat.

STRAUSS: Why are you limping?

JORDAN: I've got some bum cartilage in my right knee. I was hoping the weight loss would take care of it.

STRAUSS [*as she puts files away*]: You do look svelte.

JORDAN: Tell that to my knee.

STRAUSS: You are a shadow of your former self.

JORDAN: When the press corps stops using descriptive words like "presence" and "carriage" and starts using words like "massive" and "hulking," you know it's time for a little spinach. Also, Nancy promised me a bike if I took off sixty pounds by Labor Day.

STRAUSS: You dare ride a bike in Washington?

JORDAN: As a matter of fact I don't. By Labor Day I had lost only fifty-seven pounds. I never got the bike.

STRAUSS: She didn't buy you the bike?

JORDAN: She wouldn't budge. It's nice to see you again.

STRAUSS: You were three pounds off the mark, and she didn't—

JORDAN: And people think *I'm* tough.

STRAUSS: Good Lord.

JORDAN [*picks up the phone and holds out the receiver*]: You want to call her in Texas, Bob? Because I still really want the bike.

STRAUSS: Maybe I'll drop her a line.

JORDAN: Smart man.

[*She hangs up the phone and dives for a cigarette.*]

What can I do for you?

STRAUSS: Well, I don't know. We'll see.

JORDAN: Oh, shit.

STRAUSS: What?

JORDAN: You've quit, haven't you?

STRAUSS: That's okay, go ahead.

JORDAN: No, no. I won't corrupt you.

[*She returns the cigarette to the pack.*]

How did you finally manage it?

STRAUSS: You've got to *want* to quit. That's really the key.

JORDAN: Well, now, there's got to be another key, Bob, because I will never "want" to quit, I can tell you that right now.

STRAUSS: Lung cancer is another good way.

JORDAN: Thanks, Bob.

[*She eases back in her chair.*]

Okay. So what gives?

STRAUSS: I've come from Ed Williams.

JORDAN: Is this about John Connally?

STRAUSS: What have you heard?

JORDAN: Will he be indicted?

STRAUSS: It looks that way.

JORDAN: Just when I think I've heard it all—

STRAUSS: Watergate is over, Barbara. This is different.

JORDAN: What does he want from me?

STRAUSS: Justice. Now I know how you feel about the man.

JORDAN: Wait a minute—

STRAUSS: Ed Williams will be representing him.

JORDAN [*overlapping*]: How can *I* give the man justice?

STRAUSS: Ed asked me to stop by and see if I could enlist your help.

JORDAN: To do what?

STRAUSS: He wants you to intercede as a character witness on John's behalf during the proceedings.

[*She hoots.*]

I'm not kidding, Barbara.

[*She chuckles. He smiles ruefully and shakes his head.*]

JORDAN: Why me?

STRAUSS [*reminding her*]: "My faith in the Constitution is whole, it is complete, it is total. I am not going to sit here and be an idle spectator"—

JORDAN: All right.

STRAUSS: That speech made quite an impact on this country, Barbara.

JORDAN: It was nothing but common sense.

STRAUSS: Common sense is hard to come by on the Hill.

JORDAN: Lyndon once gave me a great bit of advice: "When it comes to asking for a political favor, don't go for it unless it's already in your pocket." I assume Ed Williams understands that piece of wisdom.

STRAUSS: I believe you could say he's playing a long shot. I told him you might kill the messenger.

JORDAN: That must be the reason he didn't come and speak for himself.

STRAUSS: No doubt.

JORDAN: What makes Edward Bennett Williams think I would lift a finger to help his smug son-of-a-bitch client?

STRAUSS: Here we go.

JORDAN: I'll tell you why he wants me up there. D.C. is a black town, that's why, and a D.C. jury is going to be front and center.

STRAUSS: Wait—

JORDAN: I've come a long way, Bob, sometimes in *spite* of my color and sometimes *because* of it. I put it to you: Have I *earned* my place in the spotlight or was it *handed* to me because of my pretty black face? This is a question designed to occupy fools. Therefore, it rarely troubles *me*. However, I do cringe, I do become slightly hostile, when a man who has ignored me for half a lifetime suddenly wants to rub my nappy little head for good luck. Can you understand that? The bells and whistles go off.

STRAUSS: Yes.

JORDAN: I actually have an intestinal response to the whole idea, Bob.

STRAUSS: I understand—

JORDAN: Apart from that, this is what my *reason* tells me about John Connally. He made *hay* after JFK was assassinated.

STRAUSS: What?

JORDAN: I never saw so much fund-raising come out of one bullet.

STRAUSS: Just a goddamned minute! That one bullet went through John Fitzgerald Kennedy's neck into John Connally's back! He fell into a pool of his own blood on Nellie's lap!

JORDAN: That one bullet did more for his political image than anything he ever did as the governor of Texas, and he wasn't even trying!

STRAUSS: Well, forget it! Just forget it!

[*He is on his feet, headed for the door.*]

JORDAN: Robert, stop.

STRAUSS: I don't believe I've ever heard anything so—

JORDAN [*overlapping*]: Come back!

STRAUSS: —so deliberately cold!

JORDAN: Robert, please!

STRAUSS: I know you've never seen eye to eye with John, but Jesus Christ!

JORDAN: Sit back down.

STRAUSS: He and Nellie went to hell and back!

JORDAN: I know; I know that!

STRAUSS [*overlapping*]: Look, I'll just tell Williams—

JORDAN: What time is it?

STRAUSS: What *time* is it?

JORDAN: Yes!

STRAUSS: You don't think *I* feel the pressure?

JORDAN: I am asking in the literal sense, Bob. My clock is on the fritz. Just look at your watch and tell me what time it is.

STRAUSS: Oh.

[*Beat.*]

Five-thirty. Why?

JORDAN: A little Scotch is going to make this meeting go a whole lot better.

STRAUSS: Damn straight. Break it out.

[*He works his way back into the room.*]

Good Lord!

[*Eventually he sits back down.*]

JORDAN: I was out of line, okay? I know he is your good friend, but if John Connally is asking Barbara Jordan for a favor, it gets complicated. Whether or not you've noticed, I have a considerable agenda on the Hill. I stand at the *bottom* of it pushing every bill I introduce *up* it! One false move could scrap my plans.

[*She hands him a drink. He takes it, swishes it around a bit.*]

STRAUSS: I would not put your career in jeopardy.

JORDAN: I don't give a shit about my career. You could wreck my work.

STRAUSS: You'll take a little heat from the Left.

JORDAN: Have you noticed my constituents happen to be pretty left-handed?

STRAUSS: I don't know if John is using your . . . pretty black face. Something happened to him after the assassination. He is a changed man . . . a bit more self-preoccupied, perhaps. A little more conservative.

JORDAN: A tad more Republican.

STRAUSS: Who do you think you're talking to? Do you suppose for a minute that fact is wasted on me? John believes we Democrats have all lost our minds. I believe he thought he was following his integrity into the Republican Party.

JORDAN: Right into Richard Nixon's camp? Now there's some integrity, mm, mm, *mmm.*

STRAUSS: I'm telling you—

JORDAN: John urged Nixon to burn the Watergate tapes. He advised Nixon to bomb Hanoi. He reminded the president that nuclear weapons were an option.

STRAUSS: Nixon's program to stimulate the economy in '71? Everybody on the Hill knew that was John's idea. Did anyone ever hear John take credit for its success? Nixon used John the way he used everybody else, but John couldn't see it.

JORDAN: "The only case on record of a man swimming *toward* a sinking ship."

STRAUSS: Which only bolsters my contention that he is innocent! He had no idea what was happening. This indictment is nothing but vicious political maneuvering. It's a travesty of everything this country—

[JORDAN *grabs her Scotch and crawls under her desk.* STRAUSS *stops and looks under the desk, then stands.*]

What are you doing?

JORDAN: In high school I learned this was the appropriate response to bullshit, both foreign and domestic.

STRAUSS [*laughing*]: You are such a rotten bitch, Jordan.

[*He comes around the desk and looks at her.*]

Come out.

JORDAN: Keep talking, buddy. Now that I'm safe, I'm all ears.

STRAUSS [*peering under the desk*]: I'd love to. But if I did, your secretary would take this golden opportunity to bring in a gaggle of Texas tourists, and then where would we be?

JORDAN: Good Lord, you're probably right.

STRAUSS: Are you okay? Do you need help?

JORDAN: My right leg is asleep.

STRAUSS: Let me help you. How can your leg be asleep?

JORDAN: Sue me. It's sound asleep.

STRAUSS: You might need surgery on that knee.

JORDAN: Thanks. I'm fine. Where were we?

STRAUSS: The special prosecutor has two witnesses—both highly suspect—and a safety deposit box full of cash. The serial numbers don't add up, and anyone could have tampered with the money. That's not evidence. They haven't one ounce of proof.

JORDAN: The special prosecutor seems to think it is.

STRAUSS: The special prosecutor is out of control. I know you think John abandoned the Democrats, but we fumbled the ball during two elections. George McGovern for president? That left-wing pacifist? The McGovernites stole the party in broad daylight. They made up new rules as they went along and didn't bother to tell the rest of us what they were.

JORDAN: We did not fumble in '68. They shot our nominee, remember?

STRAUSS: Point of clarification.

JORDAN: Okay.

STRAUSS: The Republicans did not shoot our nominee.

JORDAN: Details, details.

STRAUSS: Sixty-eight was a tragedy. Seventy-two was a travesty. John is convinced we're going to blow it again in '76. He believes that we have lost our way, that we are so involved appeasing the Far Left, we have forgotten about the folks in the middle who make up the majority of the party. And let's face it, to a certain extent, maybe we have. He believes that the only place a thinking man can go is . . . is to—

JORDAN: The other side.

STRAUSS: You don't think that takes courage? To leave your party because you have a private conviction, an absolute purpose?

JORDAN: Connally's "absolute purpose" is to win the presidency next year.

He will do it through the Democrats, the Republicans, or his local Moose Lodge, it won't matter. He will go with the machine that can get him elected. The man is desperate. Electability isn't everything!

STRAUSS: Chris Dixie tells a story about you.

JORDAN: Well, now, there's a head-spinning change of subject.

STRAUSS: You know how the story goes?

JORDAN: Probably not. Chris is a loose cannon.

STRAUSS: After you were defeated in your second bid for a seat in the Texas senate, he says he came to you, as your campaign manager—

JORDAN: Yes?

STRAUSS: —and he said, "Well, we've got the analysis for you."

JORDAN: Oh, that.

STRAUSS: And you said, "I'll give you the analysis: I didn't win. There, now we've got it analyzed."

JORDAN: It changes with the telling.

STRAUSS: One thing doesn't change. It demonstrates in plain English what every politician knows. Electability *is* everything! You can't do one damn thing for the people unless the people put you in office . . . You surely won't refuse to testify because the man changed horses in midstream?

JORDAN: Why won't I?

[*Beat.*]

STRAUSS: I swear to God, Barbara, if they convict him, I'll resign.

JORDAN: It's personal.

[*He acknowledges this quietly.* JORDAN *considers.*]

Well, then. I'd like to know what his plan for the nation is. It certainly doesn't include *my* constituents, the people who put *me* in office. As governor, Connally did everything he could to diminish black voter registration.

STRAUSS: Barbara, I don't think that was his—

JORDAN: I'm telling you, I was there! He did everything but shut down the businesses where we were signing up black people to vote. He killed one newspaper article after another. "Well, the Negroes don't really read the papers. What's the point?" You don't know from grass roots how hard we had to fight just to register voters!

STRAUSS: He had to fight, too, Barbara.

JORDAN: For his *right to vote?*

STRAUSS: He was picking cotton when he was five years old. He understands what poverty is. He did everything he knew how to do to raise up the people of Texas.

JORDAN: I took a trip across this country in 1954, with my all-black college debate team. We were on our way to debate Harvard! We slept in the car by the side of the road all the way to Boston. We had to pack our own food because there was no restaurant from Tulsa to Youngstown that would serve us . . . We couldn't get a drink from a water fountain in any public park. We had to pee in the woods, Robert. I'm not talking a hundred years ago. This was twenty-one years ago. I just wanted to eat. Just wanted to use the toilet. Wanted a clean bed at the end of the day . . . Who led the fight against public accommodations in Texas?

STRAUSS: Barbara—

JORDAN: If we're gonna talk, we're gonna talk truth!

STRAUSS: John did.

JORDAN: John Connally, you got that right. He fought Lyndon every step of the way when it came to civil rights.

[Beat.]

STRAUSS: What else?

JORDAN: Isn't that enough?

STRAUSS: It's enough, but I can tell it's not all.

JORDAN: Where were you when Martin was shot?

STRAUSS: Why? Where were you?

JORDAN: I was at the Texas state capitol, sharing an outdoor platform with John Connally.

STRAUSS: Jesus.

JORDAN: There was a crowd of about eight hundred Texans looking up at us. Election time, wouldn't you know it? In the middle of Connally's speech there were sudden stirrings in the crowd. Some message was working its way to the podium. It was written on a torn scrap of paper. Big John received it and stopped talking. I watched him read in silence. He looked up and said, "Martin Luther King has been shot. Reverend King has been shot and killed . . . Well," he said to the crowd, "well . . . those who live by the sword die by the sword."

[Silence.]

STRAUSS: I am at a loss.

JORDAN: Why?

STRAUSS: I can't presume to know what that did to you.

JORDAN: Go ahead. Presume. You can stand in my shoes from time to time. In fact, I insist that you do. I understand that you come at matters from a different vantage point. "E pluribus," sure. It's the "unum" thing we all seem to have trouble grasping! Why is that?

STRAUSS: I don't know.

[*Beat.*]

Why don't we just cut to the chase?

JORDAN: Why not?

STRAUSS: Do you know for a fact that John Connally took a bribe?

[*Pause.*]

JORDAN: No, I do not.

STRAUSS: Has he ever misled you or lied to you?

JORDAN: No.

STRAUSS: He ignored you when you were in the state senate, didn't he?

JORDAN: Completely.

STRAUSS: So you don't owe him any favors now that you've come to the House?

JORDAN: Absolutely not.

STRAUSS: That makes you a great character witness, you know. All you have to do is tell the truth. Make no mistake, if you testified on behalf of John's character, it would be one hell of a symbolic gesture.

JORDAN: I don't much care about that.

STRAUSS: I assume you do care whether or not he gets a fair trial.

JORDAN: There ain't no way he's gonna stage a political comeback, if that's what you're hoping.

STRAUSS: No . . . He's gone too far with Nixon.

[*She is quiet.*]

So, anyway. There's my pitch. Don't answer just yet. Take a week to think things through, and give my office a call.

JORDAN: I don't need a week.

STRAUSS: I don't think I can bear to hear you say no right now.

JORDAN: I'm not going to say no.

STRAUSS: You can   what?

JORDAN: I will testify on behalf of the character of John Connally.

STRAUSS: Don't toy with me.

JORDAN: Would you like another drink, Bob?

STRAUSS: Just my seat.

[*He sinks back into his chair.*]

You'll do it?

JORDAN: For various reasons. Interested?

STRAUSS: Very.

JORDAN: From what I know of the evidence, they may indict, but they have no legal grounds for a trial. The two witnesses are contradicting each other. Mind you, Connally doesn't have perfect recall, either, but when all is said and done, there is no hard proof.

STRAUSS: Nothing.

JORDAN: I also get stuck on the idea that a multimillionaire with his eyes on the presidency could be enticed by a few thousand dollars. That just doesn't make sense.

STRAUSS: Right.

JORDAN: If I testify, I'll score some points with conservatives, and since I love to build support across the board, that suits me just fine. It's no real reason to testify, but I just love gathering those chits.

STRAUSS [*laughing*]: Absolutely.

JORDAN: The main thing is, I'd really *love* to be the one to extricate that anti–civil rights corncob from out between Connally's lower cheeks. It's the charitable thing to do, I expect. I want to *see* the expression on his face when he looks around and realizes it is a black hand that is bringing him comfort. So . . . I'll do it. Okay, Bob?

STRAUSS: I have . . . no words.

JORDAN: I'll try to jot down a few ideas on how I might best serve the defense. I assume Williams will be wanting a few strategy sessions with me before I testify?

STRAUSS: You knew.

JORDAN: What?

STRAUSS: You knew you were going to say yes before I even came in here.

JORDAN: I had a pretty fair notion about why you were coming to see me, but I had by no means—

STRAUSS: You knew exactly what you were going to do. You knew it all along!

JORDAN: I thought I explained it to you, Bob: I'm new to the House. A lot of this political wagering goes over my head. I can't afford to fall behind. You would like another drink, wouldn't you?

STRAUSS: Why did you do that? Why did you let me go on as I did?

JORDAN: Good grief, Robert. I had no idea how you were going to pitch it. You might have said something to make me change my mind!

[*Pause.*]

STRAUSS [*rising*]: Thank you, Barbara. Thank you.

JORDAN: Are we square?

STRAUSS: We're square. [*Suddenly*] What are you doing tonight?

JORDAN: I'm going to the library.

STRAUSS: Let me take you to dinner instead.

JORDAN: Only if I pay.

STRAUSS: Barbara.

JORDAN: My treat.

STRAUSS: Forget it.

JORDAN: Some other time then.

STRAUSS: It's a meal.

JORDAN: Right. It's a meal.

STRAUSS: I hear you're tight with a dollar.

JORDAN: Let me take you to dinner; you can find out for yourself. I'll make the reservation.

STRAUSS: I'll stop back.

JORDAN: Around eight.

STRAUSS: Barbara?

JORDAN: Yes?

STRAUSS: The next time you start to wonder about how much you earned and how much was handed to you because of your "pretty black face"?

JORDAN: Yes?

STRAUSS: Give me a call. I know the answer.

[*He exits.* JORDAN *clears the glasses and the Scotch back to a small shelf that serves as her bar. As she does so, she addresses the audience.*]

JORDAN: "The spirit of liberty is the spirit which is not too sure that it is right; the spirit of liberty is the spirit which seeks to understand the minds of other men and women; the spirit of liberty is the spirit which weighs their interests alongside its own without bias; the spirit of liberty remembers that not even a sparrow falls to earth unheeded; the spirit of liberty is the spirit of Him who, nearly two thousand years ago, taught mankind the lesson it has never learned, but has never quite forgotten; that there may be a kingdom where the least shall be heard and considered side by side with the greatest."

[*The lights fade. Intermission.*]

ACT 3

[*The end of February 1990.* JORDAN *sits on her terrace. She is reading a news clipping. There are other news clippings stacked in a pile next to her. There is also a dirty ashtray and a pack of cigarettes and matches lying next to it. A four-pronged cane is propped beside her. A young woman stands quietly with her back to* JORDAN, *looking out at a garden.* EARL *enters with a tray with tea things and a plate of cookies. She puts it down on the table.*]

EARL: Here we are.

DUNN: Thank you, Nancy. You didn't have to go to the trouble.

EARL: No trouble.

JORDAN: Nancy loves to fuss. You've got to try her herbal tea. She makes it out of tree bark.

EARL: I do no such thing.

JORDAN: Tastes like tree bark.

EARL: And the horse you rode in on.

JORDAN [*picking up a cookie*]: What are these?

EARL: Fat-free oatmeal.

[JORDAN *immediately puts it back.*]

DUNN: The garden has changed so much since I was last here. It's beautiful.

EARL: This time of year there's not much to see. Are you sure I can't convince you to stay with us?

DUNN: I've got to meet some friends downtown for dinner. I can crash with one of them tonight. I've got an early flight in the morning.

[JORDAN *takes the last cigarette from a pack and crumples the pack.*]

EARL: Next time you're in town, give us a little notice.

DUNN: Will do.

EARL: Plan to spend a night or two.

DUNN: Okay.

EARL [*to* JORDAN]: Do you have everything you need?

[JORDAN *puts the cigarette between her lips and goes for the matches.*]

JORDAN: Thanks.

EARL: I'll let you two get on with it then.

[*She grabs the cigarette, snaps it, puts it in the ashtray.*]

Call me if you need me.

[*She exits.*]

DUNN: She looks great.

JORDAN: She holds up pretty well, yes.

DUNN: So. [*Referring to the clippings*] What's next? What do you think?

JORDAN: Well, you've managed to pick open a hornet's nest, I'll say that much.
Who is Charles Macon?

DUNN: A reporter from the *Inner City Press.*

JORDAN: What's his connection to you?

DUNN: He's an old college buddy. He went out of his way to get himself
assigned to my campaign. I had always supposed he was sympathetic.

JORDAN: Are these quotes accurate? Did you *say* these things?

DUNN: It was supposed to be off the record.

JORDAN: Good Christ! Didn't I teach you anything at all?

DUNN: The whole campaign had stopped for the day. We were all sitting
around headquarters watching the speech when Charles stopped by to join
the celebration. We listened to the speech, and then we sat there for the
rest of the evening talking about it. The guy had his feet up on my desk.
He was drinking my whiskey and debating right along with the rest of us.

JORDAN: How did you come to make these remarks?

DUNN: Mandela was acknowledging the ANC and seemed to be encouraging
the armed resistance. The whiskey had been flowing awhile, and I just . . .
said it. It never once dawned on me that Charles would write about it. This
was clearly an off-the-record discussion between friends.

JORDAN [*picks up a clipping and reads*]: You said, "We must put a stop to white
America's methodical genocide of the African American male"?

DUNN: I did.

JORDAN: And this? "The Nazis may have been quicker and more efficient, but
if African Americans don't take action, the end result will be the same."

DUNN: It was stupid. But it's done. I've gone on record with a denial, but
that alone won't bail me out. This could have a huge effect on my money
base.

JORDAN: You denied saying it?

DUNN: I had no choice. You don't understand. My polls were dazzling. I'm
not even sure now if I'll make it through the primary. Ballard is going to
work these quotes as long as he can. He's foaming at the mouth. I've got to

do something to stop him. Now . . . we have something on him, Barbara, and it's—

JORDAN: What?

DUNN: My campaign manager and some of the people who advise me think I should leak a certain piece of information about Ballard that we've been sitting on. I've resisted all along because I didn't want to run that sort of campaign. But now I'm wondering if I've been wise. What we know about this man could seriously affect his ability to lead.

JORDAN: So you have the goods on your "worthy opponent." I assume it has something to do with his personal life?

DUNN: How do you know?

JORDAN: Every time one politician questions another's "ability to lead," it turns out to be personal and almost always irrelevant. You didn't think it was ethical to use this information before, but suddenly, because you made a fool of yourself in the newspapers, now it's okay?

DUNN: Ballard isn't above going after me with his "family values" crap. He has actually dragged my divorce into the spotlight. Now he is using these remarks—remarks I made in private—to twist everything I've ever said in public. I need your support. The denial I've made to the press can only work if I also have someone with a certain amount of prestige to come to my defense. You're the only one I know who has the stature to put this matter to rest once and for all. You understand my position on the issues. It would take one phone call. One statement to the press.

JORDAN: I see. Yes, but from what I read here, your politics have shifted since we last spoke. [*Referring to an article*] You call for "all black juries when the defendant is black."

DUNN: The *law* calls for "a jury of one's peers." Seventy percent of the black prison population is serving time for nonviolent drug offenses. Black jurors bring a different perspective to these kinds of cases.

JORDAN [*turning back to the page*]: You also call for "separate schooling for young black males."

DUNN: I'm not the first to propose funding for independent schools for black youth. The time is coming.

JORDAN: It's the first I've heard of it.

DUNN: Our children need to be separated from a system designed by and for whites which encourages them to fail because of the color of their skin. The dropout rate for blacks is three times higher than it is for whites. Our male children, in particular, are in danger. They need sheltering.

JORDAN: I was sheltered as a kid. My whole world revolved around the Good

Hope Baptist Church. I came into contact with white people every once in a while, but I didn't pay them much mind. They were somewhere . . . over there. I thought I had it all. What I didn't realize was that I was always measuring my ambitions in terms of what a "black" person could do, rather than what "any" person could do. It wasn't until I went to law school in Boston that I understood my world had been limited. There were books, there was music and art, all kinds of ideas that were totally new to me—my education, my experience, my religion, my achievement, even my imagination were not what they could have been simply because . . . I was held separate.

DUNN: First black woman in the Texas senate, first black woman from the Deep South elected to the United States Congress. How can you poormouth the upbringing that gave you so much? If that's what a little segregation does for a person, then I say bring it on.

JORDAN: You will never convince me that the citizens of this country should live apart. It's wrong. No matter what kind of face you put on it or how many frills you attach to it, separate is not equal.

DUNN: You're African American, Barbara. You understand the—

JORDAN: I am no such thing. I am an unhyphenated American. It is my birthright. "African American" is simply a way of continuing separatist thinking.

DUNN: It is a way of embracing the history and cultural heritage that was denied us for centuries!

JORDAN: There are other, more appropriate ways to honor our cultural heritage. But when you insist on defining yourself as a separate entity, you ask to be treated as such.

DUNN: Barbara, you're a heretic.

JORDAN: I realize it's not a popular view, but that doesn't concern me in the least. I am an American woman who happens to be of African descent.

DUNN: You are a black woman, Barbara, and in America that comes with heavy baggage.

JORDAN: I've dropped the baggage. I'm done with the baggage. The question is, how do we proceed? And one thing of which I am thoroughly convinced is that the races must move on together.

DUNN: Why must they?

JORDAN: You took my ethics class. Do I even have to answer that?

DUNN: An abiding faith in constitutional law, I know. Has it ever occurred to you that the framers of the Constitution were eighteenth-century farmers?

JORDAN: And Papa was a rolling stone. What's your point?

DUNN: Don't you think it's possible that when they wrote it, they were not envisioning the kind of world we live in today?

JORDAN: No, I do not, but even if I did, that's what the amendment process is for. You can't do much better than the Bill of Rights. Articles 13, 14, 15, and 19 did a lot for you and me, kiddo.

DUNN: Barbara, I really didn't come here for a lecture. I'm asking for a simple favor. Will you make a statement in support of my campaign or not?

JORDAN: I don't think so, Julie.

DUNN: What?

JORDAN: No, I will not issue a statement in support of your candidacy.

DUNN: I don't believe this. You're supposed to be my friend.

JORDAN: I am your friend.

DUNN: I'm only asking for your endorsement.

JORDAN: I understand that.

DUNN: You're retired from politics. How can it possibly hurt you?

JORDAN: It can't.

DUNN: Then why?

JORDAN: Because I don't waste my time on hopeless politics. I never have.

DUNN: Is that what you think of me? That I'm hopeless?

JORDAN: When you compare white America to the Nazi regime, then I begin to wonder about your motives, Julie. Are you trying to bring us together or drive us apart?

DUNN: I told you, I denied saying it.

JORDAN: And don't think for a moment your denial won't come back to bite you in the ass, because you *did* say it. And if you truly feel this way, then I understand why you are driven toward isolationism, but I can't go there with you.

DUNN: Let me get this straight. You'll speak up for white guys like John Connally, but you will not speak up for me?

JORDAN: Apples and oranges.

DUNN: Not from where I stand. You don't like my politics? Fine. But you gave Robert Byrd, a former Klansman, for God's sake, a glowing introduction at the midterm convention. Are you telling me his politics were okay?

JORDAN: I wasn't endorsing him. I was simply introducing him.

DUNN: Ah, *that's* the difference.

JORDAN: I believe people can change, and you can help them change more quickly at times by defining them. Byrd called me after the introduction and acknowledged he owed me a debt of gratitude, and that I'd never be sorry. I wasn't, and I'm not.

DUNN: In other words, he had power, and you wanted some of it.

JORDAN: Slow down.

DUNN: You wanted power. The good old boys had it. I understand the nature of the beast. However, I find myself in the embarrassing position of having nothing I can offer you in return, except my gratitude.

JORDAN: Don't insult me!

[*Beat.*]

Don't do that.

[*Beat.*]

I understand you're in trouble back home, but . . .

DUNN [*overlapping*]: I'm sorry, Barbara. I'm sorry. It was so stupid. I understand. It was such a stupid thing to say!

JORDAN [*overlapping*]: It was a mistake, yes, but look on the bright side: you'll never make the same mistake again.

DUNN: Believe me! . . . I knew the guy was a reporter. Why shouldn't his job be as important to him as mine is to me? He had to write about it, of course he did. I should have kept my mouth shut.

JORDAN: Now we're getting down to it: you concede the remarks you made were stupid, not because the whiskey was flowing and you overreached yourself, but because you simply should have kept your beliefs to yourself? You were speaking with conviction?

[*Beat.*]

DUNN: Eight years in the public defender's office was a real wake-up call for me.

JORDAN: How so?

DUNN: These kids who come through my door every day—you know, they've been stopped by the police, put under arrest for possession of—well, fill in the blank—marijuana, crack, heroin. The first thing they do is let me know they are fucking tough. They can size up anybody. They sit down, they look at me, and they wait. They know most people think they are disposable. That's cool. The majority rules, okay, they get it. So they wait to see how I will cast my vote. Will I pay them with the usual lip service, or will I actually give a damn? If I somehow make the right connection, they will show me who they really are, the children that they really are: attentive, eager, ready to do better if they can. These are our children. Sometimes I just want to grab them and run.

JORDAN: So. Separate schools.

DUNN: I always hear the things you said when I speak. I've felt your guidance.

JORDAN: I have never guided you toward disunion. I taught you to use the power of reason. Fear and anger are the real enemy, and you are surrendering to both.

DUNN: How?

JORDAN: Do you understand that you cannot separate the political moves you make from your integrity? You can't fake integrity.

DUNN [*indicating the articles*]: I just told you I believe what I said.

JORDAN: Then stand by it, and take the hits. But you decide no, you can't! You call an honest reporter a liar. You consider smearing your opponent to get out of the stupid mess that you created. My God, I was never above playing politics, but I could always look myself in the eye the next morning.

DUNN: The man has no problem bringing my divorce into the public arena!

JORDAN: I don't care about him. Fuck him! . . . I'm talking about you now. I'm asking you to cut through the fear and the anger and the usual knee-jerk responses and use your powers of reason.

DUNN: Yes, I remember you were always big on the "power of reason." My *reason* tells me there is a methodical genocide taking place in this country, and it is aimed at the young African American male. I can sit here all night and give you reasonable explanations for why I think it. I can cite the AIDS crisis that continues unchecked, the government's pathetic inability to get drugs off the street. I can cite welfare reform, the inner-city land grab, the white fraternity of the lower courts, outrageous sentencing policies, and a penal code that is designed to provide cheap labor for big business! I've been on the front lines as a public defender for eight years, and I know what I know! I see it on a daily basis, and it is killing our race. My reason also tells me it is political suicide to speak of such things in public, even though it is the truth. And, yes, the truth makes me afraid and angry! It makes me very angry!

JORDAN: Stay angry and see where it gets you. I can tell you where it's going to get you, Julie.

DUNN: You may not like the words I use to describe—

JORDAN [*on her feet*]: Words have power! That's what you don't understand! When you assert that, taken together, these issues add up to a conscious wholesale slaughter of one race by another, of "genocide," then you don't understand the power of words! Once spoken, they are a moving force that can build up walls or break them down. They can engender love or hate! They are always a reflection of the person who utters them. If you use them carelessly, without forethought or reason, they come back to haunt you; they slip under the door in the middle of the night; they wake you and they hold you accountable. Julie, until you understand the power of the spoken word, you will be helpless to come to the defense of anyone, much less the young black defendants who walk through your door every day. Reason! Not passion!

DUNN: Barbara, I understand. I've made mistakes. I understand I have a lot to learn. However, I do believe I can be an effective congresswoman. I need you to speak for me. There's no one else I can turn to.

[JORDAN *shakes her head no. Beat.* DUNN *begins to pack up her things.*]

I should have known it was a fool's errand. People tried to tell me, but I thought I knew you better than they did.

JORDAN: Julie, wait—

DUNN: Would you please say good-bye to Nancy for me? I appreciate your time, Barbara, I really do.

JORDAN: Julie—

DUNN: Maybe you're right. Maybe I don't deserve a voice in Washington. I understand I have been reckless. I do have a problem with the anger I feel, and right now I am so angry with you!

JORDAN: Julie—

DUNN: You must have experienced anger over the years. What did you do with it? When the Texas good old boys needed to prove America worked, they trotted out Barbara Jordan. Why not? You were eloquent, articulate. There was no danger of black militant rhetoric, no harassment of whites, and absolutely no sympathy for black protest. But I have to wonder, as you *bowed* and *scraped* for guys like Robert Byrd, has there never been a bit of resentment or, yes, even anger at how they used you? Was it worth it? Did you get what you wanted?

[*She looks out over the garden.*]

Well. Look at this place! Onion Creek. So beautiful. A dream come true, living here with Nancy. The rose beds, the rolling hills, the woods. The secluded drive, almost impossible to find from the main road. So idyllic, so . . . *isolated.* You can't see who or what I am anymore, because you've lived white too long. You've forgotten me. And when you forget me, you forget . . . everything.

[*She picks up her briefcase and exits.* JORDAN *stands immobile. Eventually, she turns and addresses the audience. Keynote address: Democratic National Convention 1992.*]

JORDAN: "There appears to be a general apprehension in the country about the future.

"That apprehension undermines our faith in each other and our faith in ourselves.

"The idea that America today will be better tomorrow has become destabilized.

"The American dream is slipping away from too many people. It is slipping away from too many black and brown mothers and their children.

"The American dream is slipping away from the homeless of every color and every sex. It is slipping away from those immigrants living without water and sewage systems.

"We are one, we Americans. We're one, and we reject any intruder who seeks to divide us on the basis of race, creed, or economics.

"This is the great danger America faces. That we will cease to be one nation and become instead a collection of interest groups: city against suburb, region against region, individual against individual. Each seeking to satisfy private wants.

"If that happens, who then will speak for America?

"Who then will speak for the common good?

"Are we to be one people bound together by common spirit sharing in a common endeavor, or will we become a divided nation?

"There is no executive order; there is no law that can require the American people to form a national community. This we must do as individuals and if we do it as individuals, there is no president of the United States who can veto that decision.

"We are a generous people so why can't we be generous with each other?

"Our history bears witness: e pluribus unum—from many, one.

"As we undergo the necessary change, we must be prepared to answer Rodney King's haunting question: Can we all get along? I say we answer that question with a resounding . . . yes!"

EPILOGUE

EARL: Are you going to go to Washington?

JORDAN: Is the rehab room that far?

EARL: No, I mean—

JORDAN: Because the rehab room looms large on my agenda at the moment.

EARL: Slow down.

JORDAN: Are you going to nag me for the rest of my life?

EARL: If you're lucky.

JORDAN [*with sudden emotion*]: You don't understand!

EARL: What, Barbara?

JORDAN: I don't know. I don't know.

EARL: Just sit down. Sit down.

JORDAN: I don't want to sit down.

EARL: What do you want?

JORDAN: I want . . . the goddamn bike!

EARL: What are you talking about?

JORDAN: And you wouldn't get it for me because I was three pounds off the mark!

EARL: Are you *still* brooding about that? You were three pounds off the mark because you went to a Texas barbecue fund-raiser and stuffed yourself.

JORDAN: They expect you to eat! And don't kid me! You never intended to give me that bike! You thought I couldn't lose the sixty pounds!

EARL: And you didn't.

JORDAN: Three pounds off!

EARL: From whom do you think I learned precision?

JORDAN: And now it's too late.

EARL: Okay. Things are a little emotional.

JORDAN: Would you call me a cold individual?

EARL: Not at the moment.

JORDAN: Have I lost touch?

EARL: With whom?

JORDAN: Where do you put your anger?

EARL: What?

JORDAN: Your anger. Where do you put it? What do you do with it?

EARL: I take it out on you, of course.

JORDAN: Ah.

EARL: Why? What do you do with yours?
JORDAN: John Ed had his bottle of gin, I think. My father had our backsides.

[*She puts a hand on her chest.*]

I think I put mine in here . . .

[*Her hand moves down to the walker.*]

I could really go for a strawberry sundae right now.
EARL: Your mind is a maze! I wander around it, and when I come to a corner, I try to remember whether to turn left or right!
JORDAN: Left, left, you idiot.
EARL [*laughs*]: Left, of course. Sit down.
JORDAN: I'm not going to fall.
EARL: Two years ago you broke your collarbone. Last spring you sprained your wrist. Don't tell me you're not going to fall.

[JORDAN *sits.*]

JORDAN: May I see the newspaper?

[EARL *retrieves the newspaper and puts it down in front of her.* JORDAN *reads it silently.*]

I was always "that black girl." I knew what it meant, and so I put my head down and plowed my way into the middle of the toughest white boys on the block.
EARL: It had to be done, and you were the only one at the time who could do it.
JORDAN: The Medal of Freedom. Good Lord. Why? . . . Where is Vernon Dahmer's Medal of Freedom? Medgar Evers's Medal of Freedom? Andy Goodman's Medal of Freedom?

[*Pause.*]

EARL: Sometimes it's enough if you only *live* for your country, Beej.

[*There is a tap at the door.* WOODRUFF *enters.*]

WOODRUFF: Okay, they're ready for you in rehab, Professor.
JORDAN: Shit!
WOODRUFF: Are we all set? Ready to go?
EARL: Just about. We're still trying to find a comb.
WOODRUFF: Take your time.

[EARL *picks up her purse and goes through it.*]

JORDAN [*as* WOODRUFF *seats herself beside* JORDAN]: Something on your mind, Doctor?

WOODRUFF: I may feel really foolish in a minute because somehow, when in the presence of a person I revere, my verbal skills are diminished . . . to say the least.

[EARL *stops fishing in her purse.*]

JORDAN: The same thing happens to me when I am engaged in conversation with a doctor of medicine, for very different reasons.

WOODRUFF: I know you've had your fill of people like me. The sight of the endless parade of white coats turns your stomach, right? Here you are in the middle of the battle of your life, and who comes to your rescue? . . . Gidget. Believe me, I know. I've had an uphill battle myself.

JORDAN: I'm sure you have.

WOODRUFF: I specialize in neurology and immunology. I *am* young. I'm thirty-four years old. But I believe I'm the best there is, all appearances to the contrary . . . For close to sixty years you've pushed the envelope, am I right? And you've made your body deal with it. Your body has had to make up for the demands and the neglect because some inner message has been so strong.

[*Pause.*]

Consider this wild possibility: if you let your body get a word in edgewise every once in a blue moon, we might just be able to keep your spirit alive and your mind cranking so that you can continue to deliver the message.

JORDAN: Do you know how many doctors I've seen in the last ten years?

[*Beat.*]

WOODRUFF: I always thought you would have made an amazing Supreme Court justice.

[*Beat.*]

JORDAN [*remembering* PATTEN]: Why?

WOODRUFF: The best judges in the world are nonjudgmental, don't you think?

JORDAN: They are—

WOODRUFF: They withhold judgment . . . until the evidence is in.

[*Beat.*]

So, I'll be just outside the door whenever you're ready.

[*Beat.*]

EARL: It will be just a moment.

[WOODRUFF *gets up and heads for the door.*]

JORDAN: Wait.
WOODRUFF [*stops her progress toward the door*]: Yes?

[*Beat.*]

JORDAN: There is one new symptom that I may have forgotten to mention.
WOODRUFF AND EARL: Yes?
JORDAN: I've been having some trouble breathing. That's a new, unexpected little treat.
WOODRUFF: Are you having trouble now?
JORDAN: No. It comes and goes like all the other symptoms. Sometimes I'll be in the middle of a breath and not know whether it would be best to breathe in or breathe out. So I just hang there, not doing either.
WOODRUFF: What else?
JORDAN: Other than that, I'm dandy.

[*Pause.*]

WOODRUFF: We're going to go over all the medications you're taking, and we're going to fine-tune them. Then we'll talk. Okay?

[*Beat.*]

I'll just wait outside then.

[*She exits.*]

EARL: Come on. I'll take you to rehab.

[*She places the walker in front of her.* JORDAN *takes out the pack of cigarettes, takes one last smell, and gives them to* EARL. EARL *trashes them.*]

JORDAN: Go over there. Go way over there.
EARL: Now what?
JORDAN: If you don't mind, I'll take the chair.
EARL: The chair?
JORDAN: The chair. "One second you're here; next second you're there," the chair?
EARL: Oh, the chair! Are you sure?
JORDAN: That doesn't mean you have to throw out the walker, Nan, okay?

EARL: Of course not.

[*She holds out her arms.*]

On three?
JORDAN: No. I would like a little privacy while I adjust to living with my eyes focused on the navels of the general populace.
EARL: All that lint.
JORDAN: You understand, as usual.
EARL: I'll be outside with the doctor. Call if you need me.
JORDAN: I always do.

[*Silence as she pulls herself into a standing position.* EARL *exits.*]

VOICEOVER OF WILLIAM JEFFERSON CLINTON: "The next recipient of the Presidential Medal of Freedom is a woman worthy of our highest regard. For twenty years Barbara Jordan has been the most outspoken moral voice of the American political system . . . a position she reached soon after becoming the first black congresswoman elected from the Deep South from her native Texas in 1972."

[*Once settled in the chair, she looks for the brakes.*]

JORDAN: Now how do I—
VOICEOVER: "From national platforms she has captured the nation's attention and awakened its conscience in defense of our Constitution, the American dream, and the commonality we share as American citizens."

[*She spots the lever and releases the brakes.*]

JORDAN: This doohickey. Right.

[*She gives a little roll back and forth. She attempts to turn a circle.*]

VOICEOVER: "As professor of ethics and public policy at the Lyndon B. Johnson School of Public Affairs, she ensures that the next generation of our public servants be worthy of the legacy she has done so much to build."
JORDAN: It's a cakewalk.
VOICEOVER: Ladies and gentlemen: Barbara Jordan.

[*The applause builds as* JORDAN *pushes herself center stage and faces the audience. There is a smile on her face.*]

BATTLE OF THE BANDS

DEAN CORRIN

PLAYWRIGHT'S STATEMENT

Writers are often asked where they get their ideas. The idea for this play appeared on January 15, 1996, in Chicago, Illinois, when I was stopped at a red light waiting to get on southbound Lake Shore Drive. A conversation began to run in my head between a husband and wife about his brother moving into their garage/studio and "getting the band back together" to escape his marital strife. The light changed, and by the time I crossed Foster Avenue, I knew who five of the characters in the play would be and that the progress of the band would provide the structure for the story. When I got to my office at DePaul University, I made some notes about the play and wrote six lines of dialogue, which I shared with my students that afternoon.

It only took me another six years to write the play.

Ideas are easy. Plays are hard. I was fortunate to have a number of people who kept the writing of this play from being lonely. My students in the winter and spring quarters of 1996 listened to a new six lines from the play each week. I wrote ten new minutes of the play in 1999 and 2000 in order to have something to read at the Victory Gardens Playwrights Ensemble PlaySlam. In January 2001, Dennis Začek asked me if the play would be ready for next season, and I said yes. To keep that from being a lie, Jim Sherman and I made a deal to show each other a scene from the plays we were working on so we *had* to have new pages every week. Thanks to Jim, I had enough pages by March for Dennis to put it on the schedule. That spring my students at DePaul read my act and a half and gave me useful notes. That summer and fall we did readings at Victory Gardens, followed by a workshop with the cast in February 2002. Several members of the ensemble attended those readings, and I received especially useful suggestions from Jim Sherman, Doug Post, and Claudia Allen. Throughout the workshop and rehearsal process Sandy Shinner and the cast gave me great information about what was happening in the play and always gave their all to any new pages I gave them.

I think that this play has turned out to be my attempt at capturing a few of my observations about the richness and complexity that is family life. Though my wife, Judy, and my daughters, Julia and Ann, would undoubtedly like it made clear that none of these characters are based on them, I hope they will accept that it was the richness of the experience of my life with them that is responsible for anything that is good in the play.

PRODUCTION HISTORY

Battle of the Bands, by Dean Corrin, was first presented by Victory Gardens Theater, Chicago, Illinois, in April 2002.

PRODUCTION TEAM

Director	Sandy Shinner
Set	Jeff Bauer
Costumes	Judith Lundberg
Lights	Rita Pietraszek
Sound	Christopher J. Johnson
Dramaturg	Rachel Shteir
Production Stage Manager	Karl Sullivan

CAST

Neal Reynolds	Justin Cholewa
Claire Sherman	Julie Ganey
Michael Burns	James Krag
Gina Burns	Karlie Nurse
Steve Burns	Phil Ridarelli
Janet Burns	Jill Shellabarger

The play was subsequently produced by the Center for the Arts, Wichita, Kansas, in April 2004.

CHARACTERS

Janet Burns, *fortyish, married to Steve*
Gina Burns, *fifteen, Steve and Janet's daughter*
Steve Burns, *fortyish, married to Janet*
Michael Burns, *two years younger than Steve, his brother*
Claire Sherman, *twenties, a new friend of Michael's*
Neal Reynolds, *seventeen, a friend of Gina's*

STAGING

Time: Late in the twentieth century
Place: Steve and Janet's home in Wichita, Kansas
Setting: The dining room of a comfortable home. The room is pleasant but not fancy. Steve and Janet probably intend to remodel it but haven't gotten around to it yet. In addition to being the dining room, it is also a center of activity. The place mail gets dropped, newspapers get read, and books and bags are dropped upon entering the home. Beyond the dining room, through two doorways, we can see the kitchen (it is possible for characters in the kitchen to move out of sight, but we can see them through the doorways as they move about). The kitchen is more modern—the result of a remodeling project in the not-too-distant past. A door in the kitchen (which does not need to be seen if we can hear it open and close) provides access to the driveway at the side of the house and the detached garage. This is the "family" entrance that is used for most comings and goings. An archway in the dining room leads to the (unseen) front door and the other rooms of the house (living room, bedrooms upstairs, etc.). In either the kitchen or the hallway to the front of the house is a visible door that opens to the steps to the basement.

ACT 1

SCENE 1

[*September. Late Friday afternoon. Offstage a radio plays. Something on the adult contemporary station, maybe John Lennon's "(Just Like) Starting Over." There is the sound of keys in the back door.* JANET *opens the door, and* GINA *bursts through.* GINA, *dressed in casual school clothes, enters the dining room and walks across it, dropping her books, purse, instrument case, backpack, etc., behind her.*]

GINA: It's not my fault practice went long. It wasn't even my section.

JANET [*closing the back door*]: I never said—

GINA: It was the drums. Ooou. You'd think they'd at least know left and right.

JANET: I just said that we had to hurry if we're going to get you there on time.

GINA: I hope you washed my new sweatshirt, because those uniforms are so itchy that if you don't wear something underneath them they'll like draw blood.

[*She exits out the front doorway.* JANET *drops her purse and briefcase in the kitchen and then steps into the rear entrance to the dining room. She wears business attire.*]

JANET: Steve.

[*She returns to the kitchen, walks through it, and appears in the second kitchen doorway.*]

Steven.

[*She walks through the dining room to the front doorway.*]

Steven?

[*She calls offstage.*]

Gina, is your father upstairs?

GINA [*offstage*]: I haven't seen him.

JANET: Steven?

[*She begins to pick up the things that* GINA *had distributed around the room.* GINA *returns, looking through the mail.*]

GINA: What's for supper?

JANET: I don't know. I thought your father was going to fix something, but it doesn't look like he's started yet.

GINA: Is he here even?

JANET: The radio's on.

GINA: He didn't bring in the mail.

JANET: He didn't?

GINA: No. It was in the mailbox.

JANET: His car was in the driveway, wasn't it?

GINA: Can I see how bad the Visa bill is?

JANET: No.

[*She goes to the front doorway.*]

Steven!

GINA: Is there any of that good bread left from the bakery?

JANET: Not before supper. Have a piece of fruit. Where else do you think he could be?

GINA: Mom. You're making such a big deal. I'm sure he didn't run away and join the circus.

[*She sits down and kicks off her shoes.*]

JANET: Hey, don't just sit there. Take some of this stuff up to your room and start getting dressed. What time are you supposed to be there?

GINA: Six-thirty.

JANET: You'd better get moving. I wonder what he was going to fix for supper?

GINA [*exiting into the front of the house*]: We could just stop and get something.

JANET: Would you turn off the radio?

GINA [*offstage*]: Taco Tico.

JANET: I'll make us a sandwich. You're not going to leave these shoes . . .

[STEVE *enters from the basement, carrying a basket of laundry. The radio is turned off.*]

STEVE: Hey.

JANET: I was calling you. Didn't you hear me calling you?

STEVE [*placing the basket on the table*]: I was changing the laundry.

JANET: Did you work late? I thought you said you'd fix dinner.

STEVE: I was . . . I just—

JANET: Bad day at the office?

STEVE: Typical.

JANET: Do you need to go in this weekend? I've got to do budgets for the client presentation on Tuesday.

STEVE: No. I wasn't going in. I'll be around.

JANET: If you could get Doug to settle on an idea for his science fair project, that would be a big help.

STEVE: Sure.

JANET: And you remember Gina has to be there early tonight? The band is marching at halftime.

STEVE: Oh, no. I forgot. I just—

JANET: And one of us has to pick up Doug at soccer at six and take him over to the Burtons' to spend the night. But you can't drop him off till seven 'cause Kenny's got football so the Burtons won't be back.

STEVE: Oh. Jeez, I—

JANET: Can I help you get something started for supper?

STEVE: Look, if Dougie isn't going to be here and Gina's got to go, maybe I should just run over and get some chiliburgers at Jack's—

JANET: There's lunch meat in the refrigerator. I'll get stuff out. Did you just get home? You didn't even pick up the mail or anything.

STEVE: Michael called.

JANET: Michael? What'd he want?

STEVE: Um, he wanted to come over tonight.

JANET: Tonight? He can't come over tonight, with the game and everything. You told him it wasn't a good night, didn't you?

STEVE: You know, he wanted—

JANET: You're not going to miss Gina's first time marching in the band just because your little brother wants to come over. You'll see him tomorrow. Debbie invited us for dinner.

STEVE: I don't think so. He was— He wanted a place to stay.

JANET: To stay?

STEVE: Yeah. I guess he and Debbie are . . .

JANET: Oh. No.

STEVE: I didn't know what to tell him.

JANET: What did you tell him?

STEVE: I told him he could stay here.

JANET: Of course. Of course he can. He's your brother.

[*Pause.*]

What happened?

STEVE: I don't know.

JANET: I should call Debbie. Should I call Debbie? Are we supposed to know? I guess we'd have to know. What do I say to her?

STEVE: I don't know. Maybe she's—

JANET: And Morgan? What's this going to do to her?

STEVE: Maybe she won't even notice.

JANET: She's almost two, Steven. She's going to notice.

[GINA *enters.*]

GINA: Mom. My sweatshirt's not upstairs. I can't stand to wear that uniform without something under it. Did my sweatshirt get washed?

JANET: Gina.

GINA: What?

JANET: We need to talk to you for a minute.

GINA: What'd I do? I didn't do anything.

STEVE: Maybe we should—

JANET: He's going to be here. She's going to know soon enough.

GINA: What?

STEVE: Gina, Uncle Mike is going to be staying here for a while.

GINA: Oh. Are they getting divorced?

STEVE: Well, they're having some trouble, and I guess they think they need some time . . .

GINA [*getting her sweatshirt out of the laundry basket*]: If they get divorced, will she still do like holidays and birthdays with us?

STEVE: I wouldn't think so.

GINA: That's boo. She always buys the best presents. Hey, Mom, you better get moving. You're not going dressed like that, are you?

[*She exits with the sweatshirt.*]

JANET: I'll get Gina to the game. If you could pick up Dougie.

STEVE: I can take Gina.

JANET: You should be here for your brother. In case he wants somebody to talk to.

MICHAEL [*offstage*]: Hey, Stevie Wonder. You want to give me a hand here?

STEVE: Or anything.

[MICHAEL *enters with a guitar in a soft case, a bag of luggage over his shoulder, and a case of beer in bottles.*]

MICHAEL: If you want to help me unload my stuff, then I'll get my car out of the driveway.

JANET: Michael.

STEVE: Let me run this upstairs.

[*He exits with the laundry basket to the front of the house.*]

MICHAEL: I don't want to be in anybody's way.

JANET: Of course not. How are you?

MICHAEL: I'm good.

JANET: You're okay?

MICHAEL: I'm fine. Yeah. How are you?

JANET: I'm fine. Fine. If there's anything we can do.

MICHAEL: A place to stay. What more could I ask?

[STEVE *returns.*]

STEVE: You ready?

JANET: I better go upstairs and move the junk out of the extra room.

STEVE: Don't worry about it.

JANET: I don't think you know what's up there.

MICHAEL: I'm going to stay in the studio.

JANET: The studio?

STEVE: It was his idea.

MICHAEL: You won't even know I'm here. I'll be out in the studio.

JANET: You mean the garage? Oh, Steven, you can't ask him to do that.

STEVE: The studio is fine.

JANET: Steven, just because your parents let you boys staple egg cartons to the walls when you were in high school does not make it a studio.

STEVE: It's a finished room. I don't know why you— If it was attached to the house, it would just be an extra room.

JANET: If it was attached to the house it would have heat. Michael, the room upstairs is no problem.

MICHAEL: It's where I want to stay.

[*Beat.*]

JANET: What kind of a mess is out there? Do we need to go—

STEVE: It's okay. I got out clean sheets for the bed and moved the cat box out of the bathroom downstairs.

JANET: The bathroom in the basement? We can't make him—

STEVE: He'll be fine. Now what time do I have to pick up Doug?

JANET: No. I'll get him. I'll swing back after I drop Gina at the game.

STEVE: You don't have to.

JANET: You should stay with your brother. Gina will understand. You should spend some time with your brother. We're not going to leave you alone here, Michael.

MICHAEL: I wouldn't be alone.

[*Beat.*]

JANET: You wouldn't?

MICHAEL: Eric and Lloyd are coming over.

STEVE: Eric?

MICHAEL: I called them.

STEVE: And Lloyd?

JANET: Michael, do you really think—

STEVE: What are you talking about?

MICHAEL: I'm getting the band back together.

JANET: Michael.

STEVE: The band? There is no band.

MICHAEL: Come on. It'll be fun.

STEVE: You don't expect me—

MICHAEL: When was the last time you got the bass out?

STEVE: When there was a band.

MICHAEL: Come on, Steven. It's just for—

STEVE: We're not in college anymore. Except for Lloyd. And now he's older than the professors.

MICHAEL: I thought after all this time we could just—

STEVE [*exiting to the front of the house*]: Gina, we better get this show on the road.

[JANET *and* MICHAEL *are left alone. Beat.*]

JANET: Michael.

MICHAEL: Yeah?

JANET: Michael, of course you're welcome here. If there's anything we can do for you . . .

MICHAEL: Thanks. I appreciate that.

JANET: If you and Debbie need some time, we'd be happy to help out with Morgan.

MICHAEL: Can I put this in your fridge?

JANET: Sure. Let me get that.

MICHAEL: Lloyd's lending me one of those little apartment refrigerators, so after tonight—

JANET [*exiting into the kitchen*]: We've got plenty of room.

MICHAEL: And I'm going to get groceries tomorrow. I'll stay out of your hair.

GINA [*entering*]: Mom, I thought you were taking me.

MICHAEL: Little Gina.

GINA: Uncle Mike.

MICHAEL: Very *Sgt. Pepper's*. Is that back in?

JANET [*returning*]: Tonight's her first time marching in the band.

GINA: If you're taking me . . .

JANET: Band practice ran late.

GINA: You'd think the drum section could at least march.

MICHAEL: Drummers are always trouble. Keith Moon. John Bonham. That guy in the Smashing Pumpkins. Stick with your piccolo.

GINA: It's a flute, Uncle Mike. A flute.

MICHAEL: They tell you I'm going to be staying here?

GINA: Well, yeah.

MICHAEL: I hope you don't mind giving my old room back.

JANET: Michael.

MICHAEL: I'm kidding.

GINA: Uncle Mike.

MICHAEL: It's all pretty now anyway.

GINA: Are we going to have dinner?

JANET: Go see if your father has any cash. We'll get something on the way.

GINA: Taco Tico?

JANET: Whatever.

GINA [*exiting*]: Bean burrito.

JANET: You know, Michael, maybe tonight it would be better if—

MICHAEL: You ever sorry you bought the old place when the folks retired?

JANET: You should maybe have some time by yourself.

MICHAEL: I'd always feel like I was living in their house.

JANET: Michael.

MICHAEL: Living with their furniture.

JANET: We haven't been able to get to everything we've wanted to.

MICHAEL: But I guess they gave you a pretty good deal.

[STEVE *enters, calling behind him. He carries a jacket.*]

STEVE: Then we've got to go right now because I have to pick up Doug. [*To* MICHAEL] Janet can give you her garage key 'cause she doesn't need it. This is the house key with the red mark on it. The lock on the back door sticks sometimes, but if you turn the key left and then right—

MICHAEL: You haven't fixed that?

JANET [*giving* MICHAEL *a key*]: It's on the list.

STEVE: I've got to pick up Doug and take Gina to the game. There's towels in the dryer.

JANET: I'm driving them.

[*She exits to the living room.*]

MICHAEL: Get out the ax, man. It'll be fun.

STEVE: I don't think this is a good idea for any of us.

MICHAEL: It's just messing around.

STEVE: I don't think that's going to—

MICHAEL: Eric and Lloyd are expecting you.

STEVE: Maybe tonight you should just take some time to yourself.

MICHAEL: Oh. So you're going to give me the big lecture, huh?

STEVE: This just isn't—

MICHAEL: I should just be more like you, then everything would work out fine.

[JANET *returns.*]

STEVE: Michael.

MICHAEL: If I could just do it like you, I would.

STEVE: What's that supposed to mean?

MICHAEL: It's not as easy for everybody else as it is for you.

[MICHAEL *exits through the kitchen. The back door slams. Beat.*]

JANET: Maybe you should go talk to him.

STEVE: You can't talk to him.

JANET: Maybe you should try.

STEVE: He wants to get the band together.

JANET: Maybe if you talked to him.

GINA [*observing from the doorway*]: Mom. It's a classic example of male interaction.

[*They both look at her.*]

Well. It is. We had this with Ms. Probst in psychology. The women of the tribe will come together to share information, discuss feelings, and make plans before they can unite and participate in a community event. The men, however, must first come together as a group, to participate together in a shared physical activity. Those members of the tribe who can display proficiency at this task will establish a bond that will allow them to share secrets and address the unspoken rules of their community. So, Mom, you can call Aunt Debbie and go have lunch and talk everything out and then go to a movie together. But if Daddy wants to talk about this with Uncle Mike, he's going to have to show him he can play in his band.

[*Beat.*]

JANET: Steven?
STEVE: Forget it.
JANET: She may be onto something.
STEVE: If he wants to call Lloyd and Eric, that's his thing.
JANET: It might make it easier to talk to him.
STEVE: I can talk to my brother.
JANET: Give you a chance to bring things up.
STEVE: I'll talk to him tomorrow.

[*Beat.*]

JANET: Gina. Got to go.

[*She turns to go.*]

STEVE: I can just talk to him.
JANET [*exiting to the front of the house*]: And I'll pick up Dougie.
STEVE: I'm taking you.
GINA: My permit's in my case.
STEVE: If we're in a hurry.
GINA: How am I going to be ready for my test?
STEVE: We'll go out tomorrow.
GINA: I can't drive with Mom.
STEVE: Tomorrow.
GINA: She jumps.

[*She exits out the back.* STEVE *starts to put on his jacket.* JANET *enters with a beat-up guitar case.*]

STEVE: I don't think so.
JANET: It might be fun. What's the worst that could happen?
STEVE: You don't remember—
JANET: That was a million years ago.

[JANET *flips open the latches on the case.*]

STEVE: Janet.

JANET: It's not the band. You're grown-ups now.

[*She lifts the bass guitar out of the case. In contrast to the dingy case, the bass gleams.*]

You can just play for fun.

STEVE: I don't think I—

JANET: Put this on.

STEVE: I haven't played since I don't know . . .

JANET: Like riding a bike.

[JANET *places the guitar strap over his neck.*]

I always paid more attention when you had this thing on. Maybe he will, too.

STEVE: You don't have to—

JANET: It seemed like they were doing okay.

STEVE: I don't know.

JANET: Had he said something?

STEVE: I never heard anything.

JANET: Did you know this was coming?

[*Beat.*]

STEVE: It'll probably just blow over.

JANET: You think? You think he figures they'll get right back together?

[*Beat.*]

I guess you never know.

STEVE: I guess not.

JANET: Are you okay?

STEVE: I'm fine. Sure. And you?

GINA [*at the back door*]: Who is taking me?

JANET: Got to go. Good luck.

STEVE: Thanks.

JANET [*stops*]: It looks good on you.

[*She exits.* STEVE *starts to remove the bass but stops. He adjusts the straps, fingers a few notes on the frets, and stops. He looks around, perhaps in a mirror, and fingers a couple of phrases. He checks to make certain no one has observed, quickly shifts the bass to one side, closes the case, picks it up, and heads through the kitchen toward the back door. He stops, takes a beer from the refrigerator, closes the refrigerator, and exits to the driveway.*]

SCENE 2

[*The next evening.* GINA, *dressed casually, is standing at a music stand finishing a flute practice.* MICHAEL *sits at the table, fingering his unplugged electric guitar.*]

MICHAEL: I don't understand how this is your fault.

GINA [*taking her flute apart*]: It's not my fault. But I'm the one laying in the middle of the football field in front of the whole school.

MICHAEL: You're really lying on the field?

GINA: Unconscious.

JANET [*offstage*]: You weren't unconscious.

GINA: Loretta says I was unconscious.

MICHAEL: Wouldn't you know if you were unconscious?

GINA: How could I know if I'm not conscious?

MICHAEL: But you're really lying in the middle of the football field?

GINA: With the rest of the band marching around me.

[JANET *enters from the kitchen.*]

JANET: She may not want to go through it all again, Michael.

GINA: Why wouldn't I want to relive the most humiliating moment of my life?

MICHAEL: She was really lying on the field?

JANET: He really nailed her.

GINA: You ever been hit by a bass drum?

MICHAEL: Not that I can recall.

GINA: Then maybe you have, because if you were you would be unconscious.

JANET [*exiting to the basement*]: It wasn't that bad.

GINA: Loretta said I just laid there for about fifteen minutes. She thought I was dead. I just wish I was.

MICHAEL: Just because he ran into you?

GINA: He spun into me. He was supposed to turn right and he turned left.

MICHAEL: Ouch.

GINA: And he had it written on his hands.

MICHAEL: What?

GINA: Left and right. After practice went so bad, Mr. Hollowell took a marker and put a big *R* and an *L* on Neal's hands.

MICHAEL: That's humiliating.

GINA: It's frightening. He's a junior and he's already got his license. Can you imagine riding in his car?

[STEVE *enters, wearing a fringed leather vest.*]

STEVE: Look what I found.

GINA: Dad.

MICHAEL: Oh my God.

STEVE: Still fits.

MICHAEL: It's a good thing it doesn't have to button.

STEVE: Was this ever cool?

GINA: Did you actually wear that?

MICHAEL: We all wore something leather because that was the name of the band.

GINA: Like the Village People?

STEVE: Not that kind of leather. It's more Buffalo Springfield, don't you think?

GINA: It's pretty Partridge Family if you ask me.

MICHAEL: I had this amazing jacket with fringe down to here on the sleeves.

STEVE: And it always got caught in your whammy bar.

MICHAEL: One time. Only one time did it ever get caught.

STEVE: It got caught all the time. Only one time did we have to cut your fringe out of your guitar in the middle of a show.

MICHAEL: At least I never missed a gig because I got carded.

STEVE: I had a youthful face.

MICHAEL: So you should bring your wallet. You got carded all the time. Not once did I have to use that fake ID you bought me.

STEVE: Michael.

MICHAEL: It's a good thing, too. What'd you pay for that thing?

GINA: You had a fake ID?

[JANET *enters from the basement with a tablecloth and plastic plates.*]

JANET: Steven, have you— Oh, my.

STEVE: Huh? Do you remember?

JANET: Somehow I remembered it . . . cooler.

STEVE: Come on. This is great.

GINA: You weren't actually seen with him wearing this.

STEVE: And she'd wear this suede halter top.

JANET: Steven.

GINA: Mom?

JANET: Steven, did you start the fire?

STEVE: Aren't we going to make—

JANET: I thought while the weather's still nice. And Michael's here.

GINA: You wore a halter top?

JANET: It was not a skimpy halter top.

MICHAEL: Yes it was.

STEVE: And these bell-bottom jeans.

MICHAEL: Don't get him started on those jeans.

JANET: Those were great jeans. What I would give to be able to wear those jeans again.

GINA: What kind of jeans?

JANET: We'd better get moving if you guys want to eat before Eric and Lloyd come over.

GINA: Can we come listen tonight?

STEVE: I don't think we're ready for that.

JANET: They don't let girls into the clubhouse.

STEVE: It's not that.

JANET: You never let me in a practice.

STEVE: It wasn't because you were a girl.

JANET: Uh-huh. You let Jeff Bryant in. And Bobby Adams.

STEVE: Well—

MICHAEL: They were our roadies.

STEVE: Yeah. They were our roadies. They were helping out.

JANET: I hauled more equipment than either of them ever did.

STEVE: I'd better start the fire.

[*He starts to go.*]

GINA: You're not going to go outside in that?

MICHAEL: I'll light the coals. You don't want your fringe to catch fire.

[*He hands* STEVE *the guitar.*]

Are there matches out there?

JANET: There's matches in the bowl by the coffee cups.

[MICHAEL *exits through the kitchen and then out the back door.* STEVE *puts on the guitar and strikes a pose for* GINA.]

GINA: Daddy, you are creeping me out.

[JANET *waits until she hears the door close.*]

JANET: Gina, should you do some homework till supper is ready?

GINA: Finished.

JANET: Or read a book or something?

GINA: I'd rather talk about your halter top and that blouse you wouldn't let me order from Delia's.

JANET: I was in college, not just turned fifteen. And I need to talk to your father.

GINA: About Uncle Mike?

JANET: Why don't you go watch TV?

GINA: But Dougie's watching golf again.

JANET: Tell him I said to change the channel. He doesn't need to watch a sport he doesn't play.

STEVE: Try to find something you won't fight over.

GINA: I'll make him watch *Fashion Emergency*. Oops. That's on in here.

[*She exits to the living room.*]

STEVE: Do we have to cook out? I got stuff for stir-fry.

JANET: You'll be trapped in the kitchen if you do that. If you're grilling, you and your brother have time to talk.

STEVE: I'm going to talk to him when I have the chance.

JANET: Did you find out anything this afternoon?

STEVE: There was a lot of stuff to do out there if he's going to stay for a while. We were pretty much just working the whole time.

JANET: Steven. You're going to have to bring it up.

STEVE: I'm going to bring it up.

JANET: You can't wait for the perfect moment.

STEVE: I just don't want him to get his back up.

JANET: Do you think he's called your parents?

STEVE: I don't know.

JANET: Should you?

STEVE: I think that's up to him.

JANET: You can't not tell them when he's living in our garage.

STEVE: It's just going to get them all upset for no reason.

JANET: But what if they try to call him? That's not fair to Debbie. To make her tell them.

STEVE: I'll see if he's called them.

JANET: 'Cause she really doesn't know what's going on.

STEVE: You talked to her?

JANET: I had to talk to her. I had to see if I could do anything. She's all alone with the baby.

STEVE: Is she okay?

JANET: Well, at least her mom's coming up for a few days.

STEVE: She called her mom already?

JANET: Of course she did.

STEVE: But if this all blows over—I mean, that really makes him seem bad if this is nothing.

JANET: It's already something, Steven, even if it all blows over.

STEVE: I just thought we'd give it some time.

JANET: I think you can understand that that's not exactly how Debbie feels about it.

MICHAEL [*standing in the doorway*]: She's pretty pissed off, I'll bet.

JANET: She's upset, of course.

MICHAEL: I bet she gave you an earful about me.

JANET: She really didn't—

[*The phone rings.*]

MICHAEL: That's okay. I don't expect you to tell me.

JANET: Look, if there was anything, I would tell you.

MICHAEL: What'd you tell her?

STEVE: Look, Michael—

[*The phone rings.*]

JANET: I didn't really have anything to tell her. I told her you were staying here. She didn't know that.

STEVE: Maybe we should—

GINA [*offstage*]: It's for you, Dad.

JANET: Is there something you want me to tell her?

MICHAEL: No. Just tell her I'll call.

STEVE [*exiting to the kitchen*]: Do we need to check the fire?

JANET: Can I tell her when you'll call?

MICHAEL: You don't have to tell her anything. I'll talk to her.

JANET: She'd appreciate that.

MICHAEL: You should hear my side, too.

JANET: I'd love to hear your side.

MICHAEL: There's probably no point.

JANET: You're making a hell of a mess if there's no point.

STEVE [*returning*]: This sucks.

JANET: Who was it?

STEVE: Eric isn't coming. They're going to dinner at Maggie's parents. What are we supposed to do without a drummer?

MICHAEL: We don't need a drummer.

STEVE: I'll call Lloyd. Maybe he knows somebody.

MICHAEL: It's just a practice.

STEVE: Yeah, but it's not the same without a drummer.

MICHAEL: But it's Eric that really needs the practice.

JANET: Will you two stop it? Stop talking about it like it's a band. It's just fishing or golfing or playing poker. It isn't a band.

[*She exits. Beat.*]

STEVE: Drummers.

MICHAEL: You said it.

STEVE: Why is it drummers always screw everything up?

SCENE 3

[*The following Friday. After school.* MICHAEL *is seated at the table grading papers. His books, papers, and grade book are spread across the table.* STEVE *enters from the basement, wearing an apron and carrying a cardboard box.*]

STEVE: Are you sure you didn't end up with the tape?

MICHAEL: Forget the tape.

STEVE: But we sounded great on that tape. We could have released that tape.

MICHAEL: Steven.

STEVE: I think maybe it's in one of these boxes. I don't know where else it would be.

MICHAEL: Aren't you supposed to be fixing supper?

STEVE: Even Eric sounded good on that tape. I bet if he heard it, he'd play better.

MICHAEL: Or if he'd come to practice.

STEVE [*looking through one of the boxes*]: Oh, man. I'd forgotten this.

[*He holds up the album.*]

MICHAEL: That's a collector's item.

STEVE: "How'd you end up inside?
   How'd you end up inside?"

MICHAEL: "I was doing fine,
   Till I sold weed to Sergeant Cline."

STEVE AND MICHAEL: "And I had no place left to hide.
   Yes, it left me no place to hide."

[*They make the guitar sounds verbally.*]

"I came home, 'cause I didn't want to roam
So I brought it back to Wichita."

[*They each remember the next lines differently.*]

STEVE: [*at the same time as* MICHAEL]: "Went to the river bend
Where I thought I'd find a friend."
MICHAEL: [*at the same time as* STEVE]: "I was doing fine,
Till I sold weed to Sergeant Cline."

[*The song breaks down. They resume and finish the verse with only the guitar sounds.*]

Whatever happened to them?
STEVE: They played the Fillmore.
MICHAEL: Yeah, but I wonder what happened to them?
STEVE: If you played the Fillmore, what difference would it make?
MICHAEL: I thought you got rid of all these.
STEVE: No. I just put them in the basement. Haven't been able to play records
since Gina started walking. [*Exiting into the living room*] The kids start
dancing, and it just skips all over the place.
MICHAEL: You know they've solved that with CDs.
STEVE [*offstage*]: I don't even want to think about what that would cost.

[*The sound of a needle being placed on a record. A couple of false starts before finding
the beginning of the track. After a couple of beats,* STEVE *reenters.*]

MICHAEL [*reading a test*]: *Trabajo. Trabajas. Trabaloo?*

[*He grimaces and marks the wrong answer.*]

STEVE: It's different when you have kids, Michael.
MICHAEL: I know all about that.
STEVE: It's not just your own money anymore.
MICHAEL: You don't have to tell me.
STEVE: It's something you get used to.
MICHAEL: So I've heard.

[*The record begins to skip.*]

STEVE: Man.

[*He starts for the living room.*]

MICHAEL: They're going to wear out sooner or later. Then what are you going to do?

STEVE: Maybe when the kids are done with college. There'll be something better than CDs by then anyway.

GINA [*entering from the living room*]: What is that?

STEVE: Gina. You've got to be more careful or the record skips.

GINA: I was just walking.

STEVE: You've got to walk lighter. That can scratch the record.

GINA: Okay. I'm sorry.

MICHAEL: It's an obsolete technology. It's not her fault. [*To* GINA] You know he built that turntable with a kit from Radio Shack.

GINA: No wonder.

STEVE: That was top of the line. It's better than what you could buy now.

MICHAEL: You can't buy one now. That's my point.

GINA: Can I turn it off so I can watch TV?

STEVE: Didn't your mother ask you to set the table?

GINA: I know. It's a little hard when . . .

[*She looks at the cluttered table.*]

STEVE: Don't get wrapped up in anything. Your grandparents will be here before you know it.

[*She exits.*]

We're going to need the table, Mike.

MICHAEL: I'm just going to finish marking these tests. There's not enough light to work out there.

[*The music is turned off.*]

STEVE: I told Janet I'd have everything ready before she got home.

MICHAEL: Al and Judy are coming. Nobody told me that.

STEVE: Of course they're coming. They always come for the kids' birthdays. When have they not come for the kids' birthdays?

MICHAEL: It makes sense now.

STEVE: What?

MICHAEL: Janet. Janet always gets tense when her parents are coming over.

STEVE: She does not.

MICHAEL: Wait'll you see what I got Doug for his birthday.

STEVE: You think she gets tense?

MICHAEL: Around Al and Judy? You haven't noticed? I got him that skating game he's been talking about for his Game Boy. And one of these lights they've got you plug into them that are like snakeheads with these glowing eyes.

STEVE: I'm not sure it's that . . . that makes her tense.

MICHAEL: They are her parents. She's entitled.

STEVE [*calling offstage*]: Your mother'll be here any minute. [*To* MICHAEL] I don't get tense around our parents.

MICHAEL: Never.

STEVE: What's that supposed to mean?

GINA [*returning*]: This isn't going to go super late, is it? 'Cause Mom said I could go to a movie with Loretta after.

STEVE: I hope not, because we have practice.

GINA: So you can't take me?

STEVE: Can't your mother take you?

GINA: Can I ride with Loretta?

MICHAEL: Loretta?

GINA: She just got her license.

STEVE: I'll have to talk with your mother.

GINA: Loretta is such a good driver.

STEVE: When your mother gets home.

[*He exits into the living room.*]

MICHAEL: You're not marching tonight?

GINA: We're not home team. Thank God. Only pep band has to go.

MICHAEL: No need for emergency medical technicians to be standing by then.

GINA: No. They're all going to wear safety goggles.

MICHAEL: What?

GINA: Oh, God. He did it again. At the pep assembly today, when they were playing "War Cry," Neal's pounding away until one of his drumsticks goes flying and catches Mr. Hollowell right in the face.

MICHAEL: Could have put an eye out.

GINA: Don't joke about that, Uncle Mike. It could have. Mr. Hollowell had to go to the nurse and everything. Wore this big bandage over his eye the rest of the day. He had no idea what the cellos were doing during orchestra.

MICHAEL: Threat to public safety.

GINA: And Neal's a junior. You'd think he'd be a little more under control by now.

MICHAEL: I hate to have to break the bad news to you . . .

[JANET *enters the kitchen with her briefcase and a shopping bag.*]

JANET: Steven. I'm home. Sorry I'm late. It was the client from hell today.

GINA: You better wind this up *muy fasto,* Uncle Mike.

MICHAEL: I'm just about there.

GINA: I've got to set the table.

JANET [*entering from the kitchen*]: Hi, Gina. How was your—

GINA: Hi, Mom. How was work?

STEVE [*entering*]: Did you get candles? I meant to call and remind you.

JANET: I thought you were going to . . . I thought Gina was going to set the table.

MICHAEL [*still working*]: I'll give her a hand as soon as I'm finished.

STEVE: Michael was working. We can all pitch in. The lasagna's in the oven.

JANET: I just thought we'd be farther along.

MICHAEL: I'm going to be out of here in just . . .

JANET: Gina, Dougie's presents are up in my closet.

[GINA *exits into the front of the house.* JANET *places the shopping bag on the sideboard.*]

MICHAEL: There's just no good place to work out there.

JANET: You know, Steven, I thought you'd make sure she—

MICHAEL: I'll be out in two seconds, as soon as I finish this.

JANET: Mom and Dad are going to be here. They're picking Doug up at soccer.

[MICHAEL *gives* STEVE *a look.*]

STEVE: Dinner's under control. I'm ready to put the bread in and start the broccoli as soon as they get here.

[JANET *begins moving things from the table.*]

JANET: I just thought it would be nice if the table was set and the room was ready.

STEVE: It won't take us that long.

JANET [*discovering the record box*]: What's this?

STEVE: I'm going to move that.

JANET: And not into the living room. I wish we could keep one room in this whole house that wasn't just a dumping area.

MICHAEL: There. Done. Finished. Finito. I'll get this stuff out of here.

JANET: It's not just you, Michael. I don't know why the dining room has to look like a warehouse.

MICHAEL: I really wanted to finish marking these tests today so I could go apartment hunting tomorrow.

JANET: Apartment?

MICHAEL: I don't want to be in your hair.

JANET: You're not. Michael. You don't need an apartment.

MICHAEL: Just have my own place.

STEVE: You can't afford an apartment.

MICHAEL: I can't stay here forever.

JANET: There's no rush. There's no hurry, is there, Steven? You don't need an apartment.

MICHAEL: That's great. I just don't want to be—

JANET: An apartment is so . . .

STEVE: An apartment is so expensive.

MICHAEL: I just don't want to be in the way.

JANET: We have plenty of room. There's the extra room upstairs if you don't want to be—

MICHAEL: It's not that. Really.

JANET: I don't want to hear any more about an apartment. You're welcome here. You're family.

[*She exits into the kitchen.*]

STEVE: An apartment?

MICHAEL: I was thinking.

STEVE: There's no rush.

MICHAEL: I don't know.

STEVE: Don't have to rush into anything.

JANET [*returning*]: You didn't frost the cake.

MICHAEL: Potato cake?

JANET: When were you planning to frost the cake?

MICHAEL: He doesn't like frosting on potato cake.

JANET: The kids expect frosting. I hope you bought frosting.

[*Beat.*]

STEVE: I can make frosting.

JANET: Steven. There's no time to make frosting.

STEVE: I can make frosting.

[*He exits into the kitchen as* GINA *enters.*]

GINA: What did you get him? They barely even fit on the mantel.

JANET: Steven. Don't make frosting. Go to Dillon's and buy a can.

GINA [*taking an elaborately wrapped package from the shopping bag on the sideboard*]: Oh. This is so cute. Did you see this, Mom?

JANET: Why don't you put that back?

GINA: We should let people see this. Douglas won't appreciate it.

JANET: Why don't you take it to the living room with the others?

GINA [*exiting*]: I bet she got him something good.

MICHAEL: Debbie must have worked on that for days.

JANET: She just wanted to make it nice.

MICHAEL: Could I borrow some paper? I haven't wrapped mine yet.

JANET: Sure. There's paper up in the extra room.

MICHAEL: I won't be able to make it so fancy.

JANET: Dougie isn't going to care how it's wrapped.

MICHAEL: What'd she get him?

JANET: Let's wait till he opens—

MICHAEL: She told you.

JANET: She just wanted to be sure we hadn't got it for him already.

MICHAEL: She get him something good? Or'd she get him a book or something?

JANET: I'm sure he'll like it very much.

MICHAEL: What is it?

JANET: If this is going to upset you.

MICHAEL: I just want to know what she got him.

JANET: It's a game for his Game Boy.

[*Beat.*]

MICHAEL: What game?

JANET: It's a skating game he wanted.

MICHAEL: And a snakehead light with eyes that glow?

JANET: Well, a light. Yes. She said a light for his Game Boy, too.

MICHAEL: That bitch.

JANET: Michael.

MICHAEL: You can't give him that.

JANET: Michael, I—

MICHAEL: She knew I would get him that.

JANET: I don't think she—

MICHAEL: That was my idea. She stole my idea.

JANET: If you both got him the same thing, it's a coincidence.

MICHAEL: We talked about what to get him a month ago. She doesn't know what he wants for his Game Boy. When we came over on Labor Day, I was the one who played with Dougie. She never paid any attention to him. She never took her eyes off Morgan the whole time.

[*Beat.*]

On the way home I told her I knew exactly what we should get Doug for his birthday.

[*Beat.*]

You can't give him that package.
JANET: Michael, she already told me—
MICHAEL: Well, I told Steve. I told Steve before she told you.

[*A series of toots from a car horn.*]

GINA [*offstage*]: They're here.
JANET: Steven. They're here.
MICHAEL: Please let me give him my present.
GINA [*entering from the living room*]: Gramma and Grampa are here.

[*More toots from the car horn.*]

Didn't anybody hear them?

[*She exits out the back door.*]

JANET: He doesn't have to open Debbie's tonight. He can open it tomorrow.
MICHAEL: Thanks.
GINA [*offstage*]: Gramma, how are you?

[STEVE *enters from the kitchen. His apron and his face have been soiled with powdered sugar and cocoa.*]

STEVE: Do we have any cream of tartar?
JANET: Get in the car, go to the store, and buy a can of frosting.

[*She exits to the living room.*]

STEVE: You're right. They do make her tense.

SCENE 4

[*October. Two weeks later. Saturday morning.* GINA, *wearing pajamas, sits at the table, reading the newspaper and eating a bowl of cereal. There is a loud sound from a ball striking the exterior wall of the house.* GINA *reacts but does not move.*]

JANET [*offstage*]: No. You're doing everything that you can . . . What else could you do? . . . Of course you can't.

[*The ball hits the house again.*]

One second.

[JANET *appears in the doorway to the kitchen with the telephone receiver in hand.*]

Gina, would you go outside and remind your brother that the house is not a soccer goal and that your father is still sleeping?

GINA: Can I finish my breakfast?

[*The ball again.*]

JANET: Now.

GINA: I'm not even dressed.

JANET: I'm on the phone with Aunt Debbie.

[GINA *responds with a "tension" face and gets up from the table.* JANET *speaks into the phone.*]

Sorry. Doug's warming up for his soccer game by kicking his ball against the back of the house . . . No, no. Gina's going to go talk to him . . . Well, of course, it's upsetting for her, but she's . . . No, no. Don't worry about that. Don't worry about her.

[*The ball again.* JANET *motions* GINA, *who has been listening, on out the door.* GINA *exits out the back.*]

You always worry about everybody else. Just worry about yourself this time . . . Do you want to go out to dinner tonight?

[JANET *moves back into the kitchen, her voice fading away.*]

We could go to a movie after or something . . . No, no. Gina can baby-sit . . . No, she doesn't have any plans . . . No, you can't pay her. She's happy just to help out.

[STEVE *enters from upstairs wearing a soccer referee's uniform, but with the jersey untucked. He carries a pair of street shoes and a pair of soccer shoes. He makes his way slowly across the room toward the kitchen. As he reaches the doorway,* GINA *returns and walks past him.*]

GINA: I told him. I told him you'd kill him. I hope you won't make a liar out of me.

[JANET *reenters.*]

JANET: Can you babysit for Debbie tonight?

GINA: Loretta's having people over.

JANET: I already told her you would.

GINA: Thanks, Mom. Thanks a lot. I have no life.

[*She exits upstairs.*]

STEVE: How's Debbie?

JANET: Good morning. Coffee's ready.

STEVE: Did you call her, or did she call you?

JANET [*folding the newspaper* GINA *left on the table*]: Where'd you go last night?

STEVE [*going into the kitchen*]: We stopped playing at ten. I didn't want to bother the neighbors.

JANET: Yeah, but then where'd you go?

STEVE: We went over to Lloyd's for a while.

JANET: Oh, Steven.

STEVE [*returning with a cup of coffee*]: No. He bought this new mixer. It's amazing. It's only about so big—

JANET: You guys aren't getting together tonight?

STEVE: No. Eric has some Maggie thing again.

JANET: Great. I invited Debbie out for dinner tonight. I think you should come with.

STEVE: I don't think Debbie—

JANET: I really think you should.

STEVE: I don't want to get in the middle of this.

JANET: Your brother's been here for three weeks. If that's not in the middle . . .

STEVE: Have you seen my glasses?

JANET: I think it's really important that you come to dinner.

STEVE: I bet she'd be a lot more comfortable if it was just you two.

JANET: She wants to talk to you.

STEVE: I don't know what I can tell her.

JANET: Maybe I should call Eric and see if he's talked to him.

STEVE: I've talked to him. He just doesn't say that much.

JANET: Sometimes you have to ask questions.

STEVE: I can't keep the scorecard if I don't find my glasses.

JANET: I told her we'd pick her up at six.

STEVE: I don't think this is a good idea.

[*The ball again.*]

JANET: If you never talk to her, it's like we're taking sides. I think we need to stick with both of them.

STEVE: What am I supposed to tell Mike?

JANET: That you're having dinner. Maybe then he'll want to talk to you.

[GINA *enters.*]

GINA: I'm trying to read and he's doing it again.

STEVE: We may want to practice tonight after all. Eric's firm is having this party, and he thinks it would be cool if we could play—

JANET: Steven. We're trying to help your brother, not Eric and his law firm.

STEVE: He refers a lot of business to me.

JANET: Steven. They don't care if the guy who does their taxes can play "Stairway to Heaven."

STEVE: You're the one who got it out of the closet.

JANET: I just wanted you to talk to your brother.

[*The ball.*]

STEVE [*heading for the back door*]: If he doesn't stop that . . .

JANET: Steven.

STEVE: I won't actually kill him.

[*He exits out the back door.*]

GINA: They aren't going to play in public, are they? 'Cause that would not be good.

JANET: The Flab Four? I don't imagine it'll get that far. Did you forget to take your bowl into the kitchen?

GINA: Doug just left his.

JANET: Thank you. Would you get it, too?

GINA: How late do I have to babysit?

JANET: It depends if she wants to go to a movie.

GINA: How much am I getting?

JANET: A warm feeling for having helped out.

GINA: But Aunt Debbie always pays me to babysit.

JANET: But I don't. And I invited her out.

GINA [*exiting into the kitchen with the cereal bowls*]: I hate my life.

STEVE [*returning with the ball*]: I disarmed him. I've got to get out of here. I'm supposed to help set up the goals.

JANET: When will you be back?

STEVE: I'm reffing Dougie's game and the game after. Noon or something?

JANET: I made a list of stuff Dougie needs from the hardware store. We've got to get him started on the science fair.

GINA [*returning with* STEVE's *glasses*]: These were in the sink.

STEVE: I've been looking all over for those.

GINA: Loretta gets eight dollars an hour to babysit her own brother. And he's ten. She doesn't have to do anything. I'd do it for half that. And Morgan is a baby. I have to play with her.

JANET: She's your cousin. You love her.

GINA: I don't know why Uncle Mike can't babysit. She's his daughter.

[*She exits to the living room.*]

STEVE: We're not going to really get into it with her tonight, are we?

JANET: It's not going to be Camp David or anything, but I'd figure the subject might come up.

STEVE: I just don't want to get in too deep. That's all I'm saying.

JANET: Her husband's sleeping in our garage. I think we're up to our asses in it.

STEVE: I just think it's better if we let them work it out. If we just give them a little space, I bet this whole thing will blow over.

[*The sound of the back door opening.* CLAIRE *appears in the back doorway. She is barefoot, wearing* MICHAEL's *shirt.*]

CLAIRE: Hi. You're up already. Great. Mike said I had to be really quiet so I didn't wake anybody up. I was really trying to be careful. I'm sorry, I've got to pee really bad.

STEVE: It's down the stairs there.

CLAIRE: There. Right. Thanks, Steve.

[*She starts to go, then stops and turns back.*]

Is that your little boy out back? He's a real cutie.

[*She exits. Beat.*]

JANET: Who the hell is that?

STEVE: I didn't know that—

JANET: *Steve.*

STEVE: Yeah. Um . . .

JANET: I want to know who's peeing in our basement.

STEVE: She's, well, she goes to school with Lloyd.

JANET: Of course.

STEVE: I didn't know she was—

JANET: She on the perpetual plan, too?

STEVE: Maybe it's not what it— Maybe she's just—

JANET: And you know her from?

STEVE: She was at Lloyd's last night.

JANET: Lloyd have a party last night?

STEVE: No. No. It was nothing like that.

JANET: So it was just you guys and the coed with the little bladder?

STEVE: No. We went by Lloyd's to check out his new mixer—

JANET: Uh-huh.

STEVE: And some people came over.

JANET: Girl people?

STEVE: Janet, it was a bunch of people. Girls. And guys. It was just people.

JANET: Like a party?

STEVE: Yeah, like a party.

JANET: You went to a party at Lloyd's last night with a bunch of college girls?

STEVE: You make it sound like . . . I didn't even know Michael was . . . I got a ride home from Eric.

JANET: You left him there? You left Michael there alone?

STEVE: I didn't think I needed to—

JANET: We're supposed to be saving his marriage, not fixing him up. You're supposed to be . . . connecting with him. You're not supposed to leave him with girls. You're supposed to keep him in the garage, not send him out on the town.

CLAIRE [returning]: Are all those your tools down there?

STEVE: Well, yeah. In the workshop.

CLAIRE: You must be really handy. I've never known anybody who had their own lathe.

[She turns to JANET.]

Janet?

JANET: Yes.

CLAIRE: Nice to meet you. What a great house. It's so homey. Claire. Claire Sherman. I'm a friend of Michael's. I guess. We'll see.

[A look.]

Matches in the bowl by the coffee cups he said?

JANET: Above the canisters.

CLAIRE: Thanks.

[She exits into the kitchen. Beat. The sound of the ball against the side of the house.]

STEVE: Where'd he get another ball?

JANET: Steven.

STEVE: I've got to run.

JANET: You're not going?

[*The ball again.*]

STEVE: I can't not go.

JANET: You can't just . . . You've got to talk to Michael.

STEVE: I can't talk to him now. I'm the referee.

[CLAIRE *returns, holding a cigarette and a book of matches.*]

CLAIRE: I'm so glad you guys were up already. Mike really wanted to let you guys sleep.

[*She strikes a match and lights the cigarette.*]

I think we're going to go out and get some breakfast. You want to come along?

STEVE: I can't because I've got to go now. But Janet . . .

JANET: I don't think—

CLAIRE: You want to come?

[*Beat. The sound of the ball.*]

JANET: You know, we don't really allow smoking in the house.

CLAIRE: No. Of course not. I wouldn't think of it.

[*She fans away the smoke.*]

If you decide you want to come, just give us a holler. It'd be fun. Have a good game.

[*She exits to the driveway.*]

JANET: I want to know what you're going to do about this.

[*She exits to the kitchen.*]

STEVE: What am I supposed to do?

JANET [*offstage*]: You'd better do something.

STEVE: I can't ground him. I can't stop him from doing anything.

[JANET *returns with a can of air freshener. She sprays.*]

JANET: In my house you can stop him from doing anything.

222 ∞ DEAN CORRIN

STEVE: You want me to ask him to leave?

JANET: I want you to tell him that he can't do this in our house.

STEVE: And if he says no?

JANET: He can find someplace else to stay.

STEVE: I think he just did.

JANET: He wouldn't do that.

[STEVE *shrugs*.]

You can't let him do that.

STEVE: Then I can't kick him out.

JANET: But you'll talk to him.

STEVE: I'll talk to him.

JANET: And no more parties at Lloyd's.

[*Beat*.]

Where's Doug?

STEVE: He's out back.

[*Beat*.]

JANET: But it's so quiet.

STEVE: I'm sure he didn't go—

JANET [*running to the kitchen*]: It's too quiet.

STEVE: Janet.

JANET [*offstage*]: Oh my God.

STEVE: What?

JANET: She's playing with him.

STEVE: What?

JANET [*returning*]: They're playing soccer in the driveway. With a cigarette in her mouth. Steven. Do something.

STEVE [*going into the kitchen*]: They're just playing soccer.

JANET: Everybody in the neighborhood can see.

STEVE [*offstage*]: Nobody's watching.

JANET: You don't know who's watching.

STEVE: Whoa.

JANET: What?

STEVE: She's pretty good.

JANET: Steven.

STEVE [*returning*]: We probably shouldn't mention this at dinner, you think?

SCENE 5

[*Two weeks later. Friday night. On the table there are a number of jars filled with water and containing a number of nails. There is a small kitchen scale on the table as well as bottles of motor oil, vegetable oil, nail polish, glue, pancake syrup, and paint. The table is further cluttered with brushes, bowls, paper towels, and such.* MICHAEL *pushes numbers on a cell phone and puts it to his ear.*]

MICHAEL: Hi. She asleep? . . . Sorry, I didn't think you'd be asleep . . . I didn't want to call while you were trying to get her to sleep . . . I couldn't call this afternoon because I was at school . . . Because I was busy, I had things to do . . . School is not a good place for me to talk . . . I don't know about what, I just wanted to let you know I've got a new number . . . No, I'm not moving. I got a cell phone . . . Yes . . . So you can call me, you don't have to bother Steve and Janet, you don't have to call at school . . . I'm at Steve's . . . Because I'm calling on the new phone . . . I've always told you the truth . . . I never said we couldn't afford a cell phone . . . I said we couldn't justify the expense of a cell phone. I think now we can, I think I need one . . . I'm paying for it . . . I can't spend any money? . . . Do you want the number? . . . Why do you want to do that? . . . Then it is a waste of money . . . Let me give you the number . . . But this way you don't have to bother them . . . At least let me give you the—

[*Beat. He flips the phone shut and puts it in his pocket. He goes to examine the display on the table.* JANET *enters from the basement, wearing an apron and carrying a basket of laundry.*]

JANET: I'm going to move it.
MICHAEL: I was just looking.
JANET: Science fair.
MICHAEL: You're growing nails?
JANET: We're preventing rust.
MICHAEL: Maybe if you took the nails out of the water.
JANET: We're testing which materials, when used to coat nails, most effectively inhibit rust.
MICHAEL: Fascinating.
JANET: Steven should be home any minute. They must have stopped to get something to eat after the game.
MICHAEL: That's okay. Lloyd's not here yet.
JANET [*handing him the basket*]: I put the load in the washer into the dryer.
MICHAEL: Thanks.

JANET: I've got to start a new load when Dougie's out of the shower.

MICHAEL: Sorry. I was going to go change it.

JANET: He managed to get as much of this stuff on him as he did on the nails. I hope we didn't get anything on the rug.

[*She picks up a nail from under the table.*]

Watch your step.

[*The telephone rings.*]

MICHAEL: Why didn't you do it in the basement?

JANET: It's such a mess down there. I'm afraid he'll step on something sharp and hurt himself.

MICHAEL: Like a nail?

[*The telephone rings again, and* JANET *exits into the kitchen.* MICHAEL *continues to fold the laundry.* JANET *steps back into the doorway, talking on the phone.*]

JANET: Hello . . . Yeah. He's right here . . . Do you want to talk to him? . . . No, he's standing right in front of me . . . I think so . . . Do you want to talk to him? . . . Oh . . . Okay . . . You want me to give him a message? . . . Well, okay . . . Yeah . . . Bye. [*To* MICHAEL] Debbie.

[*She exits into the kitchen.* MICHAEL *angrily tosses his clothes back into the laundry basket, picks it up, and starts toward the back door.* JANET *returns from the kitchen.*]

She just wanted to know if you were here.

MICHAEL: I figured.

JANET: I haven't said anything.

MICHAEL: I know.

[MICHAEL's *cell phone chirps.*]

JANET: What's that?

MICHAEL: My phone.

JANET: When'd you get that?

[*The cell phone again.*]

MICHAEL: This afternoon.

JANET: Well . . .

MICHAEL [*answering the phone*]: Hello? . . . Yes . . . How'd you get this number? . . . Since when do we have caller ID? . . . You can just ask me where

I'm calling from . . . Of course I will tell you the truth, why wouldn't I tell you the truth? . . . Debbie . . . Look . . . Debbie . . . Maybe we should . . .

[*The back door opens.* GINA *and* STEVE *enter. She wears a jacket over her band uniform pants and carries the uniform jacket and her flute case.* MICHAEL *moves into the kitchen through one door as they enter the dining room through the other.*]

GINA: There is no way.

STEVE: If you don't think flutes have enough to do.

GINA: That's not what I meant.

STEVE: It'd put the flutes right up front.

GINA: They'd give it to the clarinets. The clarinets get everything.

[*She exits into the living room.*]

STEVE: You can't do a Jethro Tull medley and feature the clarinets.

JANET: How'd it go?

STEVE: She doesn't think they have enough to do.

JANET [*following* GINA *offstage*]: Don't just dump that there. Doug's in the shower, sweetie.

STEVE: Hey, Mike, are—

[MICHAEL *stops him, indicating the phone.*]

MICHAEL: I'll pick her up then . . . Or you can call me . . . You can call me here . . . On this phone . . . The minutes are included in the plan . . . Yeah . . . Okay . . . Good-bye.

[*He flips the phone shut.*]

STEVE: A cell phone?

MICHAEL: Yeah. If I'm not going to get my own place, I figured you guys were going to get sick of running out to the studio every time Debbie calls about something.

STEVE: Or when anybody else calls.

MICHAEL: It's a phone. I don't know what the big deal—

STEVE: You haven't called . . . *her*, have you?

MICHAEL: You want to check? You want to check the numbers I've called? I guess that's why they do that. So you can be chaperoned.

STEVE: You're just separated, Mike. You don't have to turn this into . . . Don't you want this to work out?

MICHAEL: I want it to work out. That doesn't mean I necessarily want to go back.

STEVE: What about Morgan? You don't want to miss Morgan—

MICHAEL: I'm going be there for Morgan, okay? Everybody acts like I'm going to screw up Morgan.

STEVE: Michael. It's not that. Of course we don't—

MICHAEL: Then what is it?

STEVE: Think of the position you're putting us in. With the kids. With Debbie. How long do you think we can go without having to say something to Debbie? You can't expect us to lie to her.

MICHAEL: You can tell her.

STEVE: I don't want to tell her.

MICHAEL: She already knows.

STEVE: She knows?

MICHAEL: I told her.

STEVE: Told her what?

MICHAEL: I told her.

STEVE: Oh, man. Why'd you do that?

MICHAEL: You want me to be honest with her, don't you?

STEVE: Yeah, but . . . That was just . . . once . . . That was just an accident.

MICHAEL: I didn't want to lie to her.

STEVE: You don't have to lie . . . You just don't have to—

MICHAEL: I felt like I needed to tell her.

STEVE: I don't believe you. How does this make us look? We haven't said a thing to Debbie.

MICHAEL: I don't think she expects—

STEVE: She'll think we're—

MICHAEL: She's not going to blame you.

[*The phone rings.*]

STEVE: Oh, great.

MICHAEL: Come on, Steve.

STEVE: What if that's her?

[*The phone rings again.*]

MICHAEL: It's okay.

STEVE: What are we supposed to tell her?

MICHAEL: Whatever you want.

[*The phone rings again.* JANET *enters.*]

JANET: Isn't anybody going to get—

STEVE: Don't answer it.

MICHAEL: Steve.

STEVE: It might be Debbie.

[*The phone rings again. Beat.*]

JANET: Well, I think I'd want to talk to Debbie.

STEVE: Michael told her.

[*The phone rings again.*]

JANET: What?

STEVE: Were you going to tell us you told her?

JANET: Michael.

[*The phone rings again.*]

MICHAEL: Look . . .

JANET: Oh my God. Michael.

GINA [*offstage*]: Dad.

[*Beat.*]

    Phone for you.

STEVE: Me?

JANET: Steven.

STEVE: Why does she want to talk to me?

JANET: Stay calm.

MICHAEL: I'll talk to her.

JANET: She can talk to Steve.

STEVE: Is there anything . . .

MICHAEL: Whatever you want.

GINA [*entering*]: Dad. Eric's on the phone.

STEVE: Eric?

GINA: You didn't hear the phone?

STEVE: It's Eric.

GINA: You didn't hear me call you?

STEVE: It's just Eric. [*To* GINA] I'll get it down here.

[*He exits into the kitchen. Beat.*]

GINA: Didn't anybody hear the phone?

JANET: No. I guess we didn't.

GINA: Well, it was ringing. [*Calling offstage*] Doug. Will you hang that phone up?

MICHAEL: Look, I don't want you to think—

JANET [*indicating* GINA]: Not now.

GINA: Is this going to live here?

JANET: It's got to be somewhere Doug can do observations. I don't like him going down in that basement. I'm afraid he'll—

GINA: He got the idea just out of a book, right?

JANET: Nobody made it to the hardware store. We had to come up with something we had the materials for.

GINA: He better have a good paper.

MICHAEL: Not every project can be "The Effect of Homeopathic Remedies on the Growth of E. Coli Bacteria."

JANET: Michael.

GINA: It was a good idea. The judges just didn't get it.

JANET: It was a very good idea. I just can't believe we let you cultivate a deadly microorganism in the kitchen.

MICHAEL: Ew. Gross.

GINA: Uncle Mike.

MICHAEL: What'd you have to do? Go find bad hamburger?

GINA: You order it. From a catalog.

JANET: They have a complete selection of lethal microbes for the use of middle school students.

MICHAEL: Dougie didn't want to build a volcano? That's what I did.

GINA: You can't do that anymore. No human subjects, no animal dissection, and no volcanoes.

MICHAEL: That's all the good stuff.

GINA: A volcano is a demonstration, not an experiment. Were you testing a hypothesis with your volcano?

MICHAEL: Could I set a smoke bomb off in school without getting in trouble?

GINA: I didn't know you were a pyro, Uncle Mike.

[*Obnoxious music begins to blare from a boom box offstage.*]

JANET: What is that boy doing? [*To* GINA] Be positive about his experiment. He worked really hard. [*Calling off as she exits into the front of the house*] Douglas Philip Burns, I thought you were supposed to be getting ready for bed. You've got to be up for the first game tomorrow.

[MICHAEL *and* GINA *are silent for a moment after they are left alone. The music offstage is turned off.*]

MICHAEL: You know Cookie Bondurant?

[*Beat.*]

GINA: She's a senior.

MICHAEL: Yeah. She's a tutor at school.

GINA: In Spanish?

MICHAEL: No. Reading, I think. I was just talking to her. She said she knew you.

GINA: I don't think—

MICHAEL: She's on the Winter Dance committee.

GINA: I'm sure.

MICHAEL: She said they usually get a DJ.

GINA: I guess.

MICHAEL: We used to always have bands.

GINA: I've heard about that.

MICHAEL: She thought it might be cool to have a band.

GINA: Oh.

MICHAEL: Different.

GINA: Yeah.

MICHAEL: We're supposed to send them a tape.

STEVE [*returning from the kitchen*]: Eric's not coming.

MICHAEL: Again?

STEVE: Do you believe that?

MICHAEL: What came up now?

STEVE: Nothing. He just doesn't have enough time.

MICHAEL: Enough time?

STEVE: "There's so much going on right now."

MICHAEL: What about his firm's party?

STEVE: Now that he's up for partner, he's not sure if playing there would be "appropriate."

MICHAEL: He could still practice.

STEVE: He said maybe when things aren't so busy.

GINA: I guess this rules out Winter Dance, huh?

STEVE: What?

MICHAEL: This girl from Gina's school is one of our tutors. She wanted me to send an audition tape to the Winter Dance committee.

STEVE: You're kidding?

GINA: If only.

STEVE: We've got to find that tape.

GINA: Daddy.

MICHAEL: It's not a sure thing. They were planning to hire a DJ.

STEVE: Lloyd's got that drum machine.

MICHAEL: Oh, no. Come on, Stevie. Where's the fun in that? Might as well get a karaoke machine if we're going to do that.

STEVE: Just to make a new tape.

MICHAEL: Do you think if I called Eric? If he knew we had someplace else to play?

[*The doorbell rings.*]

STEVE: There's Lloyd.

MICHAEL: Wait till he hears.

STEVE: Gina, can you let him in? I've got to get the bass.

[GINA *exits to the front of the house.*]

MICHAEL: He's going to have a fit.

STEVE: Don't let Lloyd call Eric.

MICHAEL: Can you imagine that conversation?

STEVE: We'd never see Eric again.

MICHAEL: Or even his drums.

STEVE: Hey, what if Janet talked to Maggie?

MICHAEL: I don't know. That could go either way.

GINA [*returning*]: Is Lloyd here?

STEVE: I thought—

GINA: It's for him.

[CLAIRE *enters. She carries a textbook.*]

CLAIRE: Hi.

[*Beat.*]

Lloyd said he had practice tonight.

STEVE: We haven't seen—

CLAIRE: He wanted to borrow my astronomy book. We've got a test on Monday.

STEVE: I'll give it to—

MICHAEL: Lloyd should be here any minute.

CLAIRE: Oh.

MICHAEL: You want to wait?

CLAIRE: Sure. I can wait.

STEVE: We can just give him the book.

MICHAEL: You want to stay for practice?

STEVE: Mike.

CLAIRE: Would that be okay?

MICHAEL: Can you play the drums?

JANET [*entering*]: Who was at the . . .

CLAIRE: Hi.

JANET: Hello.

CLAIRE: It was just me. I had to drop off a book for Lloyd.

STEVE: Astronomy.

JANET: Oh.

[*There is a banging on the back door.*]

MICHAEL: And there he is.

CLAIRE [*taking out a pack of cigarettes*]: I hadn't heard from you. I wasn't sure
    if—

MICHAEL: I was just . . . I was going to call you today.

CLAIRE: I wish I'd known. I was driving Lloyd crazy.

[*More banging on the door.*]

   [*To* JANET] It was nice to see you.

[*Beat.*]

   You want one?

JANET: No. Thank you.

CLAIRE: You don't smoke, do you?

GINA: No.

CLAIRE: Don't start. It was nice to meet you. We'll have to talk more later.

GINA: Yeah.

[*More banging.*]

CLAIRE: I'm never going to hear the end of this. [*Exiting out the back door*]
    I'm staying for practice, Lloyd. I guess it wasn't such a dumb idea.

STEVE: You can't do this.

MICHAEL: She's just going to stay for practice.

STEVE: You can't do this in my house.

MICHAEL: Your house?

STEVE: It's our house now.

MICHAEL: If you want me to go—

STEVE: No. Of course not. But you can't just—

MICHAEL: If you want me out of your way.

JANET: Of course you can stay here, Michael. It's just—

STEVE: This puts us in a hell of a position, huh?

JANET: We just want to help you and Debbie.

STEVE: She's going to think we were—

JANET: Steven. Shut up. This is not about us.

[*Beat.*]

It's not about how we feel. [*To* MICHAEL] Did you guys just give up?

MICHAEL: It's complicated.

JANET: Isn't it worth more than that?

STEVE: What are you thinking about? It's not just about you.

MICHAEL: I don't know what you guys are so bent out of shape for. It's not like it's your marriage.

[*He storms out the back door. Beat.*]

JANET: Go.

STEVE: What?

JANET: Just go. Go play.

STEVE: Look, maybe it's none of our—

JANET: What?

STEVE: Maybe it's not going to work.

JANET: You don't think he should go back?

STEVE: I don't know.

JANET: You don't think it's worth the effort?

STEVE: Janet.

JANET: It's not important to you?

STEVE: Of course I'm not going to give up.

JANET: I need to know that.

STEVE: I just don't know if I can . . .

JANET: What?

STEVE: Nothing.

GINA: Does Uncle Mike have a girlfriend?

ACT 2

SCENE 1

[*One week later. Saturday afternoon.* GINA, *in her pajamas, sits at the table eating cereal and reading the newspaper. The science fair project has been moved to the sideboard. There is an iron and ironing board set up to one side.*]

GINA: Shouldn't there be some rust by now?

JANET [*offstage*]: What?

GINA: Shouldn't Dougie's nails be showing some rust by now? They've been sitting here for a week.

JANET [*entering from the kitchen with a measuring cup of water for the iron*]: I don't know. The book didn't say how long it would take.

GINA: Didn't Douglas do any background research?

JANET: His research was on the process of oxidation, not how long it takes for nails to rust.

GINA: When's the science fair?

JANET: We have two more weeks.

GINA: Should've done some research on nails.

[CLAIRE *enters at the back door, carrying an armload of jeans. She peeks into the room.*]

CLAIRE: Morning, everybody.

GINA: Morning.

JANET: Good morning.

CLAIRE: Michael doesn't have a clean pair of jeans. Do you mind if I run a load?

JANET: I guess not.

CLAIRE: If we're going to go out later.

[*She starts to go.*]

Does he have his own detergent?

JANET: Just whatever's down there.

CLAIRE: I'll tell him to get some.

[CLAIRE *exits to the basement.*]

GINA: Is she living out there?

JANET: No.

GINA: But she's doing laundry?

JANET: She's doing his laundry.

STEVE [*entering at the back, wearing his referee's uniform*]: Good morning.

JANET: Morning.

STEVE: Smells good.

[*He goes into the kitchen.*]

JANET: I told Debbie I'd bring the cake for Morgan's party.

GINA: So we'd have a real cake this year.

JANET: Be nice.

STEVE [*entering with a cup of coffee*]: We're not having another sugar-free whole wheat cake?

JANET: That was Morgan's first birthday. Debbie'd never even bought baby food. She didn't want to give her chocolate and sugar.

GINA: But she'd give her that cake.

JANET: This year she wants a potato cake. I told her I'd do that. Debbie's never made one.

STEVE: Are we having ice cream?

JANET: We'll bring some.

STEVE: This is turning into one wild birthday party.

JANET: How'd it go?

STEVE: We won.

JANET: How'd Dougie do?

STEVE: He played well. He was really on top of it.

JANET: No goal?

STEVE: Soccer's about more than scoring.

JANET: I just wish he'd get a goal one time. He'd feel so much better about it.

STEVE: If he keeps at it.

JANET: I'm afraid he'll want to quit if he never scores a goal.

GINA: For football? He'll never even get in a game.

JANET: I don't want him to play football.

GINA: Those football guys are nuts. He'd be the goal.

JANET: I'm just saying I would hate to see him quit soccer.

[*The sound of the soccer ball hitting the wall of the house.*]

STEVE: I don't think he's planning to quit.

GINA: We couldn't be that lucky.

STEVE: Would you go out and remind him to use the practice goal we bought him?

GINA: He uses it. He just doesn't hit it.
JANET: Gina.

[*The ball.*]

GINA: Well.
STEVE: Just go tell him.
GINA: But I've got to get dressed. I'm meeting Loretta for our Russian Rev project.
JANET: Go tell him he needs to come inside and work on his paper.
MICHAEL [*entering at the back door*]: Morning.

[*They respond.*]

I hope you don't mind. I asked Dougie to move that thing out front for a while. I don't think my head could take that pounding this morning.
GINA: Thanks, Uncle Mike.

[*She exits to the front of the house.*]

MICHAEL: Is Claire . . .
JANET: Basement.
MICHAEL: I got to have some coffee.

[*Exits into the kitchen.*]

JANET: Good practice last night?
STEVE: You know.
JANET: Saw Eric came.
STEVE: Stopped by. Didn't stay.
MICHAEL [*taking his cup of coffee to the basement*]: Claire Bear. You got those aspirin?
STEVE: Can't blame him.
JANET: What?
STEVE: It's not a practice anymore. It's Michael's time to play for his adoring fan.
JANET: Maybe that's a good reason to ask him—
STEVE: And she sits there like she's bloody Yoko or something, just staring at him.
JANET: If you're not enjoying it, maybe it's time to pull back.
STEVE: It's like now we're all just playing for him.
JANET: If it's not working—
STEVE: And the smoke. Do my eyes look red? 'Cause they were just burning.

CLAIRE [*offstage*]: Stop it.
MICHAEL [*offstage*]: What?
CLAIRE: You'll make me drop this.
MICHAEL: Let me help you.
CLAIRE: Mike.

[CLAIRE *enters from the basement with a laundry basket full of clothes.* MICHAEL *follows.*]

    Good morning.
STEVE: Morning.
CLAIRE: I put the towels in the washer into the dryer. I figured they'd go in the dryer.
MICHAEL: Maybe we should leave them alone.
CLAIRE [*taking a shirt out of the laundry basket*]: Oh, is this ever cute? Is this Gina's?
JANET: I can fold that stuff.
CLAIRE: I don't mind.
JANET: It's okay.
CLAIRE: It's the least I can do.
MICHAEL: You want to get breakfast?
CLAIRE: They've eaten already.
STEVE: I'm about ready for lunch.

[*He exits into the kitchen.*]

CLAIRE: They've been up, honey. They can't just sleep all day.

[GINA *enters, wearing jeans and her pajama top. She carries a couple of shirts.*]

GINA: Mom, do you think I should wear the— Oh.
MICHAEL: Hey.
GINA: Which top do you think I should wear?
JANET: Either one needs to be ironed.
CLAIRE [*taking a blouse out of the laundry basket*]: This would be cute, don't you think?
JANET: I don't think she wanted anything that dressy for today.
CLAIRE: She could wear it open over a strappy little tank or something. Did I see one in here?
GINA: I have a blue one that would go.
JANET: It's probably not—
CLAIRE: This one?

GINA: Those do look good together.

MICHAEL: What's that smell?

JANET: I'm baking a cake.

MICHAEL: Potato cake?

JANET: Yeah.

MICHAEL: For Morgan?

JANET: Well, yeah.

MICHAEL: That's been approved?

JANET: I was asked, if that's what you mean.

MICHAEL: Wow. That's a major step.

CLAIRE: I got Morgan these sweet little overalls embroidered with stars on the front.

[*Beat.*]

MICHAEL: You did?

CLAIRE: I hope I got the right size. Do you remember what size she wears?

MICHAEL: Those sizes are so confusing. It's always a bigger size than it seems like it should be.

JANET: She's a 4T.

CLAIRE: Ooo. I got a 2T.

MICHAEL: We can exchange them.

CLAIRE: Can we do it before the party? I want to give her the right pair.

GINA: Are you coming to the party?

[*Beat.*]

CLAIRE: It's probably not a good idea.

MICHAEL: I wouldn't make you go through that.

CLAIRE: I'll just send the gift.

JANET: You know, Michael, Debbie's mom is going to be there and everything.

CLAIRE: Oh.

JANET: It just might not be the best time.

CLAIRE: Sure.

JANET: I don't want to tell you—

MICHAEL: We can do it some other time. I'm going to have her tomorrow. We can give it to her then. That's okay with you, right?

[*The doorbell rings.*]

JANET: Gina, you want to—

GINA [*ironing the shirt* CLAIRE *picked out*]: I'm trying to—

[*The doorbell again.*]

CLAIRE: I'll get it.

JANET: Gina can.

CLAIRE [*exiting*]: I don't mind.

STEVE [*returning from the kitchen carrying a plate with a sandwich, etc.*]: I think somebody's at the door.

MICHAEL: Claire's getting it.

STEVE: Oh.

JANET: Michael, are you coming to the party?

MICHAEL: Come on. I'm not going to miss my kid's birthday.

JANET: Debbie's expecting you?

MICHAEL: She invited me.

STEVE [*examining the experiment*]: Shouldn't something more be happening here?

CLAIRE [*returning*]: Do you guys know somebody "Send"?

STEVE: Send?

JANET: No.

CLAIRE: There's a guy here looking for Send about the audition?

JANET: Audition?

CLAIRE [*speaking offstage*]: What does it say?

STEVE: I'll talk to him.

[NEAL *enters. A high school–aged kid. He is a bit tentative. He carries a flyer.*]

NEAL: This was on the bulletin board at Jenkins.

STEVE: Why don't we go out here?

NEAL: Are you Mr. Toe?

JANET: Audition?

STEVE: I think I know what this is about.

NEAL: Gina.

GINA: Hi.

NEAL: Are you in this band?

GINA: I live here.

STEVE: Why don't we just—

JANET: Can I see that?

[NEAL *gives her the flyer.*]

STEVE: We can talk in the other—

JANET: "Drummer needed." Steven.

STEVE: If you'd just let me—

MICHAEL: Can I see that?

STEVE: Look, Michael, I just thought if Eric—

MICHAEL: Listen, kid, the position's filled.

STEVE: Give him a chance, Michael.

NEAL: Are you Mr. Toe?

MICHAEL: Who's Mr. Toe?

JANET: You put up flyers with our address on them?

STEVE: I didn't want to put our phone number.

NEAL: Oh, man. I am so stupid.

STEVE: I didn't think anyone would just stop by.

NEAL: That's the name of the band.

MICHAEL: What?

NEAL: "Send Resume Toe."

STEVE: That's "send résumé to."

JANET: Are you going to fire Eric?

STEVE: Eric doesn't want to—

MICHAEL: He came last night.

STEVE: But he didn't stay. We're never going to get a chance to play if we wait for Eric to be ready.

JANET: Half your clients come from Eric. What if he stops giving you referrals?

NEAL: Then what's the name of the band?

JANET: It's not a band.

STEVE: Janet.

JANET: It's not working. Obviously. And now you're going to fire your best friend?

[*The soccer ball hits the side of the house.*]

Would somebody tell him to stop kicking that ball and come inside and do his homework?

[*She exits to the front of the house. Beat.*]

NEAL: Did the band break up?

[*The soccer ball.*]

STEVE: Why don't we go out to the studio and play a little?

MICHAEL: Steve.

STEVE: As long as he's here, let's at least let him play. That okay with you . . .

NEAL: Neal.
STEVE: Neal.
MICHAEL: Neal? [*To* GINA] Is he the spinner—
GINA: Uncle Mike.
MICHAEL: Let's see what he can do.
STEVE: Great.

[*The soccer ball.*]

Come on. The studio's out back.

[*He exits out the back door.*]

MICHAEL: In the garage.
NEAL: Great.
MICHAEL: I think there's an old catcher's mask out there.

[MICHAEL *and* GINA *share a look as he exits.*]

NEAL: Your folks seem cool.
GINA: Thanks.
NEAL: I didn't know they had a band.
GINA: No.
NEAL: That's cool.
GINA: Yeah.
NEAL: Well, I better go.
GINA: Yeah.
NEAL: Wish me luck.
GINA: Good luck.

[NEAL *starts toward the front door.*]

CLAIRE: Neal.
NEAL: Yeah?
CLAIRE: It's out the back door.
NEAL: Right.
CLAIRE: Good luck.
NEAL: Thanks.
CLAIRE: Watch your step.

[*He exits out the back door.*]

He's sweet.
GINA: I'm wearing my pajamas.

SCENE 2

[*That night.* STEVE *is playing on a Game Boy with a light attached that is shaped like a snakehead with glowing eyes. The light goes out in the kitchen.* JANET *enters with a glass of water.*]

JANET: You coming?

STEVE: Yeah.

JANET: That went okay.

STEVE: Uh-huh.

JANET: Not as bad as I thought it might be.

STEVE: Debbie's mom.

JANET: Well, you can't expect.

STEVE: Did she ever say his name?

JANET: Well, he is "Debbie's husband."

STEVE: I thought he took it pretty calmly.

JANET: What's he going to do?

STEVE: It's just, he would usually . . .

JANET: He's not exactly in a position . . .

STEVE: But he never took the bait. You got to give him that.

JANET: The dinner was good.

STEVE: Whoa.

JANET: I don't know where she finds the time.

STEVE: You think turkey was a hint that she doesn't want to get together for Thanksgiving or that she wants to have it over there?

JANET: I just think she wanted to do something nice. Have a nice meal.

STEVE: You think we should do something different for Thanksgiving? Since we've had turkey so close?

JANET: Not have a turkey for Thanksgiving?

STEVE: We could have duck. Or a goose.

JANET: I'm going on up.

STEVE: I'm just going to finish this one . . .

JANET: I was going to go into the office after church tomorrow.

STEVE: That's fine. I brought some stuff home I've got to spend some time on.

JANET: Can you help Doug write up his materials and procedures?

STEVE: No problem.

JANET: Good night.

STEVE: Good night.

[JANET *exits to the front of the house.* STEVE *continues to play. His game ends. He expresses his disappointment. He changes cartridges and restarts the game. As he begins the new game* CLAIRE *enters at the back door, carrying a basket of dirty clothes. She peeks into the room.*]

CLAIRE: Hi.

STEVE: Oh. Hi.

CLAIRE: Will it bother anybody if I start a load?

STEVE: No. Go ahead.

CLAIRE: I need clean for tomorrow.

STEVE: No problem.

CLAIRE: Is Michael . . .

STEVE: No. He stayed for a bit.

CLAIRE: Oh.

STEVE: So he could put Morgan to bed.

CLAIRE: Right. Sure.

STEVE: He'll probably be back soon.

CLAIRE: That's okay.

[*Beat.*]

That kid today was good.

STEVE: Yeah.

CLAIRE: You guys sounded great.

STEVE: It was fun.

CLAIRE: You going to hire him?

STEVE: I don't know.

CLAIRE: He's better than Eric.

STEVE: Probably.

CLAIRE: Definitely. You guys were hot. It sounded like a band. Just the three of you. It really clicked.

STEVE: He was good.

CLAIRE: And you. You really took off.

STEVE: You think?

CLAIRE: Unquestionably. You were a riot.

STEVE: It was nice. Just to be able to play.

CLAIRE: Not having to worry if Eric could keep up?

STEVE: Yeah.

CLAIRE: You guys could definitely play out with this kid.

STEVE: You think?

CLAIRE: Undoubtedly. Right now. You guys were better than half the bands working in this town.

STEVE: I don't know.

Managing director Marcelle McVay, artistic director Dennis Začek, and associate artistic director Sandy Shinner accepting the 2001 Tony Award for regional theater

Jason Allcock (Daniel Oreskes) and Mediyah (Celeste Williams),
Pecong

JENNIFER GIRARD

Mediyah (Celeste Williams), Persis (Catherine Slade), and Faustina Cremoney (Wandachristine), *Pecong*

Ted (William L. Petersen), *Flyovers*

Ted (Gary Cole), *Flyovers*

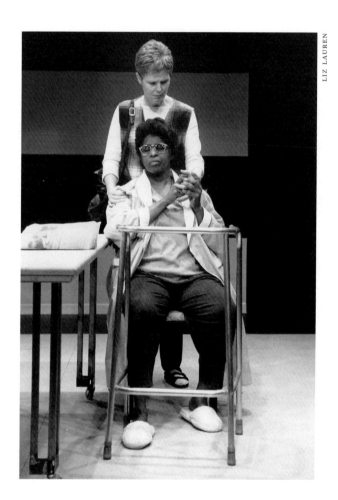

Barbara Jordan (Cheryl Lynn Bruce) and Nancy Earl
(Meg Thalken), *Voice of Good Hope*

LIZ LAUREN

Barbara Jordan (Cheryl Lynn Bruce), *Voice of Good Hope*

Steve Burns (Phil Ridarelli), *Battle of the Bands*

Michael Burns (James Krag), Steve Burns (Phil Ridarelli), Janet Burns (Jill Shellabarger), Claire Sherman (Julie Ganey), Gina Burns (Karlie Nurse), and Neal Reynolds (Justin Cholewa), *Battle of the Bands*

Eugene Moore (Ian Westerfer) and Jerome Moore (David New), *Affluenza!*

Ruth Moore (Roslyn Alexander), William Moore (Richard Henzel), Dawn (Kim Wade), Bernard (Cedric Young), Jerome Moore (David New), and Eugene Moore (Ian Westerfer), *Affluenza!*

Robert Wilson (Gary Houston), John Newton Templeton (Anthony Fleming III), and Jane Wilson (Shelley Delaney), *Free Man of Color*

LIZ LAUREN

John Newton Templeton (Anthony Fleming III),
Free Man of Color

Young Ruth (Mattie Hawkinson) and Young Lillian (Bethanny Alexander), *Hanging Fire*

LIZ LAUREN

Mr. Donny Fletcher (Les Hinderyckx), Ruth (Rachel Stephens), Lillian (Ann Whitney), Calvin (Mick Weber), and Deb (Meg Thalken), *Hanging Fire*

An artist's rendering of the mainstage theater for Victory Gardens, which opened in 2006

CLAIRE: Give yourself credit. Most bands in this town are a bunch of kids fooling around. And they sound like it. You guys've got something going on.

STEVE: Really?

CLAIRE: You bring something to it. Life experience. It shows.

STEVE: You're saying we're old.

CLAIRE: I don't mean "old." You know what I mean. I don't think you're old. You're substantial.

STEVE: You mean fat?

CLAIRE: No. Now stop it.

STEVE: Fat, old, and out of touch.

CLAIRE: I never said fat or old.

STEVE: So just out of touch?

CLAIRE: Quit. Of course you're not out of touch. That's what's so cool.

[*As she speaks, she reaches under her shirt to unfasten and remove her bra.*]

I can really talk to you. And you listen. A lot of guys it's not like that. Especially older guys. They don't really hear you.

STEVE: Uh-huh.

CLAIRE: I guess it's a sexual thing sometimes. That gets in the way. That's what's so great about you. There's none of that going on. It's like you're a guy but you're not a guy.

[*She tosses her bra into the laundry basket.*]

I always wanted a guy I could just talk to.

STEVE: Right.

CLAIRE: It's nice.

STEVE: Great.

[JANET *enters.*]

CLAIRE: Oh, hi.

JANET: Hi.

STEVE: Hey.

JANET: I left my book down here.

CLAIRE: I have to run a load of delicates for tomorrow. You have anything you want to throw in?

JANET: That's okay.

CLAIRE: I hope I wasn't keeping you up. [*To* JANET] We were talking.

JANET: Great.

CLAIRE [*exiting to the basement*]: I hope Michael's not too long. He was supposed to bring me cigarettes.

STEVE: We were talking.

JANET: I know.

STEVE: About the band.

JANET: You put your game down when you're talking to her.

STEVE: We were talking.

JANET: And listening. You listen to her when you talk. You take part in the conversation.

STEVE: Honey. Come on—

JANET: You think just talking doesn't hurt? You don't think I'd like to be involved? To be included?

STEVE: In the band?

JANET: In anything.

[*The back door opens and* MICHAEL *enters. He carries a plate covered with foil.*]

MICHAEL: Hey. You guys still up?

STEVE: Yeah.

MICHAEL: I helped Debbie clean up. After Morgan went to bed. She sent leftovers. For sandwiches.

JANET: Great.

STEVE: Don't have to wait for Thanksgiving.

MICHAEL: That was some dinner. She really put on a spread.

JANET: It was very nice.

MICHAEL: And the cake was great.

JANET: Thanks.

STEVE: You held up all right?

MICHAEL: It got easier once her mom went to bed. We had some time with just Morgan then before she conked out. She is getting so big.

CLAIRE [*returning from the basement*]: Mike.

MICHAEL: Claire. What are you—

CLAIRE: I didn't realize you were going to be so late.

MICHAEL: I didn't know you were—

CLAIRE: Did you get cigarettes?

MICHAEL: It got so late. I didn't think you were going to wait . . .

CLAIRE: You said you would.

MICHAEL: I just figured you'd gone home.

CLAIRE: Home?

MICHAEL: Yeah.

CLAIRE: Do you want me to go?

MICHAEL: Look, I'll go get cigarettes.

CLAIRE: You don't have to.

MICHAEL: It's my fault. I forgot. Let me just—

CLAIRE: What's that?

MICHAEL: This? Leftovers. For sandwiches. Turkey.

CLAIRE: Wow. She made a turkey?

MICHAEL: Yeah.

CLAIRE: For Morgan's birthday? [*To* JANET] Was it good?

JANET: Yeah. It was very good.

CLAIRE [*peeling back the foil*]: I'm glad Morgan had a good party. That's important.

[*She takes a bite of turkey.*]

Mmm.

MICHAEL: She had a good time.

CLAIRE: I didn't know Debbie was such a good cook.

MICHAEL: I guess.

CLAIRE: We'll have to do something special with Morgan tomorrow.

[*Beat.*]

I think I will have a sandwich. I never really had supper. [*Taking the plate*] Did you have mashed potatoes and dressing and gravy?

MICHAEL: Yeah.

CLAIRE: God, I wish she'd sent some of that.

[*She exits into the kitchen.*]

JANET: Well, I think I'm going to go read for a while.

MICHAEL: I'm going to bed. It's been a long day.

CLAIRE: Honey, don't forget cigarettes?

MICHAEL: This'd be a good time to quit.

CLAIRE: Ha-ha. Do you want me to make you a sandwich?

MICHAEL: No. I'm stuffed.

CLAIRE: Don't think you're getting half of mine.

[MICHAEL *exits out the back door.*]

JANET: You think . . .

STEVE: What?

JANET: He stayed a long time.

STEVE: He helped with the dishes.

JANET: I don't know.

STEVE: I don't think so.

JANET: Maybe they talked.

STEVE: Maybe.

JANET: Are you going to ask him?

STEVE: Oh, jeez.

JANET: You could give him a little encouragement.

STEVE: At practice tomorrow. We'll see what comes up.

JANET: Right.

STEVE: I'm not just going to—

JANET: Good night.

[*She exits.* STEVE *picks up the Game Boy without starting it. After a moment* CLAIRE *enters, carrying a plate with a sandwich and a glass of milk.*]

CLAIRE: Do you want a sandwich? I'm sorry. I didn't even ask.

STEVE: No. Thanks.

CLAIRE: You want half?

STEVE: I'm fine.

CLAIRE: So. Tell me about the party. Did Morgan like her cake?

STEVE: Oh, yeah. The ice cream freaked her out a little bit.

CLAIRE: What is potato cake?

STEVE: It's like a chocolate cake, but it's got some mashed potatoes in it. It's real dense. And cinnamony. My grandmother used to make them.

CLAIRE: Wow. That really is an old family recipe. I'd like to try that.

STEVE: I'm going to go on to bed.

CLAIRE: Okay.

STEVE: See you in the morning.

CLAIRE: Good night.

STEVE: Good night.

[*He exits, leaving the Game Boy on the table.* CLAIRE *looks around the table at everyone who is not there, picks up her sandwich, and begins to eat.*]

SCENE 3

[*One week later. Late Saturday morning. The stage is empty. There is a pounding at the back door. Silence. More pounding.* GINA *enters from the front of the house and crosses to the back door. More pounding.*]

GINA: I'm coming.

[*She goes to the back door and opens it. They are heard offstage.*]

  Neal.

NEAL: Is your dad here?

GINA: No. He's at soccer.

NEAL: Oh, man. Your uncle?

GINA: I don't know.

NEAL: The garage is locked. Can I bring this in?

GINA: I guess.

[NEAL *enters through the kitchen and brings a large drum case into the dining room.*]

NEAL: I'm supposed to drop these off for practice tonight. I'm a trial member of the band.

GINA: I heard.

NEAL: Your dad is so cool.

[GINA *starts to respond as he exits out the back door. She tries to move the case out of the way.* NEAL *returns with more cases.*]

GINA: Maybe you should come back when my dad gets home so you can put these in the garage.

NEAL: I would, but my mom needs the minivan to take my little brother and his friends to a movie for his birthday.

GINA: Yeah, but—

[*He exits.* GINA *starts to follow but stops and goes back to moving the cases.* NEAL *returns with more.*]

NEAL: Do you really know Cookie Bondurant?

GINA: I don't know—

NEAL: I can't believe we may be playing for Winter Dance. Wouldn't that be cool?

[GINA *doesn't respond.*]

  I got these cymbals used, but look [*opens the case*] they're as good as new.

GINA: You don't really want to play for Winter Dance, do you?

NEAL: Oh, no, that would be so gr—

GINA: With my dad? Don't you think that would be . . .

NEAL: Dweeby?

GINA: Yeah. You don't want to be dweeby.

NEAL: I don't know. I figure this can only be a step up from marching band.

GINA: You think marching band makes you dweeby?

NEAL: I'm sorry. I didn't mean—I know you're really into it.

GINA: I'm not *really* into it.

NEAL: Right. I know. And band's cool.

[*Beat.*]

You're really good.

GINA: Thanks.

NEAL: And Mr. Hollowell really likes you.

GINA: I don't know.

NEAL: But for me, playing Winter Dance . . . It would be a big step up.

GINA: But you'd be playing with somebody's parents. It's like playing with the PTA.

NEAL: No. It's going to be great. We're going to get dressed up in these, like, business suits—

GINA: I don't want to know.

NEAL: Like Paul Revere and the Corporate Ragers.

GINA: Raiders.

NEAL: Ragers.

GINA: No, it's Paul Revere and the Raiders. It's the name of a band.

NEAL: Somebody's already got our name?

GINA: It's an old band. "Him or Me." "Kicks."

[*She sings.*]

". . . just keep gettin' harder to find."

NEAL: Wow. How do you know so much?

GINA: When I was little, my dad used to make me guess the name of the group playing on oldies. He called it my "cultural education."

NEAL: Man. You should play in the band.

GINA: I don't think so.

[JANET *enters at the back door dressed casually but carrying her briefcase.*]

JANET: Gina. There's a van parked in the driveway. Do you—

[*She sees* GINA, NEAL, *and the drums.*]

NEAL: Oh. Sorry. That's mine.

JANET: Oh.

NEAL: Neal Reynolds.

JANET: I know. Of course. Neal.

GINA: He's dropping off his drums and the garage was locked.

NEAL: I better finish unloading or my mom's going to kill me.

[*He exits.*]

JANET: Is your father home?

GINA: Not yet.

JANET: Is anybody home?

NEAL [*returning with more*]: I've got just a couple more loads, Mrs. Burns, and then I'm going to have to ask you to move your car so I can get out.

JANET: Maybe there's a better place to—

GINA: Don't you have a key to the garage?

JANET: No. I gave mine to Michael.

NEAL [*exiting*]: I'll move them out there tonight. Before practice.

GINA: I've been trying to move them—

JANET: You had a boy in while you were home alone?

GINA: He's dropping off drums.

JANET: You said he's a junior?

[NEAL *drops the cymbals coming in the back door.*]

GINA: It's Neal, Mom.

NEAL [*entering*]: This is really going to be great. I bet we get our picture in the yearbook and everything.

GINA: Shut up, Neal.

JANET: Gina.

GINA: They can't play at Winter Dance. You won't let Daddy do that.

JANET: Maybe you should talk to him.

GINA: He won't listen to me.

NEAL: I always write a note to my dad. When I need him to do something. If I just tell him, he forgets.

[*He exits.*]

GINA: You've got to talk to Daddy.

STEVE [*offstage*]: Did you bang on the door? He said he'd be here.

GINA: Please?

[STEVE *enters, wearing casual clothes. He carries a soccer ball.*]

STEVE: Hey. How's it going?

GINA: Daddy . . . Oh, never mind.

[*She exits into the kitchen.*]

STEVE: What's with her?

JANET: You're taking this to the garage, right?

STEVE: As soon as Mike gets back.

JANET: Don't you have a key?

STEVE: I gave mine to Claire.

NEAL [*leaving another case by the door*]: Mr. and Mrs. Burns, if you could move your cars, I'd get out of the driveway.

[*He exits.*]

STEVE [*starting after* NEAL]: Neal, don't— I'm going to see if I can find an extra key.

JANET: Tell Doug to get in here and get to work. He has to finish his board for Tuesday.

STEVE: He's at Kenny's.

JANET: But he's got—

STEVE: Remember? He was going to watch Kenny's game this afternoon.

JANET: That's today? I thought that was next week.

STEVE: It's on the calendar.

GINA [*offstage*]: Mom. Is this lunch meat okay?

JANET: What's the date on it?

GINA: Is it supposed to look like this?

JANET [*exiting into the kitchen*]: That's today?

NEAL [*in the doorway*]: Excuse me, but if you could move—

STEVE: You won't believe who I met today.

NEAL: Mr. Burns, I told my mom—

STEVE: One of the dads on the other team knows this guy who books the lounges for these Holiday Inns in Kansas City.

[*Beat.*]

NEAL: My mom is—

STEVE: He's coming to see us at the Winter Dance.

[*Beat.*]

For an audition.

NEAL: Mr. Burns, I can't move to Kansas City. I'm only a junior.

STEVE: It's just to fill in. For like a week around Christmas. So he can give his regulars some time off.

GINA [*entering with her lunch on a plate*]: It just looked shiny to me.

JANET [*following her*]: It's moist. Your father bought it this morning.

STEVE: You want a sandwich?

NEAL: Would we be playing in a bar?

JANET: A bar?

STEVE: I'm going to have a sandwich.

JANET: You guys aren't going to start playing in bars?

NEAL: In Kansas City.

STEVE: Neal. Let's go make a sandwich.

JANET: You're going to play at a bar in Kansas City?

STEVE: It would be a lounge. At a Holiday Inn. If it happened.

NEAL: For Christmas. He met this guy at the soccer game this morning.

JANET: You're going to play at a bar in Kansas City for Christmas?

STEVE: It wouldn't actually be on Christmas. It would be around Christmas.

JANET: You can't do that. You can't go to Kansas City for Christmas.

STEVE: It really kind of all falls together. Michael and Lloyd and Neal all have a break from school. I'd only have to take a week of vacation.

JANET: You're going to take a week of your vacation?

STEVE: Maybe not even a full week.

JANET: You're going to use your vacation to play in a bar?

STEVE: It's a Holiday Inn.

GINA: You can't play in a bar.

STEVE: It's really not a bar.

GINA: Won't they card Neal?

STEVE: No. It's twenty-one to drink, but only eighteen to enter.

NEAL: Mr. Burns.

STEVE: Come on, Neal.

NEAL: I'm only seventeen.

STEVE: What?

NEAL: I'm seventeen.

STEVE: But by Christmas, though?

NEAL: Seventeen.

STEVE: You ever try and grow a mustache?

JANET: Steven. His parents aren't going to let him—

STEVE: He doesn't look seventeen.

JANET: But he is.

STEVE: Michael was only seventeen.

JANET: Yes, but—

GINA: You got Uncle Mike a fake ID.

JANET: I don't think that's—

GINA: No. Daddy told me.

NEAL: Do you know people, Mr. Burns?

STEVE: Aren't you hungry, Neal?

MICHAEL [*offstage*]: Hey ho. [*Entering*] Afternoon, all. Whoa, what is all this?

NEAL: You didn't park in the driveway, did you, Mr. Burns?

MICHAEL: Michael, remember? I'm not at work.

STEVE: Neal needs a studio key.

MICHAEL: He's Mr. Burns.

STEVE: We've got to put these out there.

MICHAEL: They let you wear long pants to the soccer game? What are you, the undercover official?

STEVE: It's the tournament. Only the senior refs were working.

MICHAEL: Look at Mr. Neal. If your drums are half as nice as these cases, you've got one sweet kit.

NEAL: Could you move your car? I've got to take my mom's van home before practice.

MICHAEL: Wait. Hold on a second. You may want to . . .

STEVE: What?

MICHAEL: I can't practice tonight.

STEVE: Michael.

MICHAEL: I'm going home.

STEVE: What?

MICHAEL: Debbie and I. We're going to try . . .

JANET: Oh, Michael.

MICHAEL: We've been talking about it.

JANET: Congratulations.

MICHAEL: We put her mom on a plane this morning and I'm going to get my stuff out of the studio.

JANET: I'm so happy for you.

[MICHAEL's *cell phone chirps.*]

STEVE: You could still practice.

JANET: Steven.

STEVE: Well?

[MICHAEL's *cell phone chirps again.*]

Are you going to get that?

MICHAEL: The voice mail'll pick up.

STEVE: Can you practice tomorrow?

MICHAEL: No. I don't think so.

[*The cell phone chirps again.*]

STEVE: You think we're just going to walk into the gym for the Winter Dance and fake our way through? There's a guy coming—

MICHAEL: Forget it, Steven.

[*Another cell phone rings with a melody.*]

STEVE: I thought the voice mail would—

MICHAEL: That's not mine.

[*The melody again.*]

STEVE: Then whose is it?

NEAL: I really need to get out of the driveway.

[*The melody again.* NEAL *takes his cell phone out of his pocket as it rings again.*]

My mom's going to have a cow.

[*He exits into the kitchen, answering the phone.*]

STEVE: If his mother grounds him, how are we ever going to be ready?

MICHAEL: We're not playing at the Winter Dance, Stevie.

STEVE: You can't just quit like this. Not now. There's a guy coming—

MICHAEL: We didn't get the job.

STEVE: But you said . . . I thought you said . . . Didn't that tutor . . .

GINA: They're going with a DJ?

MICHAEL: They hired a band.

STEVE: If we'd only found that tape.

MICHAEL: The Roadhouse Rodeo.

STEVE: The what?

MICHAEL: It's a country band.

STEVE: They're going to hire a country band?

MICHAEL: They wanted to have line dancing.

STEVE: Line dancing?

JANET: That could be fun.

STEVE: Fun? Maybe they could have square dancing. And shuffleboard. They're in high school, for Christ's sake. It's supposed to be a party, not a barn raising. I can't believe the administration won't let the kids pick their own music for the dance.

MICHAEL: They picked them. The student committee.

STEVE: Well, there must have been some kind of arm-twisting to get high school kids to hire a bunch of geezers in cowboy hats.

MICHAEL: They're college kids, and they play out a lot. In fact, their drummer just got a job in Branson with—

STEVE: Branson? Even our parents wouldn't be caught dead in Branson. [*To* GINA] You're not going.

JANET: Steven.

[MICHAEL *exits into the living room.*]

STEVE: We're not going to allow them to take the dance away from the kids with some lame two-stepping music forced on them by the administration.

JANET: Steven. You're not going to stop her from going to the dance.

GINA: I never said I was going in the first place.

JANET: Of course you're going.

STEVE: She doesn't have to go if she doesn't want to.

JANET: She wants to go. Don't you want to go?

[MICHAEL *returns, carrying his guitar in its case.*]

STEVE: You guys should boycott the dance. You should hold out for your own music.

GINA: What music would that be?

[*She exits.*]

JANET: Gina. Wait a minute. We can talk about this.

[*She follows* GINA *off.*]

STEVE: So I guess we don't need to practice.

MICHAEL: Maybe we can just get together sometime and play.

STEVE: I don't think so.

MICHAEL: I've got to get my stuff out of the basement.

[*He exits.* STEVE *picks up one of* NEAL's *drums and carries it outside.* NEAL *enters from the other kitchen door.*]

NEAL: You won't believe what—

[*He notices that everyone has left.*]

Hello? Hello?

[STEVE *returns.*]

Where'd everybody go?

STEVE: Wherever they want, I guess, Neal. Wherever they want. [*Picking up another drum*] We're not going to be practicing tonight.

[*He exits.*]

NEAL: Wait, Mr. Burns . . .
GINA [*in the doorway*]: He's a little . . .
NEAL: Yeah.
GINA: If you need to talk to him.
NEAL: Before I go.
GINA: Sure.
NEAL: That was Dennis with the Roadhouse Rodeo.
GINA: On your phone?
NEAL: They want me to sit in on all their gigs while George is doing a Christmas show in Branson.
GINA: Wow.
NEAL: I guess Mr. Hollowell gave them my number.
GINA: They're supposed to be good.
NEAL: We're playing Winter Dance.
GINA: I heard.
NEAL: Are you going?
GINA: I don't know.
NEAL: Oh.

[*Beat.*]

'Cause if you were going to go . . . I mean if you wanted to . . .
GINA: I might go.
NEAL: Really?
GINA: Yeah.
NEAL: That'd be great.
GINA: Okay.
NEAL: If you need a ride or anything . . .
GINA: Sure.
NEAL: All right then. Swinging.

[STEVE *returns.*]

STEVE: Neal.

NEAL: Yes, sir?

STEVE: You want to give me a hand with the rest of your drums?

NEAL: I was just getting them.

[MICHAEL *returns from the basement, carrying a razor, shampoo, and a bottle of laundry detergent.*]

Mr.—Mike.

MICHAEL: Yeah, Neal.

NEAL: If you could move your car.

MICHAEL: I got to get a couple more things.

NEAL: I've got practice tonight.

MICHAEL: No, Neal.

GINA: I can get that stuff, Uncle Mike.

[*She takes the things from* MICHAEL.]

MICHAEL: We're not practicing—

GINA: I can help you load your car.

NEAL: I'm playing at Winter Dance with the Roadhouse Rodeo.

MICHAEL: Way to go, Neal.

GINA: I'll be outside.

[*She exits.*]

NEAL: I'm sitting in while George is in Branson.

MICHAEL: All right.

NEAL: Winter Dance.

MICHAEL: Cool.

STEVE: So you're quitting, too?

NEAL: I thought we broke up.

MICHAEL: He got a spot with a band, Steve. You don't expect him to fool around in the garage with guys older than his parents.

[MICHAEL'S *phone chirps.*]

STEVE: We could have had a job in Kansas City.

MICHAEL: You don't want to go to Kansas City.

STEVE: It would have been great.

[MICHAEL'S *phone chirps again.*]

Would you either turn that thing off or see what Debbie wants?

MICHAEL: It's one job.

STEVE: That could lead somewhere.

[MICHAEL's *phone chirps again.*]

MICHAEL: Come on, it's not like we'd be driving around Swope Park in the Monkeemobile.

STEVE: It's just a big joke to you, isn't it? That's why you quit last time.

MICHAEL: You're the one who quit.

STEVE: I only quit because you gave up.

[*The phone chirps again.*]

That's what you do when anything gets hard. You quit on me. You quit on Debbie.

MICHAEL: I didn't quit on Debbie.

STEVE: Right. I'm sure it's all her fault.

MICHAEL: I quit on me. I'm not sure I can do it.

STEVE: You said you were going back.

MICHAEL: What if I screw up Morgan worse by being there?

STEVE: You're not going to do that.

MICHAEL: I'm not like you. I can't be the poster dad.

STEVE: Look, it's not perfect. There's a lot of things—

MICHAEL: What don't you have? The house? The wife? The ideal kids?

STEVE: There's things I wish were different.

[MICHAEL *goes to his guitar case and unzips a pocket. He takes a slim box out of the pocket and tosses it on the table.*]

MICHAEL: Is this what you want?

STEVE: Where'd you find—

MICHAEL: There's your tape.

STEVE: Have you had that—

MICHAEL: You want to trade that for what you've got?

STEVE: I never said . . .

MICHAEL: Go ahead. Rack it up on the old reel-to-reel.

[*Beat.*]

See if it's worth all that.

[*Beat.*]

NEAL: What kind of nails did you use?

STEVE: What?

NEAL: Are these all the same kind of nails?

STEVE: I don't know, Neal.

NEAL: 'Cause if they're galvanized nails, they aren't going to rust.

STEVE: They wouldn't use . . .

MICHAEL: I've got to get some clothes, Neal. Then I'll move my car.

[*He exits.*]

NEAL: They look like galvanized nails to me.

STEVE [*calling offstage*]: Janet.

NEAL: I did this by testing different kinds of nails in the same solution instead of the same nails in different solutions.

[GINA *returns.*]

STEVE: How'd it work out?

NEAL: Galvanized nails won't rust.

GINA: Neal.

NEAL: Hey.

JANET [*entering*]: You okay?

STEVE: What kind of nails did you use for Doug's project?

JANET: Old nails.

NEAL: Were they galvanized?

GINA: Neal.

JANET: Were they supposed to be? They were in the basement. You used them on the deck.

STEVE: No.

NEAL: Those are galvanized.

[GINA *exits to the front of the house.*]

JANET: I thought that was good.

STEVE: They won't rust.

JANET: The ones in the deck rusted.

STEVE: That's discoloration. It's not rust.

JANET: It looks like rust. I thought that's why you painted them.

[*The back door flies open, and* CLAIRE *enters, carrying grocery bags.*]

CLAIRE: Hi, everybody. It's me.

[*They exchange a look. She drops the bags on the dining room table.*]

I bought stuff for supper. I hope that's okay. You didn't have any plans, did you? I was going to make burritos. I promised Dougie I would. I make really good burritos. I was trying to call Michael to make sure, but he must have forgotten to charge his phone again. Is burritos okay with you? I just wanted to do something for you and I didn't think you'd want to come over to my crumby place. You can come, too, Neal, and I'll invite Lloyd because of practice.

NEAL: Did you park in the dri—

JANET AND STEVE: Neal.

CLAIRE: All these groceries and I forgot to buy cigarettes. I hope Michael's got some. I'll put the groceries away—don't worry about them. I've just got to get a . . .

[*Makes smoking gesture.*]

And I'm going to tell him to plug in that phone.

[*She exits. Beat.*]

JANET: Should we have . . .
STEVE: I don't think we could . . .
JANET: We could have warned her . . .
NEAL: I'm sorry about the nails, Mrs. Burns.
JANET: The . . . ? Oh. Yeah. Right. Plan B.
STEVE: You want to help me with the rest of the drums?

[*He exits with some of the drums.*]

NEAL: What time do you think you're going to eat?
JANET: What?
NEAL: Burritos.
JANET: I don't think we're going to . . .
NEAL: Oh. Anyway, it was nice of her to invite me.
STEVE [*returning*]: If you could unlock your van.
NEAL: Thanks, Mr. Burns. I can get them.
STEVE: I think you want to be ready when the cars start to move.

[*He picks up more equipment.*]

NEAL: It was nice to see you, Mrs. Burns.
STEVE: Neal.

[STEVE *exits.* NEAL *picks up equipment and exits.* JANET *picks up the trash can and begins dropping the jars of nails into it.* STEVE *returns.*]

I don't know how he fit everything in that van. And he certainly can't remember.

[CLAIRE *enters at the back door. She steps into the room and starts looking through the grocery bags.*]

JANET: Are you all right?
CLAIRE: No. Really. I'll get everything out of your way. I've just got to get my stuff.

[*She exits to the basement.*]

STEVE: Do you want me to . . .
JANET: Go help him pack up.
STEVE: 'Cause if you want me to . . .
JANET: Just get that kid out of here.
STEVE [*exiting with more equipment*]: Holler if you need anything.
GINA [*entering*]: Mom, if Uncle Mike is—
JANET: Oh. Gina. Maybe you should wait up—

[CLAIRE *enters from the basement with a basket of laundry.*]

   Can I help you?
CLAIRE: Oh, yeah, well that's, um. I don't know. I don't think so.

[*She drops the basket of laundry.*]

JANET: Can I get you anything?
CLAIRE [*returning to the grocery bags*]: I don't know why I keep looking. I know I forgot to buy cigarettes but I keep hoping I'll find some.
JANET: If you want some time . . .
CLAIRE: I know that's your laundry basket. I'm not going to take it.
JANET: If you need it—
CLAIRE: I just need a cigarette. Really, really badly.
GINA: I've got some gum.
CLAIRE: Thanks.
GINA: It's sugarless.
CLAIRE: I won't get cancer or cavities.

[STEVE *enters.*]

STEVE: His mother's waiting on him. Sorry.
CLAIRE: Do you think maybe like a handful of aspirin would help this headache?

[JANET *gets her purse.*]

STEVE: If you give me your keys, I could just move your car.

CLAIRE: That's fine. That's great. [*Giving him her keys*] I don't suppose I could get you to run out for some cigarettes?

JANET [*producing a pack of cigarettes from her purse*]: Here.

GINA: Mom.

CLAIRE: Are you kidding me?

JANET: You can take the pack.

STEVE: What are you doing—

JANET: I smoke one a day after lunch.

GINA: Mom.

JANET: Just one.

CLAIRE: I thought you were one of us.

[*She lights up.*]

STEVE: How long have you—

JANET: One. One a day. Even when I want another one. And it's a disgusting habit. This is not an excuse for you to start.

CLAIRE [*exhaling*]: I'll take it outside.

JANET [*wafting the smoke her way*]: That's okay.

STEVE: Why didn't you tell me?

JANET: I lock the door to my office and sit by the open window for seven minutes. You're not going to begrudge me that. You're not the only one, Steven, who wants to get away now and then.

[MICHAEL *enters with a garbage bag of clothes.*]

MICHAEL: I got some of your stuff together.

CLAIRE: Oh, thanks. I would've gotten it.

MICHAEL: I just thought I'd help. Okay?

CLAIRE: You couldn't have put it in a grocery bag or something? How do you think this makes me feel?

MICHAEL: I was just trying to be helpful.

CLAIRE: If I didn't like your family much more than I do you right now, I would give you such a piece of my mind.

MICHAEL: I don't think they want you to smoke in here.

CLAIRE: That just shows how much you know. [*To* JANET] There's cheese and sour cream that should go in the refrigerator.

JANET: No, you take it.

CLAIRE: It doesn't sound good anymore. I think I'm going out for Vietnamese.

[CLAIRE *takes the clothes from the laundry basket and stuffs them into the garbage bag.*]

Be sure you warm the tortillas before you serve them. In my special burrito, and this is what I promised Doug, you use rice instead of meat. If you try it, you'll like it. I promise.

[MICHAEL's *phone chirps. Beat.*]

Stick with one a day. It is a filthy habit.

[*The phone chirps again. Beat.* MICHAEL *takes it out of his pocket.*]

MICHAEL: Hello . . . I'm just getting my stuff.
CLAIRE: Throw a ballad or two in with the rockers. It'll make a better set list.
MICHAEL: It's taking me longer than I expected, too.
CLAIRE: Give your brother a hug for me.

[*Beat.*]

MICHAEL: No, she's not here.

[*Beat.*]

Do you want to talk to Janet?

[JANET *tries to indicate that she isn't there.*]

She's right here.

[CLAIRE *takes the garbage bag and exits.*]

You don't have to call her, you can talk to her right now. [*To* JANET] Will you be home later?

[*Beat.* JANET *nods.*]

She'll be here later . . . As soon as I get off the phone.

[MICHAEL *takes his key ring out of his pocket. He proceeds to remove two keys and put them on the table.*]

The cleaners by the drugstore? . . . If you want me to . . . If you need it . . . I don't mind . . . It's not out of my way . . . I can pick it up . . . I'm leaving now . . . Right now. Do you have the ticket?

[*He exits through the kitchen.*]

I can call you from there . . . No, it's not too expensive . . . The minutes are included in the plan.

[*The back door closes.* STEVE, JANET, *and* GINA *are left alone.*]

JANET: Should we . . .
STEVE: What?
JANET: I don't know.
GINA: I'll get these.

[*She moves the grocery bags from the table into the kitchen.*]

NEAL [*entering*]: I'm all loaded up. If you could just move your cars now, I'll get going.
JANET: Just a minute, Neal.
STEVE: I'll get them, honey.
JANET: I can move my car.
STEVE: It's okay. I'll get them both.
JANET: Okay.

[*She exits to the living room.*]

NEAL: I'm sorry about the band, Mr. Burns.
STEVE: Yeah, well . . .
NEAL: Creative differences?
STEVE: Sort of.
NEAL: I've never really been in a band.
STEVE: I hope it works out for you.
NEAL: Do you have any advice for me?
STEVE: I don't think so.
NEAL: I mean, from your experience.
STEVE: Okay, Neal. One thing. Just don't forget why you're in the band.

[NEAL *ponders for a moment.*]

NEAL: Well, wouldn't that be to play the drums?

[*Beat.*]

STEVE: I'll get the cars out of the way.

[*He exits.* NEAL *does not move.* JANET *returns from the living room with several paperback books. She dumps them on the table. Beat.*]

JANET: Do you need something, Neal?

NEAL: Like?

JANET: I don't know, Neal. I was asking.

NEAL: No. I guess. I'm fine. Thanks.

JANET: Steven's moving the cars.

NEAL: I know. That's great.

JANET: If your mother is waiting.

NEAL: Right.

[JANET *exits to the basement.*]

GINA: Don't mind her.

NEAL: That's okay.

[*Beat.*]

    I guess I better go.

GINA: Yeah.

NEAL: My mom's really going to be—

GINA: I bet.

NEAL: And when I tell her I've got practice . . .

GINA: I know.

NEAL: I'll see you at school.

GINA: Okay.

NEAL: In band.

GINA: Yeah.

[STEVE *enters at the back door with parts of an old and worn drum set.*]

STEVE: Neal. I thought you had to go?

NEAL: I couldn't get out.

STEVE: I moved the cars.

NEAL: Oh, great. Thanks. I really appreciate it.

STEVE: No problem.

[*Beat.*]

NEAL: Do you need help with anything?

STEVE: Why don't you just go so I can put the cars in the driveway.

NEAL: Sure thing. Whatever you say. Good-bye, Gina.

GINA: Good-bye, Neal.

NEAL: Cool.

[*He exits.*]

STEVE: Well, at least you won't have to worry about him coming around anymore.

GINA: Right.

STEVE: So it's not all bad.

[*He exits out the back door. After a moment* JANET *enters from the basement. She carries electrical wire, tape, nails, a flashlight, etc. She puts them on the table and sits down to organize them.*]

GINA: Is Daddy really going to be mad if I go to the dance?

JANET: Of course not.

GINA: That's good.

JANET: Are you thinking about going?

GINA: I guess so.

JANET: I'm sure you'll have a good time if you go. All your friends will be there.

GINA: I don't know what I'd wear.

JANET: We could go look for something.

GINA: Really?

JANET: Sure.

GINA: Would it be okay if I got a ride?

JANET: Well, sure. If you and Loretta—

GINA: With Neal?

JANET: I guess. I thought— Did he ask you out?

GINA: I think so.

JANET: You think so?

GINA: I have to call Loretta.

JANET: Wait, wait, wait.

[GINA *exits.* JANET *starts to follow but stops.* STEVE *enters, bringing more of the old drum kit into the dining room.*]

Steven. What are you doing?

STEVE: Getting Eric's drums out of the way.

JANET [*resuming her work on the project*]: I think we've got enough going on in here.

STEVE: So we can put your car in the garage.

JANET: Steven.

STEVE: Get some good out of it.

[*Beat.*]

I can take them by Eric's later. Get the rest of Michael's stuff out of there.

JANET: Should I call Debbie?

STEVE: You think?

JANET: See if there's anything . . .

STEVE: I don't know.

JANET: We did the right thing.

STEVE: Did the best we could.

JANET: Maybe she'll call.

STEVE: Probably later.

JANET: Did you get potatoes at the store?

STEVE: I was going to make spaghetti.

JANET: Do you think an apple would work?

STEVE: What are you—

JANET [*showing* STEVE *the book*]: For testing factors affecting voltage, amperage, and resistance in an electronic circuit.

[*Beat.*]

It was Dougie's first choice. I thought the nails would be easier.

STEVE [*looking at the book*]: I could go get potatoes.

JANET: I think we've got everything else.

STEVE: Shouldn't we wait and do this with Doug?

JANET: It's due on Tuesday. If we can make it work, we'll do it again with Dougie.

[*Clearing things off the table, she uncovers the tape box.*]

What's this? Where did you find this?

STEVE: Michael had it.

JANET: How's it sound?

STEVE: I didn't—

JANET: Put it on.

STEVE: I don't think so.

JANET: Don't you want to hear what it sounds like?

STEVE: It can't possibly be as good as we remember.

JANET: Sure it can.

STEVE: Nobody's that good.

JANET: Come on.

[STEVE *continues to hold the box.*]

STEVE: I didn't tell you about the game today.

JANET: They going on?

STEVE: They lost.

JANET: Oh. So that's the season. Dougie disappointed?

STEVE: He was okay. Scored a goal.

JANET: Dougie?

STEVE: Yeah.

JANET: Oh. I wish I'd seen it. I can't believe I wasn't there. Tell me about it. What'd he do?

STEVE: I missed it.

JANET: What?

STEVE: I didn't see it. I was talking. To that guy. I was talking to that guy about the Holiday Inn and I missed it.

JANET: Steven.

STEVE: Dougie ran by. He was beaming. Jumping up and down. He came over to me. He wanted to see me. I got all excited. Gave him a big smile. He doesn't know. He thinks I saw it.

JANET: That's good.

STEVE: But I didn't.

JANET: You were there, Steven. You were there for him. That's what matters to him.

STEVE: But I wanted to see it.

JANET: Well . . .

STEVE: That's what I really wanted.

JANET: You'll see the next one.

STEVE: That's assuming there is a next one.

JANET: Steven.

STEVE: You don't think it was a fluke?

JANET: It just took him a while to get the hang of it.

STEVE: That's probably what it is.

[STEVE *carries the tape to the trash can. He drops it in.*]

JANET: Steve.

STEVE: They'll be okay, you think?

JANET: Mike and Debbie?

STEVE: Yeah.

JANET. Water under the bridge.

STEVE: Right.

JANET: Just needed some time.

[*Beat.*]

STEVE: You know, if you want to smoke in the house . . .

JANET: I don't. Really. I really don't want to. [*Taking the tape out of the trash*] I'm going to put it behind your grandmother's platter so the kids will find it when we're dead.

[*She puts it in the sideboard or on the plate rail.*]

You want to put on a record?

STEVE: A record?

JANET: You don't have to.

STEVE: If you want me to.

[*Offstage the stereo is turned on midsong. It is something like "My Generation" or "Born to Be Wild."*]

JANET: Never mind.

STEVE: Brought her up right.

[*They begin to move to the music, tentatively at first. As they relax into it, the song is interrupted by the sound of the radio tuner scrolling down the dial.*]

Hey.

[*The tuner stops on a station in the middle of a country song.*]

What is that?

JANET: Steve.

STEVE [*calling offstage*]: Gina?

JANET: Steven.

STEVE: I don't have to listen to that junk in my own house.

[*JANET steps away and takes a seat at the table.*]

JANET: You know, Steven, that ain't entirely accurate.

[*Curtain call. As the cast members enter to take their individual bows, they bring on microphones, guitars, and the remainder of the drum kit. After they complete their bows, the full cast should play and sing a short version of a rock classic. Something like "Kansas City/Hey! Hey! Hey!" would be ideal.*]

AFFLUENZA!

JAMES SHERMAN

The business of comedy is to present in a general way all the
defects of men and, in particular, those of our own age.

Molière

PLAYWRIGHT'S STATEMENT

Step 1: In 1988, visiting Stratford-upon-Avon, I saw a production of a play by Ben Jonson, *Epicoene, or the Silent Woman.* It concerns two young men who play a dastardly trick on their uncle, Mr. Morose (a man who likes no noise), who is in love with the lovely young Epicoene. The young men succeed in their plan, and Mr. Morose is defeated. This bothered me because I was hoping that Mr. Morose would somehow turn the tables on the young scoundrels and have the last word. Perhaps, I thought, someday I will write my own version of the story.

Step 2: In 2000, much to my dismay, George W. Bush was elected president of the United States. The rich get richer.

Step 3: In 2001, Enron collapses. Over the next couple of years, I follow the stories of congressional hearings, subpoenas issued, and indicted executives. More stories of corporate malfeasance come out concerning the likes of Tyco, WorldCom, and Adelphi. But the rich keep getting richer.

Step 4: I think I'd like to write a play about greed. I remember *Epicoene.* What if I set the story in today's time? What if I had two young scoundrels who were born into a rich family and never had to work but still want to be richer and richer, and they conspire to acquire their uncle's (make it father's) fortune, and the father has a new young wife who he loves and an ex-wife who he hates, and they're all after the money except that, unlike in *Epicoene,* the father will have the last word because he is a self-made man from the "honest buck for an honest day's work" generation and he turns the tables on them and all the greedy people are defeated? I realize that I'm thinking about a contemporary story using archetypal characters from Restoration comedy. The cuck-olded husband, the coquette, the fop. Add a wily servant à la Sganarelle. I love the plays of Molière. What if I wrote the play in the style of Molière, in verse?!

Steps 5, 6, 7, and 8: Read all the Molière plays. The Richard Wilbur translations. Marvel at their beauty and intelligence. Begin to understand why Molière himself wrote his plays in verse. The heightened language satirizes the baseness of the characters' objectives. The use of verse exemplifies the wit of the characters. (Later, my director, Dennis Začek, will say that the play depends on "wit and out-wit.") And most important of all, the plays are wonderfully funny. Get inspired.

Step 9: Write *Affluenza!*

Step 10: Premiere it at the Victory Gardens Theater on November 14, 2003.

PRODUCTION HISTORY

Affluenza! by James Sherman, was first presented by Victory Gardens Theater, Chicago, Illinois, in November 2003.

PRODUCTION TEAM

Director	Dennis Začek
Set	Mary Griswold
Costumes	Judith Lundberg
Lights	Chris Phillips
Sound	Andre Pluess and Ben Sussman
Production Stage Manager	Tina M. Jach

CAST

Ruth Moore	Roslyn Alexander
William Moore	Richard Henzel
Jerome Moore	David New
Dawn	Kim Wade
Eugene Moore	Ian Westerfer
Bernard	Cedric Young

The play was subsequently produced by the New Theatre, Coral Gables, Florida, in January 2004; American Heartland Theatre, Kansas City, Missouri, in February 2005; and the Jewish Theatre of the South, Atlanta, Georgia, in September 2005.

CHARACTERS

William Moore, *a rich old white guy*
Jerome Moore, *William Moore's son*
Eugene Moore, *William Moore's nephew*
Ruth Moore, *William Moore's ex-wife*
Dawn, *William Moore's girlfriend*
Bernard, *William Moore's employee, African American*

STAGING

Time: During the reign of George W. Bush
Setting: The play takes place in the penthouse belonging to William Moore. It is an old building in Chicago overlooking Lake Michigan. The floors and walls are made of solid oak, which suggests age but also permanence. William Moore has lived here for many years. His home is immaculately maintained, but it is obvious that nothing new has been added to the furnishings for a long, long time. Two large ornate doors open into the main living area. There is a door that leads to William's bedroom. There is a hallway that leads off to the kitchen and Bernard's living quarters. There are glass doors that open out to a balcony. And somewhere in the room is an ornate trifold screen large enough for someone to hide behind.

PROLOGUE

[EUGENE]

[EUGENE *addresses the audience.*]

EUGENE: If "affluenza" is a new word for you,
    Please listen 'cause I can give you a clue.
    These days, the rich people are numerous.
    Our poet thinks they're rather humorous.
    They look for all the ways they can explore
    How to get more. And more. And more. And more.
    Except, of course, for my great-uncle Bill.
    This is his house. Man, it is such a thrill.
    Come in, dear ladies and kind gentlemen.
    Please notice—you can see Lake Michigan.
    We're up so high. The view is kind of scary.
    But when the weather's right, you can see Gary.
    He's lived up here since 1965.
    That's way, way back. Before I was alive.
    He'd started a construction company
    And he ran it very successfully.
    So he is rich. But it is kinda funny.
    He doesn't act like he has much money.
    Now his ex-wife. Well, I must tell the truth.
    There's no one who can shop like my aunt Ruth.
    And then there's Jerry, who is my first cousin.
    He'll go and shop and buy things by the dozen.
    I'm not here to pass judgment or condemn.
    I'm sure there's no one here who acts like them.
    Just recently, I graduated college.
    And so I'm here to get a little knowledge.
    I think it will be educational.
    And also, maybe, recreational.
    Between us guys, these people play hardball.
    One person, at the end, will have it all.
    So now you can put down your bets and wagers.
    And please—turn off your cell phones and your pagers.

ACT 1

SCENE 1 [JEROME, EUGENE]

JEROME: No.

[*Pause.*]

EUGENE: Now.
JEROME: No.

[*Pause.*]

EUGENE: Now.
JEROME: No.

[*Pause.*]

EUGENE: Now.
JEROME: No.

[*Pause.*]

EUGENE: Now.
JEROME: No.

[*Pause.*]

EUGENE: Now.
JEROME: Be quiet, will you please? You don't know how
    To do this. Quiet. I must concentrate.
    Stand over there, don't move, shut up, and wait.
EUGENE: You're running out of time.
JEROME: Shut up. I'm not.
    Don't tell me what to do, you idiot.
    For when it comes to cruising online shops,
    Particularly on eBay, I'm tops.
    Where bidding has become a high-tech art.
    Here, on this Web site, I am very smart.
    On eBay, shopping victory depends
    On watching closely when the auction ends.
    The bidders bid, I watch with veins of ice,
    'Cause I know I can always beat the price.
    The time goes by until the final sec.

And in that micro, final sec, I peck.
With perfect timing and with cool dispatch
I overbid a price no one could match.
I've let some cocky dunderhead assume
He has the final winning bid and boom!
I'm there! "Hello! A little bulletin!
You lose, you worthless piece of slime. I win!"
EUGENE [*pointing to the screen*]: You really want this?
JEROME: Yes, you stupid lout.
This kind of thing is what I'm all about.
The raison d'être of all this razzmatazz
Is so I have a thing nobody has.
I'm happy as a puppy when I find
Something that is unique. One of a kind.
Like this. A perfect specimen, you jerk.
The captain's chair once used by Captain Kirk.
I love to be the guy who goes and buys
His own piece of the starship *Enterprise*.
The price is up to sixteen thousand bucks.
So now I—auction ended? Well, this sucks.
Why you—
EUGENE: It's not my fault.
JEROME: You wanna bet?
I always get the things I want to get.
It's killing me. I really cannot bear
The thought that someone else has won my chair.
EUGENE: A little disappointment. It will pass.
JEROME: Don't talk to me. This really chaps my ass.
Allowing you to watch. What a mistake.
I'll bind your feet and toss you in the lake.
EUGENE: Ahhh! Spare me from your violence, if you please.
My asthma kicks in, and I start to wheeze.
JEROME: You're nothing but a worthless piece of crap.
You're nothing—

SCENE 2 [BERNARD, JEROME, EUGENE]

[BERNARD *enters*.]

BERNARD: Mr. Moore is takin' a nap.

JEROME: Hello, Bernard.

EUGENE: Hello, Bernard.

BERNARD: Hello.

EUGENE: We were just—

BERNARD: I know. It's time to go.

    It's always such a thrill to see you boys.

    But Mr. Moore, you know, don't like no noise.

    You woke him up just now. I think you best

    Take off now so that he can get his rest.

JEROME: I'd like to see my father. Let him know.

EUGENE: You heard, Jerome. The man said we should go.

JEROME: Excuse me? Just a sec. I'm at a loss.

    Remember? He's the worker. I'm the boss.

    He sits around here all day, worry free,

    And does it for a hefty salary.

BERNARD: I understand you think I'm lazy here.

    I'm working. Not *Driving Miss Daisy* here.

JEROME: Well, tell him that I want to see him then.

BERNARD: What happened? Your allowance gone again?

JEROME: Well, aren't you a joker and a half?

    That was so funny, I forgot to laugh.

    Just focus on being an employee.

    It's private, what's between my dad and me.

BERNARD: He's had a busy day. A lot's transpired.

    He's got to rest. The man is simply tired.

JEROME: Oh, stop it, please. Just stop the whole routine.

    We know what's up.

BERNARD: I don't know what you mean.

JEROME: She's coming here. The little girlfriend.

    So drop the act. You don't have to pretend.

    'Cause we know all about it. Don't we, Gene?

    Their picture's in *Chicago* magazine.

    Eventually, we surely had to know

    That Daddy's got himself a little ho.

EUGENE: Don't talk that way. You don't know that for sure.

JEROME: I'll say a gold digger, if you prefer.

BERNARD: She's just a woman that he's come to know.

JEROME: And he's a man who has a lot of dough.

    A woman with a man like that? What for?

    She knows what he is worth. Need I say more?

His charming wit and grace? You think that wins?
She's doing it just for the Benjamins.
And so he's gonna get his trousers pressed.
No wonder that he needs to get his rest.
BERNARD: So you'll be going now. Go grab some hats.
JEROME: I'm having dinner with the Democrats.
A fund-raiser. A thousand bucks a plate.
To meet the politicians. Cultivate
Some friendships. Makes good sense.
In case I ever need some influence.
The mayor will be there, and Maggie, too.
I'm at their table. Very *entre nous.*
It's in the ballroom down at Navy Pier.
Until it's time to go, I'll hang out here.
BERNARD [*to* EUGENE]: Do you have anything to say to me?
EUGENE: I'm having dinner with the GOP.
JEROME: Republicans should also get their due.
We help them with a little revenue.
A cocktail party up in the Sears Tower.
In case, by chance, they ever come to power.
Relax, Bernard. Chill out. I'm gonna make
Myself at home until he is awake.
BERNARD: You want to see your father? Sure. Okay.
But just be warned. He's had a cranky day.
If you upset him—if you are so rude—
You will not find him in a gen'rous mood.

[BERNARD *heads off to the kitchen.*]

"I'm having dinner with a Democrat."
I hope you choke on it, you spoiled brat.

[BERNARD *exits.*]

SCENE 3 [EUGENE, JEROME]

EUGENE: Thank God, he's gone. My God, I'm in a sweat.
You have to see your dad? If he's upset—
JEROME: Oh, that was just a plate full of baloney.
I'm really here to see the tenderoni.
EUGENE: To see the . . . ?

JEROME: Slut! The bitch! The little Jezebel!
That harlot! Fortune-hunting mademoiselle!
That tart! That trollope! Floozy! Strumpet! Chippie!
Forgive me if I sound a little snippy.
She's got my father toasted. What a whore.
I know what she is really going for.
She'll come to him so quiet and straitlaced,
Her manner is so virtuous and chaste.
But, wait, you'll see, the little porcupine
Will get her grubby hands on what is mine!

EUGENE: So tell your dad.

JEROME: I've told him. More than once.

EUGENE: And so?

JEROME: He wouldn't listen. What a dunce.
She hasn't faltered. I don't have the proof.
The biggest hypocrite since . . . since Tartuffe.

EUGENE: Since who?

JEROME: Forget about it. What I need
Is time with her to catch her in her greed.

EUGENE: But you are always saying greed is good.

JEROME: No. *My* greed. Mine. You haven't understood
The things I've taught you. Well, all right. Once more.
Back in our parents' time, in days of yore,
They got through the Depression and the war.
They knew what had to happen and what for.
They labored tirelessly with toil and strife
All so their kids would have a better life.
There was no shame. It wasn't seen as vice
To live for service and for sacrifice.
With their success, with what they could convey,
We had, indeed, a better life than they.

EUGENE: And so you're rich.

JEROME: Not rich enough. Not near.
I have developed appetites, my dear.
The values of the past are antiquated.
The need for thrift has been obliterated.
So when I see what I want to acquire,
Well, instantly, I simply must conspire.
Through any means I can, I will endeavor

To get one of my own.

EUGENE: One what?

JEROME: Whatever.

Whatever is the best or tops or rare.
When I see it's for sale, then I'm there.
One thing's for sure. One thing is guaranteed.
The more I have, you know, the more I need.
I won't be satisfied until I'm certain
I've more than Dick Cheney at Halliburton.
I want more than was ever socked away
By my hero.

EUGENE: Who?

JEROME: Enron's Kenneth Lay.

EUGENE: Be patient. You'll inherit all his wealth.
You wouldn't want to wish on him ill health.

JEROME: I did. He's still alive. And so I must
Sit patiently until he bites the dust.

EUGENE: I think he's in good health.

JEROME: Well, vive le roi.

That means there's just no hope for poor old *moi*.
To keep from giving me cash, he would burn it.
He thinks that I should go out there and earn it!

EUGENE: My God.

JEROME: Really. I mean, hey, I'm his son.

And how much aid do I get from him? None.
Our government officials can find tons
Of chances to make money for their sons.
I would be making loot hand over fist
If I could be a D.C. lobbyist.
It's beautiful, what they collect in fees.

EUGENE: But don't you have to have some expertise?

JEROME: Like what? Come on, Gene. That is not expected.

You just need an old man who is connected.
I know that I'd be getting loads of scratch
If I was just the son of Orrin Hatch.
I'd lobby in the Congress with panache
If I was Denny Hastert's little Josh.
The richest lobbyist—son of Trent Lott—
Before that, do you know what he did?

EUGENE: What?

JEROME: Before he started working for the pros
   He ran a pizza joint for Domino's.

EUGENE: Well, wait. Maybe your dad will come around.
   Maybe, in time, you'll find some common ground.

JEROME: Our president sure never had to wait.
   He got it all on a nice silver plate.
   He had his father's great big rich coattail.
   It got him into Harvard.

EUGENE: Into Yale.

JEROME: George Senior helped his son out. He was loyal.
   He made a call and got him Harken Oil.
   His daddy helped him out. There were no dangers.
   Like that, he bought and sold the Texas Rangers.
   His daddy helped him to his heart's content
   And Dubya became the president!

EUGENE: I bet, in time, your dad will reappraise
   This thing with Dawn. I bet it's just a phase.

JEROME: I can't believe I'm in this deep morass.
   I'm sure to lose out to this piece of ass.
   She'll move in, gain his confidence and trust.
   Get him to feel youthful and robust.
   She'll get him in a sexually playful mood,
   And I'm the one who's gonna end up screwed!
   I've got to get that little honeydew.

SCENE 4 [BERNARD, JEROME, EUGENE]

[*The house phone rings.* BERNARD *enters and picks up the phone.*]

BERNARD: Hello? Yes. Fine. Please send her up. Thank you.

[*He hangs up the phone and waits by the front door.*]

JEROME [*to* EUGENE]: Great. Now's my chance to get the real deal.
   Somewhere I'm sure there's an Achilles' heel.

[*Pause.*]

   I've never met the madam or the sir
   Who could slip past my bullshitometer.

The girl has no idea what's in store.

[*Pause.*]

EUGENE: It's taking—

JEROME: Well, we're on the eighteenth floor.

[*The doorbell rings.*]

Aha! Now watch as I unleash the bomb.

[BERNARD *opens the door.* RUTH *is there.*]

Well, well! What a surprise to see you—

SCENE 5 *[JEROME, RUTH,*
BERNARD, EUGENE]

JEROME: Mom!

RUTH: Hello, Bernard.

BERNARD: Hello, Ms. M.

EUGENE: Aunt Ruth.

BERNARD: You're looking very well, and that's the truth.

RUTH: That's very kind. How nice of you to say.

And you. You must get larger every day.

BERNARD: I'm feeling well. And you?

RUTH: I'm managing.

BERNARD: That's nice. So can I get you anything?

RUTH: Just passing through. I'm in the neighborhood.

Is Bill here?

BERNARD: He is in the bedroom.

RUTH: Good.

BERNARD: I'll let him know you're here. It's been a while.

RUTH: A joy to be back in his domicile.

When I think back to when I was his wife,

I can't believe that this was once my life.

I so admire your ability

To stick with him. You have such loyalty.

And I must ask you—how is Barbara?

I miss her most of all. Your dear mama.

The meals that she made were so exquisite.

I really must come by to have a visit.

The sweetest woman you could ever know.
How is she?

BERNARD: Passed away ten years ago.

RUTH: Oh, dear. But no one said . . . I should have gotten
A call or something. God, I feel rotten.
Bernard. Please, dear. Accept my deep regret.
I just had no . . . This makes me most upset.
I should have been informed of your mom's death.
I swear he—all right. Stop now. Take a breath.
My yoga teacher says, "More oxygen.
Just breathe your anger out. Don't hold it in."
I take a breath. My tension is abating.
I'm all right now.

BERNARD: I'll tell him that you're waiting.

[BERNARD *exits.*]

SCENE 6 [JEROME, RUTH, EUGENE]

JEROME: Hello!

RUTH: Hello, Jerome. Hello, Eugene.
You must be up to something. What? Come clean.

JEROME: You shouldn't be concerned what's up my sleeve.
For your sake, I would say that you should leave.

RUTH: I see. Not even stay to chat a bit?
He has the youngster with him. Is that it?

JEROME: Not now. But she will be here any sec.
I'm just here for the chance to wring her neck.

EUGENE: Not really.

RUTH: That's okay, Eugene. I'm hip.
[*To* JEROME] You're troubled by this new relationship.
Bill's with her now, and much to your chagrin
There's no way you can stop her homing in
On Bill and what she'll ask him to finance.
You want to stop her. You don't stand a chance.

JEROME: There has to be a way I can co-opt her.

RUTH: I wonder if he'll marry or adopt her.

JEROME: I don't get why you are not more concerned.
I'm not the only one who could get burned.

RUTH: I'm not concerned. It is a classic story.

Old men want to revive their former glory.
They want to resurrect their long-lost youth.
They hook up with these girls. It's so uncouth.
They find a little playmate. Have a blast.
But she has other motives. It won't last.
She'll bat her eyes and sigh with heavy breath.
And let him think he isn't so near death.
His eyes will gaze upon her posturings.
But she has got her eyes on other things.
So then she'll ask for something. Cross the line.
He'll see through her, and then it's "Auld Lang Syne."
JEROME: Perhaps you're right. I guess I should relax.
　　Hell, no! I think I'll stop her in her tracks.
RUTH: Well, I shan't worry what's with him and Dawn.
　　I just need Bill to sign this. Then I'm gone.
JEROME: Why, Mummy dear. You're here to get some dough?
　　How mercenary. Say it isn't so.
RUTH: I'm driving by and I thought, What the heck?
　　I need his Johnny Hancock on this check.
JEROME: So what's it for? To buy up some old slums?
　　And put up high-priced condominiums?
RUTH: If you must know, it's not for property.
　　It's for a special project—a new me.
　　I've found a doctor with a wondrous gift.
　　There's nothing on the body he can't lift.
　　He lifts the face, and then he lifts the eyes.
　　He lifts the breasts—you get to choose the size.
　　He sculpts the chin, reshapes the nose, and then
　　Some Botox and a little collagen.
　　He lifts the buttocks—makes them nice and tight.
　　He lifts the thighs—removes the cellulite.
　　A liposuction treatment and, for luck,
　　Some dermaplaning and a tummy tuck,
　　So every sag and wrinkle's rectified.
　　And then some perm'nent makeup is applied.
　　I'll be a woman who's no longer cursed.
　　The aging process now can be reversed.
　　Why, I'll be growing younger. Have no fear.
　　In time, I'll be the youngest person here.

SCENE 7 [BERNARD, RUTH,
JEROME, EUGENE]

[BERNARD *enters.*]

RUTH: Bernard, well, took you long enough. Where's Bill?
BERNARD: I told him that you're here. He still feels ill.
    He really doesn't mean to be unkind.
    He's sorry, and he hopes that you don't mind.
RUTH: He hopes that I . . . ? You bet your boots I mind it.
    This check's no good unless he will cosign it.
    The louse. He's got me stuck in misery.
    My hands are tied by the divorce decree.
    Unhappy is the life I must endure!
    I'm screwed unless I get his signature!

[RUTH *bangs on the bedroom door.*]

    Get out here, Bill! Get out! You cannot hide
    From me! I'm here! I will be satisfied!
BERNARD: Ms. M., I wouldn't bang upon the door.
    That's just the thing to piss off Mr. Moore.
JEROME: Hey, you. Don't tell my mother what to do.
    Lay off or I'll show you a thing or two.
BERNARD: Okay. Go 'head. You want to take a shot?
    Come on, Jerome. You show me what you got.
JEROME: I'll show you what I got. I got Eugene.
    Go 'head, Eugene. Get on him. Go. Get mean.
EUGENE: What?
JEROME: Upside the head. Give him a smack.
BERNARD: Come on. Let's go. One hand behind my back.
    I'm sick of you two brats, and that's the truth.
EUGENE: Oh, God. Oh, God. Oh, God. Oh, God. Aunt Ruth!
RUTH: Don't look at me. I cannot interfere.
    I can't—

SCENE 8 [WILLIAM, BERNARD,
RUTH, JEROME, EUGENE]

[WILLIAM *enters.*]

WILLIAM: There's too much goddamn noise out here!

In life I have one unadorned request.
Be quiet so that I can get some rest!
Take it outside. Outside into the street.
Outside the sirens blare. The car horns bleat.
Construction workers rev up their machines.
Catch music videos on giant screens.
The Humvees throbbing to the boom box beat.
The people yell on cell phones where to meet.
"I'll meet you at the Starbucks on the corner!
It's opposite the Starbucks on the corner!
A few feet from the Starbucks on the corner!
Adjacent to the Starbucks on the corner!"
Bernard!

BERNARD: Yes, sir.

WILLIAM: Has Dawn—

BERNARD: I'll let you know.

WILLIAM: And to the rest of you . . . please, please, please go!

[WILLIAM *starts to exit.*]

RUTH: Wait! Bill!

WILLIAM: Bernard. There's no way to escape her?

RUTH: I'll leave. Just sign this piece of paper.

WILLIAM: What is this?

RUTH: No big deal. Don't get tense.
Just authorize this medical expense.
I'm going in to have some nips and tucks.
Just sign it and—

WILLIAM: Three hundred thousand bucks!

RUTH: Don't holler, Bill. Remember, I can force you.
We set this up way back when I divorced you.
"The party of the first part now agrees
Forever to pay off my doctors' fees."

WILLIAM: Bernard.

BERNARD: Yes, sir.

[BERNARD *exits.*]

JEROME: Come on, Dad. Be a sport.

RUTH: Must I remind you? We could go to court.
A judge, I'm sure, will get you to comply.
I'll see you there. And please, Bill, wear a tie.

WILLIAM: Bernard will settle this.
RUTH: Bernard?
WILLIAM: No doubt.
JEROME: What, are you gonna have him throw her out?
WILLIAM: Your lawyers, judges, fill me with disgust.
    Bernard's the only man that I can trust.
    Just wait a minute. Stay right where you are.
    My man Bernard studied and passed the bar.

[BERNARD *enters in lawyer's garb.*]

RUTH: Oh, Bill. Come on. You're grasping here at straws.
BERNARD: I have a copy of the pertinent clause.
    According to this, you can rest assured
    That for your life you will be health insured.
    And also, William Moore will recompense
    All necessary medical expense.
RUTH: All right. That's it. Go on, Bill. Go and sign.
BERNARD: Except that we should legally define
    By precedent just what is customary
    To make a medical case necessary.
RUTH: It's necessary.
BERNARD: So you would opine.
    But just to be sure, I will go online.

[BERNARD *sits at the computer.*]

    With legal questions found that might perplex us,
    I look online at Westlaw or at Lexis.
    Uh-huh. I see. There is a precedent.
    If what you want's due to an accident.
    So, no, in fact, you won't be compensated.
    Except if, say, your face is mutilated.

[BERNARD *exits.*]

WILLIAM: That's it.
RUTH: But—
WILLIAM: No!
RUTH: But—
WILLIAM: No!
RUTH: But—

WILLIAM: No!

RUTH: But—

WILLIAM: No!

This meeting is concluded. You can go.

RUTH: The surgery already has been planned.

WILLIAM: What part of "no" do you not understand?

RUTH: This surgery is a necessity.

WILLIAM: It's necessary for your vanity.

RUTH: This surgery is more than just cosmetic.

It's curative. Corrective.

WILLIAM: It's pathetic.

RUTH: You're such a paragon of rectitude.

I might comment. But, no, I shan't be rude.

JEROME: Oh, say it, Mom. It's on all of our minds.

Let's talk of old men and their concubines.

WILLIAM: You think you're such a clever raconteur.

You watch it, boy. You don't speak ill of her.

[*To* RUTH] You don't know what my life has undergone.

I'll have none of your criticizing Dawn.

RUTH: I won't speak ill of her. I will not knock her.

What's sad is this decrepit *alta kocker.*

How 'bout your life, Bill? Let us face the truth.

The way you're clutching to your long-lost youth.

WILLIAM: Depart!

RUTH: I won't!

WILLIAM: I'll have him wring your neck!

RUTH: You wouldn't dare!

WILLIAM: So what?!

RUTH: So sign the check!

WILLIAM: Now listen to me, Ruth. You can be sure

There's no way that you'll get my signature.

RUTH: There's no way I'll acquire your consent?

WILLIAM: Yes. Call me if you have an accident.

RUTH: All right. I'll go. You think the die is cast?

In time, we'll find out who'll be laughing last.

[RUTH *exits.*]

WILLIAM: Good. Say good-bye to that old battle-ax.

JEROME: Oh, she'll be back. Don't think you can relax.

WILLIAM: All she can do to me is shout and cuss.
JEROME: Or throw herself in front of a school bus.
  Have a collision with the CTA?
  No. She won't stop until she gets her way.
WILLIAM: Get out of here, you two. I have to rest.
JEROME: We know. We know. Get ready for your guest.

[WILLIAM *exits.*]

  She shouldn't do that plastic surgery.
EUGENE: No. I agree. She looks okay to me.
JEROME: You think I care about her looks? No way.
  She might cost my estate 300K.

SCENE 9 [BERNARD, JEROME, EUGENE]

[*The house phone rings.* BERNARD *enters and picks up the phone.*]

BERNARD: Hello? Yes, fine. Please send her up. Thank you.

[BERNARD *hangs up the phone and stands by the door.*]

JEROME [*to* EUGENE]: She's here. Now here's my chance to catch the shrew.
EUGENE: So now you'll get the chance to call her bluff.
  Whatever you do, please don't be too rough.
JEROME: Don't worry, Cuz. This will not hurt a bit.
  I'll only hurt her with my rapier wit.
EUGENE: You promise me that talking will suffice?
  She's just a helpless girl, so be nice.
JEROME: Do you have feelings for the sneaky tramp?
  You have the hots for her! You little scamp!
EUGENE: You're just so mean, Jerome. You are. I swear.
  You make assumptions. You . . . It isn't fair.
  Hey, maybe she's exactly what she is.
  A simple, lovely, feminine . . . Gee whiz.
JEROME: Forget it. You could never land the bitch.
  It's pretty clear the guys she likes are rich.
EUGENE: I'm just concerned about this . . . rigmarole.
  I wouldn't touch her with a ten-foot pole.

[*The doorbell rings.*]

JEROME: I think, maybe, that you should step outside.
   I'll do what I will do. You go and hide.

[EUGENE *steps outside onto the balcony.*]

SCENE 10 [DAWN, BERNARD, JEROME, EUGENE]

[BERNARD *opens the door.* DAWN *enters.*]

DAWN: Good afternoon, Bernard.
BERNARD: Good afternoon.
DAWN: Does William know I'm here?
BERNARD: He'll be out soon.
   He asks for you to wait and have a seat.
   And can I get you anything to eat?
DAWN: Oh, no, Bernard. Please do not make a fuss.
   When William's here, you'll feed the both of us.
BERNARD: That's fine. I'll be around so you just call
   For me if you need anything at all.

[BERNARD *exits to the bedroom.* JEROME *approaches* DAWN.]

JEROME: Hi.
DAWN: Oh! Jerome. I did not see you there.
   Excuse me. Oh, you gave me quite a scare.
   I just came by to visit William. Is he—
JEROME: He's getting dressed. I'm here to keep you busy.
DAWN: No. Much as I would like to be with you,
   You must have lots of better things to do.
JEROME: I really don't. It's really not a bother.
   I think that we should get to know each other.
   I'd like to know about you. Where you're from.
   Who knows? It might end up you'll be my mom.
DAWN: Oh, heavens, please. Don't. Don't insinuate.
   I'm just his friend. His confidante. Soul mate.
   Before I met him, life was very grim.
   And now I have a purpose—me with him.
JEROME: I wonder what that purpose is. I do.
   My mind keeps asking, "What's in it for you?"

DAWN: For me? I ask for nothing. Not a thing.

JEROME: That's sweet. And yet I keep imagining
You're with a man whose means are plentiful.
I'd want to get some. Only natural.

DAWN: From what I've heard of you, that's half expected.

JEROME: I do not like to brag. I'm well connected.
I know a guy who lives up on Sheffield.
He's got the greatest view of Wrigley Field.
I know a guy who flew planes at Meigs Field.
But now they have the brand-new Soldier Field.
I have a skybox for the most well heeled
Of people. Well, their names can't be revealed.
Suffice to say they live on Lake Shore Drive
And work at City Hall, well, up on five.

DAWN: I understand. That's an impressive crowd.
I bet you always get your alley plowed.

JEROME: I know a gal who works for Oprah Winfrey.
You want some tickets? I can get you in. Free.

[BERNARD *enters.*]

DAWN: Bernard. Excuse me. Is Bill ready yet?

BERNARD: Yes. Almost. He's completing his toilette.
He wants to make his entrance with panache.
Perhaps you'd like to have a little nosh?

DAWN: I think I have a bit of dehydration.

BERNARD: May I suggest a sparkling, cool libation?

DAWN: Some water? If it's not out of your way.

BERNARD: Unless you would prefer a Perrier.

DAWN: Just water's fine. I must resist the urge.

BERNARD: It's quite all right.

DAWN: Oh, very well. I'll splurge.

BERNARD: And do you take it with a piece of lime?

DAWN: Is that what you would recommend?

BERNARD: Sublime.

DAWN: Well, thank you very much. Yes.

BERNARD: Very good.

[BERNARD *heads off to the kitchen.*]

JEROME: I'd like to have one, too.

BERNARD: I'm sure you would.

[BERNARD *exits.*]

DAWN: Jerome. I think that we could become friends.
　If you'd be interested—
JEROME: Well, that depends.
　You must be thinking—all of your good works
　For William Moore. There have to be some perks.
DAWN: I know you put down what I have with Bill.
　I can withstand the onslaught of ill will.
　You and others like you look aghast.
　You can't imagine that our love will last.
　But you see black and white while I see gray.
　We're not some kind of soap opera cliché.
　I don't want money. He's not out for sex.
　The feelings that we have are more complex.
JEROME: So what then? His urbane sophistication?
　His jovial wit? His sparkling conversation?
DAWN: Of course not.
JEROME: So?
DAWN: Why can't you just believe—
JEROME: 'Cause I know you've got something up your sleeve!
　But just between us, don't be too wide eyed.
　I hate to say—you'll be dissatisfied.
　He's not a gen'rous man. Won't spend a dime.
　He never shops. Thinks it's a waste of time.
　The stuff he has is old. There's no new stuff.
　Enough, he says—God help me—is enough.
　I'm on your side, Dawn. Really. My advice is
　Seduce me. I promise better prizes.
　I'm sure I have something to satisfy
　Your aspirations. Come on. Let me try.
　Let's get it on. Relax. I'll make it swift.
　And then you'll go with a nice parting gift.
DAWN: That's quite an offer, Jerry. How gallant.
　Forget it. You've got nothing that I want.
JEROME: Don't be so sure. You won't know what you've missed.
　Hey, I've got plenty. Want to see a list?
DAWN: Of what?

JEROME: Of things. Of things I've bought.
  You simply have no notion what I've got.
DAWN: So people—friends and lovers—have no worth.
  There are more things in heaven and in earth
  Than you might dream in your philosophy.
JEROME: Ooh, Shakespeare. Listen. My philosophy
  Is this: You're born alone, you die alone.
  But while you're living, you are what you own.
DAWN: Well, I am sorry for you. Yes, I am.
  There's so much we . . . And you don't give a damn.
JEROME: No, no. Not true. I do. I do. I do.
  It's just nothing can match in quality
  The happiness I get from property.
  Please don't dismiss me. Please don't be unfair.
  I'm proud of what I own. I want to share.
  So would you like to see a sample?
DAWN: Yes.
JEROME: Here.

[*He turns on the computer.*]

          Here's a list of things that I possess.
DAWN: These are your things that have the most cachet?
JEROME: No. These are just the things I bought today.
  I was online. I picked up some knickknacks.
  A prewar, mint-condition tenor sax.

[BERNARD *enters, carrying a tray with four glasses on it.*]

DAWN: Oh. Do you play?
JEROME: No. Why?
DAWN: Just wondering.
  I have to say, I find it interesting.
  If you don't play, why buy a saxophone?

[BERNARD *exits into the bedroom.*]

JEROME: It's not to play, you sil—it's just to own.
  She doesn't get it. I would like to pop her.
  Try. Get in touch with your own inner shopper.
  Attempt to have the right appreciation
  For my talent in accumulation.

[BERNARD *enters, carrying the tray with three glasses on it.*]

DAWN: Sorry. I won't be an apathist.
    Please. Show me what you've got there on your list.
    [*Reads*] A diamond ring to wear upon your pinky.
    A limited edition platinum Slinky.

[BERNARD *exits out onto the balcony.*]

    A bottle of one-hundred-year-old wine.
    A 1930s Coca-Cola sign.
    An antique piggy bank.
JEROME: It makes me laugh.
DAWN: A Cartier two-tone *français* chronograph.

[BERNARD *enters, carrying the tray with two glasses on it.*]

    A life-size robot that can walk and talk.
    A skateboard.
JEROME: Autographed by Tony Hawk.

[BERNARD *holds the tray out to* DAWN, *and she takes one of the glasses.*]

DAWN: Thank you. Should I come back another time?
BERNARD: He wants to see you looking at his prime.
    He has to comb his hair and shave his chin.
    He has to brush his teeth. And put them in.
    He has to trim his mustache. And his ears.
    I think you get the picture.
DAWN: Thank you.

[*As* JEROME *reaches for the final glass,* BERNARD *picks it up.*]

BERNARD: Cheers.

[BERNARD *clinks her glass. He takes a drink and exits off to the kitchen.*]

JEROME: Look. Let's start over. Let's just clear the decks.
    I'm sorry. Just forget about the sex.
    It's just—if acquisition is your plan,
    Don't waste your time with William. I'm your man.
DAWN: You still expect some vile larceny.
    Only because, as far as you can see,
    The only reason to be with this man
    Is to acquire anything I can.

JEROME: Well, now you're talking. It's a surefire bet
    That you are here to get what you can get.
    This? This is nothing. This is just a trifle.
    At my apartment, there you'd get an eyeful.
    'Cause when I shop, what really blows my mind
    Is when I find one of one of a kind.
    I have so many . . . Where should I begin?
    You understand they all are genuine.
    They all come with a written guarantee.
    Certificates of authenticity.
    For fifty grand I got the chance to buy
    A first edition *Catcher in the Rye.*
    It's in a special box up on the shelf,
    And it was signed by old J.D. himself.
    Rosemary's baby held by Mia Farrow.
    A parking ticket got by Clarence Darrow.
    The Great Escape? The movie?
DAWN: Yes, I've seen—
JEROME: The motorcycle rode by Steve McQueen.
    A group shot that includes Miss Greta Garbo.
    An LP that includes the voice of Harpo.
    The book of Dr. Seuss's that does not rhyme.
    "Send in the Fools" composed by Stephen Sondheim.
    The only leisure suit worn by Al Gore.
    The hat tossed up by Mary Tyler Moore.
    The rarest item ever on eBay—
    A jockstrap autographed by JFK.
DAWN: Okay. I see. It's an impressive hoard.
    You don't think, maybe, you've gone overboard?
JEROME: I have created a unique lifestyle.
    I am the world's greatest eBay-phile.
    So now, Dawn, think about this. Just for fun.
    Of all the things I have, choose any one.
    So how'd you like to have it? Tha'd be nice.
    Just dump my dad. Forget him. Name your price.
DAWN: Why do you come at me with words so vicious?
    You think that I am merely meretricious?
JEROME: Let's state the reason that you're with him, honey.
    You're with him 'cause he's got a lot of money.

DAWN: We've barely met. You've got the wrong impressions.

    I'm not here for material possessions.

    Our nature's are so different, you and I.

    I want to love. You want what you can buy.

JEROME: Oh, stop it, please. Don't give me that insult.

    It's just us here. Come on. Let's be adult.

    I think we know what's going on here, sure.

    Babes never pick an older man who's poor.

DAWN: I know from whence you get your incoherence.

    For you see only physical appearance.

JEROME: See physical appearance? No, not I.

    Perish the thought. I'm not that kind of guy.

    To me, a woman's beauty matters not.

    You really want to know what gets me hot?

    You want to know what gives my heart a thwack?

    It's power. That's my aphrodisiac.

    The times that I have had most excellent

    Have been with women in the government.

    One time in Washington, I had the honor

    Of dating Justice Sandra Day O'Connor.

    Once at a Democratic jamboree

    I passed the time away with Hillary.

    A couple years ago at Hanukkah

    I dreideled all night long with Monica.

    And then there was the night in that casino,

    Playing chemin de fer with Janet Reno.

    And how 'bout you? What makes you feel dandy?

    What is the modus of your operandi?

DAWN: My escapades with men have been quite rare.

    Compared to you, well, my life can't compare.

    In that race, you would leave me far behind.

JEROME: So you and Bill? What did you have in mind?

DAWN: I had no motive. There was nothing planned.

    If you knew me before, you'd understand.

JEROME: I'd love to hear your story. Yes, I would.

    We've got a minute. Come on. Make it good.

DAWN: There is no reason that I should be coy.

    I'm from a town in downstate Illinois.

    I'll bet you couldn't find it on the map.

My mom was poor. I never knew my pap.

[EUGENE *peeks in from the balcony.*]

You never saw such abject poverty.
For money, Mom would take in laundry.
On weekend nights, the men would come around.
I'd hide and close my ears against the sound.
One night a drunk came at her with a knife,
And now she's doing fifteen years to life.
My childhood was spent in misery.
In foster homes. Like Nicholas Nickleby.

[EUGENE *enters.*]

EUGENE: Like Nicholas Nickleby?
DAWN: Oh, yes, indeed.
What saved my life was that I learned to read.
I learned I could escape the daily grind
By living in the world of my mind.
Dickens, Shakespeare, Tolstoy, Twain, Fitzgerald,
Dostoyevsky, Shaw, and Proust. I barreled
My way through the library with relish.
I found a life that wasn't quite so hellish.
I came up here to university.
I studied hard and earned my Ph.D.
I got a teaching job to preach the truth
Of classic books to inner-city youth.
I finally found out what my life was for.
EUGENE: So how did you meet up with Mr. Moore?
DAWN: There is a willow grows aslant a brook
Near Indian Boundary Park in County Cook.
A quiet spot. Silence is guaranteed.
I often go there when I want to read.
I've spent so many days there undisturbed.
And then, one day, the oddest thing occurred.
A gentleman sat underneath a tree.
I looked at him, and then he looked at me.
I thought for sure his motives would be base.
But, no. He didn't move into my space.
He sat. And then I saw he was so sad.

The saddest man I'd ever seen.

JEROME: My dad?

DAWN: Oh, yes. The man had such a tortured look.

    I was so touched that I put down my book.

    Without a thought of what might lie ahead

    I walked on over to him and I said,

    "I do not mean to be too meddlesome,

    But I must ask you, why are you so glum?"

    He looked at me. Said he was in despair.

    Because, he said, that no one seemed to care

    About the future of all humankind.

    It seems, he said, we've grown so unrefined.

    The noise and the pollution of the earth.

    He said that we've forgotten what it's worth.

    He felt, he said, that in all likelihood

    No day would come when he would feel good.

    I said I think I have the antidote.

    You must remember what the poets wrote.

    I opened up my book. Then I began

    To read him: "What a piece of work is man."

    That day I read him all the Danish prince,

    And I've been reading to him ever since.

    You can't think I had any plan because

    I really didn't know who this man was.

    He's put his trust in me, Jer. You should try it.

JEROME: I would. Except, Dawn, sorry, I don't buy it.

[WILLIAM *is heard in the bedroom.*]

DAWN: Well, here he comes. What are you going to do?

JEROME: I'll bide my time and keep my eye on you.

[JEROME *and* EUGENE *exit through the front door.*]

SCENE 11 [WILLIAM, DAWN]

[WILLIAM *enters.*]

WILLIAM: Hello, my dear. It's nice to see you here.

    I fear it's been a year since you've been near.

    I'll say a cheer 'cause now you're in my sphere.

I shed a tear to think you'll disappear.

DAWN: Oh, my emir. Your fear is too severe.

It's clear that many others jeer and sneer.

So in your ear I'll say I'll persevere

To make your happiness my life's career.

WILLIAM: A mountaineer! Upon the highest tier

Could veer and a . . .

DAWN: Sheer cliff could interfere.

WILLIAM: A pioneer . . .

DAWN: Could reach a new frontier.

WILLIAM: A buccaneer . . .

DAWN: Could get a souvenir.

WILLIAM: How 'bout a beer? A bagel and a schmear?

DAWN: I'd like to read a passage from *King Lear*.

[*She opens a book and reads.*]

"Unhappy that I am, I cannot heave

My heart into my mouth."

WILLIAM: Dawn. I believe

King Lear does not fit in with what I've planned.

DAWN: Of course. You're right. I surely understand.

My lack of talent's obvious when I read.

That is your wise opinion. I accede.

WILLIAM: Oh, no. I love your reading. It sounds swell.

"The man who loved not wisely, but too well."

DAWN: Excuse me, Bill. *Othello*'s what you speak.

WILLIAM: It's Shakespeare. So, to me, it all sounds Greek.

Your simple student never finished school.

All I know is I am like Lear. A fool.

DAWN: You're street smart. Don't you ever ridicule

Your lack of education. That's a rule.

WILLIAM: I love to hear you read. To hear your voice.

But Shakespeare? I'm not sure it's the best choice.

DAWN: Perhaps a sonnet could be your métier.

"Shall I compare thee to a summer's day?"

WILLIAM: Well, that sounds nice. Could I hear more of it?

DAWN: "Thou art more lovely and more temperate."

WILLIAM: Oh, yeah.

DAWN: So I could be your sonneteer?

WILLIAM: Without a doubt. I think I like Shakespeare.

    After this one, can you read some more?

DAWN: Of course. There are a hundred fifty-four.

WILLIAM: I want to hear them all.

DAWN: Them all?

WILLIAM: That's right.

    So maybe you should plan to spend the night.

DAWN: I could do that. I'm not in any rush.

    In fact, down in my bag, there's a toothbrush.

WILLIAM: Good thinking. You are such a clever girl.

    Please. After you.

[DAWN *and* WILLIAM *exit to the bedroom.*]

SCENE 12 [JEROME, EUGENE]

[JEROME *and* EUGENE *enter.*]

JEROME: I think I'm gonna hurl.

EUGENE: That was so beautiful. They're just so cute.

    I can't believe you questioned her repute.

    Admit it now, Jerome. She's got you whupped.

JEROME: What are you, dense? Who's in there getting shtupped?

    She did her little abracadabra.

    Toss in a healthy dosage of Viagra

    And, whoop-de-do, he's getting his toes curled.

    It is the oldest story in the world.

    A sir will always give in to a madam.

    It's been that way since Eve came on to Adam.

SCENE 13 [WILLIAM, JEROME, EUGENE]

[WILLIAM *enters.*]

WILLIAM: Are you still here? I told you both to go.

JEROME: I'm pleading with you, Dad. Don't be a schmo.

    Forget that I'm your son. We're just two guys.

    There's so much wool she's pulled over your eyes.

    I'm watching you, and I am panic struck.

    She's working on you, man. Don't be a schmuck.

WILLIAM: How dare you think she's mercenary. Her?
   Well, I'll show you. I'm gonna marry her!
JEROME: No, please. You will be sorry, man. I swear.
WILLIAM [*calling off to the bedroom*]: Would you come in here, Dawn?
   [*Calling off in the other direction*]   Bernard! Prepare!

SCENE 14 [DAWN, WILLIAM, JEROME, EUGENE]

[DAWN *enters.*]

DAWN: What is it, Bill? What can I do for you?
WILLIAM: Stand next to me so we can say "I do."
DAWN: Oh, my. You mean . . . ?
WILLIAM: I'm down here on one knee.
   I mean it, Dawn. Will you please marry me?
DAWN: Oh, no. I can't. It's much too much to hope.
JEROME: Oh, what the hell. Go on. Marry the dope.
DAWN: You mean it, Bill?
WILLIAM: I do. Without a doubt.
DAWN: Your happiness is all I care about.
   So if you really want to share your life,
   I'll humbly say, "Yes. I will be your wife."
WILLIAM [*to* JEROME]: So there! You see! I still can close a deal.
   We'll show you and the world our love is real.
   I cut you off, you low-life reprobate.
JEROME: Yeah, sure. So now what? Now you'll set a date?
WILLIAM: So you can try to break us up somehow?
   No, sir. I'm gonna marry her right now.
   With Bernard here we do not have to wait.
   He's been ordained. He can officiate.
   Right here! This instant! She and I will marry!
   My man Bernard has been to seminary!

SCENE 15 [BERNARD, WILLIAM, DAWN, JEROME, EUGENE]

[BERNARD *enters, wearing preacher's robes.*]

BERNARD: Praise God! Can I get an "amen"?!

WILLIAM AND DAWN: Amen!

BERNARD: Oh, yes! Let's hear it once again!

WILLIAM, DAWN, AND EUGENE: Amen!

BERNARD: Step forward, if you please, you two lovebirds.

    You two will witness as I say the words.

    Will you, Dawn, be with William as his wife?

DAWN: I will. I'll be with you for all my life.

WILLIAM: For all your life, I swear, you'll be adored.

DAWN: I'll serve, love, and obey you.

BERNARD: Praise the Lord!

    Will you, William, be husband to this Dawn?

WILLIAM: I will. Our love will carry on and on.

    I will love you until the day I die.

JEROME: What's with you?

EUGENE: Weddings always make me cry.

BERNARD: Remember. Love is patient. Love is kind.

    Rejoice in truth as your lives are combined.

    Love bears all things and love believes all things.

    Love hopes all things and love endures all things.

    Oh, woe to him who is by himself when

    He falls and there is no one there.

EUGENE: Amen!

BERNARD: By the laws with which I am sanctified

    I say that you are married. Kiss the bride.

[WILLIAM *and* DAWN *kiss.*]

WILLIAM: Wait here. There's something that I have to do.

    Just wait right here. I have a gift for you.

[WILLIAM *exits.*]

DAWN: How 'bout that? Just like that a life can switch.

    This morning I was poor, and now I'm rich!

    Yee-hah! I did it! I am Mrs. Moore!

    It's party time, folks! Katie bar the door!

JEROME: I knew it! I knew that's what you would do.

    Eve Harrington could learn a thing from you!

DAWN: You got me, Jer. You're really quite astute.

    You knew that I was coming for the loot.

    You did. You really saw through my disguise.

The rest of you who didn't—well, surprise!

[WILLIAM *enters.*]

WILLIAM: I give this gift to you and to none other.
　　I'd bought it for my dear departed mother.
DAWN: Oh, no. Oh, Bill. I don't know what to say.
WILLIAM: Just promise me you'll wear it every day.
DAWN: Of course, I will. But you are all I want.
WILLIAM: I want to take you to a restaurant.
　　The finest place in town. We'll sing and dance.
　　I want to show the world our romance.
　　Is that okay?
DAWN:　　　　　　Of course.
WILLIAM:　　　　　　　　　I want to gloat!
　　Just wait right here. I'll go and get my coat.

[WILLIAM *exits.*]

JEROME: I'll blow your cover, doll. I guarantee—
BERNARD: Stop. Chill. The man is happy. Let him be.
DAWN: Oh, please. Bernard. Eugene. Jer. Let's not squabble.
　　I'm happy. Look. I got a little bauble.
　　Go sit and muse on what a son inherits.
　　What is this? Maybe six or seven carats?
JEROME: Bernard!
DAWN:　　　　　　Shut up! You all are idiots.
　　From here on out, I'm calling all the shots.
JEROME: Oh, no!
DAWN:　　　　　　Oh, yeah. You're working for me now.
　　Bernard? Yeah, babe. I am the new house frau.
　　From now on, you will follow orders, chum.
　　Get rid of Tweedledee and Tweedledum.
　　Guess what, guys. It is time for you to go.
　　I am the lady of the house!!
JEROME:　　　　　　　　　Oh, no!!!

[*Blackout.*]

ACT 2

SCENE 1 [JEROME, EUGENE]

[JEROME *is at the computer.* EUGENE *is watching him.*]

EUGENE: Your dad was hoodwinked just as you suspected.
How can you sit there calm and so collected?
JEROME: Eugene dear, just be quiet, s'il vous plaît.
I'm drowning all my sorrows on eBay.
I've found a lovely little acquisition.
A special level one-three-two magician.
With major armor, heart, and GSC,
Maxed stats and hundreds of buffed-up HP.
EUGENE: Excuse me, could I just peek at the screen?
I haven't got a clue of what you mean.
JEROME: It's *Asheron's Call*. I play it very oft.
An online game that comes from Microsoft.
We players live online in lands where we go
On exploits with our personal alter ego.
We travel miles hour after hour.
We pick up points and then increase our power.
I can't find this, no matter how I try it.
So I've no choice. It's on eBay. I'll buy it.
EUGENE: So you want what is inside of the game?
JEROME: Sure. Lots of players do it. There's no shame
In selling what you have that satisfies
Another player. That's free enterprise.
EUGENE: So what you're saying—let me get the gist.
You're buying something that does not exist.
JEROME: It does for me! It's very meaningful
To spend time in a land that's teeming full
Of life. Adventure. Landscapes. Property.
I've played there for so long so happily.
It frees my mind from all my toil and strife.
If not for this, I'd have no social life.
EUGENE: I like to be with you, Jerome. No kiddin'.
JEROME: That's nice, Eugene. Now let me get my bid in.

Well, fine. I missed it. There. You happy now?

Relax. It doesn't matter anyhow.

No, nothing matters now. I'm so depressed.

That devil woman has my dad possessed.

My life is ruined. Man, I feel so crappy.

From now on, I'm officially unhappy.

EUGENE: I hate to see you sitting there so idle.

JEROME: You want to make a plan that's homicidal?

Say, kick her down the elevator shaft?

Or on Lake Michigan tied to a raft?

I just can't stand it! I might go berserk!

You know what I just might do? Go to work.

EUGENE: Oh, no. Jerome. You mean . . . ?

JEROME: Yessireebob.

It's time.

EUGENE: But have you ever had a job?

JEROME: I don't mean wear an apron and a hat.

And smile, saying, "You want fries with that?"

It could be my ideal vindication

If I create my own new corporation.

Man, this is great! I'll be a CEO.

EUGENE: And I'll be . . . ?

JEROME: You'll be . . . something. I don't know.

EUGENE: My business knowledge isn't very formal.

I have my lib'ral arts degree from Normal.

JEROME: We'll find something you like, and you'll pursue it.

No sweat. Watch me, and I will walk you through it.

The main thing is you always have to act sure.

EUGENE: Okay. So talk. What will we manufacture?

JEROME: Please. We don't manufacture anything.

We will just do an Enron buck and wing.

I have a banker who'll lend me some dough.

We start up. Then announce an IPO.

Spread rumors. Plant some stories in the press.

The guys on Wall Street eat up that BS.

Investment bankers will break down our door.

We take the money and stash it offshore.

Create a corporate office in Bermuda.

A perfect place to harbor all the moolah.

EUGENE: You might think this is a banality,
    But aren't we talking vague legality?
JEROME: We're chummy with the Washingtonians.
    We've spread around lots of simoleons.
    The Congress passed the laws, and so the fact is
    We can avoid all corporation taxes.
    We open up our offices and then
    We get those guys from Arthur Andersen.
    They come aboard, and they'll be our cohorts
    For rosy-looking quarterly reports.
    And when the bad time comes, we'll have those gents
    To cook the books and shred the documents.
EUGENE: That doesn't seem so hard.
JEROME: No shit, Sherlock.
    Our job? Inflate the value of the stock.
    Stock options, Gene. Stock options are the key.
    Amazing, what can be done legally.
    You're chairman of the board, so to be nice
    You let me buy my shares at half the price.
    I'm CEO, so I get all the perks.
    No-interest loans. And bonuses. The works.
    Just like John Rigas of Adelphia
    I will grow wealthia and wealthia.
    Oh, can't you just imagine it, Eugene?
    Me, on the rich list of *Forbes* magazine.
EUGENE: But what if you use up what's in the bank?
JEROME: Well, then, of course, the company will tank.
    But right before the stock price starts to plummet,
    I call up Mr. Broker and say, "Dump it."
    See, when it's time, you just have to be willing
    To bail out like Enron's Jeffrey Skilling.
    And I'll be sitting pretty with my loot
    Because I have a golden parachute.
EUGENE: But what if you are called to testify?
JEROME: "But what if I am called." Well, duh! I lie.
    I can withstand congressional assault.
    I'll raise my hand and say, "It's not my fault.
    I'd like to help, but much to my dismay
    I just don't know. I'm not a CPA."

EUGENE: But what about the people who lose out?
    The people that will have to do without?
JEROME: That's life, Eugene. That is part of the game.
    Some people win. Some lose. Hey, who's to blame?
    You have to see this philosophically.
    It's money. Money has no memory.
    It knows not which hand it will occupy.
    The money doesn't feel bad. Why should I?
    I'm feeling good, Eugene. You sense the joy?
    Come on. Let's hear it. Are you with me, boy?
EUGENE: I'll try to have a positive outlook.
JEROME: Congratulations, Gene. You are a crook!
    The future's clear. The sky is bright and sunny.
    Let's sing! "We are the world. We have the money."
    Oh, yeah! Come on, Eugene. What do you say?
    First thing tomorrow, we'll be on our way.
EUGENE: We'll get up bright and bushy eyed at six.
JEROME: At what?
EUGENE: At seven? Eight, we'll hit the bricks?
    Just tell me when you'd like the clock to ring.
JEROME: I've changed my mind. Forget the whole damn thing.

SCENE 2 [DAWN, JEROME, WILLIAM, BERNARD, EUGENE]

[DAWN *enters.*]

DAWN: Hi, boys.
JEROME: Hello. Another shopping trip?
DAWN: That's right. I'm on the job. So zip your lip.

[WILLIAM *and* BERNARD *enter, laden with packages.*]

    Just put those packages down there for now.
    Oh, William dear, please let me wipe your brow.
    This shopping trip took longer than I thought.
    But thank you for the lovely things we bought.
WILLIAM: Whatever makes you happy, Dawn. Of course.
    I've never shopped like this. I'm no clotheshorse.
DAWN: Nor I, my dear. The merchandise we reap will

Benefit so many other people.

Our wealth does give us certain obligations

To help the ones who live beneath our stations.

WILLIAM: Your attitude for shopping's so voracious.

DAWN: It's not for me. We must be ostentatious.

We have to ring up lots of costly sales

To help the employees of Bloomingdale's.

It's right to spread our money helter-skelter

To help afford them food and clothes and shelter.

WILLIAM: But wouldn't it be just as right and smart

To help the employees down at Kmart?

DAWN: At Kmart? Don't be silly. Us? No way!

At Kmart? Bill. What would the neighbors say?

WILLIAM: The neighbors? I don't care. It makes me wince

To look upon all this extravagance.

DAWN: What would you have me do? Go and return it?

Or take it all downstairs and simply burn it?

Just say the word. It matters not to me.

I'll lose all of this stuff. ASAP.

WILLIAM: No. No. Please, dear. My dear. Please dry your eyes.

I'm sorry, Dawn. I do apologize.

I do not want your feelings to be hurt.

DAWN: You didn't even thank me for the shirt.

WILLIAM: I thank you for the shirt. I love it, Dawn.

DAWN: It's good on you. It's very au courant.

WILLIAM: I do not mean to doubt your reasoning.

Please keep it. Keep it all. Keep everything.

DAWN: I need to raise the limit on the Visa.

Tomorrow, would you do that for me? Please—a?

WILLIAM: Now, Dawn—

DAWN: It's our responsibility

To help the national economy.

I want to be a good American.

If we don't shop, the terrorists will win.

WILLIAM: All right.

DAWN: You've had a hectic day. You're stressed.

I think that you should go and have a rest.

WILLIAM: But—

DAWN: No. No buts. You listen to your bride.

And soon I'll come and lay down by your side.
WILLIAM: Bernard?
BERNARD: Yes, sir. It is a good idea.
    A rest right now would be a panacea.
WILLIAM: I guess you're right. My head feels like a ton.
    Good night.

[*He exits.*]

SCENE 3 [DAWN, JEROME,
BERNARD, EUGENE]

DAWN: Hot damn! I'm having so much fun!
    I crack me up. It's just hilarious.
    I play him like a Stradivarius.
JEROME: Have you no shame?
DAWN: No. Maybe I should try some.
    If I want shame, I'll have my husband buy some.
    Hey, Bernie! Babe! An extradry martini.
    And set me up some caviar and blini.
JEROME: For how long did you have this whole thing planned?
    Or was it just a chance—
DAWN: Talk to the hand.
    I shopped so hard today, and now I'm done.
    For information, dial 411.
JEROME: I might go public with your treacheries.
    There are some people I could call and—
DAWN: Freeze!
    Don't even think it, dickhead. I'm in charge.
    No way you're busting me. I'm livin' large.
    You are a guest in this house. Who's the host?
    One word from me to him and you are toast.
    You want to take me on? Well, boys, you can't.
    'Cause you're here on a Mrs. Dawn Moore grant.
    As soon as I get bored with your routines,
    You'll both be standing outside smelling beans.
    Let's go, Bernard! Chop-chop! Let's move those feet!
    You'll find your sorry ass out on the street!
    Oh, never mind. I've tot'ly lost the mood.

You see what happens when you cop a 'tude?
Man, hanging out with you is just so lame.
Do what you want. I'll be with what's-his-name.

[*She exits.*]

SCENE 4 [JEROME, BERNARD, EUGENE]

JEROME: You gonna let her talk to you that way?
How can you simply stand there, so blasé?
BERNARD: Her words are air. They can't make me a victim.
What makes me mad is how she went and tricked him.
JEROME: Exactly. Man, she treats him like a clown.
You've got to help us try and take her down.
EUGENE: Beware, Jerome. If you talk to your dad,
Without a doubt, you're gonna make him mad.
JEROME: He has to know that she is just a fraud.
You've got to help us, Gene, expose this broad.
EUGENE: I understand that you are quite irate.
She's standing in the way of your estate.
It surely will be to your benefit
If you can prove that she is counterfeit.
JEROME: It's not just for myself I want to squeeze her.
I feel sorry for the lovesick geezer.
I know that when he hears it, it might hurt him,
But we have got to risk it and convert him.
You guys, he has to know that she's a faker.
BERNARD: I love that man. The bitch is whack. Let's take her.
JEROME: All right! Okay! Let's go to work, Eugene.
We'll find a way to get her to come clean.
EUGENE: If you will trash the promise that he gave her,
You need to expose all her bad behavior.
JEROME: Yes. He himself must get some sort of peep.
What's underneath the clothing of that sheep.
Oh, man, I cannot wait till she is gone.
I see on the horizon—a new Dawn.
BERNARD: But first he has to see her flip the script.
JEROME: You're right. But how? She is so well equipped.
He buys her everything that she desires.

There must be something else that she requires.
We have to entice her to demonstrate
Her real character. But what for bait?
I can't get her with money, she's in clover.

[*Pause.*]

Of course! They're married now! The sex is over!
EUGENE: They seem to be a very loving pair.
JEROME: Get with it, Gene. He hasn't got a prayer.
With married people, sex is very rare.
It's kept on ice inside the Frigidaire.
Her life for her is one big sugar cookie.
I doubt that he is getting any nookie.
She's young. She must possess an appetite.
I'll bet she has a flame I could ignite.
Yes. Yes. I'm sure it is a safe deduction.
She should be very ripe for a seduction.
Imagine that if he could get a glance
Of his own son—me—getting in her pants.
But wait a sec. I have to say it strikes me.
[*To* EUGENE] It must be you 'cause I don't think she likes me.
EUGENE: What?
JEROME: Yes.
EUGENE: No.
JEROME: Yes.
EUGENE: No.
JEROME: Yes.
EUGENE: No.
JEROME: Yes.
EUGENE: But.
JEROME: What?
EUGENE: I cannot be a party to this plot.
JEROME: It must be you. You're perfect for the job.
EUGENE: I—
JEROME: Sure. It's you. A regular heartthrob.
EUGENE: Why can't it be Bernard instead of me?
BERNARD: No good. I have no sense of irony.
EUGENE: I don't know what to do or what to say.
JEROME: The girl's in heat. You just stand in her way.

EUGENE: Jerome, by law, the woman is my aunt.
  You really should get someone else. I can't.
JEROME: You can. In no time you will have it mastered.
  Just get in touch with your own inner bastard.
  I'm not expecting you to do the deed.
  You get her hot, and then we'll intercede.
  Just talk and move your eyes around a bit.
  You got it going, man. She'll have a fit.
  We'll just need Dad in place to overhear.
  Bernard, come on. Let's get this thing in gear.

[BERNARD *goes to the bedroom door and knocks.*]

BERNARD: Excuse me, sir. I need a word with you.

SCENE 5 [WILLIAM, BERNARD, JEROME, EUGENE]

[WILLIAM *enters.*]

WILLIAM: What is it?
BERNARD: You should listen to these two.
WILLIAM: I'm tired, man. What is this all about?
JEROME: Please, listen up. You have to hear me out.
  You think you and your wife have got a bond.
  You've got to hear this, Dad. You're being conned.
WILLIAM: I will not listen to your lies and slurs.
  How dare you insult anything of hers?
JEROME: We're not a bunch of raving maniacs.
  Let's take a moment to look at the facts.
  Since you got hitched, her shopping never yields.
  Who did she marry? You or Marshall Field's?
WILLIAM: I do not care a bit about the money.
  I find your accusations most unfunny.
JEROME: I do not say this just to be provoking.
  She'll gut you like a vulture. I'm not joking.
EUGENE: Please. Uncle Bill. It's pretty evident
  That since the wedding you don't seem content.
WILLIAM: I'm just a little tired. That is all.
  I think I need to drink some Geritol.

JEROME: You're not yourself. Now think, man. Concentrate.
    Where is the William Moore I love to hate?
    Since she's been at you dollar after dollar
    Not once have you let go a big ol' holler.
WILLIAM: Bernard?
BERNARD: I'm sorry, sir. The man is right.
    It hurts me to intrude on your delight.
JEROME: No doubt about it. She is out to screw you.
    Give us a minute, and we'll prove it to you.
    Eugene will talk to her and you will glean
    The truth about her from behind the screen.
WILLIAM: You want me—
JEROME: Yes.
WILLIAM: Behind the screen?
JEROME: For sure.
    At times like this, it's—what?—it's de rigueur.
    Before Eugene can get his pants unbuckled,
    You'll say hello to your own inner cuckold.
WILLIAM: I eavesdrop on them from behind the screen?
JEROME: And then you'll know she's just a libertine.
WILLIAM: A libertine? A libertine? Not her.
    I don't like your insinuation.
BERNARD: Sir.
    I have to say I favor this routine.
    So please—just for a moment—do the screen.

[WILLIAM *goes behind the screen.*]

JEROME: Okay, Eugene. It's time to do your thing.
    Remember—talk. And eyes. And bada-bing!
EUGENE: Can we get someone else to do the trick?
    Jerome, I think . . . Jerome, I might be sick.
JEROME: Just breathe. We're here. We'll be your chaperones.
    Just tell her that you want to jump her bones.

[EUGENE *doesn't move.* JEROME *goes to the door and knocks on it.*]

    Convince her that you're carrying a torch.
    We'll both be outside listening from the porch.

[JEROME *and* BERNARD *go outside onto the balcony.*]

SCENE 6 [DAWN, EUGENE,
JEROME, BERNARD, WILLIAM]

[DAWN *enters.*]

DAWN: Oh, William, is it time to do our reading?

[*She sees* EUGENE.]

    Oh, fine. It's you. The knocking was misleading.
    I thought the knock was Bill's. Where is the square?
EUGENE: He . . . isn't here. He went . . . away . . . somewhere.
DAWN: He went out on his own? How very weird.
    Well, that's nice for a change. The coast is cleared.
    Where is Bernard?
EUGENE: Bernard . . . went . . . somewhere, too.
DAWN: You're full of information, aren't you?
    Well, fine. Now I can rest. Put up my feet.
    I was demure all day today. I'm beat.

[*She sits on the couch and puts her feet up.*]

    You want to know how much I spent today?
    Not counting what I put on layaway?
    How many lines of credit I accessed?
    Leona Helmsley would have been impressed.
    Another day with Mr. Moneybag.
    You know what I could really use? A fag.
EUGENE: A what?
DAWN: A smoke. You know. A cigarette.
    You want to carry on this tête-à-tête?
    I'll check my bag. I think I have a pack.
    Sit down. Relax, Eugene. I'll be right back.

[*She exits into the bedroom.* EUGENE *goes over to the balcony.* JEROME *and* BERNARD *come in.*]

EUGENE: Can I be done now?
JEROME: No. Don't be absurd.
    What's with you? You have hardly said a word.

[WILLIAM *comes out from behind the screen.*]

WILLIAM: There's no point to this stupid exercise.

JEROME: Do you not see how she's dropped her disguise?
WILLIAM: She's just relaxed. There's no cause for alarm.
JEROME [*to* EUGENE]: All right. Get in there, Gene. Turn on the charm.

[*They hear* DAWN *coming back.* JEROME *and* BERNARD *go back outside.* WILLIAM *goes back behind the screen.* EUGENE *leaps onto the couch and attempts to look relaxed.* DAWN *enters.*]

DAWN: No luck. I guess that I can do without.
　　I don't suppose that you might have . . . ?

[EUGENE *pats himself down.*]

EUGENE:　　　　　　　　　　　　　　　 Fresh out.
DAWN: I see. So what's on your deficient mind?
EUGENE: I'd like to talk. If you are so inclined.
DAWN: Sure. What about your partner? Where's Jerome?
EUGENE: Jerome has . . . left the building. He went home.
DAWN: I've never seen you separate from your chum.
　　You watch yourself, Eugene. He's such a scum.
　　You should have an existence of your own.
EUGENE: He's not so bad.
DAWN:　　　　　　　　　 Compared to Al Capone.
　　He'd sell his own grandmother in a minute
　　If he could find a decent profit in it.
EUGENE: His manner always has been rather coarse.
　　When he was young, his folks got their divorce.
　　The custody arrangement was a mess.
　　They argued over who could get him less.
DAWN: The fact is that his ego's so inflated.
EUGENE: He thinks that he is so sophisticated.
DAWN: He treats all other people with such rancor.
EUGENE: He's such a crabby person.
DAWN:　　　　　　　　　　　　 He's a wanker.

[*They laugh.* JEROME *starts to burst in.* BERNARD *subdues him.*]

　　So, what? Is he the only friend you've got?
EUGENE: I try to make friends. I end up with squat.
　　It's been that way since I was back in school.
　　Most people just don't like me as a rule.
　　My playmates always used to be pretend.

    I have one good imaginary friend.

    He lives next door to me. His name is Hal.

    He's real. I imagine he's my pal.

DAWN: You'd do okay if you just weren't so shy.

    You're not such a decrepit-looking guy.

    Most girls eat up that sad and lonely schtick.

    You should be fighting them off with a stick.

EUGENE: I often talk about this with my shrink.

DAWN: Say, how 'bout this? You want to have a drink?

    Let's open up a bottle of Dom P.

EUGENE: You think that it's okay?

DAWN: Sure. It's on me.

    "We have to share our bounty with the masses."

    You pop the cork, and I'll go get some glasses.

[*She exits.* JEROME *and* BERNARD *come in.* WILLIAM *comes out from behind the screen.*]

JEROME [*to* WILLIAM]: You see?

WILLIAM: I see she wants to have champagne.

    That's fine. I see no reason to complain.

    There's nothing here that is lascivious.

JEROME: Man, how can you be so oblivious?

    [*To* EUGENE] Go get her, Gene. You pull out all the stops.

    Go on.

BERNARD: You sure this boy has got the chops?

    He's acting like he's playing patty-cakes.

JEROME [*to* EUGENE]: Go on, Eugene.

BERNARD: You gotta up the stakes.

[JEROME *and* BERNARD *go back outside.* WILLIAM *goes back behind the screen.* EUGENE *is trying to open the bottle of champagne.* DAWN *enters.*]

DAWN: Man, living here's more fun than Disneyland.

[EUGENE *is having trouble getting the cork out of the bottle.*]

    Eugene?

EUGENE: I got it.

DAWN: Let me lend a hand.

[*She takes the bottle from him and pops the cork. She pours the champagne into the glasses.*]

I love the sound of champagne. It's sublime.
Here's lookin' at you, kid. Drink up.
EUGENE: *L'chaim.*

[*They drink.*]

DAWN: Oh, yeah. That's good. I tell you, I am tired.
It isn't easy being so admired.
He wants me in the limelight all the time.
On this gig, I am earning every dime.
EUGENE: He really loves you.
DAWN: Yeah. I know, I know.
I have to chill that old lothario.
He wants to sleep with me. No way. I won't.
See, ever since I said "I do," I don't.
EUGENE: So he was right.
DAWN: Who was?
EUGENE: Why . . . Uncle Bill.
How right to wait for you. I'm sure he will.
DAWN: Yep. That's my hubby, Bill. He's quite a guy.

[EUGENE *is rolling his eyes around in an attempt to be seductive.*]

Have you got something stuck inside your eye?
EUGENE: I just think . . . Well . . . I think that I should mention
I could help you release some of your tension.
I've grabbed this chance for us to be alone.
The moment that we met—
DAWN: Now hold the phone.
Let's get this straight. Let's skip the subtlety.
You naughty boy. You comin' on to me?
EUGENE: I've loads of pent-up sexual energy.
DAWN: That's fine for you, but what's in it for me?
EUGENE: For you?
DAWN: What do I get? You imbecile.
I got all this because I slept with Bill.
EUGENE: I'm speaking of romantic celebration.
It's not a cut-and-dried negotiation.
DAWN: You want to get romantic satisfaction?
Then learn the rules of animal attraction.
The theories of our mating habits are in
The books of science going back to Darwin.

Females decide acceptance or rejection.

We are in charge of sexual selection.

EUGENE: You are in charge? That's not what I have heard.

DAWN: Behold the male spotted bowerbird.

You want to study sexual relation?

The bowerbird's a perfect illustration.

He takes up to a year to build his nest

In hopes that his abode will be the best.

With twigs and leaves and grass. Chunks of topsoil.

Some bits of broken glass or old tinfoil.

Cigar butts. There is nothing he won't try.

His nest must be the one to catch her eye.

And when he's done, he'll just sit down and wait.

There's lots of nests from which to choose her mate.

When she decides which one has made the grade,

Well, that's the bowerbird who will get laid.

EUGENE: I always thought it was the men that rule

Because they have the more aggressive tool.

DAWN: The plans of men might go right down the tubes.

I always get what I want. I've got boobs.

I'm flattered. Really, Gene, you're very sweet.

Relax. I'm gonna get something to eat.

[DAWN *exits.* EUGENE *goes over to the balcony.* JEROME, BERNARD, *and* WIL-
LIAM *appear.*]

EUGENE: Nothing will ever happen at this rate.

JEROME: You got her on the ropes. You're doing great.

[*To* WILLIAM] You see how her flimflam is feasible?

WILLIAM: She's teasing him. He's young. He's teaseable.

I've had enough of this. I'm going.

JEROME: Wait.

[*To* EUGENE] You're losing her. So try some different bait.

EUGENE: You'd better come up with another plan.

JEROME: I can't.

BERNARD: Just tell her that you love her, man.

EUGENE: Oh, no.

JEROME: She'll fall for it. I guarantee.

EUGENE: You really think she will?

BERNARD: It works for me.

[*They hear* DAWN *returning and return to their places.* DAWN *enters, carrying a tray of food.*]

DAWN: Bernard left all this food out on a tray.

    You ever have foie gras? Duck mousse pâté?

EUGENE: I love you!

DAWN: What?

EUGENE: I love you!

DAWN: Whoop-de-do.

EUGENE: I love you. Oh my God. I really do.

    You are the most exciting woman ever.

    You're beautiful and sensual and clever.

DAWN: Your ardor is a little bit misplaced.

    This stuff is really good. You want a taste?

EUGENE: I'd do whatever you would ask me to.

    You've no idea what I feel for you.

DAWN: Don't talk of love. That just gets in the way.

    You want to get it on with me? Okay.

    Why not? You want to get our bodies mergin'?

    That's great. I've never made it with a virgin.

EUGENE: I'm not.

DAWN: It's fine.

EUGENE: I'm—

DAWN: I don't give a damn.

EUGENE: I'm not.

DAWN: Come on.

EUGENE: I'm not. All right. I am.

    The world's oldest virgin. Go call Guinness.

DAWN: Forget about it. Let's get down to business.

    Let's finish this transaction you began.

    Eugene, you want to be my backdoor man?

EUGENE: What? Um . . .

DAWN: It's all right. No one has to know.

EUGENE: Oh, my.

DAWN: You'll be my secret gigolo.

EUGENE: But I . . .

DAWN: You said you've got the hots for me.

EUGENE: Oh, sure.

DAWN: We're right here where you want to be.

EUGENE: Uh-huh.

DAWN: You've given me an appetite.

EUGENE: Oh, yeah.

DAWN: You'll be my afternoon delight.
   Let's go. I'm proud to be your first affair.
   Come on. Climb up. I'll show you what goes where.

[*She pulls him down onto the sofa.*]

SCENE 7 [WILLIAM, EUGENE,
DAWN, JEROME, BERNARD]

[WILLIAM *comes out from behind the screen.* JEROME *and* BERNARD *enter.*]

WILLIAM: Oh, no!

EUGENE [*hugging* DAWN]: Oh, yes!

DAWN [*leaping up*]: Oh, Bill!

EUGENE: Oh, man.

WILLIAM: Oh, Dawn.

DAWN [*to* EUGENE]: Get off me, you heartless brute. Be gone!
   [*To* WILLIAM] Oh, Bill. Thank God you're here. That boy's insane.
   He came at me—

WILLIAM: Do not try to explain.
   What's going on in here is most clear cut.

JEROME: That's right! You are completely busted, slut!
   He heard. And so did I. So did Bernard.
   So now you're hoisted by your own petard.
   Nice going, Gene. I now owe you a lot.
   You nearly pulled it off. You got me hot.
   [*To* DAWN] So now you're at the end of all your capers.
   With pleasure, I hand you your walking papers.
   Make like a tree and leave.

DAWN: I'd like to say—

JEROME: Make like a storm and blow.

DAWN: Please. If I may—

JEROME: Make like a bee. Buzz off.

DAWN: I'd like a word.

JEROME: Make like a rock and roll.

DAWN: May I be heard?

JEROME: Make like a super chicken. Fly the coop.

DAWN: Shut up your mouth, Jerome! Now, here's the scoop.
   There's nothing you can do. May I remind you?
   I'm Mrs. Moore. I legally entwined you.
   The marriage contract has been signed and dated.
   What's more, the marriage has been consummated.
   You think I'm through? Forget it. I'm not walkin'.
   You want me out? We'll get the lawyers talkin'.
   We'll get divorced. That's fine. And I will clean up.
   You chump. You didn't make me sign a prenup.
   You want to go to court? I'll testify.
   Before I'm through, I'll hang you out to dry.
   You think I'm finished here? That's what you think.
   Bernard! Get over there. Build me a drink.

WILLIAM: Please, Dawn. I do not want to go to court.
   I love you. All I want is your support.

JEROME: Dad, aren't you listening? She is a fake.
   She's lower than the belly of a snake.

WILLIAM: I love this girl. That is all I see.
   If something's wrong, the fault must lie with me.
   It is the money that's the complication.
   I brought you here, and there's too much temptation.
   It should be just us two. Husband and wife.
   Let's go someplace and live a simple life.
   Let's go someplace where you and I can be
   Just people living in simplicity.

DAWN: Simplicity? In some cheap habitat?
   No. Sorry, babe. Not me. Been there, done that.

WILLIAM: Come live with me, my dear. It won't be hard.
   It will be just us two. Us and Bernard.

DAWN: You want to go away? That's fine, my dear.
   Just leave me—with your cash and credit—here.
   I'm playing here to win. Accept it, boys.
   I'm coming out on top. So face the noise.
   You think I'm finished? Quote me. "Never, Moore."

[*There is a knocking at the front door.*]

WILLIAM: Bernard, who is that banging on the door?

SCENE 8 [RUTH, BERNARD,
JEROME, EUGENE, WILLIAM, DAWN]

[BERNARD *opens the door.* RUTH *enters. She is wearing an arm cast and a neck brace and is walking with a cane.*]

RUTH: Oh, good. I'm glad that everyone is in.

I have something to say. Where to begin?

BERNARD: You're looking well, Ms. M.

RUTH: Thank you, Bernard.

JEROME: We heard the Mazda hit you pretty hard.

EUGENE: We hope you're getting better every day.

RUTH: Next week, I'll be with the Cirque du Soleil.

I guess the joke was on me in this case.

The accident did nothing to my face.

So plastic surgery was not required.

But soon I will get what I have desired.

Next month, all the procedures will commence.

I found out it's a corporate expense.

JEROME: Excuse me, what? Your plastic surgery?

You're gonna charge it to the company?

RUTH: That's standard business practice to the letter.

It's good for business if I can look better.

There's nothing in the bylaws that forbade it.

The board and I officially okayed it.

They also voted with their yeas and nays

That everyone of us should get a raise.

WILLIAM: You can't have votes without my full approval.

RUTH: We also voted for your full removal.

WILLIAM: You what?

RUTH: Oh, yes. There really was no tellin'

What they would do when they heard you're a felon.

Oh, dear. I hate to be a tattletale.

But you are going off to freakin' jail.

I have found out—it was big news to me—

That you, Bill, stand accused of bigamy.

WILLIAM: Of bigamy? Why, that's ridiculous.

The lawyers all were most meticulous.

RUTH: Oh, yes. They wrote a wonderful decree.

But, Bill, think back to when you married me.

The ceremony was so wonderful.
Our families came together in the shul.
There was the wedding canopy above.
We broke the glass and then said, "Mazel tov."
DAWN: That's swell. Thanks for the trip down mem'ry lane.
Is there a point to this?
RUTH: I will explain.
I found a rabbi and got a decision
That your divorce don't count in my religion.
We are not split up from each other yet.
I didn't get a get.
WILLIAM: A get?
RUTH: You bet.
When we split up, you never did present
A proper legal Jewish document.
We didn't have a ritual divorce.
WILLIAM: You think that changes anything?
RUTH: Of course.
A get was not delivered properly.
And so, I say, you're still married to me.
I'll go to court and there I will insist
As far as I see you're a bigamist.
Tomorrow, you'll be served with a subpoena.
How's that for a nice deus ex machina?
WILLIAM: Don't come at me like some great Jewish diva.
My man Bernard has been to the yeshiva!

[BERNARD *takes a skullcap out of his pocket and puts it on.*]

BERNARD: The rabbis say there is a major schism
Between the civil courts and Judaism.
The Torah says that when two people mesh
As husband and his wife, they are one flesh.
So only when the Jewish court allows
A dissolution of the wedding vows
Is anyone permitted to remarry.
JEROME: Are Jewish people strict about this?
BERNARD: Very.
A civil divorce won't be recognized
Unless the divorce has been Judaized.

WILLIAM: Bernard, you mean that this could get litigious?

JEROME: But we are not what you would call religious.

    We—

BERNARD: That is what the rabbis say, Jerome.

JEROME: But—

BERNARD: That is what the rabbis say. Shalom.

RUTH [*to* WILLIAM]: See, our divorce was never finalized.

    And so, by God, it won't be recognized.

    Because you went and had your little fling,

    Bill, you get bupkus. I get everything.

DAWN: Now just a minute, granny. Hold your horses.

    Right here is where the line forms for divorces.

    You haven't heard. Our marriage is in trouble.

    So I will start proceedings on the double.

RUTH: My little urchin, save the big outburst.

    I have the prior claim. I had him first.

DAWN: When I get through collecting what he owns,

    There will be nothing left but skin and bones.

RUTH: When I get through, you'll be out with the trash.

    And I'll be living here. Like Mama Cash.

DAWN: You think you've got a case? Well, that's too bad.

    I have a license that is ironclad.

RUTH: And I have got the teachings of the Torah.

    So you can start to pack your bags, señora.

JEROME: Man, this is great. I could watch this all night.

    I love to see two pissed-off women fight.

    This is a legal battleground, my dears.

    So, likely, you'll be stuck in court for years.

    You'll sue and countersue and . . . What a joke.

    See, pretty soon, the old guy's gonna croak.

    We'll put him in the ground, and I'll be there.

    A billionaire. His one and only heir.

RUTH: Jerome, my dear, there's something you should know.

    We should have talked about this years ago.

    I know that this will set your heart awhirl.

    But in the past I was a naughty girl.

    Way back when all my marriage woes began,

    I had relations with another man.

    You must forgive me, darling. Don't be mad.

But William Moore is really not your dad.

JEROME: That can't be true.

RUTH: It is.

JEROME: Well, who's the man?

RUTH: I can't recall his name. A salesman.

    He sold wine to my uncle's restaurant.

    He said he'd give me anything I want.

    So handsome, debonair. His charm was ample.

JEROME: You bought some wine?

RUTH: He left me with a sample.

DAWN: So, Jerry. Now the truth is out, sweetheart.

    I knew you were a bastard from the start.

JEROME: It doesn't matter. I'm still in the will.

DAWN: The worth of that old document is nil.

JEROME: So he can make a new will with me in it.

    Dad. Bill. Whatever. Sit down. Take a minute.

DAWN: A new will, William, will have to be drawn.

JEROME: Bernard, please get your lawyer costume on.

RUTH: Well, if you're gonna write another will,

    Remember all I've done for you, dear Bill.

JEROME: But I've been like a son to you. Daddy!

DAWN: I am the one you love. Leave it to me.

RUTH: All she has in her heart is larceny.

    You must leave it to me.

DAWN: No! Me!

JEROME: No! Me!

EUGENE: Eureka! Yes! Jerome. I've got it now.

    I fin'ly understand you people. Wow!

    I longed to be like you—so avaricious.

    I feel it rising in me. It's delicious!

    I have absorbed what you have tried to teach.

    I see now how to practice what you preach.

    The guiding principle that must prevail

    Is "I must win and all my friends must fail!"

    [*To* WILLIAM] *Mon oncle!* It is perfect! Don't you see?!

    The hell with them! Leave everything to me!

    I'll usher in the new millennium.

    The spirit of this country's time to come.

    I'll lead the nouveau riche in brotherhood.

I don't have much in brains, but I look good.
[*To* JEROME] You've been a model Mephistopheles
In fostering your affluent disease.
You wanted me to catch it. Well, I caught it!
I want it all! Screw you!

JEROME: By george, he's got it.

RUTH: It's up to you, Bill.

DAWN: Bill? What do you say?

JEROME: Dad?

DAWN: William?

RUTH: Bill?

WILLIAM: I want to go away.
I have to get away from all this junk.
In solitude, I'll live life like a monk.
You are the worst people I've ever known.
I want you all to just leave me alone.
I have to get away. There is no hope.
I'll live alone. Be like a misanthrope.

EUGENE: A what?

JEROME: Forget it.

WILLIAM: Time to break away.
Before I go, I have one thing to say.
You boys, Ruth, Dawn. You'll not get your windfall.
Now listen closely—*I RENOUNCE YOU ALL!*

RUTH: You're joking, Bill. You can't be serious.
If you think I'm through, you're delirious.

WILLIAM: I'm so fed up with the stupidity
You use to satisfy cupidity.
You've wrecked this country with your folderol.
You've turned the world into a shopping mall.
I've had it with your lies and degradation.
This used to be a just and moral nation.
A man would catch a fish or sell you shoes.
A man would build a house or package screws.
He'd be a railroad man or office clerk.
He'd make an honest buck for honest work.
There is enough to meet all human need.
But not enough to fill your wanton greed.
America—land of equality.

And now it's run by your plutocracy.
You never take a moment to address
The people who get by on so much less.
JEROME: The people who get by on so much less
Can get their own pursuit of happiness.
WILLIAM: You should learn to redress your apathy.
Transform your greed to generosity.
I see the very concept makes you nervous.
To think that you might live a life of service.
The egos that you have I so resent
I'm cutting you all off without a cent.
The point of leaving a bequest should be
To honor someone's love and loyalty.
The will I have will go in the junkyard.
And everything I own goes to Bernard!
DAWN: Bernard? I know I was your enemy.
But I could be your friend.
BERNARD: Get off me.
RUTH: This will be a gigantic legal wrangle.
But I assure you, I'll find every angle.
I'll fight this matter to the bitter end.
You can't give everything to just a friend.
WILLIAM: You've lost, Ruth. You have got to just accept it.
There's one more thing. I know you don't suspect it.
When we were married and the sex was rare,
In our own house I once had an affair
With Barbara, the maid. Now I admit
My man Bernard is my legitimate!

EPILOGUE

[BERNARD]

[BERNARD *steps down and addresses the audience.*]

BERNARD: Before you go and we can stand adjourned,
    Please wait a bit. But don't be too concerned
    Or head out down the aisles in a herd.
    A big black man will have the final word.
    The play is over, but our lives go on.
    Perhaps you wonder what will come of Dawn.
    She gets a nice proposal from Eugene.
    He loves her. Says he'll treat her like a queen.
    Those two might run away and tie the knot.
    Yes, wouldn't that be nice? Well, they do not.
    Eugene is selling bouquets of balloons.
    And Dawn is *shpritzing* samples of perfumes.
    Jerome, as you'd expect, is managing.
    He's getting by with telemarketing.
    Ruth gets her surgery as you might think.
    It's quite impossible for her to blink.
    Her skin got so stretched out, after a while,
    She looked just like she had the Joker's smile.
    So life goes on. The great big wheels turn.
    As we leave here tonight, what might we learn?
    When you walk out of here, out to the street,
    Please be aware of people that you meet.
    Perhaps you'll meet a man or woman who
    Will cab you home or serve a drink or two.
    They clean your house and fix your swimming pool.
    They tend your garden. Drive your kids to school.
    They wash your shirts or bag your groceries.
    They fix your car or rid your dog of fleas.
    I know you'll see them. So here's my advice.
    When you encounter all these folks—be nice.
    Go get the Good Book down from off the shelf
    And read "to love thy neighbor as thyself."
    To those of you who focus on your greed.

And *Affluenza* is your only creed.
To those who put themselves above all others
And totally forget that we are brothers.
Perhaps you will be safe, living up high.
In high-rise buildings, way up in the sky.
Perhaps you will be safe in SUVs.
Or back within gated communities.
Perhaps your life will be safe for all time.
Perhaps your life will pass in perfect rhyme.
But then again—
Maybe not.
Remember that the man who's truly rich
Is he who's happy and has found his niche.
Don't be a burnt-out lightbulb. Be the light.
I'm going back to work. So say good night.

[BERNARD *and* WILLIAM *bow to each other. Fadeout.*]

FREE MAN OF COLOR

CHARLES SMITH

The paradox of education is precisely this—that as
one begins to become conscious one begins to examine
the society in which he is being educated.

James Baldwin

PLAYWRIGHT'S STATEMENT

Free Man of Color is about John Newton Templeton, the first black man to attend Ohio University. The play is set between the years 1824 and 1828, four decades before Abraham Lincoln signed the Emancipation Proclamation. During that time, proslavery factions argued against emancipation by contending that blacks were merely children that needed to be cared for. They argued that even the blacks who appeared to be self-sufficient, smart, and educated were not smart or educated at all. They argued that these blacks who appeared to be intelligent were merely imitating whites. This same argument was later used by segregationists to support their continued call for separate schools in this country.

Today, two hundred years later, these inflammatory accusations still abound. However, the source of these accusations today is not proslavery advocates or even staunch segregationists. According to scores of politicians, social commentators, and pundits, the source of these demeaning accusations are African American children themselves. That's right. Politicians, social commentators, pundits, and even a few rich black celebrities claim that today's African American students are hostile toward education. They claim that the few African American students who excel in scholastic achievement are teased by their peers. They claim that these students are attacked, ridiculed, and accused by other African American students of "acting white." If this is true, the implications are horrifying. If true, the racists have reached nirvana: they no longer have to spend time devising ways to police Negroes to keep them in their place; the Negro children have been trained to police themselves. But I suspect something else is happening here.

There is a difference between education and indoctrination. Education is teaching a student *how* to think. Indoctrination is teaching a student *what* to think. The premise of education—real education—is that a student should be given the tools and the means by which to conduct his own intellectual inquiry. The conclusion of that inquiry should be the student's and the student's alone. When a student develops his or her own ideas, ideas that may be different from those espoused by textbooks, that student should be feted. But far too many times that student is censured and his ideas depreciated. And our children are smart; they know what's going on. Give them a few rudimentary tools and they develop their own ideas. They know what they think and they know what's in their hearts. They also know what the (usually white) authority figure standing in front of them wants them to say. Some do what is asked of them and mindlessly repeat the party line. Some refuse to parrot the party line, then ridicule those who do. Many of these students are destroyed. Only a few are lucky enough to have experienced teachers who fully support the development of the individual mind and spirit.

In *Free Man of Color*, John Newton Templeton makes a distinction between education and training, something I imagine he struggled with two hundred years ago while attending Ohio University. While it is sad that we continue to struggle with these same issues today, I find solace in the fact that many of us have successfully circumnavigated in the past, and will in the future, the mine field of education to become autonomous, free-thinking individuals. I think John Newton Templeton wouldn't have it any other way.

PRODUCTION HISTORY

Free Man of Color, by Charles Smith, was commissioned by Ohio University for its Bicentennial Celebration in 2004. It was first presented by Victory Gardens Theater, Chicago, Illinois, in January 2004. This world premiere production included performances at Ohio University and Governor's State University.

PRODUCTION TEAM

Director	Andrea J. Dymond
Set	Tim Morrison
Costumes	Michelle Tesdall
Lights	Mary Badger
Sound	Joe Cerqua
Production Stage Manager	Rita Vreeland

CAST

Jane Wilson	Shelley Delaney
John Newton Templeton	Anthony Fleming III
Robert Wilson	Gary Houston

CHARACTERS

Robert Wilson, *middle-aged white university president*
John Newton Templeton, *twenty-year-old ex-slave*
Jane Wilson, *Robert Wilson's somewhat younger wife*

STAGING

Time: 1824 to 1828
Place: Athens, Ohio

ACT 1

SCENE 1

[*Onstage are two chairs, left and right.* WILSON *sits in one of the chairs,* JOHN *sits in the other. A very rustic rendition of "Amazing Grace" plays in the background. When the music ends,* WILSON *stands.*]

WILSON [*to the audience*]: Most distinguished assembled guests, trustees, gentlemen, at this point in the program I present to you John Newton Templeton. The topic on which he will speak to you today is titled "The Claims of Liberia." Mr. Templeton.

[WILSON *exits.*]

JOHN [*to the audience*]: "*Non solum verba falsa sunt mala ipsa, sed etiam malo infligunt animam.*" For those of you who don't know, that was not "The Claims of Liberia." It was Latin. Plato. Roughly translated, it means, "False words are not only evil in themselves, but they inflict the soul with evil." That's what I was thinking on that day in 1828 when Reverend Wilson introduced me. I was thinking about my soul. Reverend Wilson was the president of Ohio University, and judging by the look on his face, he and the seventy-five other assembled guests had fully expected to hear me speak on "The Claims of Liberia," because at one point in my life, I had been claimed by Liberia. Eighteen twenty-eight. Thirty-four years before the end of slavery, I stood with my graduating class and wondered about my soul.

[WILSON *enters. He has been traveling.*]

WILSON: Here we are. I know it's a little different from what you're used to, but we consider it to be a good home. [*Calling*] Wife?

[*He listens. There is no answer.*]

I hope she's feeling better. She hasn't been in what you would call the best of health.

JOHN: Sorry to hear that.

WILSON: Have to be careful nowadays. We've had our share of the cholera. Yellow fever. Scarlet fever and smallpox.

[*He calls through the window.*]

Wife!

[*No answer.*]

> I hope she didn't walk into town again. Woman has a stubborn streak in her. Won't let anybody do anything for her. I usually have a friend check on her while I'm gone. Make sure she's all right, drive her into town if she needs it, but she'd rather walk and it's too far to walk. Town is that way, north, about four miles. We'll go in tomorrow.

JOHN: Tomorrow?

WILSON [*calling*]: Wife?

JOHN: What about my papers?

WILSON: Your papers?

JOHN: I need to get my papers in order.

WILSON: We'll take care of that tomorrow when we go into town.

JOHN: The law says—

WILSON: I know what the law says. Don't worry about the law. The law is my concern. The only thing I want you to be concerned about is your studies. You will begin your studies with nine other students and you will be treated the exact same as everyone else. Is that clear?

JOHN: Yes, sir.

WILSON: You clear on what will be expected of you?

JOHN: Yes, sir.

WILSON: Let's go over it again. How do you plan to start each day?

JOHN: With prayers at sunrise.

WILSON: Breakfast?

JOHN: Breakfast by six.

WILSON: Followed by . . .

JOHN: Morning recitations.

WILSON: Then comes?

JOHN: Morning lecture, then study until noon. Dinner will be from noon to one-thirty, after which we begin afternoon recitations, followed by afternoon lecture and study until supper. Supper is at five-thirty, followed by a half hour of relaxation and then evening debate.

WILSON: Good, John. Very good. Now, your first year will consist of the study of mathematics, science, and philosophy. Your second year will consist of the study of Latin, Hebrew, and Greek. In your third year, you will be expected to apply for admission into the Athenian Literary Society in addition to continuing your studies in Greek. And in your fourth year, you will prepare for your comprehensive exams.

JOHN: Yes, sir.

WILSON: Tell me something, John. Why do you think it's important that you study Greek?

JOHN: Why?

WILSON: That's right. Why? Why Greek?

JOHN: Greek is an important language, sir.

WILSON: Is that your answer? Greek is an important language? That's not an answer, John. That's circular logic based upon the original premise. Why is the horse white? Because it's a white horse. Does that make sense? No. All you did was chew my question and then feed it back to me in the form of an answer, but that's not an answer. You haven't added anything to it. Nothing but your own saliva, and I do not care for the taste of your saliva, John. Now let's try it again. Why is it important that you study Greek?

JOHN: I don't know.

WILSON: Didn't you study Greek at Ripley?

JOHN: Yes, sir.

WILSON: Didn't they tell you why you were studying Greek?

JOHN: They said it was important.

WILSON: Of course it's important, John. I want you to tell me why it's important.

JOHN: It's important for us to understand our language?

WILSON: Not unless you consider language to be the end, and language is not the end, it's merely a means to the end. Think about the white horse. Can you ride the words "white horse"? Will those words carry you to the store? Do you have to feed those words? No. Those words are merely a representation of the thing itself. Those words do not have a heartbeat. Those words will not leave filth in the middle of the road. Our goal is not to understand the words, John. Our goal is to understand all of the things the words represent. Have you ever studied the Bible?

JOHN: Of course I have.

WILSON: In what language did you study the Bible?

JOHN: English.

WILSON: Are you suggesting to me that Matthew, Mark, Timothy, and Samuel wrote their testaments in English?

JOHN: No, sir.

WILSON: In what language did they write?

JOHN: They wrote in Hebrew, sir. And Greek.

WILSON: That's right. And unless you are studying the Bible in Hebrew and Greek, you're not studying the Bible. You're studying what somebody else has said the Bible says, and while King James may have been a very honest man, I'd rather not stake my soul and the souls of all men on his judgment. That's the reason the study of Greek is so important, John. That's why the study of Hebrew and Latin is important, so that we may study the actual word of God in its original form. Remember, only by studying the origins of a thing can one discern that thing's true meaning.

JOHN: Only by studying the origin of a thing—

[JANE *enters. She stops and surveys the situation.*]

JANE: What's this?

WILSON: This is John Templeton. I'm sorry, John Newton Templeton. John, this is Mrs. Wilson.

JOHN: Pleased to meet you, ma'am.

JANE: You promised we were not going to do this.

WILSON: Do what, dear?

JANE: Take in runaways.

WILSON: He's not a runaway. He's a free man.

JANE: Legal free or liberated free?

WILSON: Legal free, and he's here to go to school.

JANE: School?

WILSON: John, why don't you go out and get the rest of our things.

JOHN: Yes, sir.

[JOHN *exits.*]

JANE: Robert, what're you doing?

WILSON: Reverend Hopkins come by while I was gone?

JANE: Course he came by. Every day he came by. Can't get rid of the man.

WILSON: I asked him to check on you while I was gone.

JANE: And I told you that I don't need anybody to check on me. Now I would like to know what that boy is doing here.

WILSON: He was at Ripley with Reverend Williamson. The boy is smart, Jane. He knows philosophy, mathematics, basic Greek, and Latin. And the boy is strong. He had never ridden a horse before in his life, not until he got on one to come here. But after the first day, he was riding like a professional.

JANE: You taught him how to ride?

WILSON: First thirty miles to Hillsboro were kind of hard on him. But after I showed him a few things, he got the hang of it. By the time we could see the first of the seven hills of Athens, he was riding like he had been born in the saddle.

JANE: What is he doing here, Robert?

WILSON: I told you. He's here to go to school.

JANE: You going up against the law for him?

WILSON: Nothing in the law that says he can't be here.

JANE: And that's the reason you're doing it? Because nothing says you can't?

WILSON: We minister to everyone else in this world.

JANE: We minister to colored.

WILSON: Never with substance. We preach to them, sure, we offer them the word of God, but never has anyone offered them the means by which they can obtain that word on their own.

JANE: Where's he supposed to live while he's here?

WILSON: I thought he could stay here with us for a while.

JANE: Where here?

WILSON: Spare room.

JANE: We don't have a spare room.

WILSON: The room isn't being used, Jane. He can sleep there. Won't be for long. Only a month or so.

JANE: A month?

WILSON: After folks get used to the idea of him being around, we can move him into the edifice with the other students if you like.

JANE: The gentleman from Virginia? The two gentlemen from Kentucky? You think that these men are going to sleep in the same room as a black?

WILSON: Won't be the same room.

JANE: Under the same roof. You expect these men to share a roof with a black who is not washing their clothes and serving them dinner? Is that what you're asking me to believe?

WILSON: If it doesn't work out, we can find him a room in town someplace, I don't know. The where of the matter is not important at this point.

JANE: The where of the matter is the most important. Everything in this world revolves around the where.

WILSON: If you don't want him here and if he has a problem in the edifice, we'll find a room for him in town.

[JOHN *enters with saddlebags.*]

JANE: Is he registered?

WILSON: We'll take care of that tomorrow.

JANE: Does he have money to register?

WILSON: The university is sovereign. As long as he's in our charge, he's not subject to local ordinances.

JANE: Nobody in town is going to put him up unless he's registered.

WILSON: Why must you see darkness wherever you look?

JANE: Because my life has been shrouded in darkness. I've lived in darkness for so long, it's become a friend of mine, the only companion I have.

JOHN: Pardon me, sir, but if you would tell me where to unhitch and water the horses, I'll take care of it.

WILSON: I'll take care of it, John. You get yourself cleaned up, get yourself something to eat.

JANE: Folks in town are not going to want him here unless he's registered, Robert.

WILSON: Folks in town don't have a say in the matter.

JANE: You can't continue to ignore who these people are and what they believe in.

WILSON: I don't care what they believe in. John will be here whether they like it or not. My charge doesn't come from the folks in town. I receive my charge from the trustees and the state legislature. I answer to them, and after them, I answer only to God. I do not have to answer to a bunch of provincial merchants, landowners, and pig farmers.

JANE: You may not have to answer to them, but we do have to live with them.

WILSON: I think we've been very charitable neighbors.

JANE: When it benefits you. You won't consider anything that doesn't benefit you or the university.

WILSON: I've considered many proposals.

JANE: What about the tent?

WILSON: I have no objections to that tent.

JANE: Within the square?

WILSON: Anyplace outside the gates.

JANE: Outside the gates.

WILSON: It's for the amusement and entertainment of the locals. If they want to be amused and entertained by abominations, they can erect as many circus tents as they please. Anyplace outside of the square.

JANE: There's nothing evil about the circus, Robert. They come in, they set up their tents, they tell stories. You go there and listen to stories about people and places far away from here. That's all it is. It's a diversion. It might be nice to have a bit of diversion around here.

WILSON: My students do not need diversion. My students need earnest uninterrupted study.

JANE: There are people here other than your students.

WILSON: What people? Who?

JANE: People.

WILSON: I want you to tell me whose need for entertainment and diversion you think is more important than the education of my students.

JANE: Nobody's. I'm sorry I brought it up.

WILSON: Draw some water for the boy so he can get cleaned up. And he needs something different to wear. Look around and see if we have some clothes that'll fit him. Shirt, pants, maybe a hat.

JANE: There's nothing here that will fit him.

WILSON: Why don't you look-see?

JANE: I don't have to look-see. I know. There is nothing here that will fit him.

WILSON: Draw him some water so he can get cleaned up. I'll be back in a bit.

[WILSON exits.]

JOHN: If it's all the same to you, ma'am, I can draw my own water.

JANE: Of course you can. You can and you will. I will not draw water for you while you're in this house.

JOHN: No, ma'am.

JANE: Washbasin is in there under the table.

JOHN: Yes, ma'am.

[He moves to exit. He stops.]

I didn't come here to cause trouble, ma'am. Reverend Wilson asked me if I wanted to come here and go to school. He said he was looking for young men of high moral content; young men who would eventually serve in honor of the public good. I believe I am such a man. Reverend Wilson also believes that I am such a man, and I am grateful that he's given me the chance to prove it.

JANE: So . . . you want to serve the public good.

JOHN: Yes, ma'am.

JANE: And just how do you plan to do that? . . . What's your name again?

JOHN: John, ma'am.

JANE: John what?

JOHN: John Newton Templeton.

JANE: Just how do you plan to serve the public good, Mr. John Newton Templeton?

JOHN: I'm not quite sure, ma'am. I thought that maybe I'd become a preacher like the Reverend. Spread the word of God. Maybe one day even open my own school. School for colored. That's what I'd like to do.

JANE: That's very sweet of you. Tell me something, Mr. John Newton

Templeton—you born free? Or is liberation a relatively new experience for you?

JOHN: I was freed when I was seven, eight years old, ma'am.

JANE: You don't remember the day?

JOHN: I remember the day. It was June 17, 1813. That was the day the good Reverend Marster Thomas Williamson of Spartanburg, South Carolina, died. Yes, ma'am, I remember the day. What I meant to say was, I don't know how old I was on that day. I was born the winter of '06–'07. Don't know which month. All I know is that I was born during a hard snowfall, which is rare for South Carolina. That would've made me seven, maybe eight years old on the day that me, my mama, and my daddy were freed. Yes, ma'am, I remember the day. Just don't know how old I was on that day.

JANE: What're you doing here?

JOHN: I believe I just told you, ma'am. I come here to prove myself.

JANE: You didn't come here, Mr. John Newton Templeton. You were brought here. What I'm trying to figure out is if you know the reason you were brought here, 'cause it sounds like you don't know.

JOHN: All right then. I was brought here to prove myself. Reverend says that I'm special, because of my birth. Reverend says that if I came here, I'd be treated the same as everybody else. I'd like to believe that I'm at least as good as most men. Better than some. Not as good as others.

JANE: You probably think you're pretty smart, don't you?

JOHN: Smart?

JANE: Intelligent.

JOHN: I would like to think I possess a modicum of intelligence, yes.

JANE: You don't sound so smart to me. Not so smart at all. See, your desire to prove yourself only put you in a place where you could be seen. But that is not the reason you were brought here, and make no mistake, you were not only brought here but brought here for a reason. You were chosen, Mr. Templeton. Out of all the rest of them out there, they chose you. You might as well had been standing on the block. "How about dis one chere?" "Issy healthy?" "Healthy as a mule, looka him kicking." "How 'bout his mind? Issy crazy?" "Nope, dis here nigger has a nice, even temperament. Look at dose eyes. Who can resist dose puppy dog eyes?" Yes, sir, Mr. Templeton, they fished you out of a lake of misery. And I bet you thought you were pretty lucky when they pulled you outta that putrid lake. But what you should've done before patting yourself on the back for being so lucky, what you should've done was ask the reason why. If you knew the reason why, that lake of misery you were swimming in might not have looked so bad.

JOHN: I know the reason why.

JANE: Do you? You come here to be a houseboy? That the reason you're here?

JOHN: I come here to prove to this world that the colored race is capable of climbing to the same heights—

[*He stops himself.*]

JANE: Same heights as white?

JOHN: Yes, ma'am. Same heights as white.

JANE: Is that what you believe? Or is that what somebody told you?

JOHN: That's what I believe.

JANE: And you think that's the reason Reverend brought you here? To prove that colored is as good as white?

JOHN: I know that's the reason he brought me here.

JANE: Is that what he said to you?

JOHN: Is that what he said to me?

JANE: Did he come out and say those words? That he brought you here to prove that colored was as good as white?

JOHN: Maybe not those exact words.

JANE: Then you didn't hear him say it.

JOHN: Didn't have to hear him say it exactly. I know what's in his heart, what's in his mind.

JANE: So, you supernatural on top of everything else? You able to look inside a man's heart and his mind? That's quite a trick. With skills like that, what you need to go to school for?

JOHN: Don't have to be supernatural to divine what's in a man's heart. All you have to do is listen to him speak. I know what he believes.

JANE: You know what? You remind me a little bit of my youngest boy, David. He was ignorant, you're ignorant. Just a fool. No idea of what's going on around them. Huge wheels turning, grinding the world into shattered bits of bone and shredded flesh. And you, like him, are ignorant, oblivious to the sounds, the screams. Tell me something, Mr. John Newton Templeton. What would happen if you found out that the reason you were brought here was different from the reason you think? What would that do to your intelligent colored thinking?

JOHN: I don't understand your meaning.

JANE: You think you as good as white?

JOHN: I've studied Latin, Greek, and many of the classics in the canon.

JANE: I asked if you thought you were as good as white.

JOHN: That depends.

JANE: Depends on what?

JOHN: Depends on what you mean by "good."

JANE: Are you trying to play a word game with me? Is that what you're trying to do?

JOHN: I'm trying to understand your meaning, ma'am.

JANE: I asked if you thought you were as good as white. It's not a very complex question.

JOHN: I believe that, given the chance, I can achieve anything that a white man can achieve. And that's the reason I'm here. To prove that I'm a man of high moral content. A man who is capable of serving in honor of the public good.

JANE: Oh, you will serve. Make no mistake about that. I'm sure you will serve nicely.

[JANE *exits.*]

JOHN [*to the audience*]: I hated that woman. Every time I looked at her, I kept visualizing my fingers wrapped around her throat, and you don't have to tell me: I know that was not a very good visualization. So I made up my mind to stay as far away from her as possible. I started to think of the many ways I was going to avoid her. Unfortunately, I wasn't able to think quite fast enough.

[WILSON *enters.*]

WILSON: One thing you have to understand about the others, particularly the gentlemen from South Carolina as well as the gentlemen from Virginia and Kentucky: they've never been around anybody like you before. I mean, they've been around plenty of blacks, but they were always blacks that they or somebody else owned. You can understand, it must be very difficult for them.

JOHN: I can imagine.

WILSON: And sleep is a very important part of a man's life, John. Even God had to rest. If these men are unable to sleep in the same room—

JOHN: Under the same roof. Not the same room. We'd be sleeping under the same roof.

WILSON: Under the same roof, you're right. These are their shortcomings, John. You have to understand.

JOHN: What about me? They need to rest, what about me? I need rest, too.

WILSON: Haven't you been resting comfortably here in the house?

JOHN: Course I have.

WILSON: Then what's the urgency? You've been comfortable here in the house; we've been comfortable having you here. There's no problem. There's no urgency.

JOHN: I should be in the edifice with the other men.

WILSON: Of course you should be. Unfortunately, the world is full of "should be's," John. And it wouldn't be so bad to live here in the house with Jane and me. In fact, Jane would like it, to have somebody else around. She needs somebody to keep her company. Somebody to drive her into town when she needs it.

JOHN: No, sir, it wouldn't be right.

WILSON: What wouldn't be right?

JOHN: You said if I came here, I'd come here as a charity student and that charity students didn't have to pay.

WILSON: That wouldn't change. You still wouldn't have to pay.

JOHN: If I was in the edifice, I'd be with other men, some of whom also didn't have to pay. But living here in the house with you and Mrs. Wilson, I wouldn't feel right, not paying. I'd at least want to pay for my room, pay for my meals.

WILSON: All right. You stay here with me and Mrs. Wilson, and in exchange, you can do a little work around the house. What do you think about that? Cut wood, clean squirrels, rabbits, serve dinner, that sort of thing.

JOHN: Like a houseboy?

WILSON: That's an unfortunate way to put it.

JOHN: Unfortunate but true. I'd be a houseboy.

WILSON: I'd prefer not to use that terminology, John. I'd prefer to look at it a bit differently. We'll call it something else. Something a bit kinder.

JOHN: Something like what?

WILSON: Student servant. That's what you'll be. You'd be a student servant.

JOHN: Just because we call it something different doesn't change the fact of what it is.

WILSON: We're not trying to change the fact of what it is. We're calling it something different because it will be something different. If you were a houseboy, you would do exactly as I told you to do when I told you to do it. If you were a houseboy, you would follow my orders without question or hesitation, or face severe consequences. But that's not who you will be, John. You will be a student servant, almost like one of the family. Student servant means that you're a student, first and foremost. Your primary duty will be to attend classes and to keep up with your studies. Student servant means that you and I together will decide what your secondary duties will be. If you don't find cutting wood and serving dinner to be acceptable, we'll find something else for you to do. Something that you do find acceptable. Like taking care of the horses. You said you liked being around horses. What do you think about that? You can take care of the horses, and we could continue your riding lessons. You and I, we could go out once a week riding. What do you think?

JOHN: That would be nice. Yes.

WILSON: Then it's settled. You'll stay here in the house with us and, in exchange, take care of the horses. Now tell me something. Elections coming up. If you were allowed to vote, who would you vote for?

JOHN: Sir?

WILSON: I'm sure you've kept up with politics and must have formed an opinion on this debacle of an election.

JOHN: No, sir.

WILSON: No, you haven't formed an opinion, or no, you don't keep up with politics?

JOHN: No, I haven't formed an opinion.

WILSON: We're talking about the future of the United States of America here, and you haven't formed an opinion?

JOHN: I learned a long time ago not to waste my time thinking about what I would do in a situation that I know will never happen. Why should I waste my time thinking about who I would vote for in a world in which I cannot vote?

WILSON: But that's where you're wrong. You can vote, John. However, at this point in time, you're not allowed to vote. There's a difference.

JOHN: None that I can see.

WILSON: Can't vote means that you're physically or mentally unable to vote. Not allowed to vote means that you're physically capable of voting, but just not permitted. Understand?

JOHN: Physically capable . . .

WILSON: But not permitted.

JOHN: What would happen if I went into town and tried to vote? Would somebody block my way?

WILSON: Probably.

JOHN: Would I be beaten?

WILSON: Most likely.

JOHN: Killed?

WILSON: You're drifting from the point, John.

JOHN: I thought the point was whether or not I was physically capable of voting. If somebody blocked my way, beat me, and tried to kill me, I would say that I would not be, at that point in time, physically capable, so not only am I not allowed, but I can't.

WILSON: All right. Let's put it this way. If you were allowed and if you could, who would you vote for?

JOHN: I don't know, sir. I think they're both very fine gentlemen.

WILSON: But they're nothing alike. Adams is the son of a Federalist. He was born with a silver spoon in his mouth. His daddy was president, and some think that makes him qualified to be president, too. Jackson is a military hero. No silver spoon here—no, sir. He was born with a shovel in his hand. Jackson is a self-made man who never asked anybody for anything. If you could choose between the two, which one would you choose?

JOHN: All things being equal, I imagine that if I could vote, I would vote for that Mr. Adams fella.

WILSON: Adams? Why Adams?

JOHN: He's against slave owning. His daddy was against slave owning.

WILSON: So you do know something about the candidates.

JOHN: All I know is that Mr. Adams is against slave owning, so if I had to choose, I would choose him.

WILSON: That all you know about the man? That he's against slave owning?

JOHN: Isn't that enough?

WILSON: To make a decision like that based upon a single issue is selfish and irresponsible, John. The future of a nation cannot rest on a single issue.

JOHN: What other issues are there?

WILSON: I thought you said you kept up with politics.

JOHN: I never said that. You said that.

WILSON: There are plenty of issues, John. There's the issue of the Monroe Doctrine; is it good policy or merely a prelude to war? There's the question of the Twelfth Amendment; should the House of Representatives be deciding who our next president should be? And Andrew Jackson is one of the founding members of the ACS, did you know that?

JOHN: The ACS?

WILSON: American Colonization Society, John. They want to do great things for you and your people.

JOHN: They want to ship us all back to Africa.

WILSON: That was a very uninformed and uneducated opinion. What the ACS wants to do is establish a civilized, democratic, Christian society where your people can live sovereign. A place where your people can rule themselves, John. A place where your people can determine their own destiny. A place that looks a lot like America.

JOHN: Why should the colored of America have to leave America in order to live in a place that looks like America?

WILSON: Why should the colored of America be any different from all the other people of this world? Men have had to roam the face of this earth in search of a place to call home for thousands of years. My father did it. When the English came to Ireland, they took my father's land, they burned his house, they tried to relocate him and my mother to some remote strip of barren land that couldn't even yield a single potato or carrot. He tried to fight, and when it became clear that he couldn't win, he and my mother stole upon a ship bound for America. I was born one year later in Lincoln County, North Carolina. And my father was not the only man who has had to do this. World history is replete with people searching for the land of promise, a place to call home. Think of Moses. Exodus, chapter three, verse ten, and God said to Moses, "Come, I will send you to the Pharaoh that you may bring forth my people, the sons of Israel, out of Egypt." To say that all the ACS wants to do is send your people back to Africa reveals your ignorance, John. What the ACS wants to do is free your people from bondage.

JOHN: Perhaps I should study the issue a bit more.

WILSON: Perhaps you should. Your master freed you at a very young age, but only through training and education will you be able to retain your freedom.

[JANE *enters.*]

JANE: Tent's going up on the green. Half the town's turned out to see it. They say they have women who do trick riding, bareback and saddled. That's what I wanna see. Women on horseback. I'll tell you, there hasn't been this much excitement around here since Mrs. Mavis's cow gave birth to that two-headed calf.

WILSON: Abominations.

JANE: Pardon me?

WILSON: All of it's an abomination.

JANE: Have to admit, the two-headed calf was a bit strange. I want to thank you again for allowing them to put up the tents.

WILSON: I asked you not to thank me.

JANE: Now, Robert, there's no need to be shy. You did a good deed, and I believe in giving credit where credit is due.

WILSON: It wasn't a good deed.

JANE: I know you were against the idea . . .

WILSON: Still am. Nothing's changed.

JANE: Whenever a man goes against what he believes in order to make somebody else happy, it should be recognized.

WILSON: I didn't do it to make anybody happy.

JANE: You made me happy.

WILSON: That's not the reason I did it.

JANE: Whatever reason you did it, I want to thank you.

WILSON: It was Miller. He wouldn't give John his papers. He said he had to pay a five-hundred-dollar bond, and nobody has five hundred dollars. I told him, I said the university is a sovereign entity. As long as this boy is in the charge of the university, we didn't need to pay a bond, but he wasn't having it. Said the way he read the law, the boy has to pay his bond whether he's in the charge of the university or not. Finally, I asked him, what would happen if the university allowed the circus to put up its tents on the green? And you know what he said? He said that if we allowed the circus to put up its tents on the green, he might be inclined to read the law the same way I read the law, so I agreed to it. But just 'cause I agreed to it doesn't change how I feel about it. I'm still against it and would appreciate it if you would stop thanking me for it at every turn. Every time I hear you say it, it puts a bad taste in my mouth.

JANE: And here I thought you had committed an act of compassion. Turns out you had to be forced into it.

WILSON: You consider this an act of compassion? Having a hand in helping folks gawk at a collection of misery, misfortunes, and abominations is an act of compassion? Or is it entertainment? Isn't that what you called it? Misery, misfortune, and abominations here for your amusement and entertainment.

JANE: I learned early in life to love life's bounty, be it misery, misfortune, or abominations.

WILSON: You love abominations? Is that what you're saying?

JANE: I don't think you really want me to answer that, do you? I washed the boy's bedclothes. They're out hanging on the line. When is he going to be moving into the edifice with the other students?

[WILSON *and* JANE *exit.*]

JOHN [*to the audience*]: Sure enough, the next day a wagon rolled through town with a washboard jug band on the back. The band played music announcing to anyone who didn't already know that the circus had officially come to town. The same day that wagon rolled into town, Reverend Wilson rolled out of town. Said he had to meet with some men in Chillicothe, but I thought the real reason was that he didn't want to be here when the circus arrived. The circus consisted of an assortment of wonderful oddities and delights. There was a man who had six fingers on each hand, a woman who was covered with hair from head to toe, and a boy who could twist himself into all kinds of unnatural-looking shapes. And, of course, they had the women who did trick horseback riding, bareback and saddled. They also had an elephant, a lion, a zebra that they called a striped horse, and an ostrich that caused a lot of excitement. I don't think anybody had ever seen a seven-foot bird before. I think a whole lot of folks wanted to eat it. But by far the most popular attraction, the one thing that amazed young and old alike, was Mongo the Trained Ape. Mongo was an ape who had been trained to perform various tricks. He drank water from a cup. He smoked a cigar. He sat at a table, and when it came time to eat, he used a spoon. This was a particularly remarkable feat, especially when you consider that at least half of the population of town at the time did not use or even own a spoon. But the most disconcerting part of this animal's act was that they had outfitted him with a hat, shirt with a collar, and pair of trousers. Mongo attracted fairly moderate attention for almost a week. But this was nothing like the sensation caused later when, late one night, somebody sneaked into the encampment and defaced the board that stood in front of Mongo's tent. To the shock of some, and to the delight of others, on the board announcing Mongo the Trained Ape somebody had crossed out MONGO and written in its place JOHN NEWTON TEMPLETON.

[JANE *enters.*]

JANE: What you reading?
JOHN: Cicero.
JANE: Can I see?
JOHN: It's in Latin.
JANE: I didn't ask you what language it was in.

[JOHN *hands* JANE *the book. She starts to page through it.*]

I need you to go into town and pick up a few things.
JOHN: I can drive you if you want to go.

JANE: Did I tell you I needed a ride? Go see Mr. Burke. He's going to give you some hog's blood.

JOHN: Hog's blood?

JANE: For the garden. Keeps the animals away. That's gonna be one of your jobs now. Keeping the animals out of the garden.

JOHN: What kind of animals?

JANE: Deer, mostly.

JOHN: Reverend said my job was to take care of the horses.

JANE: And take care of the garden. That's now another one of your jobs. They have deer where you come from in South Carolina?

JOHN: I know about deer.

JANE: Then you know that they have to be kept away, or they'll get in and eat up the fruit of four months of our labor. And what they don't eat, they'll trample into the ground. From now on, your job will be keeping them from doing that.

JOHN: With hog's blood?

JANE: You spread it around. Make a big circle around the garden, around the house. Makes the whole place smell of death. Animals don't like the smell of death.

JOHN: Some animals. Others might be attracted to it.

JANE: I don't know of any animals that are attracted to the smell of blood.

JOHN: Bobcat. Bear. Coyote.

JANE: You don't know much about the wilderness, do you?

JOHN: I know that the smell of blood will attract vermin.

JANE: Vermin, maybe, but not bobcat, bear, and coyote. Bobcat, bear, and coyote are killers. They're not interested in what's already dead. They're looking to kill something. They kill, they eat. That means they're looking for something alive. The more alive, the better. Now go do like I told you. The man's name is Mr. Burke.

JOHN: May I have my book back, please?

JANE: You'll get it after you do like I told you.

JOHN: If I took it with me, I could read along the way.

JANE: You can read and ride at the same time?

JOHN: I'm getting fairly good at it.

JANE: Multitalented. You see the newspaper? Your man was appointed president.

JOHN: My man?

JANE: Adams. Reverend's going to be disappointed when he hears about that.

JOHN: How did Adams get to be my man?

JANE: Weren't you pulling for him?

JOHN: I wasn't pulling for anybody.

JANE: You told Reverend you wanted him to win.

JOHN: I said that if I had to choose, I would choose him.

JANE: 'Cause he's against slavery?

JOHN: Isn't that good enough reason?

JANE: All I did was ask a question. You'd choose Adams 'cause he's against slavery?

JOHN: That's right.

JANE: The Reverend and Andrew Jackson went to school together. That means that the three of you are practically kinsmen.

JOHN: Kinsmen?

JANE: They're from North Carolina; you're from South Carolina.

JOHN: Andrew Jackson killed over six hundred Indian men, women, and children. He is not my kinsman.

JANE: But isn't that how men forge their bondships? Using pieces of land and boundaries drawn on a map?

JOHN: Some men.

JANE: All men. Everything in this world is about the where of the matter. Look at the men from Kentucky. They are united in the fact that they hate the men from Virginia. The Virginians got their own handshake, their own song. And you, the Reverend, and Andrew Jackson are all from the Carolinas. Seems to me that if you could choose, you would have chosen him, he being your kinsman and all.

JOHN: But I can't choose now and couldn't have chosen then. So who I would have chosen, if I could have chosen, is irrelevant, now isn't it?

JANE: That's why I am so perplexed. Seeing how your opinion on the matter is absolutely irrelevant, I don't understand why you didn't just shuffle yo' feet, nod yo' head, and agree with the Reverend.

JOHN: This may come as a shock to you, but I am a free thinker. I don't shuffle my feet or nod my head in sycophantic agreement with any man.

JANE: Sycophantic?

JOHN: That's right. Sycophantic. You know what it means?

JANE: I know what it means. Do you?

JOHN: It means I am not some bent-back slave who stands at the elbow of the master agreeing with everything he says. I am a free man. A free man of color. Now if you would please give me my book back . . .

JANE: Then how come you didn't pay your bond?

JOHN: My what?

JANE: The law says that every free man of color has to post a bond upon entering the state.

JOHN: I know what the law says.

JANE: Then how come you didn't pay?

JOHN: Reverend says that the university is sovereign. Reverend says as long as I'm here, I'm sovereign.

JANE: Reverend says, Reverend says. What do you say?

JOHN: I agree with the Reverend. The university is sovereign. That means as long as I'm here, I'm sovereign.

JANE: If you consider yourself sovereign living here and now, then you must have also considered yourself sovereign when you were a slave living on that plantation back in South Carolina.

JOHN: I think there's a difference.

JANE: Do you? Do you remember your life before liberation?

JOHN: What kind of question is that?

JANE: It must've been hard work for a boy of seven, eight years old, picking all that cotton.

JOHN: I didn't pick cotton.

JANE: Then you were a pickaninny.

JOHN: A pickaninny?

JANE: A slave living on a cotton plantation who didn't pick cotton is called a pickaninny.

JOHN: I know what it's called.

JANE: 'Cause you didn't pick any. I'm guessing you ran around half naked, maybe wearing a burlap bag if you were lucky.

JOHN: I didn't wear no burlap bag.

JANE: You had nice clothes.

JOHN: Hand-me-downs.

JANE: Hand-me-downs?

JOHN: From the son of Reverend Master Williamson.

JANE: Nice clothes. Better than what you're wearing now, I'm guessing.

JOHN: Somewhat better.

JANE: What about the beatings? You must've been beaten on a regular basis.

JOHN: May I have my book back, please?

JANE: Answer my question first. Were you beat as a little boy?

JOHN: I was never beaten.

JANE: Were you hungry?

JOHN: We were well taken care of.

JANE: They teach you to read?

JOHN: Like I said. We were well taken care of.

JANE: You didn't pick cotton. You didn't work in the fields. You had nice clothes, at least better than what you're wearing now. Plenty to eat, never mistreated. They even schooled you, boy, taught you how to read. So explain to me the difference between your life then and your life now.

JOHN: That's easy. You see, I have something now that I didn't have back then. Now I'm the one who makes the choices about my life. I control my direction, and I control my destiny. I remember the first time I saw my daddy do that. My daddy was a carpenter. Supposed to have been one of the best around. Man came to my master's house one day and wanted to hire my daddy out. He said they were building a new city called Washington, and they were looking for the best masons, the best carpenters they could find. By then my master, Master Williamson, had found religion. He had received what he called second sight. He was no longer Master Williamson. He had become Reverend Master Williamson and no longer hired his slaves out to anybody who had a dollar. So Reverend Master Williamson did something he had never done before. He told the man that he would have to ask my daddy and then let my daddy decide if he wanted to go help build this new city or not. My daddy listened to the man talk about the great buildings they were building—a tower, a rotunda, a great house. And then, at the end of it all, my daddy carefully considered, nodded his head, and said if it was that great, that he wanted to go there and be a part of it all. I had never seen my daddy do that before. To consider, nod his head, then decide. I thought it was the most wonderful thing in the world. Now I have that power, and that's the difference between then and now. Now I have the power to consider, nod my head, then decide.

JANE: I can't tell if you're mixing up this stew for my benefit or if you actually believe this hog slop you're trying to serve me on a silver platter. You do not have the power to decide anything that happens in your life. You gave up that right when you failed to pay your bond. When you failed to pay your bond, you became a charge of the university. We are responsible for you and everything you do. That means you can nod your head all you want, but you're not making any decisions, not around here. That's the reason folks in town wanted you to pay your bond. Ohio is a free state. They don't like the idea of slavery. Neither do they like the idea of indentured servitude.

JOHN: I'm not an indentured servant.

JANE: You work here, you don't get paid, the university is responsible for you. You're indentured whether you like it or not. That means the only difference between now and back then is back then you were a little better dressed because back then you got hand-me-downs from your master's son, but that's the only difference. Now go into town and do like I told you. You'll get your book when you get back.

SCENE 2

[JOHN *and* WILSON *onstage.*]

WILSON: I saw what somebody wrote on that board in front of that monkey cage. When did it happen?

JOHN: Couple weeks ago.

WILSON: It's been like that since I left? Nobody took it down?

JOHN: Not if it's still there.

WILSON: I'm sorry, John. I allowed them to bring their wickedness here. I knew something like this would happen.

JOHN: It's not your fault.

WILSON: I'm gonna go see Miller, and I'm gonna give them twenty-four hours to tear down that tent, pack their wagons, and get off government property. If they're not gone by the morning, I will go out and tear down that tent myself.

JOHN: With all respect, sir, you tear down that tent, all you gonna do is antagonize folks.

WILSON: Folks need to be antagonized. They can't do something like this without expecting retribution. To compare a man to an ape. A man is not an ape.

JOHN: But we don't even know if they're the ones who did it.

WILSON: Who else could have done it?

JOHN: Most folks in town can't even read, much less write, and you saw the sign. That sign was done up in a very nice hand. Most of the folks I met had to have somebody read to them what it said, and a lot of them didn't find it funny. The only folks who found it funny were the folks here on campus.

WILSON: What folks?

JOHN: The gentleman from Virginia, Mr. Drake. And the gentleman from Kentucky, Mr. Ward. They thought it was funny. In fact, Mr. Ward was the one who told me about it.

WILSON: You suggesting that Mr. Ward did this?

JOHN: I'm suggesting that perhaps we've been too harsh in our judgment of the folks in town. I don't think they had a hand in this.

WILSON: They knew the sign was there. And nobody, not one man, stepped forward to remove it. The tent goes the first thing in the morning.

JOHN: What about my papers?

WILSON: What about them?

JOHN: Miller agreed to waive my bond in exchange for the right to put up that tent. If you make them take it down . . .

WILSON: It'll send a message that we are serious about you being here. It'll send a message that we will not tolerate any type of tomfoolery.

JOHN: What happens if they revoke my papers?

WILSON: That's not gonna happen.

JOHN: What if it does?

WILSON: Half the town owes the university money for lands they've leased. If they threaten to revoke your papers, I will be forced to demand full payment for every lease that's now in arrears. And they can't pay, John. They don't have the money to pay. I don't think you have to worry.

JOHN: I don't like this. I don't like being in the middle of this.

WILSON: You're in the middle, John, whether you like it or not. You know who I met with when I was in Chillicothe? I met with members of the ACS. Congress just gave the ACS one hundred thousand dollars, John. They're ready to charter a ship. They're ready to purchase ironworks for a sawmill and a gristmill, tools, muskets, gunpowder, fishing equipment—everything men would need to settle a new land. The only thing they need now is someone to govern that land, and I believe that someone is you.

JOHN: Me?

WILSON: There are three other men in this country, free men of color, who are receiving education and training to undertake this endeavor. There's one at Amherst, one at Bowdoin College, and one at Dartmouth. But you, John, you have something these other men don't. You have a mandate from God. I believe that you are the man God chose to lead his people to a new land.

JOHN: Liberia?

WILSON: Liberia.

JOHN: But I don't know anything about Liberia.

WILSON: The only thing you need to know is the word of God. Look at this area. The men who settled this area didn't know anything about the area before they came here. Twenty-five years ago this was nothing but wilderness. No human habitation at all. Wild animals, deer, bobcats, and Indians. The men who came here knew nothing but the word of God. But we have blessed this land with civilization, culture, and education. We came here and brought God to a godless region. And that's what God is asking you to do, John. To lead your people through the wilderness to a new land. To bring God to a godless land.

JOHN: God is asking me to do this?

WILSON: All you have to do is look at your origins.

JOHN: What origins?

WILSON: The circumstances surrounding your birth, John.

JOHN: The snowfall?

WILSON: After the snowfall. What happened that summer, the summer after you were born?

JOHN: What do you mean?

WILSON: There was a man named Gabriel Prosser. You remember Gabriel Prosser?

JOHN: I remember.

WILSON: Who was he?

JOHN: A blacksmith. A slave.

WILSON: And what did Gabriel Prosser do?

JOHN: They said he tried to organize a revolt.

WILSON: Was the revolt successful?

JOHN: No.

WILSON: What happened?

JOHN: They were discovered.

WILSON: Discovered?

JOHN: He and thirty-five others.

WILSON: What happened after they were discovered, John?

JOHN: They were hanged. Thirty-six of them were hanged in the public square.

WILSON: Then what happened?

[JOHN *doesn't answer.*]

John? What happened after they hanged the men responsible for planning the revolt?

JOHN: After they hanged the men responsible for planning the revolt, the night riders came. They went from house to house. They took only the boys. The baby boys. All of the black-skinned, the brown-skinned, and the yellow-skinned baby boys.

WILSON: And what did they do with the baby boys?

JOHN: They killed them. They shot them. They drowned them in buckets. They cut their throats. They smashed in their skulls with stones. They ran them through with wooden stakes and stuck them to trees. They left shredded bits of bone and flesh scattered along the roadside that led to and from town.

WILSON: What happened to you?

JOHN: My mother said she tried to hide me, but she couldn't hide me. She tried, but my mistress, my mistress found me. She took me in. She hid me until the danger had passed.

WILSON: Your mistress may have been the one who hid you, but she was guided by the hand of God. It was God who saved you out of all the others who died.

JOHN: You think God saved me to go to Liberia?

WILSON: To lead your people to Liberia, John. It couldn't be any clearer if God himself appeared and wrote it on the wall.

JOHN: I always thought that I would be a preacher. Or a teacher. I had always imagined myself standing in front of a classroom full of colored children, little brown and black boys and girls. I always thought that was my purpose, that that was the reason God had saved me. I would have never imagined this.

WILSON: That's the reason I'm here. To teach you. To guide you. To open the door to the path of your true calling.

JOHN: Liberia?

WILSON: Liberia.

JOHN: What do I have to do?

WILSON: Keep up with your studies. The officers of the ACS will come here sometime next year. They want to meet you, talk to you, get to know you to decide if indeed you are the man they are looking for.

JOHN: They're not convinced?

WILSON: They don't know. Not like I know. But don't you worry. We'll convince them. In the meantime, I'm going to get rid of that tent. I think you would agree that we cannot allow the future governor of Liberia to be compared to an ape.

JOHN: Reverend?

WILSON: Yes?

JOHN: One more thing, a small thing.

WILSON: What is it?

JOHN: I'm almost embarrassed to ask because I don't want to sound like I'm ungrateful . . .

WILSON: Spit it out, boy. What is it?

JOHN: I would like to be paid.

WILSON: Pardon me?

JOHN: For the work I do around the house. For being the student servant and taking care of the horses, taking care of the garden. I would like to be paid.

WILSON: Our agreement was that you would do it in exchange for your room and board.

JOHN: I understand that, sir.

WILSON: It's an even exchange, John.

JOHN: But I would still like to be paid. Even if it's an even exchange, I want to be paid for the work I do. I want to hold the money in my hand. I want to put the money in my pocket. Even if I give it right back to you after you give it to me, I still want to be paid.

WILSON: All right. I think I understand. Have you thought about how much you would like to be paid?

JOHN: You said it was an even exchange . . .

WILSON: All right, even exchange. How often would you like to be paid?

JOHN: How often do the men in the edifice pay for their room and board?

WILSON: Once a month.

JOHN: Then once a month. You pay me, I'll pay you.

WILSON: Okay, John. I think we can arrange that. Anything else?

JOHN: No, sir. Nothing else. Thank you.

[WILSON *exits.*]

[*To the audience*] Over the next few months, I tried to figure out who had defaced that sign and written my name over that of Mongo the ape's. Later, after I was invited to join the Athenian Literary Society, I got the opportunity to spend time with Mr. Ward. He was the president of the society, which gave me ample opportunity to read his handwriting. This is where my suspicions about him turned into certainty.

[JANE *enters with a shirt, hat, and pair of men's trousers.*]

JANE: Here. This is for you.

JOHN: What?

JANE: New clothes. Not exactly new. New to you. Shirt, hat, trousers. They're cleaning you up. That's the first thing they do. They clean you up, then they get you fat. After that, ring the dinner bell 'cause it's suppertime.

[*She offers him the clothes. He only looks at her.*]

What you waiting for? Take it. Better than what you're wearing now. You ever wear a collared shirt before?

JOHN: No.

JANE: Better get used to it. It's going to be around your neck for a long time. It'll be your albatross.

JOHN: My what?

JANE: Albatross. From *The Rime of the Ancient Mariner* by Samuel Taylor Coleridge. Ever hear of it?

JOHN: No.

JANE: That's right, I forgot. You've taken up the Reverend's penchant for studying only dead men who wrote in Greek and Latin, and Coleridge is very much alive. He's English. But we won't hold that against him, now will we? He's a poet who wrote a poem about a sailor who kills a magical albatross that was trying to help him. For this crime against nature, the sailor was forced to wear the corpse of the bird around his neck. "Ah! well-a-day! what evil looks had I from old and young! Instead of the cross, the Albatross about my neck was hung." This collared shirt will be your albatross. Go ahead. Take it.

JOHN: If I have done something to disrespect you, I apologize.

JANE: Disrespect?

JOHN: All I've done since I've been here is try to please you. And all you've done in return is show me contempt.

JANE: Perhaps my contempt stems from your incessant attempt to please. You ever think of that? You claim to be a free man of color, a man who is in control of his own destiny, but all I see you doing is running around here, nodding your head and smiling. And the type of head nodding you're doing is not the type your father did. Now if that is who you are, all you have to do is say so, John. All you have to do is tell me that you don't want any trouble. Just tell me that the reason you're here is to make everybody happy, and I will leave you alone, I swear. Never again will you ever hear another cross word from me; butter won't melt in my mouth. But if you are the man you say you are, your desire to please makes my stomach turn.

JOHN: What's wrong with trying to please people?

JANE: Nothing. If that's the reason you're here. Is that the reason you're here? To dance for us, maybe sing a li'l song every now and then? To make everybody happy?

JOHN: I am here to be educated.

JANE: Educated? Such a big word for such a little boy.

JOHN: I have been chosen. Chosen to be governor of a new nation. Governor of a new world.

JANE: You say that as if it's something I didn't know. Is this news to you? I told you this when you first came here. They're training you. They're getting you ready. They're going to clean you up, get you fat, then prop you up in the window for the entire world to see. And you don't even give a damn. Like a hog gorging itself on slop, you don't care that the sound you hear in the background is that of a blade being sharpened. I have to admit, Robert knew what he was doing when he chose you. Here. Here's your clothes.

JOHN: I wasn't chosen by the Reverend. I was chosen by God.

JANE: Course you were. Here's your clothes.

[*He takes the clothes.*]

And I want to apologize. I apologize for everything I've said to you. I promise, you won't hear anything like that from me again. It's just that, when this moment came, I had hoped that somebody else would be standing where you're standing. But that's not your fault. You can't help who you are. You're just a poor ignorant beast being trained for something that you don't understand, and I have to understand that that's not your fault. I'm sorry. I promise, I'll do better in the future.

[*She exits. After a moment,* JOHN *starts to undress and eventually puts on the clothes.*]

JOHN [*to the audience*]: I had been called names before. Ignorant. Coon. Beast. Nigger. Of course, a colored man living in this country has seen hatred, sometimes on a daily basis. And any colored man living in this country who says that he has not been the object of hatred is either lying to you or hasn't been paying attention. So it was not the name-calling that bothered me. I think it was the pity with which she did it. While I had been, in the past, the object of hatred, I had never before been the object of naked pity.

[*He has finished putting on the shirt, trousers, and hat.*]

Look at this. They fit. The trousers, the hat, the shirt, they all fit like they had been made for me. I had never worn a collared shirt before and expected the collar to be tight around my neck, but the shirt fit fine. In fact, the shirt was very comfortable. Except for one thing. It had an odor, a faint odor that I couldn't quite identify. After I tried on the shirt, the trousers, and the hat, I sat in my room thinking about the pity that the wife of the Reverend had heaped upon me. Her pity became my pity, and while I should have been very happy, the only thing I could think about was Mongo the ape.

[*Lights fade.*]

ACT 2

SCENE 1

[WILSON *alone onstage as "Amazing Grace" plays in the background.* WILSON *appears to be uneasy. As the music plays, he keeps glancing offstage. Finally, the music comes to an end.*]

WILSON [*to the audience*]: Most distinguished guests, trustees, gentlemen . . .

[*He stops, glances offstage.*]

At this point in the program, I present to you John Newton Templeton.

[*He glances offstage.*]

The topic on which he will speak to you today is titled . . . is titled . . .

[JOHN *enters.* WILSON *and* JOHN *exchange looks.* WILSON *exits.*]

JOHN [*to the audience*]: The men of the American Colonization Society were an interesting bunch. While the organization claimed members from every state in the Union, the ones who came to visit were from parts of Ohio, Pennsylvania, Virginia, Carolina, and Washington, D.C. Counting the good Reverend Wilson, there were twelve in all, and as far as I could tell, all were pastors, preachers, ministers, and missionaries. Reverend Wilson had arranged this as the first of what was to be two meetings. It was scheduled during class hiatus so as not to interrupt my very important studies. The men arrived throughout the day on a Monday and stayed for seven days. During those seven days, every morning I would recite for them, in either Latin or Greek, passages from Caesar's Commentaries, Cicero's Orations, and the Greek Testament. Afternoons were set aside for debate, or what they called debate. They gave me topics such as "Was the conspiracy against Julius Caesar justified?" and "Should women be allowed to vote?" After stating the topic, they would then ask questions related to that topic, and I would answer their questions. This was their idea of debate. We did this every afternoon from one until six. In the evenings, they had dinner, during which they reviewed the events of the day. Being the student servant, I had the honor of serving them their dinner. During the first few days of this routine, I thought they were trying to see how smart I was, to see how much I knew. After a while I realized that they were not trying to measure the depth and breadth of my knowledge. They were trying to determine if I was actually thinking for myself or if I was merely repeating what someone had taught me. When, on or about the fifth day, they realized that I was indeed thinking for myself, they seemed to be both delighted and surprised. Reverend Wilson was beaming like a proud new father, and there I was in my shirt, trousers, and hat performing for the gentlemen. For some reason I couldn't get the image of Mongo out of my mind.

[JOHN *sits and starts to read.* WILSON *enters.*]

WILSON: You see what your president did?

JOHN: My president?

WILSON: John Quincy Adams.

JOHN: How did he become my president?

WILSON: If you could vote, you would have voted for him.

JOHN: But I didn't vote for him because I can't vote.

WILSON: But you would have. He would have been your choice. That makes him your president. You see what he did?

JOHN: What did he do?

WILSON: He appointed Henry Clay as secretary of state.

JOHN: I heard about that.

WILSON: Which proves what I've been saying about the man all along. He is corrupt.

JOHN: Corrupt?

WILSON: Henry Clay ran against Adams for president. When it looked like Clay couldn't win, he had a meeting with Adams, withdrew his candidacy, and then threw his support behind Adams. Adams gets elected and what does he do? He appoints Clay as secretary of state.

JOHN: That's right. Clay helped him get elected. All Adams did was return the favor.

WILSON: Return the favor?

JOHN: I'd do it. If somebody helped me the way Clay helped Adams, I'd return the favor.

WILSON: Please don't tell me that. Please don't tell me that you would fall into the same trap.

JOHN: What trap?

WILSON: Adams didn't appoint Clay because he was the best man for the job. He didn't appoint him because he believed in what Clay stood for. Adams and Clay can't even agree on the color of the moon. The only reason Adams appointed Clay as secretary of state was to uphold his end of a corrupt bargain. In Latin it's called quid pro quo. You know what that means?

JOHN: Yes.

WILSON: What?

JOHN: It means something given or received in exchange for something else.

WILSON: That's right. And when applied to politics, what does it imply?

JOHN: It implies a breach.

WILSON: What kind of a breach?

JOHN: A breach in the public trust.

WILSON: That's right. Now I hope you're not telling me that you would do the same. I hope you're not telling me that you would betray your own convictions in order to return a favor that someone did for you, because if so, we've made a terrible mistake.

JOHN: I suppose I would have to consider all of the ramifications.

WILSON: What's to consider? If someone asks you to betray your own convictions, you don't do it, John, no matter what that person did for you. Look at what I have here.

[*He produces a letter.*]

It's a letter from Reverend McLain. He talks about how impressed he and the other members of the committee were with your performance.

JOHN: My performance?

WILSON: On your oral examinations. Your performance exceeded everyone's expectations. They have asked me to officially ask you if you will accept their offer to become the first governor of Liberia.

JOHN: I thought we had to have an additional meeting.

WILSON: Apparently they didn't think it was necessary. You know why? Because they believe you to be a man of your convictions, John. They believe you to be a man who thinks for himself. A man who would not find himself in debt to some other man because of some small favor. I hope they're not mistaken. I hope that you are indeed a man of your convictions.

JOHN: I believe I am.

WILSON: I believe you are as well. I'll write the committee and tell them that you've accepted the offer. They'll start the paperwork. In a couple of months, we ought to receive your official charter. Congratulations, Governor.

JOHN: Thank you. Now when do I get to meet the others?

WILSON: The others?

JOHN: The first thing I'm going to have to do is establish a provisional govern-

ment. I'm going to have to draft a political constitution and I'm going to
have to establish a church. This is going to take years to accomplish and it's
going to take more than just one man.

WILSON: Don't worry. We'll get you the help you need. Did you finish your
essay for admission into the Literary Society?

JOHN: I finished.

WILSON: Did you give it to Mr. Ward?

JOHN: I did.

WILSON: And?

JOHN: He rejected it.

WILSON: Rejected it?

JOHN: He said he wanted me to prepare a topic for debate instead.

WILSON: That Mr. Ward is a rascal, isn't he?

JOHN: That would not be the term I would use.

WILSON: No need to be nasty, John. What topic for debate did they give you?

JOHN: "Why should ex-slaves go back to a land that sent them into slavery in
the first place?"

WILSON: Interesting topic.

JOHN: Interesting?

WILSON: I'm sure you'll do just fine.

JOHN: He's baiting me.

WILSON: Probably.

JOHN: He heard about my meetings with the Colonization Society and he's
baiting me.

WILSON: He's probably trying to test your mettle. That's all. See what you're
made of.

JOHN: If he wants to see what I'm made of, all he has to do is read my essay
"The Claims of Liberia." That's what I'm made of. That's who I am. But he
doesn't want to read it.

WILSON: The topic for debate is merely an exercise, John. An exercise in the
powers of persuasion.

JOHN: I think they're looking for a reason not to admit me.

WILSON: Don't worry. You'll do fine. You know what today is? The first of the
month. Time to settle our account. How's it going with the horses?

JOHN: Going fine.

WILSON: Jane tells me that the palomino looks a little lazy moving off her
hind legs.

JOHN: She was dipping a bit under saddle, but her back right hoof needed a
little trimming. I've already done it and she's moving just fine.

WILSON: Good work, John. Thank you. How many hours do you have for the month?

JOHN: Let's see, three hours a day, six days a week, four weeks, that comes to seventy-two hours.

WILSON: Seventy-two hours at seven cents an hour . . .

JOHN: Five dollars and four cents.

[WILSON *pays* JOHN.]

WILSON: There you are.

JOHN: Thank you.

WILSON: Don't mention it. You earned every bit of it, Governor.

JOHN: I suppose I ought to settle up now as well.

WILSON: If you'd like.

JOHN: How much do I owe you?

WILSON: I'm not sure. Let's see, board is a dollar twenty-five a week.

JOHN: Four weeks.

WILSON: That comes to five dollars, even.

[JOHN *pays* WILSON.]

JOHN: There you are, sir.

WILSON: Thank you.

JOHN: My pleasure.

WILSON: Bet you never thought you'd come out ahead on the deal, did you?

JOHN: No, never thought that. By the way, I'll need a receipt.

WILSON: Pardon me?

JOHN: A receipt. For the money I paid you. I'll need a receipt.

WILSON: Yes. Of course. Let me just . . .

[WILSON *writes out a receipt.*]

JOHN [*to the audience*]: Holding true to your convictions may make your life more meaningful, but it was nothing like the thrill I got when payday rolled around and I got paid for the work I did. And then to pay for my own room and board, to pay my own way, to hold the receipts in my hand . . .

WILSON [*handing the receipt to* JOHN]: There you are.

JOHN: Thank you.

[WILSON *exits.*]

[*To the audience*] I'll tell you, it was the sweetest honey. Nothing like it in the world. I prepared for my debate to enter into the Literary Society—or

FREE MAN OF COLOR ❈ 365

at least I tried to prepare. "Why should ex-slaves go back to a land that sent them into slavery in the first place?" I could answer the first part of that question. Why should ex-slaves go back to Africa?—that part of the question I had no problem with. But why go back to a land that had sent them into slavery in the first place? Try as I might, I couldn't formulate a logical argument to that part of the question, and this bothered me. If I was going to go to Liberia, I needed to be able to answer the second part of that question.

[JANE *enters.*]

JANE: I saw that Maybell was dipping a bit under saddle.

JOHN: She needed a little farrier work on her hind hooves. I've already taken care of it.

JANE: You sure she didn't pull a muscle?

JOHN: Pretty sure.

JANE: If she pulled a muscle, she's going to need some attention.

JOHN: You want me to take her out so you can inspect her?

JANE: No, John. I trust you. I'm just concerned, that's all.

JOHN: I wouldn't let anything happen to that horse. I treat her as if she were my own.

JANE: I know that. And I appreciate it. Thank you.

JOHN: No need to thank me. Just doing my job. Just doing what I'm getting paid to do.

JANE: You know that she belongs to me.

JOHN: I know that, ma'am. It was just a figure of speech, that I treat her as if she were my own. I know she belongs to you.

JANE: No. I meant that Maybell used to be mine. Robert bought her when she was a filly and gave her to me as a present. He knew I always wanted a horse. He knew I wanted to learn to ride. Right after we moved here, my youngest boy, David, died, and I guess he thought Maybell might lift my spirits a bit, which she did. Used to be my job to go out and groom her every day. Pulling, clipping, trimming. After a while, Reverend said I was paying too much attention to her. Said that if we left her out in the pasture where she could roll around on the ground, she wouldn't need to be groomed every day. But she liked it when I would come out and spend time with her. Seems like she knew when I was supposed to be there, and if I was late, she'd let me know about it. If I was late, I'd see her hanging her head over the door. She'd see me and then start bumping the side of the stall with her hoof.

JOHN: She does that with me.

JANE: Seems like you can tell what she's thinking.

JOHN: She's a smart horse.

JANE: Yes, she is.

JOHN: How'd your boy die?

JANE: I had three boys: Matthew, Mark, and David. The oldest, Matthew, died of the cholera when he was eleven. Mark died of the yellow vomit when he was fourteen. And my baby, David, he lived to be nineteen years old. He wanted to be a preacher like his father. He wanted to prove to his father that he was good enough to march into the wilderness and spread the word of God. He thought that all you needed to go into the wilderness was the word of God, that armed with the word of God, the savages would fall to their knees and pray. But you need more than the word of God. You need to have a gun, and you need to have the heart to use it. But David didn't understand that. They found what was left of his body near what used to be a Shawnee encampment. Animals had gotten to it. And the Shawnee, they had stripped his body of everything they could use. Boots, belt, everything except his Bible.

JOHN: I'm sorry.

JANE: No need to be sorry. I'm done with my grieving. I have no more tears to shed.

JOHN: I'm taking Maybell into town. I'll make sure to pay attention to how she's riding. If anything's not right, I'll be sure to take care of it.

JANE: What you going into town for?

JOHN: Mr. Morgan ordered some iron leg traps for me.

JANE: Iron leg traps?

JOHN: Deer got into the garden again. I figured if we can't scare them away, we'll trap 'em. Maybe have ourselves a little venison.

JANE: I don't want any iron leg traps in my garden.

JOHN: I'm not putting them in the garden. I'm going to put them in the deer run along the edge of the wood line.

JANE: Do you have to do it that way?

JOHN: Don't know of any other way. Hog's blood doesn't work.

JANE: It'll work.

JOHN: Didn't work over the last two springs. Didn't work over the summer.

JANE: Just can't use it all the time. First time a deer smells blood, it scares 'em. Makes 'em think death is near. But if they smell old blood, they get used to it.

JOHN: You want me to go out there and sprinkle blood around the house and garden every day?

JANE: What you got to do is figure out when the herd is going to come, then spread the blood right before they get here. That way, it'll be fresh.

JOHN: How am I supposed to figure out when a herd of deer is going to come?

JANE: Used to be easy. They used to come every four to eight weeks. And there was a tribe of Miami that used to follow them. Small tribe. Peaceful. Maybe ten men. Twelve, maybe fifteen women. A brood of small children. You'd see them up on the north ridge. You'd see the Indians and know that the deer herd was somewhere near. But you don't see them anymore. Not around here.

JOHN: I saw some.

JANE: You saw some what?

JOHN: Indians. Three of them. Don't know what kind. Brave, squaw, and a child. I was coming back from Albany. The lower plain was flooded so I was following the ridges on the way back. I had gotten lost, a little twisted around, and that's when I rode up on the child, maybe three, four years old. He was just laying there, sleeping on a bed of pine needles. I got off the horse for a better look and that's when the brave appeared. I don't know who was more scared, me or him. Then the mother appeared, snatched up the baby, and the three were gone, just like that.

JANE: You tell anybody?

JOHN: No.

JANE: Don't. Don't tell anyone.

JOHN: Why not?

JANE: They're probably Miami. They're peaceful. No need to say anything. Just keep it to yourself.

JOHN: You think the deer herd is near?

JANE: I don't know.

JOHN: You said they follow the herd.

JANE: I want you to figure out another way to keep the deer out.

JOHN: I don't know of any other way.

JANE: There's always another way.

JOHN: You said my job was to keep the deer out of the garden. If that's my job, you should let me do my job the best way I see fit.

JANE: All right. You're right. Make sure you keep the horses away. I don't want to see my Maybell get torn up by one of those devices.

JOHN: I'll keep her away.

JANE: Thank you, John.

[*He moves to exit, stops.*]

JOHN: Ma'am?

JANE: Yes?

JOHN: Why don't you come out and ride with me one afternoon? I'll get Maybell ready, and I'll take one of the other horses, and we can go up around the north ridge if you want. It's real pretty this time of the year. Or if you want, I'll get Maybell ready, and you can just go off on your own. Whatever you prefer.

JANE: Whatever I prefer. You know what I would prefer? I would prefer that you did just that. I would prefer that you went out right now and put a saddle on Maybell and I would get on her and I would ride her into town. I would prefer to get on her and ride her to someplace far away from here. But that's not going to happen, is it?

JOHN: I could get her ready if you want.

JANE: Are you trying to be mean to me, or are you just stupid?

JOHN: Ma'am?

JANE: I've been treating you with a civil tongue and would prefer if you did the same.

JOHN: I'm not trying to be mean to you.

JANE: Then you're just stupid.

JOHN: I'm sorry if I said something to offend you.

JANE: Men ride horses, John.

JOHN: What do you mean?

JANE: Men ride horses and I am not a man.

JOHN: I've seen women ride horses.

JANE: Sidesaddle. But you can't climb a hill sidesaddle. You can't ford a stream sidesaddle.

JOHN: What about the women in the town? Miss Clark? Miss Thompson? And the women in the circus. They don't ride sidesaddle.

JANE: Miss Clark, Miss Thompson, and the women in the circus are not considered to be women. They look like women. They got the parts of a woman but they smoke tobacco. They spit. They're unmarried. They have no home, they have no God. These are not women, John. They're freaks. Aberrations. Abominations.

JOHN: Abominations?

JANE: A woman would never ride with her legs splayed open astride a beast, and I am a woman. I'm not supposed to ride with my legs splayed open. I have to ride in the buckboard or in a wagon. I have to have a man drive me to anyplace I want to go. But you, you can ride. An ex-slave gets on my horse and rides but I can't ride. I'm not allowed. I'm not allowed because I'm a woman.

JOHN: I didn't know that.

JANE: What do you know other than Latin and Greek?

JOHN: I'm sorry.

JANE: Nothing in the Bible says a woman can't ride a horse. At least, I don't think there is, but I don't know for sure 'cause I can't read Hebrew. Least, I can't read it well enough to tell. And the English Bible, the King James Bible, they say that's not God's word. They say it's what King James said the Bible says. So until I learn how to read Hebrew, I won't know whether the Bible is against it or not.

JOHN: Would you like to learn?

JANE: Learn what?

JOHN: Learn how to read Hebrew.

JANE: You going to teach me?

JOHN: I could.

JANE: That's very sweet of you.

JOHN: I could do it.

JANE: You think that would change things? You think teaching me how to read Hebrew or teaching me how to read Greek is going to stop this awful, hateful thing from growing inside of me? They brought you here and they let you go to school but they won't let me go to school. My husband is president of the university and I can't even step foot inside the door. Not unless I'm looking to do laundry. Wash the sheets. Clean the floors. Every time I found out I was going to have a child, I would pray to God and ask God to please God please don't let it be a girl. I would rather it be born dead and I'd feed it to the hogs than it be born a girl. 'Cause I wouldn't know how to explain to a girl that the hunger she had inside would never be satisfied. I wouldn't know how to teach a girl to never look to the stars but to keep her head bowed down in subservient submission to some man. So I asked God to please give me boys and God answered my prayers. One by one, he gave me three beautiful healthy boys. And then, one by one, he took those boys away. I grieved for them, one by one, and then I stopped grieving. Then you came. You could teach me how to read Hebrew and you could teach me how to read Greek, but that isn't going to change anything. I still can't step foot inside the door. I am still forced to stand here and watch while they let you in over me. They let you in. They welcome you with open arms. They give you this gift and what do you do? You squander it.

JOHN: I'm sorry you feel that way.

JANE: Why are you sorry? If you're going to be a houseboy for the slave owners of this world, don't be sorry about it. Stand up and be proud that you're their houseboy.

JOHN: I'm nobody's houseboy.

JANE: You go to Liberia, you're going to be the houseboy for every man that has ever bought, sold, or traded in human flesh in this world. "Yes, sir, master, you got some niggers you done using? Ah'll take ker of 'em fer ya."

JOHN: Sometimes the limitations of your comprehension are downright embarrassing.

JANE: The limitations of my comprehension?

JOHN: I am truly sorry that you feel the way you do. However, ultimately, what you think, how you feel, your opinion on what I'm about to do is of absolutely no consequence to me. You want me to stand up for what I believe in? I am standing. You want me to be proud of the choice I've made? I am proud, I am happy, and I am humbled to be able to carry out the will of our Lord God Jesus Christ.

JANE: Typical nigger. Don't know the difference between the will of God and the will of a slave owner.

JOHN: I don't know any slave owners. The only slave owner I know died a long time ago.

JANE: Who do you think is running the ACS? They're slave owners, John. All of them. They all either own slaves now or did own slaves at one point in their lives. That's their bondship. That's the thing that binds them together. And you're too stupid to see that you're doing exactly what they want you to do. You go to Liberia and take all of the free men of color with you, who will that leave here in this country? Only the slaves, John. Only the slaves. And what will happen if they ever let a woman get anything other than an elementary school education? Will she have to leave the country as well? Is that the price we have to pay for challenging what they believe, for challenging their dogma? Banishment? I can't go to school. I can't ride a horse. Maybell is my horse. Reverend gave her to me. He said she was mine. But all I can do is look at her. All I can do is stand there and watch while somebody else rides. They're giving you your own country. Will you be able to ride?

[JANE *exits.*]

JOHN [*to the audience*]: The Indians I saw, I saw as I was on my way back from Albany. I had ridden out there because I heard rumors about a free man who had opened a school, and since it was only about ten, twelve miles out, I wanted to go see for myself. The man's name was Jonathan Goodman, and when I got there, all I saw was one room that also served as his living quarters. In that room he had three books: one Bible, the English King James Version, a very elementary book on world geography, and a book called *The Life of Gustavus Vassa, the African*. There was not one volume of Latin verses, not one volume of Greek philosophy, and after talking to him, I found out that he didn't even have any students. Hardly the ingredients of what I would call a school. I asked him, I said, "Where are the students?" Poor man, he looked around the empty room and said, "They are here. They're here." Not wanting to embarrass him by leaving straightaway, I picked up *The Life of Gustavus Vassa* and started to page through it. I found out that Gustavus had been a slave in Africa before being sold to an American slave trader. But his description of what he called African slavery bore no resemblance to the institution we came to know in America. While he was certainly owned while in Africa, the African sense of ownership was different from ours. Gustavus seemed to be owned by the entire community, and he had a place in that community. He was never required to do any more work than the other members of the community, he was allowed to own his own property, and he was allowed to have a family and that family was kept intact. There was none of the cruelty and inhumanity that permeated American slavery. In fact, the only similarity between African slavery and American slavery was that they were both, for some reason, called slavery. This was not what I had been led to believe about Africa. "Why should ex-slaves go back to a land that was the birthplace of slavery?" Because Africa was not the birthplace of slavery. At least not the type of slavery that had a stranglehold on America. I thought this was the answer. The answer to the only question I had left. Until I realized that I would soon be there in Africa. That I would soon hear all these different languages and see for myself all these strange customs. I realized that these were the people that I had been chosen to bring civilization to. That's when I started to have my first real doubts, because from what I read during those couple of hours, it didn't appear as if these people were the ones who needed the civilization.

[WILSON *enters with a leather bag containing a flintlock pistol, powder, ball bag, and horn, all of which he starts to unpack.*]

WILSON: John? How about after supper you get the horses ready and you and I go out riding? I want to look around down near the river.

JOHN: Sounds good to me.

WILSON: And I heard back from Reverend McLain. He's found a man he wants you to meet. Another free man of color who could assist you in Liberia. Reverend McLain is going to bring him when he comes for your graduation. You can meet this man, talk to him, and if you like him, he can stay here and begin his training in the fall.

JOHN: Don't you mean his education?

WILSON: I'm sorry?

JOHN: You said he can begin his training in the fall. I think you meant to say his education.

WILSON: Training, education. Same thing.

JOHN: Not quite. "Training" comes from the Latin *traginare*, meaning to draw out and manipulate in order to bring about a desired form. When you train something, you manipulate it to follow, to come after or behind. But the word "educate," it comes from the Latin *educare*, meaning to develop the power of reasoning and judgment. Manipulate to follow, come after or behind. Autonomy, power, reasoning, and judgment. Two words. Two very different meanings.

WILSON: My, my, aren't we the scholar?

JOHN: Just pointing out the difference, that's all.

WILSON: All right. He can come for your graduation, and if you like him, he can begin his education in the fall. Is that better?

JOHN: Thank you.

WILSON: And that essay you wrote for Mr. Ward, "The Claims of Liberia"? I want you to use that as your graduation speech.

JOHN: I had thought about doing a Latin oration.

WILSON: Latin oration?

JOHN: Something from Plato's Symposium.

WILSON: All of your classmates will be doing Latin orations, John.

JOHN: That's the reason I would like to do one.

WILSON: There's nothing special about a Latin oration. And the trustees are already questioning the value of a liberal arts education. We need to show them that we're doing more than simply studying Latin and Greek. We need to show them that we are actively engaged in shaping the face of America, engaged in shaping the future of the world. "The Claims of Liberia" will do that for us. Forget about doing a Latin oration. I think nine Latin orations will be quite enough, thank you. You ever load and fire a Kentucky flintlock pistol before?

JOHN: No, sir.

WILSON: You ever load and fire any type of pistol before?

JOHN: No.

WILSON: You must always remember to make sure that the ball is seated firmly up against the powder charge. If you try to fire with the ball off the charge, the thing'll blow up in your face. Here, look at this. She's a beauty, isn't she?

[*He hands the pistol to* JOHN.]

First thing you do is check to make sure the barrel is clear. Go ahead. Check.

JOHN: You want me to carry a pistol to the next meeting of the Literary Society?

WILSON: Why would I want you to do something like that?

JOHN: Because of Mr. Ward.

WILSON: Mr. Ward?

JOHN: He fired a pistol at Mr. McCoy. During debate. I thought you knew.

WILSON: No.

JOHN: They were debating the merits of religious devotion and Mr. Ward was losing the debate. When somebody started to laugh, Mr. Ward pulled out a pistol and fired it at Mr. McCoy. Mr. McCoy fell to the floor. We all thought he was dead.

WILSON: Was he hit?

JOHN: He fainted. Which of course meant that Mr. Ward won the debate.

WILSON: Nobody told me anything about this.

JOHN: I thought that was the reason . . .

WILSON: Somebody spotted some Indians not far from here. That's the reason for the pistol.

JOHN: Indians?

WILSON: Every now and then you come across a couple of stragglers. That's what these probably are. Stragglers living in the caves in the outlying regions. Nothing to worry about. The government's going to send out some riders to track them down. They'll find them, relocate them. Send them to live with the rest of their people.

JOHN: If there's nothing to worry about, why do you need a pistol?

WILSON: You never can be too safe. Besides, you're going to need to know how to fire a pistol once you get to Liberia. Now, check to make sure that the barrel is clear. Once you're sure that the barrel is clear, you add your powder charge.

JOHN: What do I do about the people who are already there?

WILSON: Already where? What people?

JOHN: In Liberia. When I get there, what do I do about the people already there?

WILSON: It's a wilderness, John. There are no people there.

JOHN: Natives. What do I do about the natives?

WILSON: That's up to you. You offer them the word and if they refuse that word . . .

[*Beat.*]

JOHN: If they refuse?

WILSON: I suggest that you give them the option of determining their own fate. If they refuse the word then one option would be to relocate them. Not you personally of course. You'll have men to do that for you. Now check your barrel. Make sure it's clear.

JOHN: Where does it stop?

WILSON: Where does what stop?

JOHN: I relocate the people who are there; they relocate someone else. Where does it stop?

WILSON: Relocation is only an option, John. They don't have to be relocated. They can accept the gift of civilization.

JOHN: I'm not quite sure it's a gift.

WILSON: What're you talking about?

JOHN: We seem to be caught in this vicious circle. The English came to Ireland, the Irish came to America, now you're sending me to Liberia. Where do the Liberians go?

WILSON: I'm sure you'll be able to find a place for them.

JOHN: The way Andrew Jackson found a place for the Shawnee?

WILSON: Are you trying to be insolent?

JOHN: I don't think I'm the right man for this.

WILSON: Course you are, John.

JOHN: I feel like I'm giving up without even trying. You said your father fought against the English. But he fought. He didn't give up when somebody asked him to move. He fought, he struggled, he tried to keep his home before striking out to find a new home. And even then he didn't abandon that fight until after it became clear that he couldn't win that fight. Here I am, I haven't even tried.

WILSON: Tried what?

JOHN: Tried to make this my home. I've given up without even trying.

WILSON: But this is not your home, John. Your home is in Africa.

JOHN: My home is here in the United States.

WILSON: But your people are from Africa.

JOHN: And your people are from Ireland, but I don't see you getting on a boat to go back. My family has been in this country for six generations. Five generations longer than your family. My father cut and fitted by hand every single piece of wood in the main library of the White House. But yet, you tell me that I'm the one who has to go? No, I'm sorry, but I can't do it, I won't do it. Not without first trying to make this my home.

WILSON: This will never be your home. Your people will never be able to live in harmony with the white race here in America. And this was not my doing, this was God's design. God made your people black, not me. And unless you can figure out a way to change your color, you will never be able to integrate into this society.

JOHN: You talk as if it's already been determined.

WILSON: It has been determined. Determined by God. God brought your people here as slaves, as savages. Now God has opened the way for you to return to Africa laden with the fruits of civilization.

JOHN: God did not bring my people here.

WILSON: God opened the way.

JOHN: Slave traders brought my people here.

WILSON: They were the instruments guided by the hand of God.

JOHN: Are you saying that slavery was part of God's design?

WILSON: I am saying that everything in this world is part of God's design. We may not always understand the reasons that God does what he does, but if we have faith and do not question his word, in time, he will reveal the truth and he will reveal the way. Now, I'm going to try to forget everything you just said. I'm going to try to forgive you but I never want to hear anything like that from you again. You're nervous. I understand that. You have concerns. But you're also educated, John. You should know better. Now, you know what today is? First of the month. Time to settle our accounts. How many hours do you have for the month?

[*Beat.*]

John? How many hours?

JOHN: Seventy-two.

WILSON: Same as always. Seventy-two hours at seven cents an hour. That's five dollars and four cents for the month.

[WILSON *pays* JOHN.]

There you are.

JOHN: Thank you.

WILSON: Don't mention it. You earned every bit of it. Governor.

JOHN: I have work to do.

[JOHN *moves to exit.*]

WILSON: John?

[JOHN *stops.*]

Aren't you forgetting something? Don't you think you should settle your account as well?

JOHN: Who founded the ACS?

WILSON: Pardon me?

JOHN: I want to know who founded the ACS.

WILSON: You know who founded the ACS.

JOHN: Tell me again.

WILSON: You know them. You met them. Many of them. Reverend Jacobs. Reverend McLain.

JOHN: Who else?

WILSON: Andrew Jackson.

JOHN: Andrew Jackson.

WILSON: Francis Scott Key.

JOHN: Slave owners.

WILSON: Maybe, at one point in their lives.

JOHN: What about you?

WILSON: What about me?

JOHN: Are you a former slave owner?

WILSON: What I used to do or who I used to be is none of your concern.

JOHN: Only by studying the origins of a thing—

WILSON: Language, John. I was talking about language.

JOHN: But language is not the end. Our goal is not to understand the words. Our goal is to understand all of the things the words represent, and if I am being asked to leave my country, to leave the land of my birth, I have the right to know who's doing the asking.

WILSON: God is doing the asking.

JOHN: Slave owners and former slave owners are doing the asking.

WILSON: You're named after a slave owner. Did you know that? You're named after John Newton, who bought and sold hundreds of slaves. But he received second sight. God allowed him to see the wickedness of his ways and then God inspired him to write a song of praise about it. "Amazing Grace." You ever hear it? [*Sings.*] "Amazing grace, how sweet the sound that saved a wretch like me. I once was lost, but now am found, was blind, but now I see." You should be grateful for former slave owners because they are the only friends you have. The abolitionists are not your friends. The only thing the abolitionists are doing is exacerbating the problem. But the former slave owners have seen the problem firsthand, they have sat at the table and dined with misery, they have had intercourse with suffering, they have conducted commerce with the devil himself, and now they have second sight. They see a world that they've never seen before and that world looks different, John. Like the morning you were born. The entire world looks different.

JOHN: A world that looks white. Is that how they see the world with their second sight? A white world cleansed of all their sins? Is that the reason they want to ship all of the niggers back to Africa? So that they won't have to be reminded of their sins?

WILSON: How dare you speak to me that way.

JOHN: I won't do it, Reverend. I refuse to take part in the whitewashing of this country.

WILSON: You don't have any choice in the matter.

JOHN: I've always had a choice.

WILSON: You never had a choice. Never. From the day you were born, this was your destiny. This is the reason God saved you. This is what God has chosen you for.

JOHN: Then why doesn't God tell me that? Why doesn't God speak to me and tell me that?

WILSON: Have you been listening? Have you been open to receive the word of God?

JOHN: I've been listening all right. But the only voice I hear is a voice telling me that if I go to Liberia, the only thing I will do is contribute to more bloodshed and more death.

WILSON: Bloodshed and death are parts of life, John. Life is blood and there could be no life without death. Civilization grinds on. Men who refuse to be a part of civilization's progress are crushed under her slow-moving weight. You try to back out of this now and you will be crushed. I will not let you graduate, the entire time you spent here will be wasted, and you will leave here as a failure. Your failure will confirm many people's suspicions that your people don't have the discipline or the intelligence for higher education. You back out of this now and you will be the last free man of color to attend university here or anywhere else in this country, I guarantee it. There are a lot of eyes upon you, John. And you've been doing well. Don't falter. Now, I think it's time to settle your account.

JOHN: I'll settle my account when I get ready.

[JOHN *exits.*]

SCENE 2

[JANE *onstage.* JOHN *enters.*]

JANE: You find it?

JOHN: I found it.

JANE: What was it?

JOHN: I don't know.

JANE: You don't know?

JOHN: By the time I got there, there was nothing left. Nothing but blood. Pieces of bone. Small pieces of flesh.

JANE: The coyotes got to it.

JOHN: I didn't see any coyotes.

JANE: I saw them. They were feeding on it.

JOHN: I didn't see any coyotes.

JANE: That's because by the time you got there, there was no reason for them to still be there. There was nothing left. Something got caught in that iron leg trap of yours and the coyotes got to it. They killed it. They ripped it apart.

JOHN: It was probably just a deer.

JANE: Wasn't a deer.

JOHN: How do you know?

JANE: I saw it. It was too small to be a deer.

JOHN: Then a fox. It was probably a fox.

JANE: I told you to be careful where you put those iron leg traps.

JOHN: It was just a fox. That's all it was. There's nothing to worry about. I'll go out and collect the rest of the traps. Give them back to Mr. Morgan.

[JOHN *moves to exit.*]

JANE: John? Robert says you've changed your mind about going to Liberia.

JOHN: That's right.

JANE: He also said you plan to give a Latin oration for graduation.

JOHN: If I'm not going to Liberia, I shouldn't give a speech supporting the idea, should I?

JANE: John . . .

JOHN: I guess I should thank you.

JANE: Don't thank me.

JOHN: But you were right, Mrs. Wilson.

JANE: No, John.

JOHN: You were right about everything.

JANE: The only thing I was concerned about was myself, John. I shouldn't have spoken to you the way I did.

JOHN: I was being trained for something I didn't understand.

JANE: I want you to give your "Claims of Liberia" speech.

JOHN: Why?

JANE: Robert won't tell you this, but the university is in trouble. Financially. The people in town can't pay the money they owe, and we were depending on that money to stay open, but there is no money. And the trustees, the trustees won't release any more money until they have had a look at the graduating class. They want evidence that the work Robert is doing here has an impact on the world outside. I'm not asking you to go to Liberia, John. But I am asking you to give your speech. "The Claims of Liberia" will be the evidence Robert needs to prove that the work he's doing here is important. But if you give a Latin oration, all the trustees will see will be more of the same of what they've seen in the past. They will not give us the money we need and the university will close.

JOHN: You're asking me to enter into a corrupt bargain.

JANE: You really don't believe that, do you?

JOHN: I don't believe you're asking me to do this.

JANE: I'm asking you to help a man who has treated you like a son.

JOHN: A son?

JANE: He brought you into this house, he protected you. I see the way he looks at you, the way he treats you, he doesn't treat any of the other students that way.

JOHN: False words are not only evil in themselves, but they inflict the soul with evil. That's what you're asking me to do. You're asking me to inflict my soul with evil.

JANE: Is that the only thing you're concerned about? Yourself? Your soul?

JOHN: If I don't look after my soul, no one else will.

JANE: You know what an ape is? An ape is a beast that lives a solitary existence aware of only one thing. Its own needs, itself in the present. That's what you are. A goddamn ape. Oblivious to everything except yourself.

JOHN: I may have been an ape once but not anymore. Here. Here's your shirt.

[*He takes off the shirt and throws it at her.*]

Stinking ape shirt. Smell of that shirt made me sick. Reminded me of everything I was doing. I'd wash it and wash it but the smell of that shirt wouldn't come out.

JANE: This shirt used to belong to my baby boy, David. Robert tried to make me give you this shirt, but I wouldn't do it. He said I was suffering from female hysteria but still I wouldn't do it. Then he took you out riding. The only other person he would go riding with was David. I remember one afternoon looking out the window and seeing you two on horseback, hearing your voices, you riding alongside Robert, and for a moment, I thought that my son had come home. That's when I realized why he wanted me to give you the shirt. So I gave you David's shirt, his hat, his pants.

[*She smells the shirt.*]

And that smell is David's smell. His sweat. God, how I used to love that smell.

[*She smells the shirt.*]

Only now, his smell has gotten all mixed up with your smell and I don't know whether to embrace it or fall away in utter revulsion.

[WILSON *enters.*]

WILSON: They found the Indians. There were Miami. They had to kill the brave.

JOHN: What do you mean they had to kill him?

WILSON: He was a savage, John.

JOHN: But why did they have to kill him?

WILSON: He came out of the woods and charged us. He was on foot and tried to attack six men on horseback. One of the men in the party, he spoke Algonquian. He shouted, "We're not here to hurt you. We want to help you." But the brave, he had a knife. He kept cutting and slashing. If they hadn't killed him, he would have certainly injured or killed one of us.

JOHN: What about the woman?

WILSON: We found her sitting at the foot of an oak tree. We rode up on her and she just sat there. She didn't try to run. She didn't try to fight. She just sat there, staring out, covered with blood. Looked like she had been attacked. Bitten. Probably coyote. She had bites on her arms, her hands. Looks like she had to fight them off.

JOHN: And the child?

WILSON: What child?

JOHN: There was a child. Three, four years old.

WILSON: There was no child.

JOHN: A little boy. I saw him.

WILSON: There was no child. We looked, but there was no child to be found. We found the brave and we found the squaw. If there was a child, don't you think we would have found him as well?

JANE: Told you it wasn't a fox. God, it wasn't a fox.

JOHN: What are they going to do with the woman?

WILSON: Send her to live with the rest of her people. She'll be happier there. This is your pistol, John. I bought it for you. I was going to teach you how to use it and then give it to you as a gift for graduation. I made that mistake once. You want it?

JOHN: No.

WILSON: You're going to need it, John. Where's your shirt?

JANE: Here.

WILSON: It's midday, man. Why aren't you wearing it?

[*Beat.*]

Put it on.

JOHN: No.

WILSON: No?

JOHN: I'm not wearing it anymore.

WILSON: Would somebody please explain to me where I went wrong with you?

[*No one answers.*]

The trustees are going to be here in two weeks. I need to start putting together a program for commencement. Would you like to be included in that program? Have you decided what you're going to do?

JOHN: I told you what I was going to do.

WILSON: Tell me again.

JOHN: You're going to have to find somebody else to go to Liberia.

WILSON: You're turning your back on God?

JOHN: Your God, maybe, but not my God.

WILSON: There's only one God, John.

JOHN: I think I read the Bible a bit differently than you do.

WILSON: And there's only one way to read the Bible.

JOHN: Your God brought slaves here in chains. My God wept while it was happening.

WILSON: That's blasphemy. Not only do you turn your back on God but you blaspheme while doing it? I think you should collect your things, John. It's time for you to leave this house.

JOHN: And go where?

WILSON: That's up to you. You have your papers, I imagine you can travel anyplace in the state you please, but you have to leave here. The university. The town.

JOHN: What about graduation?

WILSON: You're not graduating.

JANE: You can't do that, Robert.

JOHN: I've completed all the requirements for graduation.

JANE: You can't do this.

WILSON: If he doesn't go to Liberia, if he fails to recognize the overwhelming facts pointing to him being the one chosen to do this, then he has failed in his education.

JOHN: My education or my training?

WILSON: Your education.

JOHN: I still don't think you understand the difference between the two.

WILSON: And you have no idea of what's at stake here. You want to prove that you're as good as white? Stand up and embrace your destiny, John. You have to become a leader. That's the reason I brought you here, that's what the trustees want to see. They allowed me to bring you here and now they want to see a man who is on his way to becoming a leader.

JOHN: If I'm going to be a leader I need to do it how I see fit. Not in the way you think I should. My people don't need to wander through the wilderness to find a new home, they've already been on a journey, and that journey was to come here. Now if you set out to train me, you're right, I have failed in that training, you were unsuccessful in teaching me how to blindly follow orders, I do not sit up and speak on command. But if your goal was to educate me, then I would like to congratulate you, because you did a very good job. You taught me how to think for myself, you taught me about a world I didn't even know existed. But if that was your goal, if your goal was to educate me, then you must now give me the freedom to come to my own conclusions.

JANE: He's right, Robert. You have to let him go.

WILSON: No.

JANE: Let him go, Robert.

WILSON: God sent him here for me. God took away my sons and then he gave me John. Don't you see? You are mine, John. God gave you to me. You belong to me.

JANE: He doesn't belong to you, Robert.

WILSON: God gave him to me.

JANE: He doesn't belong to anyone.

JOHN: Here. This is the five dollars I owe you for last month's room and board. Thank you for taking me in. I'll get my things.

JANE: Wait, John, no. You don't have to go. You can stay here. Robert? Tell him he doesn't have to go. Robert?

WILSON: Five dollars? After everything I gave you, this is what you give me in return? Five goddamn dollars?

JOHN: If you want me to give "The Claims of Liberia" speech, I'll do it. You know why? Because I have carefully considered and come to the conclusion that it's the right thing to do. You're right, you have done a lot for me and I would like to return the favor so I'll give the speech. But don't ask me to go to Liberia. If it means I won't graduate, if it means I have to leave this house today, then I'll leave. But I'm not going to Liberia, Reverend. I'm not going to do it.

WILSON: I'll add your name to the program.

[WILSON exits.]

JANE: John? Would you like to have your shirt back?

JOHN: Thank you.

[She hands him the shirt, then exits.]

[To the audience] I gave the speech but never did go to Liberia. And I did graduate with nine other men. We all received diplomas, which were, by the way, at the time, real sheepskin.

After graduation I moved around a bit and eventually ended up in Wheeling, Virginia, now called West Virginia, where I started a school.

I had a little money. I had saved four cents a month for almost four years. That gave me exactly one dollar and twenty-two cents, which I used to purchase three books for my new school. I purchased an English King James Version of the Bible, an elementary book on world geography, and a copy of *The Life of Gustavus Vassa, the African*. Two weeks after opening my school, I was arrested and jailed for teaching colored folks how to read. But that didn't stop me. I taught in parts of Ohio, Virginia, and Pennsylvania.

And I was not the last free man of color to go to school at Ohio University. Four years after I graduated, Edward Roye was admitted. I imagine that his life here was much like mine, except for one small difference. He eventually became president of Liberia, where he reigned for a year and a half, until the day that the captain of his army walked into his office and arrested him on charges of embezzlement. Corruption. So it began.

For a long time I was worried about my soul. I worried that I had failed to live up to God's plan, that I had failed to fulfill my destiny. But I now realize I didn't have to go to Liberia to start a new life, to work my way through the wilderness, to discover a new frontier. I had worked my way through the wilderness and had discovered a new frontier and that new frontier was inside me.

[WILSON *enters.*]

WILSON: Ladies and gentlemen, most distinguished assembled guests, at this point in the program, I present to you John Newton Templeton.

[*Lights fade.*]

HANGING FIRE

CLAUDIA ALLEN

*To my "fairy godmother," the fabulous Julie Harris, great lady of
the American stage and my dear great friend*

PLAYWRIGHT'S STATEMENT

For some people, the great love of their life is their husband, wife, or lover. For others, the person they're most deeply connected to may be a longtime friend, a sister or brother, mother or father. In *Hanging Fire*, two sisters (Ruth and Lillian) are the great loves of each other's life. They're often annoyed with each other, but there's no one they'd rather fight with, cradle to grave. *Hanging Fire* is set in a small town in northern Michigan on July 3 and 4, 2000. The play also includes flashbacks from Ruth's and Lillian's younger lives. In the summer of 2000, Ruth has survived a stroke and is getting on with her life despite some speech difficulties. Lillian is trying to persuade Ruth to sell her house and move into the Golden Years, a retirement facility where Lillian is currently languishing. Lillian's mama's boy son, Calvin, is on her side until he experiences a night of passion on a picnic table with Deb (Ruth's friend and boarder) that convinces him people should stop hanging fire and live their lives fully. There's yet another romantic complication in the person of Mr. Donny Fletcher, the seventy-five-year-old boy next door who has come home to court Ruth after more than fifty years away. He's hoping she finally needs him. She doesn't; she's fine. But she might just want him after all. Ruth and Lillian are not easy women. Loving them isn't easy. But it's worth it.

The playwright would like to thank the following people for their generous support: Toni and David Mathis, Frank and Karen Schneider, Ron Ford, Sally Neely and Susan Riter, Dr. Fred Zar and family, Bill Barnes of the Clearwater School and friends, Ann Whitney, Kathryn Bowden, and Deb Mier.

PRODUCTION HISTORY

Hanging Fire, by Claudia Allen, was first presented by Victory Gardens Theater, Chicago, Illinois, in November 2004.

PRODUCTION TEAM

Director	Sandy Shinner
Set	John C. Stark
Costumes	Carol J. Blanchard
Lights	Rita Pietraszek
Sound	Andrew Hopson
Production Stage Manager	Tina M. Jach

CAST

Young Lillian	Bethanny Alexander
Young Ruth	Mattie Hawkinson
Mr. Donny Fletcher	Les Hinderyckx
Ruth	Rachel Stephens
Deb	Meg Thalken
Calvin	Mick Weber
Lillian	Ann Whitney

The play's co–world premiere was presented by Florida Stage, Manalapan, Florida, in January 2005.

PRODUCTION TEAM

Director	Louis Tyrrell
Set	Richard Crowell
Costumes	Douglas J. Koertge
Lights	John McFadden
Sound	Matt Briganti Kelly
Production Stage Manager	James Danford

CAST

Ruth	Patricia Conolly
Mr. Donny Fletcher	Richard Henzel
Young Ruth	Leanna Hieber
Young Lillian	Autumn Horne
Calvin	Colin McPhillamy
Lillian	Harriet Oser
Deb	Blair Sams

CHARACTERS

Ruth, *feisty, funny retired schoolteacher and principal in her seventies; survived a stroke so has some difficulty with speech but still manages to speak her mind*

Lillian, *Ruth's younger sister; also in her seventies, also a retired teacher; worries a lot*

Deb, *Ruth's roomer and friend; thirty-five to forty-five years old*

Mr. Donny Fletcher, *seventy-five-year-old buoyant spirit band conductor; former "boy next door"*

Calvin, *Lillian's only child; food inspector; a good-hearted middle-aged mama's boy*

Young Ruth, *Ruth from her teens to her thirties*

Young Lillian, *Lillian from her teens to her thirties*

STAGING

Place: Small-town Michigan
Time: Many Fourth of July weekends, 1940 to 2000

ACT 1

SCENE 1

[*The past: July 2, 1940.* YOUNG RUTH, *sixteen, and her sister,* YOUNG LILLIAN, *fifteen, are watching it rain.*]

YOUNG RUTH: I hate rain.

YOUNG LILLIAN: Me too, me too. Ruth oh Ruth, do you think it's going to keep raining right through the Fourth of July and ruin everything?

YOUNG RUTH: No.

YOUNG LILLIAN: Says who?

YOUNG RUTH: Says me.

YOUNG LILLIAN: I promised to watch the fireworks display with Donny Fletcher.

YOUNG RUTH: Donny Fletcher?

YOUNG LILLIAN: I just hate hanging fire about whether it's going to happen.

YOUNG RUTH: Donny Fletcher?

YOUNG LILLIAN: If it keeps raining buckets for *three* days they'll cancel the fireworks and that will ruin *everything.*

YOUNG RUTH [*it's beyond belief*]: You "like" Donny Fletcher?

YOUNG LILLIAN: He likes *me.*

YOUNG RUTH: Lillian oh Lillian.

[*Pause. They stare out at the rain.*]

Rain bores me.

YOUNG LILLIAN: Me too.

YOUNG RUTH: I realize that we need it. Mama's geraniums, Papa's garden, we all need a good soak now and then, but that doesn't mean I have to like being trapped inside like a rat today at the very *height* of summer.

YOUNG LILLIAN: Exactly.

YOUNG RUTH: Oh Lillian oh Lillian, stop complaining.

YOUNG LILLIAN [*bleats*]: Me?!

YOUNG RUTH: Remember what we used to do when it rained? When we were children?

YOUNG LILLIAN: No.

YOUNG RUTH: Oh yes you do.

YOUNG LILLIAN: No, I mean no, I won't do it; we're too old. And much too dignified.

[YOUNG RUTH *is on her feet and at the Victrola choosing a record and winding the machine.*]

YOUNG RUTH: Oh Lillian, you're not old, you're just stuffy. Get up!
YOUNG LILLIAN: Be careful. If you break that—

[*But* YOUNG RUTH *has finished winding, and the sounds of a Sousa march begin to ring out.*]

YOUNG RUTH [*the sergeant major*]: On your feet!
YOUNG LILLIAN: Yes, sir!

[*She can't resist. She hops to smartly.*]

YOUNG RUTH: Follow me!

[*They begin to march vigorously to the sounds of the Sousa march,* YOUNG LILLIAN *following* YOUNG RUTH. *There's a crack of thunder.* YOUNG RUTH *crashes her hands together as if they're cymbals and the thunder her music. They "sing" "dah's" and "dum's" rather than the words as they march. When the music ends, they collapse, breathless, pushing and punching at each other fondly, little girls again for just a moment, then they settle down.*]

"Fireworks" with Donny Fletcher?
YOUNG LILLIAN: He likes me. [*Shrugs.*] Well, truth be told, he likes *you,* but you won't give him the time of day and I will.
YOUNG RUTH: Aim high, Lily. Don't settle.
YOUNG LILLIAN: I could do worse.

[*Lights dim on the girls, though they remain onstage. Lights rise on* RUTH, *who we realize has been watching this memory.*]

RUTH [*speaking to the* YOUNG LILLIAN *in her memory, wryly*]: And you did.

SCENE 2

[*Summer 2000.* RUTH's *living room.* DEB *is reading. She reluctantly wears glasses to read. The phone rings.* DEB *answers the phone after removing her glasses.*]

DEB: Hello. This is Deb. Can I—may I—

[*She keeps being interrupted, so she finally gives up and just listens.*]

[*After a listening pause*] Nellie Briggs.

[Brief listening pause, then louder and slower] Nellie! Briggs! You're welcome.

[She hangs up. RUTH *enters, dust rag in hand. She gestures to indicate the phone.]*

RUTH: Who?
DEB: Nellie Briggs. She couldn't remember her name.
RUTH: Oh, dear.

[She shakes her head; it's a sad, bemused shake.]

DEB: At least she remembered your phone number. You two must've talked a lot.

*[*RUTH *nods but then frowns. She has spotted a speck of dust and is on it like a hawk.]*

You dusted that this morning.

[But now RUTH *is scowling at the lampshade. She adjusts it.]*

Ruth, this house is spotless. No one can find fault with your housekeeping, not even your dear sister Lillian and that son of hers.

*[*RUTH *gives her a look—oh yes they can.* DEB *puts down her book and the phone, her hands on the arms of her chair, ready to stand.]*

Okay. Then at least let me help.
RUTH: Sit.
DEB: Now don't you dare tell me I'm company. I've been rooming with you since—
RUTH: Sit.

*[*DEB *sits.* RUTH *dusts.* RUTH *stops suddenly, tilts her head to listen, then shakes her head.]*

Not them.

[She shakes her head again.]

DEB: Nope. Buddy Beasley's Honda Civic. What does Calvin drive?
RUTH: A B-B—
DEB: A Buick?
RUTH: Like me.
DEB: That was one grand old car.

RUTH: Was.

DEB [*always sensitive to* RUTH, *changes the subject*]: My it's humid. Do you think it's going to rain on the parade tomorrow?

RUTH: No.

DEB: Says who?

RUTH: Me.

DEB [*chuckles*]: Well, I hope you're right. The float for Bill's Campgrounds always has his cousins dressed in squirrel suits. Not good wet.

[RUTH *perks up, listens. We hear a car. We hear tormented brakes squeal.* DEB *looks at* RUTH.]

Them?

[DEB *looks at* RUTH.]

Wow. I never felt so sorry for a car.

[RUTH *nods solemnly, miming a very sad face. She starts to smile, then remembers to be nervous. She puts a hand to her hair, realizes the dust rag is in it. The dust rag falls to the floor.* DEB *hops up to get it.*]

Please, honey, I'll get rid of this. You go greet your company.

[RUTH *checks herself in a windowpane.*]

Now stop primping and go!

[RUTH *shoots* DEB *a look of "Oh, you!" and "Help!" combined, then exits.* DEB *looks at the rag, almost shoves it down behind a couch cushion, thinks better of it, shoves it deep into her pocket. We can hear the door open, hear* RUTH *exclaiming, "Hello! Welcome!"* LILLIAN *calls out, "Happy Fourth of July!"* CALVIN *greets* RUTH: *"Hi, Aunt Ruth."* RUTH *enters the living room with* LILLIAN *and* CALVIN, *who is blinking rapidly.*]

CALVIN: Something's in my—my eye. A speck of—of dust—flew in the—the—car window.

DEB: Hello, Lillian. Hi, Calvin.

CALVIN: Hi, Deb.

LILLIAN: Finally!

RUTH: Traffic?

LILLIAN: Awful. And they all drive eighty miles an hour.

CALVIN: I obey the speed limit. Better safe than sorry.

LILLIAN: You'd think those maniacs were driving an ambulance.

DEB: Boy, I sure burned rubber getting Ruth to the hospital after her—

CALVIN [*firmly cuts her off*]: Shhh.

DEB: Stroke.

LILLIAN: Deborah, let's not—not in front of her.

DEB: Ruth had a stroke. She'll be the first one to say it.

RUTH: Stroke.

DEB: Exactly. So how are you, Lillian?

LILLIAN: Stiff as a board. All that riding, all that sitting. My bones just freeze up if I can't stretch my legs. [*Pointed look at* CALVIN.]

CALVIN: We stopped.

LILLIAN: Once.

DEB [*baiting* LILLIAN]: I remember how stiff we both got sitting in that hospital waiting room after Ruth had her—

LILLIAN: Awful! One of the worst nights of my life.

RUTH: Me too.

CALVIN: Mother, can you look-see if you can see something in my eye?

[*He contorts to put his eye where* LILLIAN *can peer into it.* DEB *and* RUTH *exchange a look.*]

LILLIAN: The light's not very good. [*Peers some more.*]
Ruth, I have some hundred-watt bulbs in my suitcase.

DEB: Maybe you should just go outside.

LILLIAN: It wouldn't be any trouble to change the lightbulb.

DEB: We like this light.

LILLIAN: Fine. Go blind. Calvin, tilt. Move your head, tilt . . .

CALVIN [*straightening up, blinking rapidly with a martyred melodrama*]: Oh, oh, never mind. I'll be fine. [*Blinks rather pathetically.*]

DEB: Maybe it's a floater. I have one of those floating around in my eye. It looks a little like a mosquito.

[RUTH *buzzes.*]

Sometimes I'll see it and swat at the air—at nothing.

[*As* CALVIN *says his next lines,* RUTH *buzzes, gives a subtle mosquito impression, and then pretends to be swatting at a real mosquito.*]

CALVIN: I do not have a floater. I have a speck. And it hurts.

DEB: How'sabout I help you with your suitcases? They still in the car?

LILLIAN [*to* RUTH]: I need to use the [*lowers voice*] little girls' room.
RUTH [*giving her a testily astounded "Are you asking my permission?" look*]: So go.
DEB: I'd be glad to [*show you*]—
LILLIAN: I grew up here. I know where it is.

[*She exits.*]

CALVIN: She's a little crabby 'cause I made her wait.
DEB: Nice.
CALVIN: I stopped once. A three-hour drive soon becomes a five-hour drive if I stop at every Wendy's on the way. I'm going to get the bags.
RUTH: Do.

[*She scares him a little. He hurries out.*]

DEB: You scare him.
RUTH: Good.
DEB: And Lillian. I still can't believe she was a teacher. How could anyone that fussy teach high school? What in the world did she teach?

[RUTH *mimes stirring cookies.*]

Ahhh.

[*They both nod knowingly.*]

Home ec. I hated home ec.
RUTH: Me too.
DEB: I had to cheat to pass. My friend Darlene sewed my three-cornered scarf for me.
RUTH [*feigns shock*]: Bad. Bad girl.
DEB: I burned everything I tried to cook. Of course, once I grew up it would have saved me a lot of trouble if I'd learned more in home ec.

[*They have a moment.*]

I'll bet Lillian's never burned a cookie in her life.

[LILLIAN *reenters, flapping hands to finish drying them.*]

LILLIAN: Ruth, remind me to show you how to get rid of the lime around the drain in your tub.
DEB: Why were you in the tub?
LILLIAN [*ignores* DEB]: Ruth, it is too too hot in here. It's not good for you.

RUTH: Summer. It's hot.

LILLIAN: My unit [*we can see* RUTH *mouthing "unit" to* DEB] at Golden Years Retirement Village has air-conditioning. All the units are air-conditioned.

RUTH: I'm, I'm, I'm not.

LILLIAN: You're not—not—

DEB: She's not—air-conditioned.

RUTH: No. No, not, not . . .

[LILLIAN *meets* RUTH's *eyes; they exchange a long eye-narrowing look.*]

LILLIAN: She's not moving.

RUTH: Yes. [*With a furrowing of her brow, a settling of her mouth for* LILLIAN's *benefit*] No.

DEB: Well, of course she's not moving. Who thinks she should move?

[CALVIN *enters, carrying the bags.*]

CALVIN: One of these days someone's going to go right through those front steps, Aunt Ruth. Don't you get worn out keeping up this old barn?

DEB: Ah.

CALVIN: It's too much for you now, you know it is.

[RUTH *gives a scathing look.*]

Mother's so grateful I talked her into selling her old place and moving into Golden Years, aren't you, Mother?

LILLIAN: I like the air-conditioning.

CALVIN: There's bingo.

LILLIAN: I miss my flowers, miss spring in my backyard, miss—but I know I made a wise choice, made it before someone had to make it for me.

DEB [*taking a bag from* CALVIN]: Here, Calvin, let's put these in your rooms, so you two can freshen up before lunch. We thought we'd eat a nice leisurely lunch outside.

CALVIN: Isn't the parade this afternoon?

DEB: The pontoon parade is today. The parade parade is tomorrow.

LILLIAN: The parade I can do without. All those children. All that dust. But I do look forward to Old School Night. It's always interesting to see who shows up. Who's on oxygen.

CALVIN: It is fun. Though no one from my class reunion ever remembers me.

DEB: What a great way to have a reunion—just have everyone who's ever graduated from CHS get together over the Fourth.

LILLIAN: Well, the classes were so small in our day reunions didn't really work. Last year I was the only one from my class to come. And I didn't have much new to tell myself.

[DEB *laughs, glad she's finally finding something in* LILLIAN *to like.*]

CALVIN: You won't be going, will you, Aunt Ruth?
RUTH: I—
LILLIAN [*cuts her off*]: Of course she's not, are you, Ruth? You've always been so proud. [*To* DEB] She'd be like those poor souls tugging their oxygen tanks with them. [*To* RUTH] You don't want people to see you like this.

[RUTH *just sets her jaw and glares at her.* DEB *is furious, fuming but silent.* CALVIN *nods.*]

CALVIN: It would be such a shock to people.
DEB [*explodes*]: Why?! There's nothing wrong with Ruth. [*Pointedly*] Not with Ruth.
LILLIAN: Well, she's not herself. Not who she was at all. My word, the woman's had a—
RUTH: Stroke. But [*struggles for the words*] still me.
LILLIAN [*to* DEB]: In our day, if someone was maimed or crippled, they didn't flaunt it.
DEB: For God's sake, you've obviously had a lobotomy and no one holds that against you!
LILLIAN: Don't you dare—I love my sister! [*Splutters*] Sometimes Ruth needs to be protected from herself. She needs to worry what people will think. She needs—
RUTH: Oh, shut up.

[RUTH *exits.*]

DEB: You have no idea what she needs. [*After a good glare at* LILLIAN] I'm going to go help her with lunch.

[DEB *exits.* CALVIN *and* LILLIAN *look at each other.*]

LILLIAN: She has her nerve. What did I say?
CALVIN: You're just trying to help.
LILLIAN: I am.
CALVIN: You are. Your intentions are pure.
LILLIAN: And Ruth. She can barely talk but she still pushes me around.
CALVIN: Some things never change.

LILLIAN: I need to lie down.

CALVIN: I need to find my eyedrops.

[*Each picks up a bag.*]

LILLIAN: We must look out for Ruth, because she obviously can't look out for herself.

CALVIN: It's the right thing. It's for her own good.

LILLIAN: You'll stand by me?

CALVIN: Of course, Mother. I'm on your side. Which doesn't mean I'm not on her side too. Poor Aunt Ruth.

LILLIAN: Where is her pride? She used to be so proud.

CALVIN: I know.

LILLIAN: Is this my bag? Where is my bag?

CALVIN: I've got it, Mother. You've got mine.

LILLIAN: See?! They've got me all flustered. My heart's just a-flutter. We didn't drive all this way for me to be insulted.

CALVIN: Do you want to just turn around and go home?

LILLIAN: It would serve them right.

[*Long suffering pause.*]

But she is my sister. And she needs us. Whether she knows it, whether she'll admit it or not, she needs me. I'm staying.

CALVIN: You're a good person, Mother.

LILLIAN: Thank you, Calvin.

CALVIN: Here, let me carry both bags.

LILLIAN: You're a good son.

CALVIN [*as they exit*]: I've still got that speck in my eye.

LILLIAN: You poor thing. You're so brave. I'll bet it just hurts like the dickens.

SCENE 3

[*The past: summertime 1946. The yard.* YOUNG LILLIAN *and* YOUNG RUTH *are sketching.*]

YOUNG LILLIAN: Is that—a—what is that you're sketching, Ruth?

YOUNG RUTH: A frog.

YOUNG LILLIAN: Oh. [*Looking*] Oh. Oh, it's jumping, isn't it?

YOUNG RUTH: No. [*Glancing over at* LILLIAN's *artwork*] Nice fruit.

YOUNG LILLIAN: Well it is.

YOUNG RUTH: Lillian, I said it was nice. Very nice. Immaculate.

YOUNG LILLIAN: You can make even the sweetest compliment sound cutting.

YOUNG RUTH: It's a gift.

YOUNG LILLIAN: I'm almost afraid to have you meet Hubert.

YOUNG RUTH: Is he the boy that shoots rats at the dump? Oh, he's that efficiency expert who works for Ford. No chin?

YOUNG LILLIAN: He has a chin. Who told you that?

YOUNG RUTH: So where'd you meet this paragon? I hope he's on the up-and-up.

YOUNG LILLIAN: I met him in line at the Tastee-Freeze. His parents have a cottage at Little Long Lake.

YOUNG RUTH: Daddy says he's short.

YOUNG LILLIAN: He is not short. Daddy's just tall.

YOUNG RUTH: So what does an efficiency expert for Ford do exactly? Ride around in automobile trunks and listen for rattles?

[*Pause.*]

YOUNG LILLIAN: As a matter of fact, yes.

YOUNG RUTH: Well I'm sure we all will benefit. It's lucky someone's willing to do that.

YOUNG LILLIAN: You're doing it again. Cutting.

YOUNG RUTH: So what happened to Donny Fletcher? You two corresponded all the years he was in the Pacific. All those years I was away at college, I thought you two were going steady.

YOUNG LILLIAN: Not after I finally faced the truth.

YOUNG RUTH: And just what is "the truth"?

YOUNG LILLIAN: He prefers someone else.

YOUNG RUTH: Who? Some Hawaiian gal in a grass skirt?

YOUNG LILLIAN: I'd rather not say.

YOUNG RUTH: Okay. [*Returns to sketching. Points at her pad.*] That's a bug. [*Adds smudges.*] And that's a dragonfly.

YOUNG LILLIAN: Don't you want to know?

YOUNG RUTH: What? Oh, whom Mr. Fletcher prefers? No, not particularly.

YOUNG LILLIAN: You're maddening.

YOUNG RUTH: Thank you. I like to think so.

YOUNG LILLIAN: That's not a dragonfly. That's a smudge.

YOUNG RUTH: It's a dragonfly if I say it is.

[*They sketch in silence for a long moment.*]

YOUNG LILLIAN: He prefers you. He always has.

YOUNG RUTH [*explodes*]: What?! He told you that?

YOUNG LILLIAN: In so many words.

YOUNG RUTH: How many words exactly?

YOUNG LILLIAN: It's the bitter truth. And you know it.

YOUNG RUTH: Well, I don't want *him*. Doesn't that count for anything?

YOUNG LILLIAN: Ruth, you are twenty-two years old.

YOUNG RUTH: Lillian, do you know you have a brilliant talent for stating the obvious?

YOUNG LILLIAN: Twenty-two. And I'm nearly twenty-one. All of the men are out of the army, home from the war, but here we sit. Alone. Hanging fire, waiting for something to happen, waiting for *our* lives to happen. Ruth oh Ruth, are we doomed to be old maids and live together into our dotage?

YOUNG RUTH: Lillian, there are worse fates.

[*Pause.*]

YOUNG LILLIAN: Was that a compliment?

YOUNG RUTH: Lillian oh Lillian, stop snuffling. You know you'll marry. Someone.

YOUNG LILLIAN: Maybe Hubert.

YOUNG RUTH: Maybe. Though I for one would never marry an efficiency expert. Aren't they awfully fussy? I think he'd be a regular fusspot to live with. All that fussing and fretting over every little detail would get on my nerves. But you do whatever makes you happy.

YOUNG LILLIAN: Thank you *so* much.

YOUNG RUTH: You're *so* very welcome.

YOUNG LILLIAN: You're going to be an old maid schoolteacher, aren't you? I just know it.

YOUNG RUTH: I refuse to waste my fertility on children.

[*Lights dim on the past.* LILLIAN *has been watching this scene, so she of course has a comment.*]

LILLIAN: But of course that's just what she did. Ruth spent her life teaching—and dating. She never saw the need to marry or have children and now look at her. Alone in her old age. Poor Ruth.

SCENE 4

[*Summer 2000.* RUTH *and* DEB *are in the yard sitting in Adirondack chairs.* RUTH *takes an occasional strum at a ukulele as they sing some of Stephen Foster's "Beautiful Dreamer." * RUTH *has a problem or two with getting words out but generally does well with and enjoys the singing.*]

RUTH AND DEB [*sing*]: "Beautiful dreamer, wake unto me,
   Starlight and dewdrops are waiting for thee;
   Sounds of the rude world, heard in the day,
   Lull'd by the moonlight have all pass'd away!"

[DEB *applauds as they finish.*]

RUTH: Bravo.
DEB: Yeah, this is fun therapy. And thank God—[*eyes upward*] thank you, God—we didn't wake the nappers.
RUTH [*sings*]: "Beautiful dreamer . . ."

[*They laugh.* MR. FLETCHER *enters, singing.*]

MR. FLETCHER: "Beautiful dreamer, out on the sea,
   Mermaids are chanting the wild Lorelei . . ."
   Shame on you, you left out some of the man's best verse!
   [*Sings*] "Beautiful dreamer, queen of my song . . ."
   Sing with me, Ruthie! Don't stop.

[*But* RUTH *has stopped and is looking at him, studying him.* MR. FLETCHER *addresses* DEB, *but it's for* RUTH'S *benefit.*]

   She's trying to place me, trying to remember . . . who in the blazes is this handsome singing stranger? Is he a stranger or is he just strange? Think younger, younger, fifty years or more younger. More hair.
RUTH: Donny.
MR. FLETCHER: Yes indeedy, Donny Fletcher in the flesh. Finally home after all these years. Did you miss me? Don't answer that. [*Gesturing in* DEB's *direction*] Is this our love child all grown up?
RUTH [*slapping at him with the ukulele*]: Stop.
MR. FLETCHER [*to* DEB]: That's what she always said, which is why you're not.
DEB: Not . . . ?
MR. FLETCHER: Our love child. Dear, try to keep up. Ruth, Ruth oh Ruth, how lovely you look.

[RUTH *bows.*]

Ruthie, I almost hoped you'd be humpbacked or sporting a hooked nose, something to make me glad you spurned me all those years ago. Instead here you are, the same glorious creature I pined for all my childhood; here you are, not a day over sixteen. Think of all the decades I missed out on seeing you across the breakfast table.

DEB: Worse yet she missed out on seeing you.

MR. FLETCHER: Exactly!

DEB: Am I confused or didn't you used to date Lillian?

MR. FLETCHER: Briefly.

[RUTH *holds up five fingers, mouths, "Five years."*]

DEB: Five.

MR. FLETCHER: Only five years? It seemed so much longer. Five years, oh Ruth, you can't count all those years I was in the Pacific and she was here, apparently flirting with that 4-F she eventually married, but I'm not bitter. The woman dumped me for a dimwit who rode around in car trunks. But I hold no grudge. She wanted to come first in someone's heart, and she realized she'd always be second to you in mine.

DEB: Wow. Does he always [*go on like this?*]—

RUTH: Yes.

MR. FLETCHER [*clapping his hands*]: I'm just jumping out of my socks I'm so thrilled to be here, and who can blame me?

RUTH: Why—what—

MR. FLETCHER: Brings me to your doorstep? The reunion, of course. Old School Night. The Fourth of July. You. Ruth, I'm homesick.

RUTH: But I'm not—

MR. FLETCHER: Home? Don't you underestimate yourself, dear Ruth.

DEB: You sure do—

MR. FLETCHER: Finish her sentences for her? True, true. Is that good or bad? Helpful or infuriating? You tell me, Ruth oh Ruth. May I stay to dinner?

RUTH [*shrugs mightily as if overpowered; perhaps she mimes throttling him*]: God!

MR. FLETCHER [*to* DEB]: She's overwhelmed with emotion.

DEB [*dryly*]: I've never seen her this giddy.

MR. FLETCHER: You are single, aren't you, Ruth? I don't want to be cutting in on some old geezer's territory—

RUTH: I'm not—

MR. FLETCHER: —territory.

DEB: Not available.

MR. FLETCHER: Not interested? No, it can't be that.

RUTH: Sit.

DEB: Maybe we should have some iced tea; cool him down.

RUTH [*rises immediately*]: I'll get [*it*]—

MR. FLETCHER: I used to hang over the back fence and gaze at Ruth, and she'd soak me with the garden hose. Not even that could cool my ardor, nothing could. Not even time, all those years away, all those miles and marriages. All I had to do was see her again and I'm a lost man.

[CALVIN *emerges from the house, blinking.*]

CALVIN: What's all the ruckus?

DEB [*to* Fletcher]: Another love child. Your demon seed.

CALVIN: Darn, I've still got that speck in my eye. [*Finally spots* MR. FLETCHER] Oh, hello. More company, Aunt Ruth?

RUTH: Oh, yeah.

MR. FLETCHER: "Aunt" Ruth? Don't tell me you're Lillian's bouncing baby boy?!

[CALVIN *blinks, bewildered.*]

Why if I'd had a thing for car trunks I might have been your father!

DEB: Don, Donny, "Mr." Fletcher. Calvin, Lillian's son.

MR. FLETCHER: Charmed.

CALVIN: You're Donny Fletcher? [*A rather low-key, contemplative*] Wow.

MR. FLETCHER [*to* DEB]: Overwhelmed another one. It's the new teeth. Ruth, how's about I help you fetch some iced tea?

RUTH: No!

MR. FLETCHER: I promise to behave. [*Winks.*]

[*She waves him off and exits, rolling her eyes.*]

DEB [*to* MR. FLETCHER]: She's warming up.

MR. FLETCHER: She can't resist me forever.

DEB: Well, she has resisted you for seventy-five years. And she has a new garden hose.

MR. FLETCHER: Ah, but I've brought my umbrella.

[*And he has. He brandishes it at* CALVIN.]

Young man, how's your mother? Alive, I hope. Always a dangerous assumption at our age.

CALVIN: My mother is very much alive. In fact, she's right inside. Emerging from her nap. She still talks about you.

MR. FLETCHER: I'm touched but hardly surprised. I am the road not taken, the life she might have lived, unblemished by the truth of daily living. I am the beautiful dream.

CALVIN: She said you liked to talk.

MR. FLETCHER: Has it been a happy life for Lillian?

CALVIN: I guess.

MR. FLETCHER: You don't know? You should know.

CALVIN: Mother has led an exemplary life.

MR. FLETCHER: Oh, dear, how drear.

CALVIN: She has been a pillar of the community.

MR. FLETCHER: Good gravy, poor Lillian. She may need me more than Ruth.

DEB: Aren't you assuming an awful lot, Mr. Fletcher?

[CALVIN *nods and blinks in agreement.*]

MR. FLETCHER: I assume nothing. I know for a fact that I am God's gift to women. I can provide you with testimonials.

DEB: But no wife beaming with satisfaction.

MR. FLETCHER: I have outlived not one but two wives. Both died of natural causes after many years of marital bliss. I was committed to commitment. I miss it. I need it. I crave it. I must have it.

DEB: Well, we'd be glad to commit you.

MR. FLETCHER [*to* CALVIN]: Do you always blink like that? It's like you're watching us frame by frame.

CALVIN [*points at his eye*]: Speck. Hurts.

DEB: Mr. Fletcher, why did you leave here and why have you come back? Why now?

MR. FLETCHER: Is this for the social column in the *Clarion*?

DEB: I'm Ruth's friend. And I'm protective.

MR. FLETCHER [*a brief moment of sincerity*]: I do appreciate that. She's lucky. [*Back in character*] Okeydokey, artichokey. I left to go to war. During the war my family relocated to Lima, Ohio, don't ask me why. I came back once. Lillian was engaged and Ruth was as ferociously determined as ever not to have me. And I gave up too easily. I met a woman in college, Vera Jean, and we hit it off. She was from Bloomington, Illinois, so we moved there after we married. And I never came back. Probably never would have if my cousin Lucy hadn't called and told me about Ruth's stroke. That was the kick in the pants I needed. Don't get me wrong; I have had a full life. Bloomington is the birthplace of presidential contender Adlai Stevenson, so of late I have been touring the schools with my one-man show, *Adlai:*

Last but Not Least. And for many years before that I was a band conductor at a small high school surrounded by corn, endless corn, nothing but
corn. Both of my late wives were musical; one was a soprano, the other
thankfully was not. They were good women, and I enjoyed them, but they
weren't Ruth. [*To* DEB] Honestly, my dear, you don't have to protect her
from me. Ruth can take care of herself. But maybe just maybe my time has
come. Let me hope.

CALVIN: She sure is taking her time with that tea.

DEB [*smiles but not in a mean way at* MR. FLETCHER]: She's hiding out.

MR. FLETCHER: I can't help it that I'm breathtaking. So tell me about you.
[*Points at* DEB] You first. What gallant endeavor pays your rent?

DEB: I teach. English.

MR. FLETCHER: Of course.

DEB: That's how I met Ruth. She'd retired as principal, but they'd call her in
to substitute. We became friends patrolling the restrooms for smokers.

MR. FLETCHER: Tell me, do you love teaching? Did you choose the classroom
over far more sensible, better-paying jobs in the insurance industry out of
love or are you just coasting to an early retirement?

DEB: To be honest I got into it to make a living. But one day, at the end of
summer, I realized how eager I was to get back to work, and I knew teaching was the great love of my life. No man would ever make me as happy
as watching a roomful of kids read *To Kill a Mockingbird* for the first time.
That's one of the reasons Ruth and I really "get" each other. She loved
teaching, loved everything about it. She was a tough teacher; she set high
standards; she asked so much of them but gave more.

CALVIN: And used herself up.

DEB: I don't see it that way.

MR. FLETCHER: You there blinking away, don't you love your own work with
a passion?

CALVIN [*blinking*]: Actually I do.

MR. FLETCHER: And what *do* you do?

CALVIN: I'm a food inspector. I inspect restaurants for contamination,
improper food storage—

MR. FLETCHER: Rat turds.

CALVIN: Find 'em all the time.

MR. FLETCHER: Botulism, salmonella—

CALVIN: Are evil and easily avoidable if we practice due diligence.

DEB: Breed one home ec teacher with an efficiency expert and you get—

CALVIN: Me.

MR. FLETCHER: Destiny.

CALVIN: It is my calling, my life's work to force the Chinese restaurants of lower Michigan to serve their egg foo yung free of roaches and rat turds. Just don't ask me about my work too close to dinnertime unless you're dieting.

[DEB *laughs, then frowns. She doesn't want to like* CALVIN.]

MR. FLETCHER: So what in the world's happened to my iced tea? Ruth didn't escape out the side door, did she? She used to do that when we were teenagers. Or she'd hop out a window. The woman devastated my ego, but I had to admire her athleticism.

CALVIN: Aunt Ruth has been gone quite a while. Maybe Mother's helping her with the tea.

DEB: No wonder it's taking so long.

MR. FLETCHER: They always were inseparable, chattering away, marching to Sousa on a rainy day, inseparable. I was an only child so I envied them their camaraderie.

DEB: You're kidding. Ruth and Lillian?

CALVIN: They've never gotten along.

MR. FLETCHER: Inseparable. Oh they argued, but that was the spice. Haven't you ever had a lover you just loved to argue with?

CALVIN: No.

DEB [*a darker said with subtext*]: No.

MR. FLETCHER: You poor wretches, listen to you. You're perfect for each other.

CALVIN: We aren't—

DEB: No, we are not.

MR. FLETCHER: Pity.

SCENE 5

[*The past, just before the wedding.* YOUNG LILLIAN *is in her wedding suit and demure veil.* YOUNG RUTH *is wearing pedal pushers and a T-shirt.*]

YOUNG RUTH: Don't do it.

YOUNG LILLIAN: Get dressed.

YOUNG RUTH: I *am* dressed.

YOUNG LILLIAN: Do not ruin this.

YOUNG RUTH [*points offstage*]: Look at him. Look at what you're marrying. Lillian, don't do it! Your life, all of our adventures will be over.

YOUNG LILLIAN: Ruth, why are you doing this to me?! They're all here, waiting for us by the rose trellis. Ruth, put on your dress *now*!

YOUNG RUTH: Lillian oh Lillian, there's gas in the car. Come to Venice with me. Please, Lillian, please, let's go to Italy.

YOUNG LILLIAN: In your car?

YOUNG RUTH: OK. Let's go to Detroit. Anywhere but here.

YOUNG LILLIAN: Ruth, you go ahead. See Paris. See Rome. I can't. Please. Please get dressed. You can go to Italy tomorrow.

YOUNG RUTH: I want you to be happy.

YOUNG LILLIAN: So do I. Ruth, this is my day. Please.

[*Pause.*]

YOUNG RUTH: Give me a couple of minutes.

YOUNG LILLIAN: Don't forget to comb your hair.

YOUNG RUTH: Lillian, don't tell me what to do—any day except today. Today is your day. Lotsa luck, kiddo.

YOUNG LILLIAN: Thank you. Give my regards to Venice.

YOUNG RUTH: Next year. I swear I'm going to Venice next summer.

YOUNG LILLIAN: I hope you do.

[*Lights dim on the past.*]

LILLIAN [*commenting on this scene*]: . . . But Mama got cancer that summer. Ruth stayed home.

SCENE 6

[*Summer 2000. Screen door slams open.* RUTH *enters, carrying a pitcher of iced tea.*]

RUTH [*furious*]: No!

[LILLIAN *enters with a tray of glasses, hot on* RUTH'S *heels.*]

LILLIAN: Ruth, let me carry that, don't be foolish. Now don't drop it; you're going to drop it.

RUTH: No! I'm—I won't—shush.

DEB [*to* Fletcher]: They don't look that happy to me.

MR. FLETCHER: That's where you're wrong.

RUTH [*has set the tea down*]: Tea.

LILLIAN [*setting down the tray of glasses*]: I thought it would be nice if we served it with lemon, so I went ahead and cut up a lemon and *she threw it in the trash.*

RUTH: It's not—not—

LILLIAN: Lemonade; it's tea. Well, I know that. Of course I know that. But a slice of lemon—

RUTH: Ruins it.

MR. FLETCHER: Or it adds a zing, a little spice. Doesn't it, Lillian?

[LILLIAN *has been too busy managing her tray and arguing with* RUTH *to spot* MR. FLETCHER, *until now.*]

LILLIAN: Omigosh, Donny Fletcher.

MR. FLETCHER: Bull's-eye! Ah, Lillian could see the boy in the man or the man in the boy! Or Ruth told you I was here.

LILLIAN: Donny Fletcher, I would have known you anywhere, anytime.

MR. FLETCHER: Back at ya, kid.

[*There's a fond moment here—no overwhelming lust but perhaps a trace of warmth from leftover first kisses.*]

CALVIN: Mother?

[*Pause.*]

Mom!

LILLIAN: What?

CALVIN: Is there sugar for the tea?

LILLIAN: Sugar? [*Shakes from her reverie; perhaps for just a fleeting moment she was once again out behind Grandpa's chicken coop with Donny.*] Oh my, dear me, I forgot the sugar.

DEB [*starting to rise*]: Let me.

LILLIAN [*flapping about*]: Oh no. I'll go.

[*She spins around, looking for where she set down her tray.* RUTH *is getting some cranky but merry enjoyment out of watching this, but she takes pity and finally guides* LILLIAN'S *gaze to the small table where they've set the tea things.*]

Oh, dear, I did forget the sugar. I'll just be a minute.

[LILLIAN *exits all a-fluster.*]

MR. FLETCHER [*following her out*]: May I help?

[*He exits, close on* LILLIAN'S *heels.*]

CALVIN: She needs help with a sugar bowl?

DEB: You are truly clueless when it comes to romance, aren't you, Calvin?

CALVIN: He likes Aunt Ruth. He told us so. Besides, she's not—Mom's not—

RUTH: Ahhh. [*Eyes dancing, she starts making love to her own arm. She loves to torment* CALVIN; *she can't help herself.*]

CALVIN: Quit it, Aunt Ruth!

[DEB *stands near him and gives her own arm a big wet one.*]

  [*To* DEB; *he's pissed, but his eye contact lingers*] Quit it!

[DEB *returns the eye contact.*]

DEB: Make me.

[*A moment, then she somewhat breaks free from it by mock dusting off his shirtfront or straightening his already straight collar—some gesture she doesn't mean to be intimate but is.*]

  And he's staying for dinner.

CALVIN: Great.

[CALVIN *looks appalled. But there's something, something going on between him and* DEB. *Just the hint of something beginning.* RUTH *has been watching them.*]

RUTH [*means it*]: Great.

SCENE 7

[*The past.* YOUNG LILLIAN *is pregnant.* YOUNG RUTH *is swigging a Coca-Cola from the bottle.*]

YOUNG LILLIAN: My that Coke looks good.

YOUNG RUTH [*hands on chair arms, ready to stand*]: Want me to get you one?

YOUNG LILLIAN: I don't believe it would be good for *the baby.*

YOUNG RUTH [*has heard about all she can stand about the baby*]: One Coke isn't going to turn your little genius into a frog, Lillian. Oh, Lillian, you are such a goose. Have a Coke.

YOUNG LILLIAN: That's not just Coke.

YOUNG RUTH: No?

YOUNG LILLIAN: No.

YOUNG RUTH: I can fool Mama, but I can't fool you.

YOUNG LILLIAN: So don't even try.

YOUNG RUTH: It's just a little rum.

YOUNG LILLIAN: "Just a little rum." Since when did you become a lush?

YOUNG RUTH: Lush! Since when do you get to tell me what to do?

YOUNG LILLIAN: Since I'm now the married sister with a child on the way.

YOUNG RUTH: So you think that suddenly gives you seniority? Bullshit.

YOUNG LILLIAN: Ruth!

YOUNG RUTH: That was Papa's favorite curse word.

YOUNG LILLIAN: Ruth, you are going to get a reputation, and it won't be for conjugating verbs. You're a teacher, for heaven's sake. You need to set a good example. You need to be above reproach.

YOUNG RUTH: Not in my own damn living room.

YOUNG LILLIAN: It's the *drink* talking.

YOUNG RUTH: Lillian, don't tell me what to do. Never tell me what to do.

[*Furious standoff.*]

YOUNG LILLIAN: Well, you shouldn't swear in front of the baby.

YOUNG RUTH: If it ever comes out, I won't.

YOUNG LILLIAN: Don't call it "it."

[*After a moment, she realizes what she's said and has to laugh at herself. They both laugh.*]

YOUNG RUTH: Okay, I won't.

[*Lights dim on the past.* CALVIN *has been observing this memory.*]

CALVIN: I still don't think they should have been calling me "it." [*As if the audience is looking askance at him for "remembering" this flashback*] Hey, this is part of my memory, too. I was there. I could hear *every word*. No wonder I didn't want to come out.

SCENE 8

[*Summer 2000.* RUTH's *kitchen table.* RUTH *is stirring potato salad.* LILLIAN *is watching her like a hawk.* RUTH *stops and stares at* LILLIAN. LILLIAN *stares back.*]

RUTH: Stop.

LILLIAN: Stop what?

RUTH: You know.

LILLIAN: What am I doing wrong now? Ruth, I'm not doing anything. You won't let me do anything.

RUTH: Stop. Watching.

LILLIAN: What on earth is wrong with watching? Of course, that's not the way I make potato salad, but I didn't say a word.

[RUTH *mimes the evil eye.*]

Oh, nonsense. I was *not* giving you the evil eye. I'm sure that's going to taste, well, just fine. I've never been one to put pickle juice in *my* potato salad, but I know that's the old-fashioned way. You probably saw Mama or one of the aunts splash some in their potato salad when you were a little girl, so you thought that was the right way to make it. You never studied food preparation like I did, so you still do it the old-timey way. And I'm sure it'll taste just fine.

[RUTH *holds the large mixing bowl full of potato salad over the wastebasket.*]

You wouldn't. Ruth oh Ruth, don't!

[RUTH *drops the potato salad into the wastebasket.*]

RUTH: Don't! Tell me! What to do!

[DEB *enters.*]

DEB: What's all the commotion?
LILLIAN: Ruth just threw away our dinner.
DEB [*looks down into the wastebasket*]: Aha. Potato salad.
LILLIAN: Childish.
RUTH: You—you—drive me—*nuts*!
DEB [*still looking down at the wastebasket*]: It's upright. Didn't spill. It landed on the eggshells and some paper towels. Here.

[*She plucks the bowl out of the trash and sets it back on the table.*]

It'll be our little secret.
LILLIAN [*recoiling*]: Oh, no. No no no no no no no. You can't—we can't possibly—my son is a government food inspector! [*To* RUTH] I blame the—
RUTH [*interrupts*]: No.
LILLIAN: Fine. You're right; it's not the stroke. You always were—what's a nice way to put it? Pigheaded!
RUTH: Oink.
LILLIAN: You were a paragon in the classroom, but for goodness' sake, you dated a priest!
RUTH [*with a special little smile*]: Jerry.
DEB: You dated Father Jerry? He's still over there.
RUTH: Bless him.
LILLIAN [*more worried about the potato salad*]: You're not really going to serve that, are you?

DEB: I know. I'll put it in a clean bowl.

RUTH [*slams knife down on table; to* LILLIAN]: Ham. Cut. Now.

DEB: Paper plates or china?

[DEB *looks at them.*]

Paper it is.

SCENE 9

[*Summer 2000. The yard. Paper plates and glasses are strewn about.* DEB *stands with a garbage bag about to "do the dishes." Everyone is stuffed.*]

CALVIN: I don't believe I've ever had a better potato salad.

[LILLIAN *rolls her eyes.* RUTH *smiles a* Mona Lisa *smile.* DEB *chuckles as she begins picking up paper plates, napkins, etc., and stuffs them into her garbage bag. She swats at a mosquito on her arm—evening is coming on.*]

MR. FLETCHER: I remember going to block picnics and Ruth and Lillian's mother would bring a veritable vat of her potato salad—just the best, most mouthwatering potato salad—and it would be gone, every last molecule, by midpicnic. Ruth, kudos. You have captured your mother's potato salad, every delectable nuance, down to the faint tang of pickle juice. Bless you.

LILLIAN: I too have always admired Ruth's potato salad.

CALVIN: Then why didn't you eat any? Mom, are you feeling okay?

[DEB *muffles a whoop of laughter; bends to pick up a wad of paper towel.*]

MR. FLETCHER: Lillian's right as rain, aren't you, Lillian? So what's on the docket for tonight? It's almost the Fourth of July. We should be celebrating.

LILLIAN: Remember how they used to have a band concert in the park? Then television came along and people started watching their concerts on PBS.

MR. FLETCHER: Well, I walked in on a fabulous concert this very afternoon right on this very spot. Ruthie, Deb, how about an encore?

DEB: Oh jeez no.

RUTH: No no no.

LILLIAN: Now, Donny, Mr. Fletcher. You're embarrassing my poor sister. You know she can't sing since her—

RUTH: Stroke! Stroke. You. What—do you—know?!

[*She looks about, rescues the ukulele.* RUTH *strikes a pose, strikes a chord.* DEB *drops her bag when she hears the chord. They begin to sing Stephen Foster's "Camptown Races."*]

DEB: "Camptown ladies sing this song."
RUTH: "Doo-dah, doo-dah."
LILLIAN: "Doo-dah" does not constitute singing.
RUTH: "Doo-dah!"
MR. FLETCHER: "Camptown racetrack's five miles long, oh—"
RUTH AND MR. FLETCHER: "Doo-dah day."
DEB: "Gwine to run all night."
CALVIN: "Gwine"?
MR. FLETCHER: "Gwine to run all day."
DEB: "I bet my money on a bobtailed nag . . ."
MR. FLETCHER: "Somebody bet on the—"
RUTH AND MR. FLETCHER: "Bay!"

[CALVIN *slaps a mosquito on himself.* MR. FLETCHER *begins playing an imaginary kazoo, aping the sound very effectively.* CALVIN *covers his glass with his hand and starts rattling and shaking the ice cubes to provide percussion.* LILLIAN *glares at him and he stops.*]

LILLIAN: You've all lost your senses.

[MR. FLETCHER *kazoos in her face.*]

DEB: Whew.
CALVIN: Do dah.

[*Silence, then a struggling but determined voice.*]

RUTH [*sings*]: "I'm—I'm a—oh, I'm I'm—"

[*They all pause briefly to look at her.*]

MR. FLETCHER: You're a grand old flag?
CALVIN: You're a believer?
DEB [*to* CALVIN]: The Monkees?

[LILLIAN, *despite herself, exchanges a long look with* RUTH.]

LILLIAN: She's a Yankee Doodle Dandy.

[RUTH *begins to sing George M. Cohan's "Yankee Doodle Dandy."*]

RUTH [*sings*]: "I'm—mmma . . ."

LILLIAN: "Yankee . . ."

LILLIAN AND RUTH: "Doodle Dandy."

RUTH AND MR. FLETCHER: "A Yankee Doodle, do or die."

DEB AND CALVIN [*surprised to be singing together*]: "A real live nephew of my Uncle Sam."

RUTH: "B-born on the—"

ALL [*bellowing*]: "Fourth of July!"

[MR. FLETCHER *resumes his imaginary kazoo playing, leading them all in a march around the yard as they attempt to sing the words—or just "da" and "doo" and "dum." Even* CALVIN *is tooting an imaginary horn.* RUTH *has managed to pull a protesting* LILLIAN *into the fun. Finally, they all collapse, giggling at themselves.*]

LILLIAN [*though laughing*]: We should all be locked up.

[RUTH *takes* LILLIAN's *hand and squeezes it.* LILLIAN *is embarrassed but pleased.* MR. FLETCHER *stands, hand on breast, and in an almost boyish but sincere voice, a cappella, begins to sing Cohan's "Grand Ol' Flag."*]

MR. FLETCHER [*sings*]: "You're a grand old flag,
You're a high flyin' flag,
And forever in peace may you wave.
You're the emblem of
The land I love.
The home of the free and the brave.
Ev'ry heart beats true
'Neath the Red, White, and Blue,
Where there's never a boast or brag.
Should auld acquaintance be forgot,
Keep your eye on the grand old flag."

[*A moment of stunned silent appreciation, then* RUTH *applauds, followed by the others.*]

RUTH: Bravo.

DEB: Mr. Fletcher, you brought tears to my eyes.

MR. FLETCHER: My voice used to have that effect on my wife's poodle. [*Sincere again for a moment*] Thank you, my dear.

LILLIAN: That was just what this evening needed. Donny, you put the Fourth back in the Fourth of July.

RUTH [*giving him an appreciative look—is there finally some hope?*]: Wonderful.

MR. FLETCHER [*after just a moment of sincerely returning* RUTH's *gaze*]: Now where's my ice cream? My old aunties always rewarded me with strawberry ice cream.

DEB: Golly, I don't think we have any.

[*She and* RUTH *look at each other; shake their heads.*]

I'm so sorry. I was on a diet and Ruth was humoring me.

MR. FLETCHER [*thunders*]: A diet! Young woman, there should be more of you, not less! Now I absolutely insist on ice cream for everyone.

DEB: And you shall have it! I'll just run out to the store. Let me go get my car out of the garage.

LILLIAN: Why is your car in Ruth's garage?

CALVIN: Where's Aunt Ruth's Buick?

[*There's a pause.* DEB *looks at* RUTH. RUTH *exhales air, shrugs. They're caught.*]

DEB: She doesn't have it anymore.

LILLIAN: Well, thank heavens. Finally a sensible act. [*To* RUTH] You realized you shouldn't be driving . . .

RUTH: No. Kaboom!

DEB [*to* CALVIN, *in case he still missed it*]: She had an accident.

LILLIAN: Oh, dear Lord, when? Why wasn't I informed? [*To* RUTH] You could have been killed.

RUTH: I wasn't. But the Buick—

[*She mourns.*]

DEB: She loved that car. It was a grand old car.

MR. FLETCHER: Totaled?

[DEB *nods.*]

LILLIAN: First, you wouldn't let me help you with your rehab. Now this. Ruth oh Ruth, promise me you will not buy another car.

[*After a glare-off.*]

RUTH: Let's go.

CALVIN: Where?

DEB: To buy Ruth a new car.

RUTH: Yes.

LILLIAN: No!

MR. FLETCHER [*sings*]: "Wouldn't you really rather have a Buick?"

LILLIAN: No!

DEB: Oh, for God's sake, Ruth already gave up her license. On her own.

RUTH: Don't—

LILLIAN: Tell you what to do.

MR. FLETCHER: Ice cream? My treat.

SCENE 10

[*Summer 2000.* RUTH *is sitting on the edge of an Adirondack chair, sketching.* LIL-LIAN *enters.*]

LILLIAN: Hi.

[*Silence.*]

[*Trying to make up*] Whatcha doin'?

[*Silence.*]

Oh no, are you still trying to draw?

RUTH: Shut up.

LILLIAN [*leans closer*]: What is that? [*Closer.*] Why that's a—he's—Ruth!

RUTH: As . . . a . . . a . . . jay—

LILLIAN: As a jaybird.

RUTH: Jaybird.

LILLIAN: Ruth, why can't you just draw fruit?

[*Silence.*]

The others are all off to the lawn mower races. I don't go for those danger-ous sports.

[*Silence.*]

Tomorrow Donny wants to go to the pancake breakfast over at the fire-house. I told him how Daddy keeled over at the pancake breakfast in 1952, but that didn't affect his enthusiasm. Isn't it lucky we didn't marry him? He'd wear me right out.

[*She looks a little closer at* RUTH'S *drawing.*]

That young man— those chicken legs—that's not—

[RUTH *nods.*]

Donny?

[RUTH *nods.*]

RUTH [*echoes*]: Donny.

LILLIAN: No. Really? Well, thank God I never had to look at that. When did you [*have sex with Donny?*]—

[RUTH *shakes her head no.* RUTH *mimes swimming.*]

    Oh, you went swimming

RUTH: Sk—ski—ski—

LILLIAN: You went skinny-dipping with Donny Fletcher? Where was I?

[RUTH *puts her head on her hands miming sleep, snores.*]

    I miss out on everything, don't I?

[RUTH *shrugs, nods, suddenly smiles devilishly, rises, takes* LILLIAN's *hands, begins to pull* LILLIAN.]

    What are you up to?

[RUTH *mimes swimming, tugs.*]

    I will not go skinny-dipping with you at the gravel pit. What if someone sees us? Dear Lord, what if we drown and they find us floating naked or beached like a couple of old whales? People would never stop talking.

[RUTH *starts humming or kazooing a Sousa march, tugging at* LILLIAN.]

    Well, I am not taking off my clothes. You think you can make me do anything. Skinny-dipping! The very idea.

RUTH: Yes.

LILLIAN: No.

RUTH: Yes.

[RUTH *is leading* LILLIAN *offstage, humming.*]

LILLIAN: No, no, no, no, no.

RUTH: Yes. Yes. Yes.

LILLIAN: No, no, no . . . maybe.

RUTH: Yes.

LILLIAN: If I drown, I'll never forgive you.

[*Intermission.*]

ACT 2

SCENE 1

[*July 2000.* RUTH *and* DEB *are waving to* MR. FLETCHER, *who is offstage, driving away.*]

DEB: See you tomorrow, Donny! [*To* RUTH] I am surprised he didn't just curl up on the rug next to your bed.

RUTH [*swatting at her*]: Bad.

DEB: You really missed out. Nellie Briggs's daughter won the lawn mower race. She's really cutthroat. [*Lightly touching* RUTH*'s hair*] Your hair's a little damp. Did you have to take a cold shower?

[RUTH *swats her again.*]

Look, the moon's nearly full, shall we howl?

[RUTH *and* DEB *howl.*]

Why would anyone want to walk around up there, stomping all over the poetry and the mystery of it? Bringing it down to earth. Power, I suppose. Ego.

[RUTH *nods along.* CALVIN *enters from the shadows.*]

CALVIN: Adventure. Mystery. Poetry. Power. Ego. When I was a little guy, I wanted to be an astronaut so bad. I read all about the planets. Walking in space, walking on the moon was my dream.

DEB: What stopped you?

CALVIN: Me.

[*Brief pause.*]

And Mother.

RUTH: Is she—?

CALVIN: Asleep? Yes. She took a pill with some warm milk. She means well. She's just scared of losing you, Aunt Ruth. We all are.

RUTH: We all—die. But—do we   *live?*

CALVIN: She wants you to move to the Golden Years with her. An apartment down the hall just opened up.

[RUTH *snorts, indicates, mimes to indicate it's vacancy by death.*]

The previous tenant didn't die *in* the apartment, if that's any comfort. She died in the hallway.

[RUTH *rolls her eyes.*]

They cleaned the carpet.

DEB: Ruth has a home.

CALVIN: Let's be reasonable. This is too much house for someone her age.

RUTH: Me. Talk—to [*patting her chest hard*] me.

DEB: Don't talk about Ruth around Ruth like she's not here.

CALVIN: Sorry. [*He is.*] I'm sorry, Aunt Ruth. Nobody wants to give up their old life, their old ways. Mom sure didn't. Change is hard. Facing the need to change is hard. But just how long do you really and truly think you're going to be up to living in this big old house alone?

DEB: "Alone"? For crying out loud, Calvin, *I'm* here.

CALVIN: For how long?

DEB: For however long she'll have me.

CALVIN: What if you get married?

DEB [*a dark laugh with subtext*]: I won't.

CALVIN: Are you gay?

DEB [*penetrating look with a lot of subtext*]: Would that I were.

RUTH: Nosy.

[*She slugs* CALVIN *in the arm.*]

CALVIN: Ouch.

DEB: I was married. For nearly ten years.

CALVIN: What happened to him?

DEB: He died.

CALVIN: You didn't kill him, did you?

DEB [*after an odd pause*]: No. But I think my brother did.

CALVIN: You're kidding.

[*Pause.*]

You're not kidding.

DEB [*shaking her head*]: My husband was a wife beater. I wore long sleeves at the height of summer and made up endless stories of tripping over throw rugs that no one believed. One morning I was trying to cover two black eyes with makeup so I could go to the store—we were out of eggs; God forbid we should run out of eggs. The doorbell rang. I looked out and there was my brother John. He lives—lived—in San Francisco, so I was surprised but so excited to see him out there. I forgot about how I looked and flung open the door and threw my arms around him. I don't know who was more shocked. He'd lost sixty pounds and just disappeared in my arms. He saw the bruises, saw my eyes—he'd heard rumors from our cousin, but he'd never actually seen. I couldn't stop crying; my eyes were looking worse by the minute. John took my hands and looked at me, looked deep inside me, and he said, "Debbie, I've got a death sentence on my head. I'm gonna die soon. Would you like me to take that bastard with me?" The one time I tried to leave, Dick tracked me down and put me in the hospital for a week. I knew one of these days he was going to kill me. But I couldn't ask John, poor, sick John, to do that.

[*Brief pause.*]

But I think he did it anyway. It looked like suicide. Dick was upset about being laid off at the plant. He'd been drinking. It looked like he just leaned back in his La-Z-Boy and blew his brains out. Nobody ever really questioned it. Nobody liked him well enough to question it. The angle of the gun seemed right, his prints were on it, it was open and shut. I was subbing at a school in Dearborn, so I wasn't there. I think John was. I never asked him. When we were kids I would protect him on the playground. He was a "sissy"—kids always called him that and tried to pick on him. I was a big muscular girl and I'd protect him. This was his turn to protect me. Now we're even, aren't we, Johnny? After he died, I moved up here, moved here to start a new life, a fresh life, safe, the life that John gave me back.

CALVIN [*wipes at his eyes*]: I'm so sorry, Deb. Just so sorry about all of it.

DEB: When I moved here, when I met Ruth, she asked if I had family here. I said no. And she said, "Then I'll be your family."

[RUTH *squeezes* DEB's *shoulder; covers* DEB's *hand with her own.*]

Ruth's the only one up here, anywhere really, who knows. Please don't tell anyone else. It's private. It's my story to tell—or not.

CALVIN: Of course. Thank you for telling me.

[*Sudden hand to eye.*]

Darn it.

RUTH: What?

CALVIN: I've still got that speck or hair or whatever it is, or a new one, ouch, in my eye.

DEB: Oh, c'mere.

[DEB *leans* CALVIN *back on part of the picnic table.*]

CALVIN: Hey!

DEB: Take it easy, buddy. Ruth, hit the porch light, would you? Mama needs some light.

CALVIN: What are you—

[RUTH *hits the porch light.*]

DEB: Shhh. Shhhh. Now I can see. *Shhhh.* Shh. Just let me—

[DEB *leans in/lies on* CALVIN *full body and licks at his eye.*]

   There. All better.

[LILLIAN *appears.*]

LILLIAN: Dear God, what are you doing to my boy?!

CALVIN [*blinks, ignores his mother*]: What did you—how did you—it's gone. You're incredible.

LILLIAN: Calvin.

DEB [*also ignores* LILLIAN]: Haven't you ever seen a mother cat do that? With her tongue?

LILLIAN: Calvin, get up this instant.

CALVIN: Wow.

RUTH: Wow.

LILLIAN: Calvin, go to bed.

[RUTH *laughs.*]

   Oh shut up, Ruth. You know that's not what I meant.

CALVIN: Mother, go to bed.

LILLIAN: You are *all* depraved, all of you.

[*She exits into the house.*]

RUTH [*to* CALVIN *and* DEB]: Night.

[*She points to the moon, points to* CALVIN.]

   Walk—on—moon.

[*She exits into the house.*]

CALVIN: I used to be so scared of Aunt Ruth.

DEB: That doesn't mean she's scary.

CALVIN: That doesn't mean she's not.

[*They laugh. She's very close.*]

DEB: Were you a sissy boy, Calvin?
CALVIN: Yes. I suppose I was.
DEB: I like sissy boys.

[DEB *leans in and gives* CALVIN *quite a kiss.*]

Do I scare you, Calvin?
CALVIN: Yes you do. Oh yes.

[*They kiss and more. The porch light clicks off. Perhaps we can see* RUTH'*s face as she pulls a blind.*]

SCENE 2

[*The past.* YOUNG RUTH *and* YOUNG LILLIAN *and a bassinet.* YOUNG LILLIAN *is all stirred up.*]

YOUNG LILLIAN: I'm a terrible mother.
YOUNG RUTH: No, you're not.
YOUNG LILLIAN: Yes, I am. *I am!* Don't argue with me.
YOUNG RUTH: Fine. But may I ask a question?
YOUNG LILLIAN [*sullen*]: Okay. What?
YOUNG RUTH: Why do you think you're a bad mother?
YOUNG LILLIAN: Sometimes—sometimes I want to kill him.
YOUNG RUTH: I don't think that's uncommon.
YOUNG LILLIAN: He cries and he cries and he cries, and I just can't *take* it. My
    nerves. I just can't. [*Whimpers.*]
YOUNG RUTH: Lillian oh poor Lillian, I honestly think that's normal. Most
    people just don't admit it.
YOUNG LILLIAN: He just cries and cries, and he won't take his bottle.
YOUNG RUTH: Well, for God's sake, give him what he wants.
YOUNG LILLIAN: I try everything. I rock him, I bounce him, and I bark like a
    dog and make funny faces.
YOUNG RUTH: Do that for me sometime, will you? Bark like a dog?
YOUNG LILLIAN: I'm serious! He's driving me crazy!

[*Very brief pause.*]

Not this minute but night after night after night. What can I do?
YOUNG RUTH: Lillian, feed him.
YOUNG LILLIAN: But I—

YOUNG RUTH: He doesn't want a bottle.

YOUNG LILLIAN [*finally gets it*]: Oh.

YOUNG RUTH: I know you love to fuss over pots of boiling water sterilizing Calvin's bottles, but, Lillian oh Lillian, he wants you.

YOUNG LILLIAN: But the book says—

YOUNG RUTH: Never mind the book.

YOUNG LILLIAN: But how do you know? You've never had a baby.

YOUNG RUTH: Neither has the book! Lillian, I've heard women whisper that they like it.

YOUNG LILLIAN: Only hussies would—

YOUNG RUTH: Aunt Dortha.

YOUNG LILLIAN: No. Really?

YOUNG RUTH: I think that's why she had six. Remember those pendulous bosoms.

[*A graphic gesture with her hands.*]

YOUNG LILLIAN [*horrified*]: Dear God.

YOUNG RUTH: I don't think just one will do that to you.

YOUNG LILLIAN: I guess—I guess I can try. I'd do anything for Calvin. You know I would.

YOUNG RUTH: I know.

[*Lights fade on the past.* LILLIAN *has been watching this memory.*]

LILLIAN: And this is the thanks I get.

SCENE 3

[*Summer 2000. A crack of thunder.* LILLIAN, RUTH, DEB, CALVIN, *and* MR. FLETCHER *are sitting inside the house in silence.* LILLIAN *is furious.* CALVIN *is trying not to look at her; he's also sneaking peeks at* DEB, *who is staring off into space.* RUTH *is watching everyone, amused.* MR. FLETCHER *has no idea what is going on.*]

MR. FLETCHER: Can you believe it's raining on the Fourth?! It never rains on the Fourth, but here it is raining cats and dogs. You should see the tourists out at the Holiday Inn—I still can't believe this town has a Holiday Inn—you should see the tourists in their shorts with their golf clubs and their powerboats, bored out of their skulls. No idea how to entertain themselves. Thank God there's cable television for people like that.

[*Silence.*]

Thank God we don't need cable. No indeed.

LILLIAN: No indeed. Some of us are very adept at entertaining ourselves and others without the benefit of television.

[*She glares pointedly at* DEB, *whose eyes have finally focused.* DEB *stands.*]

DEB: Yes, in fact I think I'll go read. Perhaps a nice murder mystery.

[*She treats* LILLIAN *to just the slightest smile.* CALVIN *hops up.*]

CALVIN: We could read it together.

LILLIAN: Sit.

CALVIN: Mom, don't talk to me like that, like I'm a—a—

RUTH: A *child.*

CALVIN: Exactly.

LILLIAN: I am the only sane person in this family.

MR. FLETCHER: Well, don't let that stop you.

LILLIAN: From what?

MR. FLETCHER: From whatever it is you want to do that you don't think you should so you never will.

LILLIAN: I'm perfectly satisfied with my life.

RUTH: Hah.

LILLIAN: There's nothing I need or want to do, not for myself. I receive a sufficient pension. My son [*brief but long suffering pause*] is healthy and apparently has a mind of his own. Just what every parent wants. And my sister refuses to recognize her limitations. I'm fine, I am perfectly fine, but no one else is.

MR. FLETCHER: Lillian, you're a grand old flag.

LILLIAN: No more singing.

CALVIN: Mother.

LILLIAN: Don't "Mother" me. I saw you last night.

MR. FLETCHER [*to* RUTH]: Last night?

[RUTH *makes a surprisingly crude but clear gesture to indicate sex.*]

Wouldn't you know, I missed the orgy.

DEB: It wasn't an orgy!

CALVIN: It was for me.

LILLIAN: Calvin!

CALVIN: What? Mom, I'm happy. What's wrong with happy?

LILLIAN: You've been corrupted. You have changed sides.

CALVIN: I realized I was on the wrong side.

LILLIAN: Well, I never. Now what? Are you and that—that—
RUTH: Deb.
LILLIAN: Are you going to—going to—

[RUTH *hums the wedding song.*]

DEB: Are you kidding?! It was one night on a picnic table!
MR. FLETCHER: Good gravy, I really did miss out.

[RUTH *nods.*]

CALVIN: It was amazing. There we were. Under the stars.
MR. FLETCHER: Splendor in the grass.
DEB [*to* MR. FLETCHER]: He wouldn't do it in the grass. Lyme disease.
MR. FLETCHER: So Calvin threw caution to the wind with caution. Good for
   you, Calvin. Others here could learn from you.

[*He looks pointedly at* RUTH, *then at* LILLIAN.]

CALVIN: I have splinters in my butt and I don't even care.
LILLIAN [*standing, ready to march out*]: I can't listen to any more of this.
DEB: I'll go. I'm going to read. *And Then There Were None.*
RUTH: Stay. [*To both women*] Play nice.
CALVIN: I know. How about cards? You still keep a drawer full of them, Aunt
   Ruth?

[*He tugs on a drawer and looks.*]

   Right where I remembered. What do we have here? Hearts?
LILLIAN AND DEB: *No!*
MR. FLETCHER [*looking at the deck in* CALVIN's *hands*]: Old Maid.
RUTH: No!
MR. FLETCHER: I know! Forget the cards. Let's play charades!

[*He is greeted by a deafening silence.*]

   Oh, come on. It'll be fun. The perfect party game for the perfect party.

[*He pulls a small pad from his pocket.*]

   I'll just jot down a few titles and act as emcee. Come on, it's raining. The
   only Fourth of July fireworks so far today are in this room. Come on, it'll
   be fun.

[*He spots* DEB *and* LILLIAN *about to escape.*]

Sit. No one leaves this room. That way no one ends up dead in the library. Now, damn it, let's have some fun.

RUTH: But—

MR. FLETCHER: No buts, my dear Ruth, not even from you. Everyone.

[*We can see the band conductor in him.*]

Play now. Play nice. Play together.

[*He has put the folded pieces of paper in his hat.*]

Who wants to go first?

CALVIN: Aren't we supposed to play in teams?

[*He tries to catch hold of* DEB*'s hand, but she scoots her chair out of reach.*]

MR. FLETCHER: Let's just compete amongst ourselves, shall we? [*Sotto voce*] That could get ugly enough. [*Louder, rattling hat*] Ruth. Oh, Ruthie.

RUTH: No, no, no, no, no.

[*She makes an "I don't wanna go first oh please don't make me go first" face.*]

MR. FLETCHER: As our dearly beloved hostess, you get the great honor of going first.

RUTH: Crap.

[MR. FLETCHER *rattles the hat under her nose. She grabs his wrist, gripping it just a little harder than she really needs to to put a stop to the rattling. She plucks out a piece of paper.*]

MR. FLETCHER: Now don't show us what it says.

[RUTH *gives him a withering look.*]

LILLIAN: She's not an idiot, you know.

RUTH: Thank you.

LILLIAN: You're welcome.

MR. FLETCHER: Yes, thank you, Lillian, for your kind input. All right, Ruth, do you need to know any of the basics of the game? Such as [*rolls an imaginary motion picture camera*] this means you're going for the title of a—

[*He rolls some more imaginary film.*]

CALVIN: Movie!

MR. FLETCHER: Good, Calvin. But we haven't officially started playing yet.

[RUTH *rolls her imaginary movie camera at* CALVIN.]

CALVIN: Movie!

[RUTH *points at* CALVIN—*he's got it.*]

MR. FLETCHER [*race announcer voice*]: And they're off!

[RUTH *holds up four fingers. Silence.* DEB *and* LILLIAN *are too disgruntled to speak;* CALVIN *doesn't get it.* MR. FLETCHER *finally can't stand it and bursts forth with the obvious.*]

Four words.

[RUTH *points, taps her nose. She holds up two fingers.* MR. FLETCHER *pokes* LILLIAN.]

LILLIAN: All right, already. Second word.

[RUTH *mimes a fish. She swims around.*]

CALVIN: Shark! *Jaws!*
MR. FLETCHER: Four words. Four.
CALVIN: Oh. *Jaws IV*! Kidding.
LILLIAN: Skinny-dipping.
CALVIN: I never heard of that one.

[RUTH *is still gamely swimming about.*]

DEB: Carp. Carpe diem. *Seize the Day.*
MR. FLETCHER [*enunciating painfully*]: Four words. Second word. Work with her, people, work with her.

[RUTH *is making a fish mouth, breathing through her gills.*]

DEB: Fish.
CALVIN: *A Fish Called Wanda*!

[RUTH *nods, gasps, breathes a sigh of relief.*]

MR. FLETCHER: Exemplary work, Calvin. I knew you had it in you. Splendid. You're next.

[*He rattles the hat at him.*]

CALVIN: Oh, no, oh, jeez, oh, no. I can't.
MR. FLETCHER: Oh course you can. Look at the fun Ruth had.

[RUTH *shoots him a look.*]

Here, dear boy, pick one.

CALVIN: I mean it. I can't. Stage fright. I'm too dull, too stupid; I'll wet my pants.

LILLIAN: Donny, leave him be.

MR. FLETCHER: Poor dear Calvin. I suppose you're afraid you'll look like an idiot in front of your girlfriend.

DEB: I am not [*his girlfriend*]—

MR. FLETCHER [*to* DEB]: Honey, give it a rest. The boy needs building up.

DEB [*sullenly*]: Go for it, Calvin.

LILLIAN: He already did.

CALVIN: Mother!

[RUTH *plucks a slip of paper out of the hat without looking at it and hands it to* CALVIN.]

RUTH: Play.

CALVIN: I'm sorry, Aunt Ruth. I can't.

[LILLIAN *snatches the paper.*]

LILLIAN: Oh, give me that.

[*She looks at it.*]

Well, I won't do this.

RUTH: Play.

LILLIAN: Darn it.

[*She peeks again.*]

Oh, fine. [*Aside to* MR. FLETCHER] You're a dirty old coot.

MR. FLETCHER: True.

[LILLIAN *holds up her hands like a book.*]

CALVIN: Book.

[LILLIAN *holds up four fingers.*]

Four words. [*To anybody who's listening*] I can do this part.

[LILLIAN *holds up four fingers again.*]

Fourth word.

[LILLIAN *points at* CALVIN.]

Son?

[LILLIAN *gives* DEB *a look.* DEB *returns it.* LILLIAN *mimes ecstasy—as best she can.*]

DEB: Sex.

[*She and* LILLIAN *exchange a glaring stare.*]

The Joy of Sex.

LILLIAN [*tapping the end of her own nose*]: You're on the money, honey.

[*Then, with a disapproving look for them all,* LILLIAN *exits.*]

DEB: Ya gotta give her credit.

RUTH: Yes.

CALVIN: She's got more guts than I do.

RUTH [*pats his arm*]: There, there. True, but there, there.

CALVIN: One-on-one I can face down any redneck fry cook who won't wash his hands after he uses the toilet. But show me a podium or a blind date and I'm useless.

DEB: I wouldn't say that.

MR. FLETCHER [*always a friend to romance*]: Hey, Ruthie, I think the rain's letting up. How about taking a spin with me? We can drive around and you can point out what's been torn down. Buy a watermelon. See if they're going to try to put on the parade after all.

DEB: Let's all go.

CALVIN [*a bit crestfallen*]: Oh okay. If that's what you want.

MR. FLETCHER: Honey, take a hint.

RUTH [*watching* DEB's *face as he says this to her*]: Oh oh.

DEB: Honey doesn't want a hint. Thank you very much. I think it's time to go read. Have a nice ride.

[*She is about to exit.*]

CALVIN: Give me a chance.

DEB: I did. It was nice. Now it's done. Adios.

[*She exits.*]

MR. FLETCHER: She's just scared. Don't take it personally.

CALVIN: Don't take it personally?! That was one of the most embarrassing moments of my life.

[*Brief pause to ponder.*]

And it didn't kill me. Hmmm. I have spent my life in mortal fear of being embarrassed, of being vulnerable, hanging fire waiting for something to happen but afraid to death it might because I might get rejected. I was afraid to be anything but alone. But look at me. My heart's on my sleeve. The woman just kicked me below the belt *in public*. And it didn't kill me.

RUTH: Good for you.

CALVIN: Heck, I'm not even discouraged. I'm gonna go right in there after her.

RUTH: Maybe—not.

MR. FLETCHER: It might be wise to give her a few minutes, give her a little space.

CALVIN [*caves immediately*]: Okay.

SCENE 4

[*The past.* YOUNG LILLIAN *and* YOUNG RUTH *are watching the parade.*]

YOUNG LILLIAN: He was so nervous. What if he falls off his bike?

YOUNG RUTH: Lillian, you and I never fell off our bikes. Look! There he is!

[*She waves.*]

Right behind the guy in the squirrel suit. Calvin! Look at Auntie Ruth!

[*She puts the camera to her face.*]

YOUNG LILLIAN: Oh no. Oh no!

YOUNG RUTH: What?

YOUNG LILLIAN: He's peed his pants.

YOUNG RUTH: Oh, jeez. Poor guy.

YOUNG LILLIAN: Oh, Calvin!

[*They run offstage to rescue* CALVIN *as the present damp parade blends in with* RUTH *and* MR. FLETCHER *watching, standing at the edge of the stage, under a large, damp, black umbrella. They are watching something rather awesome and awful as it crosses in front of them and exits—it's the end of the Fourth of July parade.*]

RUTH: That was—

MR. FLETCHER: A very wet parade. And that last float—what were those poor people supposed to be anyway? Bedraggled beavers?

RUTH: Squirrels.

MR. FLETCHER: Really? Well, God love 'em. I give 'em all credit. Especially the band. I have marched in many a drizzle myself and afterward you can smell every person who ever wore your band uniform.

[RUTH *laughs; mimes marching with a trombone and then cymbals.*]

I remember. When you and I were in band, we *were* the band. Us and Gunderman with his grandpa's tuba.

[RUTH *nods; waves to someone.*]

You know everyone in town, don't you?

RUTH [*shrugs*]: Taught them. [*Points*] Flunked him.

MR. FLETCHER: Sometimes I think I should have stayed. But I needed to go.

RUTH: Why?

MR. FLETCHER: Because I couldn't have you.

RUTH: Heavens.

MR. FLETCHER: Oh, Ruthie, you know I always loved you. Even when we were seven and you tied me up with your jump rope and held me hostage while you robbed my piggy bank. Or soaked me with your garden hose. I just always loved you. But you never saw me as boyfriend material. And good golly, it's not your fault you're the love of my life.

RUTH: Donny.

[RUTH *is embarrassed but also touched; she doesn't look away.*]

MR. FLETCHER: Cousin Lucy called me about your stroke. She still lives out in the country, still makes maple sugar candy, maple leaves and acorns, just like her father did. Lucy'd just heard rumors, so she painted a bleak picture. So I thought, Finally. Finally Ruth needs me.

RUTH: I don't. I'm fine.

MR. FLETCHER: I can see that.

RUTH: But—

[*She stops, looks at him, takes his hand, laces her fingers through it, kisses his hand, then continues to hold it.*]

Maybe.

MR. FLETCHER: Maybe?

RUTH: Maybe.

MR. FLETCHER: Maybe works for me.

SCENE 5

[*The past.* YOUNG RUTH *is sipping "iced tea" in an Adirondack chair.* YOUNG LIL-
LIAN *is sitting on the edge of the other chair, looking off, looking stern.*]

YOUNG LILLIAN: Calvin, leave that dog alone! How many times do I have to
tell you not to pet strange dogs!?

YOUNG RUTH: I know that dog. That is not a strange dog. I have known that
dog for years.

YOUNG LILLIAN: You can't take chances if you're a mother.

YOUNG RUTH: Well, thank God I'm not. What kind of a life is a life without
chances?

YOUNG LILLIAN: You're a fine one to talk. You're still living in the house you
grew up in. At least I moved to the city.

YOUNG RUTH: You moved to Kalamazoo. Zoo-zoo-zoo-zoo.

YOUNG LILLIAN: Kalamazoo is a lovely, hilly, educated city. Ruth, are you
drinking?

YOUNG RUTH [*singing*]: "I got a gal . . ." [*Trails off.*] "Kalamazoo."

YOUNG LILLIAN: Drinking. In broad daylight.

YOUNG RUTH: Iced tea. It's a holiday. And it's hot.

YOUNG LILLIAN: I saw the vodka. In the kitchen. Behind the refrigerator.

[*But* CALVIN *is distracting her.*]

Calvin! Don't you dare go near that tomcat!

[*She watches him for a moment, then settles back a little.*]

Speaking of tomcats, how is Father Shannon?

YOUNG RUTH: Oh, Father Jerry is fine. He'll do for now.

[*She sips her tea.*]

YOUNG LILLIAN: It's sinful. But he is a man. And many men just take what
they can get. But, Ruth, women need more than that.

YOUNG RUTH: Don't generalize.

YOUNG LILLIAN: Calvin! Calvin, I don't want you climbing that tree!

YOUNG RUTH: Oh, Lillian, let him climb it. *We* did.

YOUNG LILLIAN: It was a smaller tree then.

YOUNG RUTH: Let him fall. He needs to fall. We all do.

YOUNG LILLIAN: You could still find someone, still marry.

YOUNG RUTH [*slowly, spelling it out*]: I don't want to.

[*After a moment, she really looks at her sister.*]

Okay, so I don't really like living alone. I miss the sound of Daddy cough-
ing in the hall. I miss hearing Mama talking to the cat through the screen
door in the morning. I miss *sounds*. At night, alone, it's so quiet. I don't
think this damned old house even has any ghosts. Maybe I need to take in
a boarder.

YOUNG LILLIAN: He'll murder you in your sleep.

YOUNG RUTH: Maybe a young woman. Another teacher. I don't need
a lot of companionship—I don't want a husband or children. But I do
want—something. Someone clearing their throat. Something. [*Looks*]
Calvin's about to fall out of that tree.

YOUNG LILLIAN: Gracious! Calvin!

[*She runs off.*]

YOUNG RUTH: Let him fall.

[*Lights fade on the past, rise on* CALVIN.]

CALVIN: I fell. Right on top of her. Broke her nose. She should've let me fall.
Good practice. Well, it's never too late.

SCENE 6

[*Summer 2000.* DEB *enters, walks slowly along the front of the stage.* CALVIN *follows a few steps behind, carrying an umbrella, not with her but not far.* DEB *stops.*]

DEB: You're following me.

CALVIN: No, I'm not.

DEB: Don't lie. You're a terrible liar.

CALVIN: Share my umbrella?

DEB: Why? It's barely sprinkling.

CALVIN [*venturing a hand out from under the umbrella to check*]: Oh.

[*But he stays protected—for now.*]

DEB: Besides, my umbrella-sharing days are over.

CALVIN: Look, Deb—Debbie—Deb—

[*He finally folds up the umbrella and faces her.*]

I'm kind of an old loner myself. Honestly? I don't know if I can let you in
either. But I'd like to try.

[*Deafening silence.*]

Could we—just [*shrugs shoulders*] "keep company"? I can drive up every—let's say every other; I don't want to crowd you—every other Saturday. We can watch some TV for a few hours, then I'll drive home.

DEB: You live three hours away.

CALVIN: So?

DEB: You'd drive three hours here and then three hours back just to watch a little TV with me?

CALVIN: Yes. Gladly.

[DEB *shoves him up against a tree and kisses him thoroughly.*]

DEB: I don't watch TV.

[*Her meaning sinks in and he smiles.*]

CALVIN: Okay. We'll do whatever you want. Wherever you want it.

DEB: Just don't get any ideas down the road. I'm not moving. I'm happy here, rooming with Ruth.

CALVIN: That's fine. I don't really have a lot of extra room in my apartment. I have a teapot collection.

DEB: Tonight's Old School Night. Have you got a date?

CALVIN: Well, Mother. [*Brightens*] Would you like to come with us?

DEB [*eyes to the heavens*]: Dear God, this isn't going to be easy.

SCENE 7

[*The past. The yard.* YOUNG RUTH *is drinking;* YOUNG LILLIAN *isn't.* YOUNG LILLIAN *is glowering.*]

YOUNG LILLIAN: Quit. Now.

YOUNG RUTH: Quit what?

YOUNG LILLIAN [*points at* YOUNG RUTH*'s glass*]: Quit *that*. Especially right here in the yard in front of God and the Beasleys.

[*She waves and smiles unconvincingly to the Beasleys as they obviously walk by.*]

YOUNG RUTH [*gives a big wave*]: Have a beautiful day, Mrs. Beasley! [*Nods to the man.*] Bertram. [*To* YOUNG LILLIAN *once the Beasleys are barely out of earshot*] He's such a lump. I wonder if *she* drinks? She must.

YOUNG LILLIAN: Ruth, you're a schoolteacher. For heaven's sake, you need to worry what people will think.

YOUNG RUTH: That's assuming they *do* think. Lillian oh Lillian, lighten up. I've seen you tipple the Mogen David on Christmas Eve.

YOUNG LILLIAN: Yes. Once a year. You're drinking every day.

YOUNG RUTH: How do you know that? You don't know that. You don't see me every day. You don't see me every week. You see me at holidays, and *that's when most people drink.*

YOUNG LILLIAN: I don't.

YOUNG RUTH: I'm not you.

YOUNG LILLIAN: The school board is thinking about firing you.

YOUNG RUTH: They wouldn't dare—who told you that?

YOUNG LILLIAN: I still have a few friends around here.

YOUNG RUTH: And I'm sleeping with the president of the school board, so trust me, Lillian, it's never going to happen. Besides, I'm the best damn teacher they've got. They would be insane to fire me.

YOUNG LILLIAN: I came here to warn you. I've warned you. I've done my duty. Now I'm going home.

YOUNG RUTH: Aren't you going to stay for the parade?

YOUNG LILLIAN: Seeing you was spectacle enough for one day.

[*She's leaving.*]

YOUNG RUTH: I can quit anytime I want, you know.

YOUNG LILLIAN [*turning back to face her*]: No, I don't know. Prove it. Do it. Quit. Now.

YOUNG RUTH: Don't tell me what to do. [*Brief pause; deeper, more affected voice*] "Don't tell me what to do." [*Chuckles at herself; regular voice*] Oh, Lillian, promise me you'll put that on my tombstone.

YOUNG LILLIAN [*the slightest crack in her facade; she almost smiles*]: Don't tell me what to do.

[*They both are standing, facing each other.*]

YOUNG RUTH: I only do it, drink, because it helps.

YOUNG LILLIAN: How does liquor help?

[*Pause.*]

YOUNG RUTH: I'm not very satisfied with myself. I expected more of me. This [*raises glass*] helps me not care.

YOUNG LILLIAN: Well, I think you'd better start caring about yourself and soon. For pity's sake, Ruth, you don't need booze to be who you are. You're the Eighth Wonder of the World, drunk or sober.

YOUNG RUTH: Do you love me?

YOUNG LILLIAN: Yes. Of course.

YOUNG RUTH: Without a moment's hesitation?

YOUNG LILLIAN: Yes.

YOUNG RUTH: I need someone to love me. I didn't think I did, but I do.

YOUNG LILLIAN: Well, I do love you and I always will, so throw your darned bottle away and remember who you are in this town—and how much you mean to me.

YOUNG RUTH: But what about after you leave? I wish you didn't have to leave.

YOUNG LILLIAN: I wish I didn't either. I've always been happiest here with you.

[YOUNG RUTH *pours the liquor out of the bottle, pitches it, stretches a hand out to* YOUNG LILLIAN.]

YOUNG RUTH: Let's go watch the parade.

YOUNG LILLIAN: Yes. Let's.

[*Lights dim on the past.* LILLIAN *and* RUTH *have been watching/remembering this scene.* RUTH *exits.* LILLIAN *speaks.*]

LILLIAN: Ruth did stop drinking. That very day. But I still kept checking the cupboards. She could have bought a new bottle. She could have—but she didn't. I could have had more faith.

SCENE 8

[*Summer 2000.* LILLIAN *is sitting alone on an Adirondack chair. Give her a moment to be lost in her thoughts and her memories. Then we hear a car and then a car door. We hear* RUTH's *and* MR. FLETCHER's *voices offstage.*]

MR. FLETCHER: I'll pick you up at quarter to six! We'll be the prettiest couple there!

RUTH: Drive safe.

[*The car pulls away as* RUTH *enters.* LILLIAN *waves a lackluster hand to* MR. FLETCHER *as he drives away.*]

You missed—

LILLIAN: The parade.

RUTH. Yes. Very soggy. Mud mud mud.

LILLIAN: Where's he off to?

RUTH: Primp. [*Mimes either imaginary tightening knot of tie or shooting her cuffs.*] Trim. Hair. [*Mimes trimming voluminous male nostril hair.*]

LILLIAN: Deb says you want to learn mime. Was that mime? That—

[*She twitches her hands about, miming mime.*]

I thought you had to wear white gloves.

[RUTH *doesn't bother to answer any of this. She sits next to* LILLIAN *in an Adirondack chair.*]

You're going tonight, aren't you? To Old School Night?
RUTH: Yes.
LILLIAN: What will people think? I worry about what people will think. I worry.
RUTH: Too much.
LILLIAN: And you never worried enough. I don't want them feeling sorry for you. Pitying you.
RUTH: Stop.
LILLIAN: Well I don't. I can just hear them, "Poor Ruth this" and "Poor Ruth that." I'm trying to protect you.
RUTH: From—what?
LILLIAN: Life! Everything! Ruth, you are not all right. You aren't. You can't even say my name.

[*They glare at each other.*]

RUTH: Uhl . . . Lll—

[*She can't. She tries, but can't.*]

Too . . too—
LILLIAN: Too many *l*'s.
RUTH: Yes.
LILLIAN: There are a lot of *l*'s in this world, Ruth.
RUTH: My. Lost. Words. I know! I! Know!

[*The poignance of this admission from her proud sister penetrates.*]

LILLIAN: Ruth. I'm—I'm sorry.
RUTH: Go home.
LILLIAN: I am home.
RUTH: Go. Away.
LILLIAN: You need me!
RUTH: No no no.

LILLIAN [*quieter*]: I need you.

RUTH [*too angry to listen just yet to* LILLIAN's *needs*]: Not ashamed! You! Want—want [*hits her chest*] hide. Won't. Hide. Not from—my life.

LILLIAN: Please, Ruth. For my sake. Take that unit at Golden Years. All of the staff there knows CPR.

RUTH: Damn it, you—hate—you hate it there!

LILLIAN [*caught; a rat in a trap*]: No, I don't.

RUTH: Yes you do.

LILLIAN: I do not hate it there. I'll grant you it's a little [*very brief pause*] dull. I haven't made many friends, and when I do, they die. But it's clean. Sterile. And if you can't get out of the tub, there's a button to push—though please shoot me before that ever happens. Calvin drives over and takes me to a movie or even a play at that barn theater most Saturdays. But now I suppose he'll be trotting up here all hot to trot.

[RUTH *mimes her crude mime for sex.*]

Oh be quiet.

RUTH: I am.

LILLIAN: It would be so much better if you lived there too.

RUTH: No. Wouldn't.

LILLIAN: I used to be so afraid we'd be two old maids living in Mama and Daddy's house, collecting tons of newspapers and *Saturday Evening Post*s which would eventually collapse and smother us to death. Or that we'd be down the hall from each other at the nursing home, not speaking.

[*Brief contemplative pause.*]

I do worry a lot.

RUTH: Yes. Stop. Please.

LILLIAN: So are you *finally* dating Donny Fletcher?

RUTH: Maybe.

LILLIAN: No wonder you don't need me. You've got Mr. Fletcher. And Deb. And Deb's got my Calvin. You don't need me. No one does.

[RUTH *slugs* LILLIAN *in the arm.*]

Oww! Ouch!

[RUTH *slugs her again but not as hard.*]

RUTH: I *do.*

LILLIAN: Really?

RUTH: Of course. Oh, Sister.

LILLIAN: I hate my unit. I wish I'd never sold my house. I need a yard. Windows to wash. A draft in winter that I can complain about. And a view of something other than the Ionia prison.

[*They look at each other; it's a long, measuring, revelatory look.*]

RUTH: No. Yes. No. Okay maybe.

LILLIAN: I'll pay the utilities.

RUTH: Deb.

LILLIAN: I'll be nice to her. I'll try. I promise.

RUTH: Mr. Fl—Fle—Don?

LILLIAN: I'll keep my hands off him.

RUTH: You better.

LILLIAN [*looks in the distance*]: Look, there's my Calvin. With Deb.

[*She makes a big effort to smile, wave.*]

I wonder where they've been?

[RUTH *is about to make her crude sex gesture.*]

Don't you dare.

RUTH: Don't—

LILLIAN: Tell you what to do. Fine.

[*She makes the sex gesture.*]

Satisfied?

RUTH: For now.

LILLIAN: Ruth, look, you don't have to. You don't have to let me move in. It's your house.

RUTH: It's a—big house.

[*Moment. Then they're off and running.*]

LILLIAN [*glances at her watch*]: Goodness gracious, Old School Night. We've got to get dressed. Let me set your hair.

RUTH: No.

LILLIAN: Then how about—

RUTH: No! [*Brief pause.*] But thank you.

LILLIAN: You're most welcome.

[*That's the close of the play, except for the closing number, special lighting effects, and curtain call, which all happen now without a blackout.* MR. FLETCHER *enters, all duded up, tipping a real or imagined hat to the ladies, singing Cohan's "Yankee Doodle Dandy" in a rendition that starts quietly and slowly, then builds as others join in for the finale. Following* MR. FLETCHER *are* CALVIN *and* DEB, *both dressed nicely. Carrying jackets and hats, they simply and efficiently dress and spruce up* RUTH *and* LILLIAN *for Old School Night.* YOUNG LILLIAN *and* YOUNG RUTH *appear off to the side in period clothing and a special diffused light. Small flags emerge from sleeves, perhaps sparklers (if the fire code allows), as everyone onstage joins in to sing a rousing, old-fashioned version of "Yankee Doodle Dandy" and perhaps do a little Sousa march at the curtain call as the light board simulates fireworks bursting. "Should old acquaintance be forgot: keep your eye on the grand old flag." Curtain.*]

VICTORY GARDENS THEATER PLAYWRIGHTS ENSEMBLE

Claudia Allen

Claudia Allen's play *Hanging Fire* premiered in 2004 at Victory Gardens Theater in a co–world premiere with Florida Stage. Author of more than thirty plays, she has been widely produced around the country. Her other premieres at Victory Gardens include *Winter* and *Fossils* (both starring Julie Harris), *Cahoots*, *Hannah Free*, *Deed of Trust*, and the Joseph Jefferson Award–winning plays *Still Waters* and *The Long Awaited*. She received a Trailblazer Award in 2000 from Bailiwick Rep. In 1999, *Chicago* magazine named Allen best playwright. Her play anthology *She's Always Liked the Girls Best* was a finalist for an American Library Association Award and a Lammie. Her play *Unspoken Prayers* was a finalist for the 2003 Susan Smith Blackburn Prize. Allen was a recipient of the Chicago Adapt Disability Arts and Culture Award. She teaches playwriting at the University of Chicago, Lake Forest College, and the Victory Gardens Training Center.

The Freedom Rider (1980)
Raincheck (1984)
The Last of Bilky Ciliax (1984)
Eulah (1985)
Roomers (1987)
They Even Got the Rienzi (1987)
The Long Awaited (1989)
Movie Queens (1990)
The Usher (1991)
The Child Within (1991)
Still Waters (1991)
The Gays of Our Lives (1991)
Ripe Conditions (1992)
Hannah Free (1992)
Deed of Trust (1993)
Change (1993)

Reunion: The Glass Ceiling Play (1993)
The Christmas Spirit (1997)
Winter (1997)
A Gay Christmas Carol (1998)
Xena Live! (1999)
Cahoots (2000)
The Human Bat and Other Attractions (2000)
Fossils (2001)
Xena Lives! The Musical (2001)
Unspoken Prayers (2003)
Dutch Love (2003)
Hanging Fire (2004)
Presenting Normally (2004)
I Sailed with Magellan (2006)

Lonnie Carter

Lonnie Carter has spent more than thirty years writing plays that jump racial and ethnic boundaries. Premieres at Victory Gardens include *The Sovereign State of Boogedy Boogedy, Lemuel, Necktie Party*, and *Concerto Chicago*. *The Romance of Magno Rubio* (winner of eight Obie Awards in 2003) was produced at Victory Gardens in 2004 and has gone on to be produced at the Long Wharf Theatre in New Haven, Connecticut, its seventh production in three years. These plays and others have also been performed at LaMama, E.T.C., the American Place Theatre, and Yale Repertory Theatre. *Wheatley* premiered at Victory Gardens in the 2005–6 season, and *The Lost Boys of Sudan* will premiere at the Children's Theater in Minneapolis as part of their 2006–7 season. Carter's *Organizing Abraham Lincoln* (with Rich Klimmer) was the winner of the Two-Headed Challenge sponsored by the Playwrights' Center and the Guthrie Theater. Carter has taught playwriting at New York University since 1979. He is a member of New Dramatists.

Iz She Izzy or Iz He Aint'zy or Iz They Both (1969)	*Brer Clare* (1989)
	Chocolate City (1990)
If Time Must Have a Stop, Space Is Where It's at, Here at Dead Center of America (1970)	*Gulliver Redux* (1991)
	I. B. Randy, Jr. (1995)
The Big House (1971)	*Lemuel* (1996)
Cream Cheese (1974)	*Holofernes* (1997)
The Sovereign State of Boogedy Boogedy (1976)	*China Calls* (1999)
	Wheatley (2000)
The Odd Women (1979)	*The Romance of Magno Rubio* (2002)
Bicicletta (1983)	*Bollywood* (2003)
Necktie Party (1987)	*Concerto Chicago* (2003)
Mothers and Sons (1987)	*The Lost Boys of Sudan* (2004)
Gulliver (1988)	*Organizing Abraham Lincoln* (2005)
	Blunkett (2005)

Steve Carter

Steve Carter received the Living Legend Award at the 2001 National Black Theatre Festival. He was Victory Gardens Theater's first playwright-in-residence beginning in 1981 and has also served as playwright-in-residence at George Mason University. Carter's *Pecong* (winner of the Joseph Jefferson Award for New Work) premiered at Victory Gardens in the 1989–90 season and received subsequent productions at London's Tricycle Theatre, American Conservatory Theater in San Francisco, and

Newark Symphony Hall. His plays *Eden* (winner of an Outer Critics Circle Award, an Audelco Award, and the Los Angeles Drama Critics Circle Award) and *Nevis Mountain Dew* received Midwest premieres, and *Dame Lorraine, House of Shadows, Shoot Me While I'm Happy, Spiele '36,* and *Root Causes* all premiered at Victory Gardens. Carter has recently finished a draft of his new play *Paradise* and is currently teaching writing workshops at the Restoration Center for Arts and Culture in Brooklyn.

One Last Look (1967)	*Primary Colors* (1984)
Terraces (1974)	*Shoot Me While I'm Happy* (1986)
Eden (1975)	*Walking Graffiti* (1988)
Nevis Mountain Dew (1978)	*Pecong* (1990)
Dame Lorraine (1981)	*Spiele '36 or the Fourth Medal* (1991)
House of Shadows (1984)	*Root Causes* (1997)
The Inaugural Tea (1984)	*Paradise* (2004)
Mirage (1984)	

Gloria Bond Clunie

Gloria Bond Clunie's Victory Gardens premieres include *North Star* (winner of the Joseph Jefferson Award for New Play, the 1994 Theodore Ward Prize for African American Playwriting, and the 1999 American Alliance for Theater and Education Distinguished Play Award) and *Shoes* (2005 Black Theatre Alliance New Play Award). Other produced credits include *Secrets, Sing! Malindy, Sing! Dream, Basket of Wishes—Bucket of Dreams, Mirandy and Brother Wind,* and *Sweet Water Taste* (winner of the 2004–5 Theodore Ward Prize for African American Playwriting). Since 1981, Clunie has been a full-time drama specialist in Evanston's School District 65. She is the winner of the 1997 Alice Walker Short Fiction Award, a 1996 Illinois Playwriting Fellowship, a 1993 Arts Education Fellowship (NEA/CBE), and the 2000 Scott McPherson Playwriting Award. In 1986, Clunie was given the Evanston Mayor's Award for the Arts.

Dream: A Tribute to Dr. Martin Luther King, Jr. (1981)	*North Star* (1994)
Sing! Malindy, Sing! (1987)	*Some Enchanted Evening* (1997)
Basket of Wishes—Bucket of Dreams (1989)	*Mirandy and Brother Wind* (2001)
Secrets (1990)	*Living Green* (2005)
	Shoes (2005)
	Sweet Water Taste (2005)

Dean Corrin

Dean Corrin's Victory Gardens premieres include *Butler County, Gentrification, Expectations,* and *Battle of the Bands.* His plays have also been produced at Northlight Theatre, the Actors Theatre of St. Paul, Tacoma Actors Guild, Stage #1 (Dallas), the Addison Theatre Centre (Dallas), New York Stageworks, Polaris Repertory Company (New York City), Wichita Center for the Arts, and the Cape Cod Festival of New American Plays. *Threadheads,* a musical for young audiences about Mother Jones and the child labor movement, was commissioned by Chicago Playworks and premiered at the Merle Reskin Theatre. Corrin is currently the associate dean of the Theatre School at DePaul University and is a board member of the Sansculottes Theater Company.

Play It Again, Mr. Goodbar (1979)
Matinee Idyll (1981)
Double Feature (1982)
Butler County (1984)
Gentrification (1986)
Expectations (1987)
The Blue Baby (1995)

Quite Contrary (1997)
King of Craft (1998)
Threadheads (1999)
Battle of the Bands (2002)
Longing (2003)
Filling Our Hearts with Food (2006)

John Logan

John Logan's Victory Gardens world premieres include *John Wayne Movies, Music from a Locked Room,* and *Scorched Earth* and Equity premieres of *Never the Sinner* and *Hauptmann,* which moved to off Broadway in 1992 and received a Drama Desk nomination. Logan's play *Speaking in Tongues* received the Kennedy Center/Fund for New American Plays grant and was produced by New Playwrights Theater in Washington in 1988. Logan received Academy Award nominations for best original screenplay for *The Aviator* and *Gladiator.* Other screenwriting credits include *The Last Samurai, Any Given Sunday, RKO 281,* and *Star Trek: Nemesis.* Logan is currently working on the screenplay of Stephen Sondheim's *Sweeney Todd.*

Never the Sinner (1985)
Hauptmann (1986)
John Wayne Movies (1987)·
Speaking in Tongues (1988)
Music from a Locked Room (1989)

Riverview: A Melodrama with Music
  (1991)
Scorched Earth (1991)
Showbiz (1993)
The View from Golgotha (1996)

Nicholas A. Patricca

Nicholas A. Patricca is an internationally published and produced playwright, poet, and essayist. Victory Gardens premieres include *The Examen, Gardinias 'n' Blum*, and *The Fifth Sun*. In the spring and summer of 2005, Patricca's play *An Uncertain Hour* was produced at Spirit Square Theatre in Charlotte, North Carolina, and at the Virginia Holocaust Museum in Richmond, Virginia, by ASU Ensemble. The live performances of these productions were broadcast over the Internet by CSCi Multimedia. Patricca's play *The Defiant Muse* is scheduled for future production at Victory Gardens. Patricca is a senior professor emeritus of theater at Loyola University Chicago. He has been the recipient of many honors and awards, including National Endowment for the Arts and the Illinois Arts Council fellowships and grants, USIA and Chicago Artist Exchange Program awards, and the Cunningham Prize for Playwriting from DePaul University.

The Examen (1980)

The Weight Room (1981)

The Decline of the West (1982)

La Pequeña Estrella de Gran Valor (1982; 1996 new version)

The Fifth Sun (1984; 1992 one-act version)

Gardinias 'n' Blum (1987)

The Octave (1988)

Hail Mary I (1988)

Hail Mary II (1989)

The Pursuit of Happiness (1989)

Dream Machine (1989)

The Lemon Tree (1989)

Homeboy (1990)

The Idea of Chaos (Sex, Death, Life, and Order) at Key West (1991; 1994 new version)

Three Turns with Susan R.: A Remembrance (1992)

Oh, Holy Allen Ginsberg, Oh Holy Shit Sweet Jesus Tantric Buddha Dharma Road! (1993)

An Uncertain Hour (1994; stage and radio versions)

El Quinto Sol (1995)

Radiance of a Thousand Suns: The Hiroshima Project (1995)

E LiLiʻ u E (2003)

Radiance of a Thousand Suns: The Hiroshima Project (2004; radio version)

The Defiant Muse (2005)

An Uncertain Hour: A Memory Play for Radio (2005)

False Dawn (2006)

Douglas Post

Douglas Post is the author of some twenty-five plays and musicals, which have been produced in New York, Chicago, Los Angeles, England, Germany, Austria, and Russia. Victory Gardens productions include the Midwest premiere of *Earth and Sky*, the American premiere of *Murder in Green Meadows*, and the world premieres of *Drowning*

Sorrows, Blissfield, and *God and Country.* He has also been commissioned to write screenplays for Warner Bros. and NBC, teleplays for WMAQ-TV, and several radio adaptations of his scripts. Post has received the L. Arnold Weissberger Playwriting Award, the Midwestern Playwrights Festival Award, the Cunningham Commission Award, and two Playwriting Fellowship Awards from the Illinois Arts Council. He has also been nominated for a Joseph Jefferson Award and an Emmy Award.

Prospero's Saxophone (1981)

The Other Wise Man (1981)

Drums (1982)

Everyman (1984)

The Caucasian Chalk Circle (1985)

The Wind in the Willows (1985)

Belongings and Longings (1986)

The Long River Passes (1986)

Detective Sketches (1987)

Suffering Fools (1989)

The Real Life Story of Johnny De Facto (1989)

Earth and Sky (1991)

Escape from Groovytown (1991)

Murder in Green Meadows (1992)

At Night in the Asylum (1992)

Somewhere on the Coast of Belize (1993)

Drowning Sorrows (1996)

Forty-two Stories (1997)

Gethsemane (1999)

Blissfield (2000)

God and Country (2002)

Personal Effects (2003)

Somebody Foreign (2006)

The Kingdom of Grimm (2006)

James Sherman

James Sherman is observing twenty years of collaboration with Victory Gardens. Premieres there include *The God of Isaac, Mr. 80 Percent, The Escape Artist, Beau Jest, This Old Man Came Rolling Home, Jest a Second! Romance in D, From Door to Door, The Old Man's Friend* (winner of the Streisand Festival of New Jewish Plays), *Affluenza!* and *Half and Half,* which will premiere in the 2005–6 season. His plays have been produced across the United States and around the world. Sherman currently teaches at Columbia College Chicago and DePaul University. He has been the recipient of fellowships from the MacDowell Colony, the Ragdale Foundation, the Virginia Center for the Creative Arts, and Yaddo.

Magic Time (1981)

The God of Isaac (1985)

Mr. 80 Percent (1986)

The Escape Artist (1988)

Beau Jest (1989)

Romance in D (1991)

This Old Man Came Rolling Home (1992)

Jest a Second! (1995)

The Old Man's Friend (1998)

From Door to Door (1999)

Affluenza! (2003)

Half and Half (2006)

Charles Smith

Charles Smith's plays explore issues surrounding the perception of race and politics from an African American point of view. Victory Gardens premieres include *Takunda, Jelly Belly, Cane, Freefall, The Sutherland, Knock Me a Kiss,* and *Free Man of Color* (commissioned for the Ohio University bicentennial; winner of the 2004 Joseph Jefferson Award for New Work; winner of the 2004 John W. Schmid Award). These and other plays (including *Les Trois Dumas, Pudd'nhead Wilson,* and *Black Star Line*) have been produced at the Goodman Theatre, Penumbra, St. Louis Black Rep, New Federal Theatre, Seattle Repertory Theatre, and Berkeley Repertory Theater. His play *Jelly Belly* was recently published by Northwestern University Press in *Seven Black Plays*. Smith is currently finishing the book for the musical *Shoot the Piano Player* in addition to the new play *Denmark* for Victory Gardens to open its new home at the Biograph Theater in 2006.

Jelly Belly (1985)

Takunda (1987)

Golden Leaf Ragtime Blues (1987)

Young Richard (1989)

Cane (1991)

City of Gold (1992)

Freefall (1993)

Black Star Line (1996)

The Sutherland (1997)

Les Trois Dumas (1998)

Knock Me a Kiss (2000)

Pudd'nhead Wilson (2002)

Sister Carrie (2002)

Free Man of Color (2004)

Denmark (2006)

Jeffrey Sweet

Jeffrey Sweet has been affiliated with Victory Gardens Theater for more than twenty-five years. Victory Gardens premieres include *Porch, Ties, The Value of Names, Stops Along the Way, Hard Feelings, With and Without, Flyovers, The Action Against Sol Schumann, Immoral Imperatives, Bluff,* and *Berlin '45*. These and other plays have been produced around the world. He is currently serving his third term on the Council of the Dramatists Guild and is on the faculty of the University of the Arts in Philadelphia. His writing has won numerous honors, including the Outer Critics Circle Award, a "Best Plays" designation, the Kennedy Center Fund for New American Plays Award, two American Theatre Critics Association Playwriting Prizes, the Joseph Jefferson Award, the Society of Midland Authors Award, the Writers Guild of America Award, and an Emmy nomination.

Winging It! (1970)

Wicked John and the Devil (1975)

Porch (1979)

Hard Feelings (1979)

Responsible Parties (1980)

Ties (1981)

Holding Patterns (1981)

Stops Along the Way (1981)

Routed (1981)

The Value of Names (1982)

George's File (1983)

What About Luv? (1983)

American Enterprise (1991)

I Sent a Letter to My Love (1995; revised 2002)

With and Without (1995)

Flyovers (1998)

The Falcon's Pitch (1998)

Bluff (1999)

The Action Against Sol Schumann (2001)

Stay Till Morning (2001; formerly *Immoral Imperatives*)

Berlin '45 (2005)

Kristine Thatcher

Kristine Thatcher's plays at Victory Gardens include *Among Friends* (winner of the 1997 Scott McPherson Memorial Award), *Emma's Child* (winner of the 1995 Susan Smith Blackburn Prize, a 1997 Illinois Arts Council Fellowship, the 1997 RESOLVE Award for Excellence in the Arts, the 1997 Cunningham Prize for Playwriting from DePaul University, and the 1997 After Dark Award for Outstanding New Work), and *Voice of Good Hope* (nominated for the 2000 Joseph Jefferson Award for New Work). Her play *Under Glass* premiered at Luna Stage in 2005. She has taught at Columbia College Chicago and Lake Forest College and is the newly appointed artistic director of the BoarsHead Theatre.

Waiting for Tina Meyer (1985)

Niedecker (1985)

Under Glass (1991)

Emma's Child (1992)

Apparitions (1993)

Among Friends (1999)

Voice of Good Hope (2000)

ACKNOWLEDGMENTS

The editors would like to thank Richard Christiansen, Carrie Gleason, Susan Hahn, Mark Witteveen, the members of the Playwrights Ensemble, and the staff of Victory Gardens Theater.

SANDY SHINNER joined Victory Gardens Theater in 1979. The theater's associate artistic director, she has directed more than one hundred productions, most recently the world premieres of Claudia Allen's *Hanging Fire* at Victory Gardens; Joanna McClelland Glass's *Trying,* which transferred off-Broadway after its Victory Gardens premiere; and Kathleen Tolan's *Memory House* at Actors Theatre of Louisville's Humana Festival and Victory Gardens.

DENNIS ZAČEK has been the artistic director at Victory Gardens Theater since 1977 and has directed more than 175 productions. He was honored with the Artistic Leadership Award by the League of Chicago Theatres and is a professor emeritus at Loyola University Chicago.